Conflict talk

Studies of language use in social contexts have multiplied in recent decades, yet relatively little attention has been paid to the important area of conflict talk.

The eleven studies in this volume fulfill this need, using analytic and interpretative perspectives to examine the disputes of adults and of children. Most of the studies are based on audio or sound-image records of naturally occuring discourse arising in a variety of contexts. These range from street to school, from courtroom to hospital, and from home to workplace. Allen Grimshaw has provided a short introductory chapter and extensive theoretical conclusion to the studies, which come from a variety of disciplines: the authors comprise anthropologists, linguists, sociologists, a lawyer and a psychologist. The book will appeal to researchers and advanced students in all of these areas, and also to counselors, legal professionals, and negotiators.

Conflict talk

Sociolinguistic investigations of arguments in conversations

Edited by
ALLEN D. GRIMSHAW
Indiana University

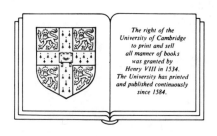

Cambridge University Press

Cambridge

New York Port Chester Melbourne Sydney

Published by the Press Syndicate of the University of Cambridge
The Pitt Building, Trumpington Street, Cambridge CB2 1RP
32 East 57th Street, New York, NY 10022, USA
10 Stamford Road, Oakleigh, Melbourne 3166, Australia

First published 1990

Printed in Great Britain at the University Press, Cambridge

British Library cataloguing in publication data

Conflict talk: sociolinguistic
investigations in conversations.
1. Oral communication. Sociolinguistic aspects
I. Grimshaw, Allen D.
401'.9

Library of Congress cataloguing in publication data

Conflict talk: sociolinguistic investigations of arguments in
conversations / edited by Allen D. Grimshaw.
    p.   cm.
Bibliography.
Includes index.
ISBN 0-521-33544-2. ISBN 0-521-33550-7 (pbk)
1. Conversation. 2. Verbal self-defense. 3. Conflict management.
4. Sociolinguistics. I. Grimshaw, Allen Day.
P95.45.C65 1990
306.4'4–dc20 89–31714 CIP

ISBN 0 521 33544 2 hard covers
ISBN 0 521 33550 7 paperback

Contents

The contributors

John M. Conley, School of Law, University of North Carolina
William A. Corsaro, Department of Sociology, Indiana University
Donna Eder, Department of Sociology, Indiana University
Charles Goodwin, Department of Anthropology, University of South Carolina
Marjorie Harness Goodwin, Department of Anthropology, University of South
     Carolina
Allen D. Grimshaw, Department of Sociology, Indiana University
Teresa Labov, Department of Sociology, University of Pennsylvania
Hugh Mehan, Department of Sociology, University of California, San Diego
William M. O'Barr, Department of Cultural Anthropology, Duke University
Katherine O'Donnell, Department of Sociology, Hartwick College
Susan U. Philips, Department of Anthropology, University of Arizona
Thomas A. Rizzo, Department of Psychiatry, Northwestern University Medical
     School
Deborah Schriffrin, Department of Linguistics, Georgetown University
Deborah Tannen, Department of Linguistics, Georgetown University
Samuel Vuchinich, Department of Human Development and Family Studies,
     Oregon State University

Preface

Conflict and talk are two features of human social life which are both pervasive and intellectually fascinating; they have attracted the interest of scholars and humanists for at least as long as we have records – and have necessarily been attended by group members as long as there have been groups. This species-long history of interest notwithstanding, systematic interest in and research on the phenomenon of *conflict talk* is both rarer and more recent. My own interest in conflict talk has roots in ameliorative as well as in intellectual concerns. I have been studying social conflict for more than thirty years and talk for more than twenty-five. My enthusiastic embracement of sociolinguistic data and analytic and interpretive perspectives following my first introduction to them resulted in part from a strong presentiment that better understanding of talk and better understanding of social conflict would turn out to be complementary. I believe this has been demonstrated. My hope then, and now, is that such increased understanding may, over the longer run, contribute to reduction of species-threatening varieties of social conflict. Such a reduction remains only a hope. I have an undocumented but strong sense that most of the contributors to this book have been similarly motivated.

There has been a quantum increase in publication on sociolinguistics, discourse analysis, and related arenas of investigation in the last decade. As I sampled these growing literatures, however, I came to realize that, while conflict talk was often recognized and discussed in the course of analyses of other matters, research on conflict talk and on conflict *in* talk was reported only rarely. Five years ago this summer, several of us whose work appears in this volume had a "show and tell" mini-conference during the course of which we viewed a large number of sound-image records particularly rich in conflict talk. This experience further convinced me of the potential value of more explicit attention to conflict talk. I therefore invited a number of colleagues who seemed to me to have interests or data which would make them valuable contributors to a book on conflict talk to write chapters on the topic. This volume is the result.

To a greater degree than is perhaps ordinarily the case with edited volumes, this is very much a co-operative venture. In addition to the meeting mentioned above, sub-sets of contributors discussed the project at disciplinary annual meetings and several of us gave versions of chapters at the Eleventh World Congress of the International Sociological Association in New Delhi in 1986. We agreed that, while any attempt to make general statements about the nature of conflict talk will require studies of the phenomenon in different cultures, societies, speech and language communities, etc., an initial attempt would probably best be limited to instances of English. It will be seen, however, that inclusion of comparative materials from Italian has substantially enhanced the value of Corsaro and Rizzo's studies of children. In my original invitation to participants I mentioned my hope that all might attend in some way to the intepretive usefulness of what I have called the "sociological variables" (i.e., relations of power and of affect and considerations of utility). Several contributors resisted such a constraint; in the event it seems to me that those variables are shown to be importantly implicated in determining the initiation, course, content, and outcomes of conflict talk. Finally, each contributor read my introductory and summary chapters. I have incorporated some, but by no means all, of their comments, corrections, and suggestions – and have ordinarily indicated where I have been stubborn. I am most grateful for their help.

I have not always had good experiences with collaborative projects and I had some hesitation about involving myself in this one. My first thanks are owed to the contributors whose papers follow – and whose counsel and encouragement kept me going when I wondered not only when, but if, we would finish. I am thankful to Susan Allen-Mills of Cambridge University Press who encouraged us to undertake the project and showed patience when I fell behind on this, and other, commitments. We are all grateful also to Penny Carter of Cambridge University Press, who provided us with both expeditious editing and production and encouragement when she took over our project when Susan Allen-Mills left the Press. We are each individually indebted to colleagues who read our chapters at various stages of writing; I am particularly indebted to Randall Collins, who has been a helpful and encouraging reader in this as in other instances. Richard D. Lambert guided my early work on social conflict and social violence and I gladly acknowledge my debt to him. Leonard D. Savitz told me about the importance of language in conflict many years before I fully understood what he meant; I am grateful to him also – even if I have been tardy in accepting his gift.

ALLEN D. GRIMSHAW

1 Introduction

ALLEN D. GRIMSHAW

1. Introduction

Discourse is species specific but pervasive and ubiquitous within our own species – we tend to take it for granted and not to consider it as problematic in ways which are likely to affect our lives very much. Conflict is pervasive and ubiquitous among all living organisms (sentient and non-sentient). We recognize it as threatening both to ourselves and, in extreme manifestations, to our species; we expend massive energy and resources on conflict at the interpersonal (perhaps intrapersonal), intergroup, and international levels and not inconsiderable resources and energies in attempts to understand and control it. This concern with conflict – and particularly with violence – notwithstanding, we have done little to try to understand how discourse and conflict (and violence) may be related among humans. Each of the contributors to this volume has a profound professional interest in how talk in social contexts is employed to get the social accomplished; to varying degrees each is also involved in investigation of "conflict talk" because of hope that such study may help us to understand conflict as a social process and, at some juncture, to control the more dangerous manifestations of conflict which threaten all of us.

This introductory chapter attempts to do three things. The remainder of this introductory section provides background information on our collaborative project. The following section explores the rationale behind studying conflict talk – as an important feature of everday life, as a source of drama in literature, and as a critical consideration for the maintenance of humanity in the age of nuclear weaponry. The third section is a brief description of what investigators of conflict talk build on and add to in their research, most particularly a long tradition of work on social conflict as a process and, more recently, a literature on discourse analysis and, specifically, on argument, dispute, etc. The final section provides brief overviews of the studies which follow, concentrating on the questions they have addressed – and indicating other questions which either have not or could not be addressed. The book's concluding chapter discusses the findings of the studies, possibilities for generalization, and directions for further work.

1.1 Background

As a sociologist I have been studying conflict as a social process for some thirty years; as a student of social control and social accomplishment by means of talk in social contexts I have been engaged in the analysis of discourse for the last twenty. While there are long and rich traditions of both theoretical and empirical sociological work on social conflict, when I began trying to combine my interests in social conflict and discourse about ten years ago there was only a handful of pioneering studies on the topic (e.g., Brenneis and Lein, 1977; W. Labov, 1972a and 1972b; W. Labov and Fanshel, 1977; Mitchell-Kernan and Kernan, 1975), none of which directly focused on conflict talk. However, by the time I started to talk about this book in the early 1980s with the colleagues who have joined me in writing it, there was a rich and growing literature on conflict talk which included contributions by anthropologists, lawyers, linguists, psychologists, and sociologists – fields which are represented in this volume. A recent literature review by Brenneis (1988) includes references to over 200 items on "language and disputing."

Over the last fifteen years there has been an exponential increase in publications analyzing spoken discourse. This work, which has engaged the attention of sociologists as well as scholars in disciplines more traditionally interested in discourse studies (i.e., humanists, linguists, and natural language philosophers), has increasingly focused on naturally occurring conversation. It has often focused also on social interaction which has important consequences for participants, i.e., events in bureaucratic, educational, legal, medical, and work settings. Conflict occurs in each of these settings as well as in less formal interaction in families, friendship groups, and casual encounters, and many investigators have considered conflict in the talk they have studied. However, there has been surprisingly little research on the special features of "conflict talk." One of the purposes of this volume is to address this deficiency in the discourse analytic literature.

The anthropologists, linguists, and sociologists whose chapters appear here include many of the discourse analysts who have attended specifically to conflict talk in their own past work. An attempt has also been made, however, to provide a sampling of theoretical perspectives, of methods, of foci of interest in different dimensions of talk, of types of participants, of scenes (or settings) of interaction, and of conflict topics. There are also differences in the nature of the data sets examined, which include both audio and/or video (or film) records of conflict talk, transcripts, ethnographic records of varying extensiveness and, in one instance, dramatic scriptings.

There is a generally accepted belief that dispute modes vary developmentally, by gender, by participant relations of affect and of power, and by the nature of the matter under dispute. For this reason, an attempt has been made to maximize variability in the personal and role-specific characteristics of whose conflict talk is examined in these studies: conflict-talk participants include small children, adolescents, children of varying ages interacting with each other and with adults, and adults with different relations of power and of affect pursuing quite different sorts of goals. The settings of the events studied include nursery schools, a junior high school cafeteria, the streets, domestic kitchens, living rooms, a meeting room in a municipal utility, a food co-op, courts, and a therapist's office. It will be seen that there are differences in disputes involving different kinds of participants in different settings and with different interactional goals; it will also be seen that there are significant similarities and identifiable underlying dimensions in all the conflict talk studied. We suspect that these similarities and underlying dimensions are not all specific to conflict talk in English-speaking North America, but limitations of space have kept us from including reports of comparative material. (Chapter 2 identifies some non-trivial differences between the disputes of American and Italian pre-schoolers.)

2. Why study conflict talk?

Conflict talk is at the same time so complex a phenomenon and one so deeply implicated in every dimension of human social life that it would be possible to identify dozens of reasons why it should be a focus of systematic inquiry; by the same token one would be left wondering why its study has been so neglected. For present purposes I will identify and comment on only four of the many reasons why we study conflict talk – and will leave the question of its neglect to others. My four reasons are: (1) disciplinary development, that is, specification of theoretical and methodological issues in the relevant social science disciplines, in linguistics, and in sociolinguistics – and of directions of research which may help in answering questions generated by that specification; (2) development of humanistic studies, that is, specification of theorectical and methodological issues in relevant specialities in the humanities, for example, comparative literature and/or critical studies in drama, fiction, and poetry; (3) improved theoretical understanding and empirical knowledge of specific substantive areas such as (in the studies following): child and adolescent socialization, race and ethnic relations, labor relations, language and law, etc.; (4) socially relevant applications on the interpersonal (and, perhaps, *intra*personal), intra-institutional, community, and international levels. I can do no more than to sketch some of the main points which would need to be covered in a full discussion of these four reasons.

2.1 Disciplinary development

Social scientists are interested in specification of the operation of conflict as a social process and in optimal ways of engaging in that specification. Linguists want to known how language works and, depending upon their own theoretical orientation, how that "working" can be specified formally or in terms of pragmatic functions. The final chapter of this book suggests some preliminary answers to the question of how study of conflict talk can lead to both more refined and better-documented understanding of the sociological dimension of social conflict as a process. As the studies here show, some questions, such as "What are the circumstances/conditions under which conflict talk is likely to occur?", are of such generality that it has been possible to posit some (possibly "testable") propositions. Other questions, such as the nature of conflict groups or the role of third parties in conflict talk (and conflict more broadly), are visible clearly in only some of the studies following.

I have for some years employed a heuristic distinction between (1) social-interactional rules governing social behavior within social structures having such features as role, hierarchy, exchange requirements and (2) sociolinguistic rules governing the use of resources of spoken and written language *within sets of social structural constraints* (Grimshaw, 1980b). If, as Simmel (1955 [1908]) argued, conflict is to serve to *organize* and perhaps even facilitate interpersonal relations then, if parties are going to engage in conflict talk, they must *select* appropriate manners of speech (both codes and prosodic and lexical variants), follow sequencing rules and, for example, know *when* to display anger. While answers to linguistically oriented questions about "how language works" are not foregrounded in the studies below, I believe that they both validate the heuristic usefulness of the social-interactional rule/sociolinguistic (selectional) rule distinction and allow interested readers to see directions which research on specification of linguistic and sociolinguistic resources might profitably follow.

2.2 Development of humanistic studies

Some years ago a humanist scholar friend, who did not conceal a contempt and dislike for sociology, humphed that he was going to have to read Erving Goffman, "in order to be able to keep up with literary criticism," where, he complained, everyone was busy citing the sociologist. The reason that humanists begin to read and cite a Goffman or a Geertz or a Levi-Strauss is that they find in the scholar cited new ways of perceiving and interpreting the materials which constitute their work – the same process works in the other direction as social scientists (sometimes quite uncritically) loot the work of Chomsky or Derrida or Foucault or Peirce. If students of literature turn to Goffman because his conceptualizations of frame "shifts" and "rekeyings" and "laminations" illuminate the ways in which dramatists and writers of fiction or poetry make their narratives compelling, their characterizations believable, and their sociological insights valid beyond the boundaries of particular writings – so too will they turn to studies which display, in actual talk, *processes* of social conflict they so often incorporate into fictional renditions and specification of conditions under which conflict will or will not occur, by whom it is most likely to be initiated, etc. (see, for example, the summary propositions in chapter 13). While only Tannen has chosen to direct her attention to conflict talk in fiction and drama, I believe humanists will find the empirical findings and the conceptualizations of other contributors insightful and suggestive. In a complementary way, I believe that Tannen's contribution should demonstrate to students of language in use in social contexts the value of investigation of dramatic and fictional renderings of conflict talk – which may foreground both social-interactional considerations and sociolinguist resources more clearly than is sometimes the case with naturally occurring events (see also Burton, 1980; Watzlawick, Beavin, and Jackson, 1967).

2.3 *Knowledge of specific substantive areas*

Each of the studies here contributes to new understandings of interaction in an institutional arena, or documents empirical observations previously supported in the main by anecdotal evidence. The institutional arenas are, on the whole, familiar ones: economic (a food co-operative [Labov] and a public utility [O'Donnell]), educational (nursery schools in Italy and the United States [Corsaro and Rizzo] and American "middle schools" [Eder]), familial (at dinner time [Vuchinich], in casual talk [Schiffrin], and in the dramatic representation of the talk of members of a triangle whose relationships are at risk [Tannen]), legal (litigants in small claims court [Conley and O'Barr], and opposing attorneys and judges in criminal trials [Philips]), and medical (a psychiatric review board [Mehan]). It may be harder to find a label for the institution in which the behaviors of the Goodwins "sling shotters" are embedded ("play," "leisure"?); it is a familiar one often found in other institutional "domains" (see, especially, the studies by Corsaro and Rizzo and by Schiffrin).

It will also be seen that the studies contribute to our understanding of processual/interactional dimensions of substantive questions about child and adolescent socialization, race relations, ethnic relations, status claiming and negotiation, and so on. One way in which they differ from investigations of the same institutions and processes employing more traditional survey or other quantitative methods or even ethnographic observation is in their discovery of subtle nuances of "reportable" (W. Labov, 1968) behaviour such as the presence of a "breaking of ranks" by management representatives in front of their union subordinates (O'Donnell) or the heavy ambivalence about stressful interaction with blacks manifested by liberal whites in the food co-operative (Labov). Such mild departures from expectations should lead students of the substantive arenas and/or interactional processes of interest to contemplate modification of the social-interactional rules mentioned above (2.1) A second difference is their specification of interactional resources seldom indentified or discussed in the more traditional studies, i.e. opinions (Schiffrin), silence and pauses (Tannen), or sequencing conventions (Vuchinich). Such specification should not only lead sociolinguistically inclined students of language in use to contemplate modification of sociolinguistic *selectional* rules (2.1); it should also lead sociological students of institutions and social processes to consider previously neglected dimensions of the question of how the social gets accomplished in interaction.

It is true, of course, that *any* study of talk within these institutions and in the accomplishment of social processes would reveal features hitherto neglected by sociologists. The study of conflict talk will prove itself to be particularly productive of understanding not only of conflict, but also (non-exhaustively) of accommodation, co-operation, conformity, socialization, stratification processes, and so on, within the institutions of interest.

2.4 Amelioration of social problems

There is a strong functionalist bias in much of the major theoretical work on social conflict (see, especially, for example, Simmel, 1955 [1908]; Coser, 1956. Cf., however, Dahrendorf, 1959; Collins, 1975) and there are often emphases on the contribution of social conflict to the generation of social structure, to socialization, to the strengthening of group bonds, and so on. Most studies of conflict talk have investigated events whose outcomes are of only transient significance – however angry, or depressed, or exhilarated, or smug participants may momentarily feel; there are few studies of conflict talk in which participants appear to either intendedly or otherwise cause *serious* injury to their interlocutors. It is no less true, however, that conflict can be a literally deadly phenomenon, that thousands of persons are killed annually in events ranging from interpersonal fights to gangland rumbles, to tribal or religious struggles, to wars, and that the population of the planet itself is at risk of extinction by nuclear conflict. We also know that outcomes of conflict talk can be both immediately hurtful (because of ethical and other data problems there are few studies of such talk; see however, Watzlawick, Beavin and Jackson (1967) on *Who's afraid of Virginina Woolf?*) and momentous in their consequences both for participants and for those who may, unbeknownst to themselves, be "spoken for" (Goffman, 1981; T. Labov, 1980) by actual interloctors. Conflict is a quintessentially social phenomenon – and violence is, most of the time, preceded by talk (or some written or other symbolic "stand-in" for talk).

While I have no illusions about the likelihood that either those who act as our representatives in international disputes or the psychologically maimed and maiming who wound one another regularly in dances of hostile intimacy (see, e.g., Henry, 1965) will rush to seek our counsel, I think that students of discourse can offer two kinds of understanding which could reduce the risks of potentially dangerous conflict talk and of socially injurious outcomes when such talk is initiated, whatever may have been done to avoid it. The first kind of understanding ·is that of communicative nonsuccess (Grimshaw, 1980c) engendered by unrecognized (or known, but dismissed as unimportant) differences in norms of production and interpretation (Hymes, 1974) of written and spoken discourse; the work of Gumperz and his students is particularly exemplary here (Gumperz, 1982a, 1982b; see also, illustratively, Erickson and Shultz, 1982 and Chick, 1985). The second understanding is that of the *process(es)* of interactional accomplishment in conflict talk, i.e., in part the specification of social-interactional and sociolinguistic *rules* but also the specification of a variety of other features of such talk including its variable course, manifestations and outcomes. I believe that the studies reported here successfully contribute to our understanding of processes; a summary of some findings appears in chapter 13 below.

3. Resources for the study of conflict talk

There are three "sets" of resources for the investigation of conflict talk, namely: (1) theoretical, methodological, and substantive literatures on conflict, on discourse analysis, and (increasingly) on conflict talk itself; (2) a fairly eclectic collection of concepts from this literature and other literatures; and (3) an increasingly rich (but still limited, because of problems of access) set of ethnographically grounded data which has been electronically recorded across a range of sites and situations. I can comment only briefly on each of these resources here; but the first two are discussed in more detail in the final chapter.

3.1 Relevant literatures

A quick perusal of the references collected in the bibliography will reveal that contributors to this volume have ranged far beyond their home disciplines (primarily sociology, anthropology, and linguistics [in that order]) in their pursuit of understanding of the phenomena of conflict talk. Somewhat curiously, in my view, they have apparently not found much in the traditional theoretical literatures of the social sciences germane to their work – I say curiously because a dichotomy between conflict and system or functionalist theories is, along with distinctions between social organization and social psychology and quantitative and qualitative methods, a principal orienting perspective in sociology (and, to a somewhat lesser extent, in both anthropology and political science). It seems to me that both such precursors as Machiavelli, Marx, Pareto, Simmel, Sorel, and Weber and contemporaries like Boulding, Coser, Dahrendorf, Rapoport, Schelling, and Williams have things to say about conflict as a social process which will help us to make more sense out of conflict talk. Perhaps this will be a next step for some students.

Contributors have drawn much more heavily on a variety of analytic modes for the investigation of discourse. Simplifying grossly, it can be argued that there are two principal approaches to analysis, namely: (1) that which focuses attention on resources available to participants in interaction (traditionally primarily speakers but in recent years increasingly hearers as well), and (2) that which focuses on resources available to analysts for the discovery of meaning-in-text. The first approach, exemplified by the comprehensive discourse analysis of W. Labov and Fanshel, the conversational inference investigations of Gumperz, the systemic/functional analysis of Halliday, and ethnomethodological/phenomenological perspectives ranging from those of Wittgenstein to Schutz to Garfinkel, attempts to discover *how participants make sense of discourse produced within known and specified contexts of text and of situation* (in Halliday's sense of those terms). The second, represented by the critical analysis of text as practiced by Althusser, Barthes, or Derrida, by the conversational analysis of Sacks and Schegloff and their followers, by the research on speech acts by Austin and Searle and contemporary linguists like Green or Fraser, and by the studies of conversational implicature of Grice, attempts in contrast to *discover both referential meaning and pragmatic "intention" within the syntactic organization and/or lexical construction of the text itself*, generally invoking context only when analyses won't otherwise "work".[1] All of these analytic perspectives, as well as others, are employed in the studies in this volume – most of the contributors appear to find at least some knowledge of context(s) necessary for their investigations.

While I think my initial claim that there has not been much research on the specific features of "conflict talk" *is* correct, there is a substantial and growing body of material on conflict *and* discourse. However, while there are many studies in anthropology, criticism (both literary and dramatic), folklore, political science, psychiatry, psychology, and sociology which associate discourse with conflict as their analytic focus, only a small proportion of these investigations directly address the question of how *sociolinguistic resources are employed in the pursuit of social-interactional goals.*[2] There are exceptions, however, and analysts have investigated such features of conflict talk as the use of direct and indirect speech, particularities of sequencing and of other devices studied by conversational analysts, the employ of narratives, and so on. A goodly portion of these studies has been identified and discussed by Brenneis in his very useful review article (1988); his review is particularly useful because he underlines the fact that particularities of conflict talk vary quite considerably cross-culturally.

An important new dimension has been added to work on conflict-related discourse with the emergence in recent years of new academic-professional specialty focusing on negotiation. Leaders in the field are often lawyers and other practitioners who are very skeptical about the possibilities of learning much from analysis of the details of the actual talk of negotiations;[3] some have them have produced extremely suggestive reports and commentaries on either general strategies, such as focusing on interests rather than positions (see especially Fisher and Ury, 1981), or on how to deal with "Xs" (often the Soviets, see Sloss and Davids, 1986). I believe that discourse analysts could usefully employ the insights of some of this work – and that negotiators could learn from analyses like those which follow. Resources are available; thus far neither group appears to feel it has much to learn from the other. Brenneis' observation (1988) about our collective inability to articulate work on "broad issues of social organization, political economy and power" and the "often apparently miniscule specifics of pronoun choice, syntactic variation and turn-taking" is particularly apposite.

3.2 Theories and concepts

There is obviously no such thing as a "unified theory of sociolinguistic description" (Hymes, 1974) of conflict talk; there are a variety of axiomatic orientations, proto-theoretical perspectives, and conceptual notions which are available for use in organizing the phenomena for systematic analysis. The organizing perspectives vary considerably in level of abstraction, in amenability to identification and (particularly) measurement, and in specifiability of relevance for conflict talk as compared to talk in general; all have influenced at least some work on conflict talk by contributors to this volume and other investigators. I will focus briefly here on the following: (1) general orientations; (2) concepts drawn directly from sociological theory; (3) concepts drawn directly from general studies of discourse; (4) typologies of conflict discourse; and (5) speech-act theory and notions of interactional terms/moves.[4]

(1) In using the term general orientation, I have in mind two kinds of organizing perspectives. There are, first, such heuristics as Hymes' (1974) SPEAKING mnemonic with its reminder to would-be-analysts to take into account such elements of language in use in social contexts as Settings, Participants, Ends, and so on. There are also interpretive orientations which focus on a smaller set of notions by treating some the elements in Hymes' heuristic roughly as if incorporated into a more relational-processual frame. My (hardly novel) notion of the "sociological variables" of relations of power and of affect and of the nature of utility (conceptually subsuming salience and costs of interactional goals for participants) has given me a very

considerable interpretive leverage in a variety of studies of naturally occurring discourse. While at least some of the contributors to this volume may
reject my characterization, it seems to me that all students of discourse
(spoken or written) are guided by one or more sets of such organizing
perspectives, i.e., by what Cicourel (1980) has variously labeled "top-down
notions" and "unspoken predicates."

(2) My notion of sociological variables obviously derives directly from
some of the sociological work noted above as particularly germane for
students of interactional accomplishment in talk. Another, considerably less
global, notion which has been extremely useful for students of conflict talk is
that of consideration of the role of third parties. While rooted in the astute
observations of Roman political strategists and commentators and developed by Machiavelli and others, the modern conceptualization of *tertius
gaudens* was initially developed in the work of Simmel and some of *his*
contemporaries and further refined by a number of ours. Moreover, this
work has provided not only a productive conceptualization for ongoing
investigation of social conflict phenomena, it has, in collateral refinements
and developments such as conceptualizations of "footing" and "participation status" discovered by Goffman (our contemporary Simmel!), engendered some extremely useful work in studies of discourse.[5]

I argue in chapter 13 the usefulness of sociological studies of the development and change of social conflict in its ongoing course; while a number of
students of conflict talk have addressed similar questions about that talk, few
if any have utilized the results of the sociological work. I hope that the later
discussion will persuade some investigators to look at it.

(3) In recent years discourse analysts have developed an extremely rich
and varied conceptual apparatus. Because each of the studies here focuses
primarily on a single variety of conflict within a particular setting (although
Corsaro and Rizzo look at the same type of setting in different *societies*) some
aspects of that apparatus, for example the concept of domain, are little used.
On the other hand, however, several contributors do look at speech registers
which over the course of a single speech event in a particular setting
characteristic of an identifiable domain – *do* differ in some manner significant for interactional outcomes. At a fairly general level contributors have
focused on such dimensions/features of talk as prosodic/paralinguistic variation, sequential organization, theme, topic-shifting, etc. (but not, e.g.,
clausal structures); at the analytic level they have looked at selection of such
specific sociolinguistic resources/devices as direct and indirect speech, address forms, narrative, silence, etc. (but not, e.g., voice, or metaphor, or
anaphora). In short, participants in conflict talk have the same resources
available for that interaction as do all conversationalists – and analysts the
same interpretive apparatuses. As will be seen, neither participants in the
disputes studied nor analysts of those disputes have employed the full range
of resources available.

(4) Both folk and formal classifications of types and genres of conflict talk are available for use by participants in disputes, and by analysts. Lawyers and professional negotiators recognize and employ distinctions among adjudication, arbitration, litigation, mediation, and negotiation; they also recognize that there may occur, within any of these formally labeled types of activities, events which they (and laypersons) may reference as, variously, altercations, arguments, bickering, contentions, debates, disputes, dissension, fights, quarrels, quibbling, squabbles, and wrangles. All those who use the second set of terms are aware that they are less clearly bounded than the first set; they are also aware that there are unclearly specified but nonetheless real and interactionally significant differences in the importance of goals and in risks to participants' social relationships implied by, e.g., bicker or quibble as contrasted to fight or quarrel. Finally, culture/speech community members also recognize other varieties of conflict and conflict-related talk such as apologies, gossip, innuendoes, insults, slurs, and so on, and also that just as these last can both be embedded in various sorts of conflictful interaction and occur independently, so too can arguments, etc., occur within arbitration or, for that matter, family dinners, hospital hearings, school lunches, play (or wedding) rehearsals, seminars, and any other speech event. "Members" recognize and report the occurrence of disputes of varying sorts; meta-discussion as to just what sort of event has or is occurring is common. That researchers on conflict talk draw very heavily on shared knowledge of the phenomena can be see from the analyses below. As of this juncture, however, a very considerable amount of work remains to be done, both in specifying how different types and genres of conflict talk vary, and in developing measures for different dimensions of variation.

(5) Much remains to be done, too, in order to so transform speech act theory that it can be moved from its intuitive and deductive roots to applications in studies of naturally occurring talk, including conflict talk. There are a number of problems here, most particularly problems having to do with: (1) failing to distinguish the "names" of verbs from the behaviors of interest to investigators of social accomplishment in interaction, and (2) clarifying what constitute "member-acceptable" reports of what behaviors are, or have, occurred (see, especially, Grimshaw, 1988a, chapter 4). There appears to be some confusion over which labels refer to speech events (in Hymes' [1974] sense), which to speech-act verbs – or names of "kinds of talk," and which to interactional "terms" or "moves" as those terms have been employed by W. Labov and Fanshel in their "comprehensive discourse analysis" (1977).

Labov and Fanshell assert that the most critical step in their analysis "is the determination of the *actions* that are being performed by speakers through their utterances" (58), and continue with the observation that "crucial actions . . . are not such speech acts as requests and assertions, but rather challenges, defenses, and retreats, which have to do with the status of

the participants, their rights and obligations, and their changing relationships in terms of social organization" (58–59). Although it will not often be
articulated in these terms in the studies, it seems to me to be manifest that
conflict talk is about just such "challenges [and counter-challenges],
defenses, and retreats." Equally evident, in my view, is Labov and Fanshel's
observation that these moves, and their successes and non-successes, and
their impact on relationships among interactants, and so on, are substantially determined by considerations of relations of power and of affect (and, I
would add, by characteristics of participants' interactional goals).

I think this brief review validates the claim that the conceptual resources
available for the study of conflict talk are rich indeed. I will now comment
briefly on the range of data available for studies of conflict talk.

3.3 Data resources for the study of conflict talk

Although the use of ethnographically grounded audio recordings was
becoming routine in studies of language in use in social contexts by the time
the Committee on Sociolinguistics of the Social Science Research Council
initiated its Multiple Analysis Project (MAP) in 1972,[6] the use of sound-
image recording (SIR) in research on discourse/interaction, whether with
film or with video recording, was still sufficiently rare for the Committee to
ask me to spend some months "finding out about the new resource" before
committing itself to employing SIR in the MAP. There was talk about the
Natural History of the Interview project;[7] there had been publications on
kinesic accompaniment to talk and contribution to interactional accomplishment; and in 1973 Scheflen published his pioneering study of talk in a
four-person therapy group; none of us anticipated the massive increase in
the use of SIR which was to occur in the next fifteen years.

With the advent of ever-cheaper and *easier-to-use* video equipment,
collection of ethnographically grounded SIR of conflict talk has become
technically and financially possible almost everywhere in the world. While
there are problems of access to data collection opportunities and non-trivial
issues of ethics, in my view the most critical data problem for students of
conflict talk is that researchers haven't been able to gain access to conflict
talk in which matters of more than personal moment are disputed. In every
instance in the studies below, the data were originally collected (or, in the
case of *Betrayal* and *Titticut Follies* produced) for ends other than the study of
conflict talk. However, there is no problem in finding data useful for the
study of conflict talk, simply because the phenomenon is ubiquitous – a
feature of almost any interesting conversation and a stimulating focus for
writers of fiction, poetry and drama.

The indeterminate problem of missing data   A persistent question in the
study of social-conflict processes has been that of the extent to which

understanding of conflict can be generalized across levels, i.e., how much of what we may learn about interpersonal conflict in families or other groups can be generalized to inter-group or inter-category conflict, and, beyond that, perhaps, to conflicts between or among nation states (or would-be nation states). While it can be demonstrated that some features of the nature and course of conflict are quite similar for family arguments and strikes and community controversies, for example (some documentation for this observation can be found in the concluding chapter), it cannot so easily be shown that the same holds for international relations. There are at least two critical differences between the types of conflict talk which have been investigated by analysts of discourse and those involving the larger social aggregates. First, while the outcomes of the disputes reported here seem important, sometimes critically so, to participants, the truth of the matter is that the stakes in, for example, international negotiations, can be magnitudes greater – war and peace may be outcomes. Second, the conflict talk involving large-scale institutional structures, up to and including states, is carried on not by all of those likely to be affected but by some set of "representatives." Until we are able to obtain data on conflict talk in negotiations between large collectives up to and including nation states we will not be able to determine the extent to which findings on conflict talk (and conflict as a social process more generally) can be claimed to hold across levels of varying social complexity and, critically, importance of stakes.[8]

4. The studies

The contributors to this volume represent a range of scholarly disciplines and professions and theoretical perspectives; they have examined data generated in very different ways; and they looked at the conflict talk of participants of very different social attributes in a wide range of *domains*. However, with only two exceptions (Corsaro and Rizzo, and Tannen) they focus on conflict talk in the United States. While participants in conflict talk will always experience some sense of satisfaction or dissatisfaction over the outcome(s) of that talk, and while such matters as discharge from a mental hospital or legal judgements will be salient for those immediately affected, it is also the case that most of the conflict talk which is analysed in this volume is of relatively modest social "relevance.". This lack of major social importance notwithstanding, however, all of the conflict talk studied and reported on, including that of young children, is complex, intricate, and, occasionally, quite subtle.

The first four studies address, with varying degrees of directness, questions of how children "learn to argue.". Corsaro and Rizzo use data collected by Corsaro in Bologna to build on Corsaro's earlier work in an American preschool (1985) to demonstrate that children in both Italy and the United States initiate disputes in much the same way and over the same range of issues (i.e., things, rights, beliefs, facts). They also show, however, that children begin even at a very tender age to display patterns found in the adult culture of their own society but not of the other. This raises the intriguing possibility that children may everywhere follow innately programmed (universal?) patterns in conflict talk/behavior and that adult differences in conflict behaviors in different societies and speech communities reflect post-childhood culturally imposed/learned variation. There is very little comparative data as yet (but see, e.g., Katriel, 1985); the possibilities are exciting indeed.

Eder has studied quite different groups of children, i.e., all-female (with occasional exceptions) adolescents in grades six through eight. She has also done her investigation in a school setting – the cafeteria at lunch time. She finds that these young women are learning communication skills which will become increasingly important as they move toward adulthood, in particular: (1) how to *resolve* conflict, and (2) how to control distress resulting from both ritual insults and more subtle affronts/assaults on personal "face" (Goffman, 1967; Brown and Levinson, 1978). Eder's data show a marked enhancement of competence in conflict "talking" in the two-year difference between girls in the three grades – further evidence of the importance of learned culture-specific specialization in the phenomenon. Indeed, she identifies differences among young white females of different social class analogous to those identified by Kochman (1981) as characterizing black and white American adults. This gives further evidence that new language skills are being acquired in early adolescence and that different peer groups expose adolescents to different conflict styles.

The Goodwins report in their study on an extremely complex dimension of conflict talk which they have identified in work on urban black youngsters playing on the "street" (i.e., in their home neighborhood and away from school). The boys, who are engaged in preparation for a sling-shot battle, are not only preparing the sling shots and missiles; they are also creating/ ratifying social organizational arrangements – most critically those of hierarchy and command. The Goodwins' study differs from other investigations of argument in two particulars. First, to a much more substantial extent than has ordinarily been the case, they have focused not so much on how participants' moves in such exchanges are patterned, but rather on *what in the behaviors of their interlocutors participants must attend to in order to construct appropriate responses.* Second, they address the question of how what is said "constitutes those who are present to it (i.e., what is said in a given turn can propose that current participants occupy particular social identities *vis-à-vis* each other.)." Pursuit of the first matter allows the Goodwins to demonstrate the analytic importance of close attention to actual text (rather than, i.e., glosses) by showing that devices employed by interlocutors are deeply dependent (even to actual wording) on the talk of their conflict partners. Pursuit of the second offers clues to critically important questions about conflict group formation.

Vuchinich's work differs from that of the other contributors, and indeed most students of conflict talk, in that rather than looking in detail at a single (and ordinarily sustained) speech event, he has looked at a phenomenon common to *all* conflict talk, i.e., termination. His analyses of multiple instances of conflict talk which occurred during family dinners aim to determine both the different ways in which conflicts are ended and the frequencies of different termination modes. Vuchinich's corpus contains some 170 conflicts which occurred during the course of sixty-four family dinners representing a range of regional locations and ethnic and class attributes. He identifies and exemplifies five termination formats: submission, dominant third-party intervention, compromise, withdrawal, and stand-off. Perhaps the most salient finding in his corpus is that the most frequent termination mode is not "resolution" but overwhelmingly a stalemate between the parties. This finding contradicts claims of experimental studies of children's conflict which report higher levels of resolution; it is more consonant with ethnographically grounded studies (see, e.g., chapter 2 below). Vuchinich's study also underlines the importance of conflict stakes and of the nature of interactant relations of power in constraining conflict closings.

While the outcomes of some of the conflicts reported in these first four studies may have been of more than momentary concern for participants, observers would generally view them as transient, unremarkable, and unimportant. Nevertheless, they demonstrate that children control a remarkable range both of conflict "routines" and of conflict formats/devices which can be used differently in different settings with different interlocutors and in search of different interactional goals. Finally, however unimportant the ends (in both Hymes' 1974 senses) of conflict talk may appear to be from the viewpoint of those not involved, participants in *all* of the kinds of conflict reported engaged in activities directed to recruiting third parties as allies, supporters, or, at the least, "approvers" or "understanders" of their positions. A similar pattern is evident in those instances of adult conflict talk reported below where there are "audiences"; it may be a candidate for status as a social-interactional universal (see Grimshaw, 1981a, chapters 5 and 9).

The remainder of the studies in the volume are concerned with adult conflict talk. The chapter by Labov, unlike others, is concerned primarily with conflict narratives, i.e., participants' reports to non-present third parties on conflict(s) in which the former were involved.[9] The conflict narratives are told by white members of food co-operative who subscribe to "liberal" ideologies, which include support of both the co-operative movement and the aspirations and rights of black Americans. They all involve confrontations between white co-op members and neighborhood blacks whose behaviour is believed to have threatened the security and functioning of the co-op. The co-op members are uncomfortable about the tensions generated by their apparent inability to act in ways consistent with *both* sets of values; the conflicts reported are clearly salient for those who tell about them. Labov shows how "commitment to organizational requirements acts as a legitimating mechanism to mitigate the effects of actions which foster segregation." In the course of her analysis she raises important questions about "speaking of" and "speaking for" and shows that adults must deal with the same questions of alignments as do the Goodwins' sling shotters – but that they do so in an even more subtle and sophisticated manner.

Discourse analysts have generally argued that they must look at naturally occurring talk in its unedited form; in increasing numbers they appear to agree that it is critical to know about both the textual and the situational contexts of talk studied. The "psychiatric out-take interview" which Mehan looks at did occur, but it is edited and essentially uncontexted; he reports that he found it so interesting that he simply could not resist an essay at analysis. Mehan uses the talk of the patient and of members of the examining board – and the outcome of the review – to show "how competing definitions of the situation are constructed and revealed in ongoing interaction," and how disputes over conflict definitions of the situation are resolved in favor of those who wield "institutionalized power." Disputes between mental patients and their doctors *are* resolved; not surprisingly, doctors usually "win" such arguments. More surprising, perhaps, is Mehan's claim that different modes of reasoning (i.e., "scientific" or "oracular"), widely believed to characterize different cultures/societies can actually both be found within our modern and "scientific" society – and that they actually co-occur in the speech event studied. I find myself wondering about being in a situation in which those with the power to define the situation subscribe to an oracular perspective – and about what mix of Mehan's oracular, religious, and scientific reasoning modes may characterize international negotiations which affect us all.

Conley and O'Barr have sought to discover some features of talk that may be associated with litigant success or failure in courts without lawyers, i.e., small claims courts.[10] In earlier work on trial courts (summarized in O'Barr, 1982; Conley, O'Barr and Lind, 1978), O'Barr, Conley and their associates discovered that the credibility of witnesses was deeply influenced by their use of more or less "powerful" ways of talking, irrespective of the content of that talk, and by the ways in which attorneys constrained them to order narrative versions of their evidence. In this investigation Conley and O'Barr describe another dimension of talk that has emerged from the study of litigant naratives in small claims courts, i.e., that talk can be rule-oriented (i.e., about contracts and evidence) or relations-oriented (i.e., about social relationships); they conclude that judges in these courts prefer to hear about contracts and evidence because a narrow focus on such issues is encouraged by the conventions of legal discourse and reasoning. Read in another way, the two styles or modes of talk differ in the nature of claims made about both normative and actual interactional identities and relationships, i.e., precisely the same sort of matters that the Goodwins discovered were being negotiated in the talk of the children they studied. Conley and O'Barr conclude with the interesting observation that even those "relations-oriented" litigants who lose (a disproportionately high number, it appears) may leave the courtroom with some satisfaction simply because they have had their story "listened to."

Philips has also looked at a part of the legal process, the talk of legally trained court officers (attorneys and judges) in trials where outcomes may be of considerably more moment to defendants who, if convicted, can in some cases be sent to prison. Curiously enough, one interesting finding of her research is that *when talking among themselves* (i.e., not in the presence of defendants, witnesses, audiences, juries, etc.) court officers often *invoke* relational matters (e.g., in the claim that a mother will not leave a jurisdiction because she will not abandon a child). Another important finding is that the third-party contributions to the management of these disputes are sometimes indistinguishable in form, content, and sequential position in the discourse from that of the disputants – an apparent anomaly which raises questions about what *does* distinguish third parties interactionally. Philips' principal concern, however, is to correct what she sees as an erroneous perception of the judge's role in American criminal trials. She reports a stereotype of American judges as acting with an Olympian detachment as contrasted to their European conterparts, "handing down" correct interpretations of the law and instructing jurors, etc., where Europeans take a more active, even inquisitorial role. She shows that in the court she investigated judges took an extremely active role under the specific circumstance that only the judge and opposing attorneys were parties to the ongoing talk (mostly discussions of either the bonding of defendants or the admissibility of evidence). The arguments appear to be couched quite substantially in terms of everyday or "common-sense logic" and to be resolved by the judge by reference as much to her predispositions, hunches, or "gut-feelings" as by invocation of codified precedent. Given the tropism of magistrates in small claims courts for rule-following remarked on by Conley and O'Barr, it is interesting to speculate on why matters in which judges participate as disputants (even though as disputants who always have the final say) are discussed only in the absence of juries. The official reason is so that jurors will not be improperly influenced; one may wonder about such latent functions as shielding jurors from knowledge that judges (and other court officers) often ignore rules in actual practice – or even simply in order to hasten things along.

The audio recordings of Quality of Working Life (QWL) program meetings between labor and management functionaries of a large public utility which O'Donnell has used in her study constitute a rare and valued resource for research on talk. While the QWL meetings are *not* bargaining sessions, the issues which are addressed (e.g., authority in the workplace, safety, mutual trust, and goodwill, etc.) are among those considered when bargaining does take place and are considered matters of moment. The meetings were expected to differ in goals (shared rather than opposing), atmosphere (co-operative rather than conflictful) and format (informal rather than formal) from bargaining or grievance sessions; a quite likely unanticipated additional difference in O'Donnell's materials is an apparent breakdown of monolithic intraparty solidarity which becomes visible when one management representative criticizes another in front of union representatives. O'Donnell's analyses differ from those of other contributors not only in the corporate as contrasted to the individual identity of the conflict parties, but also in her choice of Halliday's (1978) functional/systemic perspective (particularly "tenor") to orient her investigation of how relations of power and affect are linguistically realized. As we have seen in many of the other studies, issues of identity and of group membership are both matters at issue and resources for participants in the talk studied.

The "arguments" which Schiffrin has investigated differ from many of the others studied here in that the participants, while not by any means indifferent to the matter at issue, are deeply committed to co-operative and harmonious interpersonal relations, and also to a joint activity which may lead to consensus. The issue of intermarriage is a controversial one in the lower-middle-class Jewish community in which Schiffrin did field work; in recent years it has become possible for community members to maintain less "traditional" views on the subject. Schiffrin argues that conflict talk can be a co-operative way of speaking as well as (or instead of) a competitive one. She displays talk of family members and close friends to show how the use of "stories" and of labeled "opinions" can be used to adjust the participation framework of the talk (i.e., following Goffman [1981], interlocutors' claims to be variously animators, authors, figures, and principals). She further demonstrates that these adjustments in participation status or "footing" allow participants delicately to negotiate "two of the idealized standards (truth and sincerity) underlying argument." She argues that stories can serve as devices for diffusing the responsibility for the truth of a position and identification of positions as opinions as distancing "hedges"; it will again be clear that complex matters of personal identities and of social boundaries may simultaneously be negotiated.

Basso (1970) called attention to the expressive potential and the cross-cultural relativity of silence as a means of communication. A small number of linguists has recently turned attention to analysis of dramatic dialogue as compared to dialogue in naturally occurring conversation (see, for example, Burton, 1980).[11] The chapter by Tannen combines these two interests. Tannen's concern is the portrayal of silence as a means of managing interpersonal conflict in two works of verbal art: a play, Pinter's *Betrayal*, and a short story, "Great Wits."

After discussing the status of literary material as linguistic data, Tannen questions previous accounts of the functions of pauses and silences in Pinter's plays. Following remarks by the playwright himself, and reflecting what has long been observed in at least European-based speech communities, she suggests that both silence and a torrent of words can signal great emotion. Tannen demonstrates that in *Betrayal* pauses mark mounting conflict between characters, and silences occur when such conflict reaches points of climax, that is, points at which the most potentially damaging information, or the strongest negative emotion, is confronted. In the play, and in the short story "Great Wits," silence prevents conflict from permanently disrupting relationships. With regard to the cultural component in conflict-management style, Tannen tentatively suggests that Pinter's use of pause and silence to mask, and consequently to mark, strong negative emotion, may be characteristically British, whereas American playwrights (consider, for example, Albee) may be more likely to represent anger with loud words. As is the case with Corsaro and Rizzo's children, this difference raises interesting issues about the possibilities of universals and cultural/ speech community specialization in conflict talk.

In approaching the studies, readers may find it heuristically useful to keep in mind such considerations as: (1) relations of power and of affect and the nature of stakes in determining the occurrence, intensity, etc., of conflict talk; (2) differences in the nature and course of conflict talk in different domains, with different participants; (3) possible sociolinguistic or interactional universals in conflict talk – and of cultural and speech community specialization; (4) what sociolinguistic devices are available to and employed by conflict talk participants. I will take up these themes again in the concluding chapter.

Notes

1 There is considerable variation in views about what "context" means, and when it should be taken into account. For a somewhat cryptic review of the role of context in "disambiguation" see Grimshaw, 1987.

2 On a distinction between sociolinguistic and social-interactional rules see Grimshaw, 1981a, chapter 9.

3 Once expressed to me essentially as, "What can we learn from you people that we don't already know?" (see Grimshaw, 1988b).

4 In the final chapter I will provide modest additional detail on how contributions to this volume have employed these conceptual materials.

5 Some very similar notions appear in the work of phenomenologists, structuralists and some "critical" analysts of text (see, for a useful review and discussion, Silverman and Torode, 1980). This latter work does not appear to have had much direct impact on studies of naturally occurring (especially spoken) discourse.

6 A project in which representatives of different academic disciplines *and* analytic traditions agreed to do analyses of a shared (common) data record of naturally occurring interaction. See Grimshaw, 1980a or, for fuller

descriptions, the introductory chapters in Grimshaw, 1988a and/or Grimshaw, Feld, and Jenness, 1989.

7   A project in which social scientists and therapists projected co-operative and integrated work on an SIR of an interview between a patient and her therapist. The project was never completed, though some materials reached publication. See Zabor, 1978, for details on the NHI and Grimshaw, Feld, and Jenness, 1989 for a shorter sketch and a brief consideration of why the project was not fully successful.

8   See Grimshaw, 1988b, for some speculation on why participants in critical negotiations resist discourse-analytic study of their interaction – and on what benefits they may thereby be forfeiting.

9   Studies of conflict narratives are, like Vuchinich's quantitative studies, relatively rare in the conflict-talk literature. See, however, Bower, 1984; Dittmar, Schlobinski, and Wachs, 1987; and W. Labov, 1972a, chapter 9.

10   In at least some jurisdictions, even the presiding officers of such courts have *no* legal training and, in fact, only the most minimal preparation for the responsibilities of their positions.

11   As noted in chapter 13, conflict processes have been the specific focus of earlier studies of dramatic scriptings. Note particularly Watzlawick, Beavin, and Jackson (1967), on Albee's *Who's afraid of Virginia Woolf?*

2 Disputes in the peer culture of American and Italian nursery-school children

WILLIAM A. CORSARO AND THOMAS A.
RIZZO

1. Introduction

Carlo and Paolo are building a castle with lego-type building materials. During their play they accidently knock to the floor a castle that Alberto had previously constructed. Alberto now returns:

A: Che è successo?
(What happened?)
P: Non so.
(I don't know.)
A: Non sai? 'E un disastro!
(You don't know? It's a mess!)
P: 'E colpa di Carlo.
(It's Carlo's fault.)
C: No. Non è vero. 'E colpa di Paolo.
(No. It's not true. It's Paolo's fault.)
((Stefano is playing nearby and he overhears the argument.))
S: 'E colpa di Carlo e Paolo, hai capito?
(It is the fault of Carlo and Paolo, have you understood?)
A: Si. Si. Capito. ((A now begins picking up the pieces of his broken castle, shaking his head in agreement with Stefano's statement.))
(Yes. Yes. Understood.)

One of the first things that struck me in my observations in a *scuola materna* in Bologna was the pervasiveness of language and verbal routines in the children's peer culture. It was not simply that the Italian children appeared to be more verbal in peer interaction than the American children I have observed.[1] It seemed, rather, that almost everything the Italian children talked about turned into a verbal performance. Consider the example which introduces this chapter. It is a typical dispute over the use of play materials. Carlo and Paolo have somewhat carelessly knocked Alberto's construction to the floor. When Alberto returns and sees this, he does not

21

directly accuse Carlo and Paolo, but instead he asks what happened. Paolo first reports a lack of knowledge, which is indirectly dismissed as ludicrous by Alberto (how could such a mess occur without one noticing!). This initial response is followed by two denials of responsibility in which Paolo and Carlo blame each other. At this point a third party (Stefano), who has overheard the dispute, offers his version, which is accepted by Alberto as the "true facts" he had suspected all along.

What the children have done here is to take this disputable occurrence and turn it into a verbal routine, or what Italians might refer to as a topic for *discussione*. In such debates the discussion itself becomes more important than a settlement, one's style or "metodo di persuasione" being more important than any eventual resolution.

When I observed such examples in Bologna, I would often reflect back on my experiences in American nursery schools and try to bring to mind how American children might interactively confront similar situations. For example, my reconstructed American scenario of the above interactive sequence would have the faulted child directly accusing the suspected culprit(s) with the following results.

A: You broke my castle!
B: Did not!
A: You did too.
B: Did not.
A: I'm telling the teacher.

When I returned from Italy I began to analyze the American data (videotapes of peer interaction) with these reconstructions in hand. These investigations primarily involved the analysis of peer disputes. This paper is a report of what we found in the American data regarding children's disputes and a comparison of these findings with an initial analysis of the Italian data.

2. Recent research on children's disputes

Before turning to the analysis, it is useful to review some of the recent research on children's disputes and arguments. These studies provide important insights on how to approach interactive data of this type, and in our analysis we rely on several analytic procedures which were first introduced in this previous work. Most of the recent work on children's verbal disputes can be grouped into one of three categories. In the first type, there is an emphasis on the form or structure of disputes with little discussion of the functions of disputes in peer culture or the more general implications of peer conflict for children's social and cognitive development. One of the best examples of this approach is the work of Brenneis and Lein (1977; also see Lein and Brenneis, 1978, for a cross-cultural analysis of children's disputes). In this research the authors elicited role-play arguments from elementary school children (grades 1, 3, and 4) in quasi-experimental settings. The role-play arguments were then analyzed in terms of content and style. Regarding content, the authors identified a number of different types of initial or opening acts in disputes (e.g., threats, insults, simple assertions, etc) and reactions (e.g., denials, demands for evidence, etc). Regarding style, Brenneis and Lein noted the importance of various paralinguistic cues like volume, speed, and stress. However, the main focus of Brenneis and Lein's work was on patterns of content and style which include repetition, inversion and escalation. The work of Boggs (1978) builds on Brenneis and Lein, in that he identified several basic sequences in the disputes of part-Hawaiian children. Boggs, however, collected his data in natural settings and, therefore, was able to go beyond a purely structural analysis to consider some of the functions of disputes in the peer culture of the children he studied.

A second type of research involves a primary focus on the functions of verbal disputes for children's development of cognitive and communicative skills. One of the best examples of this type of research is Eisenberg and Garvey's (1981; also see Garvey, 1984) study of what they term "adversative episodes" in peer interaction. Eisenberg and Garvey's research was based on the analysis of videotapes of peer interaction among pre-school children. The children (some acquainted and others not) were brought to a playroom setting in dyads and they were encouraged to engage in peer play for approximately fifteen-minute sessions (see Eisenberg and Garvey, 1981).

In analyzing instances of conflict in these materials, Eisenberg and Garvey first isolated adversative episodes which were defined as beginning with the first instance of opposition and ending when (1) an obvious settlement was reached, (2) one child left the scene of interaction and was not pursued, and (3) the discourse topic was altered and not resumed for a period of one minute (1981: 157). In their analysis of adversative episodes, the authors first identified several types of disputes which are very similar to those we discovered in our data (e.g., object disputes, disputes over the nature of play, etc., see below). Second, like Brenneis and Lein, Garvey and Eisenberg identified a basic structure in children's disputes involving initial opposition followed by a series of responses. For example, the authors described several types of initial opposition which usually involved some variant of a negative response to the actions or verbalizations of the other member of the dyad. These oppositions were often followed by one of a wide range of strategies or reactions to initial oppositions. Third, unlike Brenneis and Lein, Eisenberg and Garvey focused less on specifying stylistic variations in the structure of the disputes and more on identifying the effectiveness of various types of moves or responses. For this reason they examined sequential patterns in the data with special emphasis on discovering which strategies were more likely to lead to conflict resolution. Overall, in line with

Piaget (1984) Eisenberg and Garvey argue that children's conflict should not be viewed as representing the breakdown of interaction, but rather be seen as an important impetus for the development of social thought.

One limitation of Eisenberg and Garvey's work is that the data were not collected in naturalistic settings. Although the disputes themselves were not elicited, they were (because of the nature of data-collection procedures) always dyadic and their occurrence was isolated from contextual factors present in natural settings like the nursery school, home, and play group. It is the presence of these contextual factors and of additional potential participants (other peers and adult caretakers) which are of crucial importance for discovering the functions of children's disputes within peer culture.

A third type of research on children's disputes focuses directly on the form and function of disputes within peer culture. The best example of this approach is the impressive ethnographic research of M.H. Goodwin (1980a, 1980b, 1982a, 1982b, and 1985). Goodwin's work is based on the microsociolinguistic analysis of audiotaped naturally occurring peer conversations that were collected as part of an intensive ethnography of urban black working-class children in the United States. Blending analytic techniques borrowed from conversational analysis (Sacks, Schegloff, and Jefferson, 1974) with ethnographic information on the community, the children, and peer culture, Goodwin, through the investigation of the form and sequencing of verbal disputes, demonstrates how the social order of the moment is formulated, rejected, and reconstituted through talk (M.H. Goodwin, 1982a: 77).

Like Eisenberg and Garvey, M.H. Goodwin (1982a) challenges the view that argumentative talk is disorderly or unorganized. Goodwin's work clearly demonstrates the orderliness with which disputes are conducted as well as the linguistic and communicative competence black children display in argumentation. However, unlike Eisenberg and Garvey, Goodwin does not assume that the effectiveness of various argumentative strategies can be evaluated in terms of whether or not or how quickly they lead to conflict resolution. Goodwin found that the children's arguments in her study rarely ended in compromise or settlement. But instead of viewing this relative absence of resolution as being the result of the ineffectiveness of various strategies, Goodwin demonstrates that aggravated disagreements are activities that the children worked to achieve in their own right (1983: 675). In fact, Goodwin suggests that this tendency to display rather than put off the expression of opposition can be seen as an important feature of peer culture.

In line with Goodwin, it is clear in the analysis we present below that disputes (in both the American and Italian data) become mutually shareable events in the course of their production. It is clear that the nature, direction, and resolution or non-resolution of disputes are closely tied to the interactive contexts within which they occur and to the peer culture of the children involved.

3. Data and method

The data for the following analysis of peer disputes were collected in two long-term micro-ethnographic studies of peer interaction in nursery schools. The first study was conducted in a nursery school in the United States which is part of a child study center staffed and operated by a state university for education and research. The school is located in a large metropolitan city near the university campus. There were two groups of children at the school, with approximately twenty-five children in each group. One group attended morning sessions and ranged in age from 2.10 to 3.10 years. The second group (which had been at the school the year before) attended afternoon sessions and ranged in age from 3.10 to 4.10 years at the start of the school term. The occupational and educational background of parents of the children ranged from blue-collar workers to professionals, with the majority of the children coming from middle- and upper-class families. I have presented a detailed discussion of field entry and data collection for this study elsewhere (see Corsaro, 1981b, 1985). For this report, twenty-one of 146 videotaped episodes (about eight hours of twenty-seven hours of video data) were selected for analysis. Although this subsample contains all of the transcribed data and nearly all of the longer episodes, it is also representative of the entire set of video data in terms of the age and number of children involved, the nature of activity or play, and points in time over the school term. A total of 110 disputes were isolated in the subsample of video data and these materials serve as the basis for the present analysis.

The second study, in which data collection was only recently completed, was conducted in a *scuola materna* in Bologna, Italy. The *scuola materna* is a pre-school educational program which exists throughout Italy and is administered by local governments. The *scuola materna* provides child care and educational programs for children from the ages of three to six years. The *scuola materna* which I studied was staffed by five teachers and there were thirty-five children who attended for approximately seven hours (9:30 until 5:00; some children returned home at 1:00) each weekday. The general methodological procedures, which involved participant observation, audio and video recording and micro-analysis of peer interaction, were similar to those employed in the American study and described in Corsaro (1985). The Italian data were collected over a six-month period (January through June, 1984) with additional video data collected over a two-month period (May through June) a year later. The data used for this report involve the analysis of peer disputes recorded on videotape and several audiotaped episodes which have been transcribed. For purposes of this report, twenty of the twenty-seven videotaped episodes (five of eight hours) and three audiotaped episodes were selected for analysis. This sub-sample makes up the majority of the video data collected in Italy and it is representative of the entire data set (i.e., episodes recorded in field notes and on video and audio tape) in terms of the age and number of children involved and the nature of activities. Altogether, 148 disputes were isolated in the subsample of audiovisual data selected for analysis.

For the purposes of this report, disputes are defined as general disagreements in interaction which are displayed by the occurrence of some sort of opposition to an antecedent event. We do not view the antecedent event as part of the dispute *per se* but rather as its source. Therefore, disputes begin with oppositions and end with either clear settlements, physical movement of dispute participants from the interactive scene, or a shift away from the disputed event to a new topic or activity. This definition is quite similar to the one used by Eisenberg and Garvey (1981) and Genishi and di Paolo (1982), who also worked with younger children. It differs in some respects from the conceptualizations of Maynard (1985a,b) and M.H. Goodwin (1983) who studied somewhat older children, using an approach in line with conceptualizations generated in conversational analysis (see especially Schegloff, Jefferson, and Sacks, 1977). We wish to emphasize here that the question of what actually constitutes a dispute in children's discourse is one that is not easily answered. It is an issue we are presently addressing in another paper.

In analyzing the disputes we relied on a procedure first employed in an early study of children's access rituals (see Corsaro, 1979). The first step in the analysis of the disputes involved removing each occurrence from its original source (transcript of videotaped episodes) and recording them on notecards, with prior and later discourse included to preserve context. The cards were then sorted into groups (piles) bases upon (intuitive) recognition of similarity. After the sorting process was completed we inspected each group and, after some re-grouping, identified four basic types of disputes in the data. At this point, we inspected each instance of all types of disputes and specified: (1) whether or not a clear resolution occurred; (2) the number of dispute turns; and (3) discourse features of the initial opposition and reactions to opposition. In this step we worked both with the notecards and the transcripts, and in most cases returned to view the dispute sequence in the videotaped episodes.

4. Analysis

4.1 Disputes among American nursery-school children

As noted previously, we isolated 110 disputes in the sub-sample of videotaped data from the American study. Table 2.1 reports the number of different types of disputes which occurred in the American data as well as the proportion that were clearly resolved and the mean number of turns in

Table 2.1 *Types of disputes in the American data*

Type of dispute	N	%	Resolution Yes	Resolution No	Mean number of turns
Nature of play	62	56.4	33	29	2.14 (14)[a]
Object	25	22.7	14	11	5.10 (11)
Access	16	14.5	6	10	3.50 (17)
Claim	7	6.4	2	5	2.75 (12)
Total	110		55	55	

[a]Greatest number of turns in a specific dispute

the various types of disputes. This table should be seen primarily as a way of displaying the general nature of disputes in these materials. The type of dispute, resolution, and length are all dependent on social context and the number of participants involved.

However, there are several points we would like to make about table 2.1. First the types of disputes are quite similar to those found by Eisenberg and Garvey (1981) and Genishi and di Paolo (1982) who also studied nursery-school children. There are, however, a few minor differences. Both Eisenberg and Garvey (1981) and Genishi and di Paolo (1982) found that disputes over objects occurred about twice as often as disputes over conduct or the nature of play, while we found the reverse to be the case. This difference may be related to our broader conceptualization of disputes over nature of play which includes an opposition to the actions of conduct of others within play and not just to pretend transformations (e.g., plans, role allocations in pretend play, etc.). A second more important difference is the absence of disputes over access to play in the research of Eisenberg and Garvey (1981) and Genishi and di Paolo (1982). We found a substantial number of disputes over access which is in line with Corsaro's (1979) earlier work which noted the complexity of children's access rituals in these materials. In Eisenberg and Garvey's research, the problem of access to play activities was eliminated because data collection limited the interaction to dyads. Genishi and di Paolo (1982) report few instances of access/exclusion disputes but they observed a relatively small nursery group (only eight children), while the groups we observed were much larger (twenty-five or more children). In any case, as we demonstrate below, access attempts often involve collaboration or teamwork among those children defending and attempting to enter play areas.

A third point about table 2.1 is the low frequency (only 6.4%) of disputes over the expression of opinions or beliefs (i.e., what we call "claims"). This finding is similar to those of Eisenberg and Garvey and Genishi and di Paolo.

Although M.H. Goodwin (1980a, 1980b, 1982b, 1983) and Maynard (1985a,b) do not specifically report types of disputes, it is clear from examples presented in their analyses that the majority are related to claims. As we noted previously, Goodwin and Maynard worked primarily with older children, but as we shall see below in the preliminary analysis of the Italian data, this difference in the number of disputes over beliefs or opinions can not be accounted for simply by age differences.

Two final points to note about table 2.1 concern the issue of resolution and length of disputes. In line with the findings of Genishi and di Paolo (1982) and M.H. Goodwin (1982a, 1983), we found that clear resolution did not consistently occur (only 50% of the time in our data). Although Eisenberg and Garvey do not specify the percentage of clear resolutions in their data, they imply that settlements occurred in the majority of cases. The difference is probably the result of the dyadic situation in Eisenberg and Garvey's materials. As Genishi and di Paolo note, the children in Eisenberg and Garvey's study had no access to adults who could help resolve conflicts nor could the children leave the play area and seek out other peer activities (1982: 66). We should also note, in line with M.H. Goodwin (1983), that the aggravation or extension of disputes themselves can become more important than resolution for the children involved. We feel this is much more likely to be the case among children who have a history of playing together and when the peer interaction is occurring in natural play settings. Finally, regarding the length of disputes, it is clear from table 2.1 that disputes over play objects are longer overall than any other type of disputes. This finding must be evaluated with caution because length of dispute is influenced by a number of additional factors such as the number of children involved, whether or not adult intervention occurs, and the availability of alternative play materials and participants in the setting. Given these cautions, it is still useful to point out that the object disputes may be lengthier because of the children's tendency not to give up easily when vying for play materials. This possibility is explored further below, where we look at the sociolinguistic patterns in disputes over possession of play materials.

4.2 Sociolinguistic patterns in the American children's peer disputes

Disputes over the nature of play   These disputes involve oppositions to the actions of others within the play frame. In simple terms, they consist of complaints about the way an act is carried out, imperatives to stop inappropriate behavior, or disagreements about the extensions of the play frame. Of the sixty-two disputes of this type, thirty-seven were simple, in that they involved the statement of an opposition (with or without a reason supplied) and a limited number or variety of reactions to the opposition. Consider example 1:[2]

Example 1

Two boys (Graham and Larry) and several other children are playing around the sandbox with water. Each child has an individual hose.
(Larry squirts water at Graham.)
*1. G: Quit it. Don't do that Larry.
(Larry stops squirting water at Graham.)

In other cases there were negative reactions and reasons provided, but no new reasons were provided after the initial opposition-reaction exchange. Consider example 2:

Example 2

Three girls (Alice, Beth, and Vickie) are playing a card game. Alice and Beth both try to take a turn at the same time. They struggle and Beth pushes Alice away.
*1. B: No-o-o-o!
 2. A: It's my turn
 3. V: It's her turn.
 4. A: My turn, It's my turn!
 5. V: B, it's her turn.

In this episode there is a struggle over the cards and Beth supplies an opposition to Alice (1). Alice responds stating a reason (it's her turn). Vickie supports Alice and then both Vickie and Alice repeat their earlier reason. However, Beth ignores them and takes a turn anyway. We see this as a simple dispute because the children do not go beyond the initial opposition-reaction exchange to repeat their earlier reasons. In complex disputes more than one reason is provided and children also employ a range of other strategies in their responses to initial opposition. Consider example 3:

Example 3

A girl (Rita) and two boys (Denny and Martin) are involved in role play. Rita is the mother and she is pretending to make a pair of pants for Denny while he plays in the climbing bars with Martin.
(Denny climbs high on the bars then leans out, holding on with one hand.)
*1. R: Get off the porch! It's dangerous. Get off that porch. Get off it. It's dangerous. You'll fall off it.
 2. D: OK. Then make him get off the porch too. (Points to Martin.)
 3. R: Cause my brother did one day.

4. D: Well you have to share.
5. R: I'm sharing, but you're like a monkey just hanging on the porch and you're gonna fall off.
(Denny now moves down from bars near Rita.)

In this example of role play Rita, in line with her mother role, is objecting to the dangerous behavior of Denny. She tells him to stop and them offers a reason. Denny at first agrees but makes his agreement contingent on Rita's inclusion of Martin in her discipline. We see this as a counter to Rita's opposition and it is clear that Denny's alternative fits into the role-play theme. Rita ignores the counter and offers an additional and more specific reason (3), her brother once fell off the porch. Whether or not this mishap really occurred is unclear here, but it is apparent that Rita is going outside the role play to provide support for her stand within the play. At this point (4), Denny provides a reason based on a general rule of sharing in the nursery school. This reason seems somewhat strange within the role play frame, given that they are already sharing. In effect, Rita makes this same point at line 5 where she argues that she is sharing, and then goes on to repeat her prior reason for opposing his behaviour (i.e., that it is dangerous). This example nicely demonstrates the functions of disputes for the organization of role-play events of this type.

A final example of a complex dispute regarding the nature of play demonstrates how conflicts occur and are addressed during the use of play materials like blocks and toy cars.

Example 4

Two boys (Daniel and Allen) are playing with building blocks and toy animals and cars.

1. A: (holding a car): Yeah and it can go right down it. (Allen lets car slide down board) and go voom.
*2. D: Sure, but the cars can't go down a building. (Daniel removes Allen's sliding board from the building.) I know cars can't go down a building.
3. A: This car can – put that – right here. (Allen takes board from Daniel then lays it down for a shorter one.) No, I'm going to make it shorter. The car can go –
4. D: Sorry about this but they can't, see?
5. A: See watch this one. (Places car on shorter board and lets it slide down.)
6. D: No.
(Daniel now leaves to get a block and when he returns this discussion is not renewed.)

In this example we have an unresolved dispute over the pretend/real frame in the emerging play event. At line 1 Allen describes his actions to Daniel as he lets his car slide down a ramp. Daniel objects at 2, by noting that cars can't go down a building. Daniel's utterance here is complex in that he is agreeing that Allen's car went down a building, but he is also implying that cars can't go down buildings in real life. It seems Daniel wants Allen to stay within a certain play frame here. He wants Allen to reconstruct real life events with him through their manipulation of toy cars and buildings. The problem is that Allen is proposing an impossible event in real life. Allen seems to miss the point at 3 by attempting to demonstrate that the toy car can, in fact, go down a toy building. Daniel interrupts at 4 and repeats his earlier reason. At 5, Allen completes his demonstration providing the evidence as a reason for his negative reaction to Daniel's opposition. At this point (6), Daniel simply repeats his earlier opposition and temporarily leaves the play area, which terminates the discussion.

Overall, we see that children often become involved in disputes in negotiations over the nature of ongoing and emerging play. In the more complex disputes children are often trying to reach agreement on play frames, especially real/pretend distinctions. Sometimes they are successful and sometimes not, but it is clear that disputes are important in children's attempts to reach shared understanding and to jointly organize and construct play events.

Object disputes   Disputes over objects center around children's disagreements about the possession and use of materials. Such disputes are frequent in the nursery school because children often have only limited experience in sharing play materials in the home before they enter school. In fact, the nature of possession itself shifts when children move from the home to nursery school. At home children have certain possessions (toys, books, etc.) which they may, at times, have to share with friends or siblings. But these objects belong to them and remain in their possession after periods of sharing. In the nursery school things are different. Children must learn to share a range of objects in common by means of temporary possession. Negotiations over temporary possession often turn into disputes. In our data the majority of the disputes (fifteen of twenty-five) were simple in structure, and normally began with opposition and a negative reaction to opposition. These disputes often involved reference to simple temporal reasons or justifications (e.g., I had that first). We found, however, that many of these simple disputes were quite lengthy, in that the initial opposition and reactions were often repeated over and over again without elaboration. We refer to this pattern as multiple insistence and it is nicely demonstrated in example 5.

Example 5

A girl (Barbara) and boy (Richard) are playing with blocks. Richard picks up a block near Barbara and Barbara attempts to take it from him.

*1. B: No – no.
 2. R: No.
 3. B: I had it first.
 4. R: I want one.
 5. B: But I had it first.
 6. R: I want one Barbara.
 7. B: I had that first.
 8. R: I want it.
 9. B: I had it first.

(At this point a teacher intervenes and suggests that Barbara go to the shelf and get another block. As Barbara does so, Richard takes the disputed block.)

Although multiple insistence was common in object disputes, there were also several cases where the children attempted to hold their ground without relying on simple repetition. Consider example 6.

Example 6

Two boys (Daniel and Tommy) have been hammering nails into boards. They were standing on chairs and working with the hammers and boards on top of a shelf. The activity was described by Daniel as preparation for a puppet show. Several other children were sitting in front of the shelf waiting for the puppet show to begin. Daniel leaves momentarily and when he returns he sees one board on the floor and Tommy still hammering a board which is still on the shelf.

*1. D: Why did you have to – (Daniel looks down to board on the floor.) Hey, where's my board? Tommy, this is my board. (Daniel grabs board Tommy is working with.) Go get your own.
 2. T (Looks around and sees other board on the floor): My board's right down on the floor? That's your board. (Tommy now gets down next to Daniel and both inspect the board on the floor.)
 3. T (Picks up board from the floor): I wasn't working this.
 4. D: You weren't? Then who was?
 5. T: I was working yours? Not then I was working –
 6. D: That one's mine! I was working on there and that was mine, huh

(They return to shelf where Daniel pulls board in front of him.)

 7. D: That was mine. Here. You go get your own. That was mine so go get your own.

(Tommy gets board from the floor.)
    8. D: Good

In this example, Daniel reacts to Tommy's using the remaining board on the shelf by claiming the board as his own. In reality, possession of the boards was difficult to determine since the boys left and returned to the area several times. Tommy responds to Daniel's opposition with a question: "My board's right down on the floor?" The question is then followed by a denial ("That's your board") which is reason for the negative reaction to Daniel's opposition. This sequence is highly complex and stylistic. Tommy's question at 2 is, in line with M.H. Goodwin (1983), best seen as a predisagreement which is followed in the same turn with a disagreement. This use of predisagreement is then picked up on by Daniel at line 4. Here, in response to Tommy's claim that he wasn't working the board on the floor, Daniel says: "You weren't? Then who was?". Here we have a predisagreement ("you weren't?") followed by a disagreement expressed indirectly in question form. The question, "Then who was?" is actually a counter to Tommy's denial since if Tommy was not working the board who else could be except Daniel (who has already denied that the board on the floor is his)? At 5, Tommy again produces a predisagreement which shows that he interprets Daniel's turn at 4 as both a disagreement to his statement at 3 and as an accusation. That is, Tommy takes Daniel's "Then who was?" (4) to mean "you were playing with my board", to which Tommy responds with the predisagreement "I was working yours?" followed immediately by a denial and what seems to be a reason. However, Daniel interrupts Tommy before the reason can be stated and first repeats his claim to the board and then supports it with a reason produced in the form of a tag question (6). Finally, Daniel repeats his earlier directive to Tommy who decides to give in at this point.

Although example 6 is very similar to the complex form of aggravated disagreements M.H. Goodwin found routinely in her materials, such forms occurred very rarely in the American data. In fact, in every dispute where predisagreements occurred in the data the same child (Daniel in examples 4 and 6) was a participant. Further, the only two children to use predisagreements were Daniel and Tommy who are both black, as were all the children in M.H. Goodwin's study. This finding suggests that children's exposure to complex argumentation styles within racial and ethnic groups may be more important than age in developing such styles. We will return to this point when we discuss the Italian data below.

Access and claim disputes   As we have noted in previous research (see Corsaro, 1979, 1985), interaction in the nursery school is fragile, and peer activities can break down with even minimal disruption. As a result, the children often protect interactive space by discouraging the access attempts of others. Given this tendency to protect interactive space, it is not surprising

that we found a number of disputes embedded in the children's attempts to
gain access to ongoing play. The majority of these disputes (10 of 16) were
complex in that they went beyond the basic opposition reaction to opposition sequences. Many of the access disputes in the data involved collaboration or teamwork (see Maynard, 1985a,b), most especially between those
children attempting to protect the interactive space from the entry of others
Consider example 7:

Example 7

Two boys (Richard and Denny) have been playing with a slinky on the
stairway leading to the upstairs playhouse in the school. During their
play two other boys (Joseph and Martin) enter and stand near the bottom
of the stairs.
*1. D: Go!
(Martin now runs off, but Joseph remains and he eventually moves
halfway up the stairs.)
 2. J: These are big shoes.
 3. R: I'll punch him right in the eye.
 4. J: I'll punch you right in the nose.
 5. D: I'll punch him with my big fist.
 6. J: I'll – I – I –
 7. R: And he'll be bumpety, bumpety and punched out all the way
         down the stairs.
 8. J: I – I – I'll – I could poke your eyes out with my gun. I have a gun.
 9. D: A gun! I'll – I – I – even if –
10. R: I have a gun too.
11. D: And I have guns too and it's bigger than yours and it poo-poo
         down. That's poo-poo.
(All three boys laugh at Denny's reference to poo-poo.)
12. R: Now leave.
13. J: Un-huh. I gonna tell you to put on – on the gun on your hair and
         the poop will come right out on his face.
14. D: Well.
15. R: Slinky will snap right on your face too.
16. D: And my gun will snap right –
(At this point a girl [Debbie] enters, says she is Batgirl, and asks if they
have seen Robin. Joseph says he is Robin, but she says she is looking for a
different Robin and then runs off. After Debbie leaves, Denny and Richard
move into the playhouse and Joseph follows. From this point to the end of
the episode the three boys play together.)

In this example Richard and Denny had created a game – taking turns
tossing a slinky down the stairs – which they would like to protect from the

intrusion of other children. Although successful in warding off the access attempts of several children, Richard and Denny are unable to overcome Joseph's persistence.

Unable to dissuade Joseph with simple warnings, the boys turn to physical threats. These threats exhibit some of the same features isolated by Brenneis and Lein (1977) in their analysis of the arguments of first-grade children. For example, the boys used repetition, in that some threats were countered by similar threats (e.g., lines 3–4, "I'll punch him right in the eye," "I'll punch you right in the nose,") and escalation, in that in some exchanges successive statements were stronger and often longer and more complex syntactically than preceding statements (e.g., lines 7–8).

Although the data in this example are similar to the findings of Brenneis and Lein (1977), there are some important differences. These differences are primarily the result of how the data were collected. In Brenneis and Lein's study, the data were elicited by asking children to "role play" situations which would lead to arguments or disputes. For example, dyads were asked to have an argument about who was the smartest (1977: 50).

Although children may certainly argue about who is the smartest in real-life situations, such arguments are embedded in naturally occurring peer activites. Features of interactive events like the nature of the ongoing activity (e.g., "playing a game," "talking about friends," etc.), where the dispute occurred in unfolding activities, the number of children involved, etc., are important both for children's participation in disputes of this type and for researchers' analysis and interpretations of the behavior.

In example 7, the more complex threats emerged as a result of Joseph's persistence in gaining access to the play shared by Richard and Denny. In fact, Richard and Denny had verbally remarked that they were "sharing" the slinky and would not allow others to play before any child attempted to gain entry. As a result, this example contained a pattern typical of peer culture in the nursery school, "defenders versus intruders" (see Corsaro, 1985).

Given Joseph's persistence, a triadic sequence developed involving Richard and Denny defending the play area against Joseph. As a result, we see several examples of collaboration (see Maynard, 1985a,b) within this dispute. This interactive alignment led to the interesting sociolinguistic feature of several of the threats; that being the "indirect" nature of many of Richard and Denny's verbal threats. For example, Richard and Denny threaten Joseph by *telling each other* what they plan to do to him (3,5, and 7). These indirect speech acts served two functions in this context. First, the boys were able *to threaten* Joseph and attempt to counter his access attempt. Second, the indirect threats were used collaboratively *to build solidarity* in the defender dyad by *marking the team effort* of their attempt to dissuade Joseph.

A final interesting feature of the indirect threats is Richard's use of an indirect simile at line 7. Richard notes that: "and he'll [Joseph] be bumpety, bumpety and punched out all the way down the stairs." Richard is implying that Joseph (after he is punched out) will go bumpety, bumpety all the way down the stairs like the slinky he and Denny had been playing with earlier. Again it is important to note that this interpretation of the complexity of Richard's threat was based on having information on the whole episode in which the dispute was embedded.

We now come to the final part of the dispute and the children's references to "poo-poo." Almost all disputes in the nursery school were settled without physical aggression. Disputes would often escalate to a given point and then be *relieved* by some action, such as one or the other party giving in or teacher intervention. A form of *relief* often observed was the production of a cue or signal that the dispute was, after all, *part of play* and should not be taken too seriously. In example 7, and in other disputes involving verbal threats, the signal which brought about relief to an escalating series of threats was a reference to "poo-poo."

In example 7, Joseph escalated the dispute (8) by threatening to poke out Richard's eyes with a gun. Denny repeated Joseph's reference to a gun, but hesitated in escalating the dispute. Richard then noted (10) that he had a gun too, but he did not directly threaten Joseph. Denny, after taking time to think about a response to Joseph, claimed he had a bigger gun (11) and that his gun would "poo-poo down." Although Denny's meaning is not clear, it seems he is saying that his gun will shoot poo-poo. Nevertheless, Denny's reference to "poo-poo" leads to laughter and relief from the escalating dispute. After the laughter, Richard again told Joseph to leave. Joseph, however, countered with a threat (13) that also contained a reference to "poo-poo." Joseph's threat here can be seen as a positive response to Denny's earlier attempt to end the dispute. At 15, Richard again threatens Joseph, as does Denny (16). At this point Debbie enters the area and draws the boys' attention away from the dispute. Shortly thereafter, Denny, Richard and Joseph play together in the upstairs playhouse, and the three boys eventually left together to play in another area of the school.

We see in this example that the structure and functions of children's disputes are often tied directly to features of peer culture in this setting. Disputes are part of the everyday activities of children in peer settings like the nursery school (see M.H. Goodwin, 1982a; Maynard, 1985a,b; for examples of other peer settings). In this sense disputes constitute elements through which children produce and participate in a shared peer culture.

A final type of dispute involved conflict resulting from one or more children opposing the stated beliefs or opinions of another child. We refer to such instances of conflict as claim disputes. As we saw in table 2.1, claim disputes rarely occurred in the American data. Of the seven that did occur, only two had a complex structure. In both of these cases the complexity was the result of the challenged child's attempts to gain support for his/her position. Consider the following example:

Example 8

Four boys (Lanny, Graham, Peter, and Frank) are playing with water around a sand box. Each child has an individual hose. Lanny and Frank are playing alongside each other and are facing Peter and Graham. A fifth child, a girl (Antoinette), is on the far side of the sandbox positioned between the two dyads.

1. L: Look what we made Graham. We made a real waterfall. Hey we made the best waterfall!
2. F: Yeah.
*3. P: That's not a waterfall.
4. L: Yes it is –
5. P: Lanny's isn't. Lanny's isn't.
6. L: I did the – a waterfall, right F?
7. F: Yeah.
8. A: Frank's is.
9. L: Yes, Mine is, isn't it, Frank?
10. F: It's mine.
11. L: It's both of ours, right?
12. F: Right and we made it ourselves.
13. L: Yeah.
14. P: Graham, we're not gonna be Frank's and Lanny's friend, right?
15. G: I am.
16. F: I'm gonna throw water at you [Peter] if you don't stop it, and tell the teachers. And then splash water on you again.

(Both Peter and Graham laugh at Frank's threat.)

It is clear in this example that the children sometimes both make and oppose claims as a way of collaborating and competing in play. Lanny is trying very hard to gain the support of Frank in his competition with the other children. Lanny does this by claiming that he and Frank made a real and the best waterfall (1). Frank supports this claim (2), but Peter specifically denies Lanny's contribution to the building of the waterfall (5). Lanny then tries and eventually gains support from Frank (6–13). At this point Peter counters by trying to set himself and Graham apart from Lanny and Frank (14). This attempt fails, however, when Graham refuses to go along (15). The dispute then ends as a result of Frank's playful threats (16). Here, as we saw earlier in example 7, the dispute is settled through humour. Frank's threats are humorous because he mixes teacher-sanctioned behavior (i.e., throwing water) with a threat to tell the teacher. Such a strategy is contradictory and it draws laughter from Peter and Graham because if Frank actually carried out his threat, Peter could easily get back at him simply by telling the teacher that Frank threw water.

This final example from the American data is interesting because it demonstrates how children's performances in disputes over claims can be related to their status in the peer group. These children were all approximately five years and six months old. It was among the older children in the nursery school that we most often observed competitive verbal disputes of this type. It seems that as children move into the pre-adolescent years (seven to eleven) there may be a gradual change from a communal to a more competitive peer culture (see Corsaro, 1985). The work of M.H. Goodwin (1980a, 1980b, 1982a, 1982b) and Maynard (1985a,b) with older children supports such a view. However, our initial analysis of the Italian data raises questions about such an interpretation.

4.3 Disputes among Italian nursery-school children

As noted earlier, we isolated 148 disputes in the subsample of audiovisual data from the Italian study. Since sampling of episodes in the American and Italian studies was not random, any comparison of the two samples regarding the number of occurrences of various types of behaviour must be evaluated with caution. Nevertheless, the data suggests that disputes occur more often among the Italian children than among the American children. We isolated 110 disputes in twenty-one episodes in the American data, while we found 148 disputes in twenty-three episodes in the Italian data. However, what is of most interest for this report is a comparison of the types and sociolinguistic features of disputes in the two data sets.

Table 2.2 reports the frequency of different types of disputes, the proportion of disputes that were clearly resolved, and the length (mean number of turns) of disputes in the Italian data. As we noted earlier, the tabulation of this information is a way of displaying the general nature of the disputes. It is the sociolinguistic analysis that follows which captures the more context-dependent features of children's disputes. There are, however, several points to note about table 2.2.

First, there are several general similarities between the Italian data (table 2.2) and the American data which were presented earlier in table 2.1. For example, the most frequent type of dispute in both data sets involved conflict or disagreements over the nature of play. In both settings these disputes were similar in length and were clearly resolved about 50% of the time. This general similarity regarding disputes over the nature of play may be due to the overall correspondence of the two nursery schools in terms of the social ecology of the settings, the number of children attending each school, and

Table 2.2 *Types of disputes in the Italian data*

Type of dispute	N	%	Resolution		Mean number of turns
			Yes	No	
Nature of play	63	42.6	30	33	3.48 (13)[a]
Claim	47	31.8	10	37	6.59 (56)
Object	19	12.8	9	10	3.89 (10)
Routine	10	6.8	0	10	6.33 (14)
Access	9	6.0	4	5	4.00 (12)
Total	148		53	95	

[a]Most number of turns in a specific dispute

the instructional philosophy of each school which emphasizes the importance of peer play.

A second general similarity in the two data sets involves the occurrence of object and access disputes. Although there was a lower frequency of these types of disputes in the Italian data, they occurred with some regularity and their patterns of resolution and their length are similar in the two samples (see tables 2.1 and 2.2). There is an important point to note about the relative scarcity of access disputes among the Italian children. Although they were less likely to resist access attempts than the American children, the Italian children were much more likely to set restrictions on the participation of peers who were granted access. These restrictions often met resistance and frequently resulted in the occurrence of other types of disputes (e.g., claim and nature of play).

Although the American and Italian data share the general similarities noted above, there are several specific, and rather striking, differences. The main variation in the two data sets involves the frequency and nature of claim disputes. As we can see in table 2.2, over 31% of the Italian children's disputes entailed conflict arising from the expression of claims, beliefs, or opinions, while there were very few claim disputes in the American data (6.4% of all disputes, see table 2.1). Further, the Italian children's claim disputes were resolved only about 20% of the time and these disputes were quite lengthy (6.59 mean turns with one dispute containing fifty-six turns of talk). As we argue in more detail below, claim disputes often display the Italian children's enjoyment of argumentation or *discussione* – an activity that is, as we shall see, clearly a feature of the peer culture of Italian children.

This enjoyment of *discussione* is also a central factor in another notable difference between the two data sets, that being the occurrence of what we term "dispute routines" in the Italian but not the American data. Although various types of teasing routines sometimes occurred within access, object or other disputes in the American and Italian data, there were several instances (ten or 6.8% of the total disputes, see table 2.2) in the Italian data where the entire dispute involved the enactment of complex, stylistic, and aesthetically impressive routines. In these instances what appears to be a dispute is, in fact, by way of the skillful performance of the children, a mock dispute, a parody of a real dispute, an activity produced for the sheer enjoyment of its production.

4.4 Sociolinguistic features of the Italian children's peer disputes

Disputes over the nature of play   As we noted earlier in our discussion of the American data, disputes over the nature of play involve oppositions to the actions of others within the play frame. They consist primarily of complaints about the way an act is carried out, imperatives to stop inappropriate behavior, or conflict about the extension of the play frame. Of the sixty-three disputes of this type in the Italian data, forty-one were simple in structure in that they involved only the statement of opposition and a limited number of reactions to the opposition (these data are very similar to the American results discussed earlier, where we noted that thirty-seven of the sixty-two disputes over the nature of play had a simple opposition-reaction structure). Consider the following example:

Example 9

Several children have created a game we will call "il capo" (the boss). One boy (Matteo) is "il capo" while another boy, Giovanni, is his assistant. Two girls (Carla and Luisa) and several other children are workers who are gathering ants off a wall and then putting them in buckets. During the play Matteo asks Bill (the researcher) if he can hold his microphone. Bill gives the microphone to Matteo. Later several other children want to speak into the microphone.

  1. G–M: Voglio parlare un momento io.
             (I want to talk a minute.)
*2. M–G: No, non si può parlare.
             (No, it is not possible to talk.)
  3. L–M ((Reaches for the microphone)): Dai!
             (Come on!)
  4. M–L: Non si può parlare.
             (It is not possible to talk.)
  5. C–M ((Holds bucket up for M to inspect ants.)): Guarda.
             (Look.)
  6. M–B: Tieni, Bill. ((Hands microphone to B and takes bucket.))
             (Hold it, Bill.)

7. M–C: Ma cosa fai? Tieni, C.
     ((Gives bucket back to C.))
     (But, what are you doing. Hold it, C.)
8. G–M: Voglio parlare un momento io.
     (I want to talk a minute.)
9. M–G: No, solo io posso parlare.
     (No, only I can talk.)
10. M–G: Allora, parla!
     (Ok, talk!)
11. G: ((Into microphone.)): Signore e Signori ecco a voi il cantante, Lorenzo!
     (Ladies and gentlemen here for you the singer, Lorenzo!)

Although the structure of the dispute in this sequence is relatively simple, there are some interesting things to note in the exchange. Matteo's denial of Giovanni's request (2) is expressed by way of an impersonal expression ("No, non si può parlare") which we have translated as "No, it is not possible to talk." A more literal translation would be "No, one is not able to talk." Impersonal expressions of this type are common in Italian. Its usage in this instance allows Matteo to embellish his denial without giving a real reason, while at the same time distancing himself from the denial. After Matteo rejects Luisa's bids to talk and handles the inspection of Carla's work, Giovanni again requests to speak into the microphone for a minute (8). This time Matteo again says no, but now he argues that only he is able to talk. This reason is basically arbitrary, but it does fit with his role as the boss. However, immediately after this second denial Matteo gives in and lets Giovanni talk into the microphone. But, this momentary relinqui' ing of power carries certain restrictions. Matteo holds up the microp. and instructs Giovanni to talk into it (10, where he used the informal imperative, "parla"). Giovanni goes on to pretend he is an announcer on a variety show and introduces the singer, Lorenzo. Overall, the form of this dispute blends in nicely with the general theme of the nature of play in this episode. "Il capo" is in charge.

As noted earlier in the discussion of the American data, in more complex disputes over the nature of play reasons for opposition are provided which are logically connected to the ongoing play (i.e., are not arbitrary). Reactions to such opposition are, in turn, more elaborate. There were a number of such complex disputes over the nature of play in the Italian data. Consider example 10:

Example 10

Two girls (Carla and Federica) have been playing in the outside yard of the *scuola materna*. During their play the children begin rubbing small rocks on a large stone and at one point Carla notes that, "We're making it all white." Carla is referring to white powder which is being formed by the rubbing and which now covers the large stone. Carla then places her hands in the powder to make them "tutte bianche" ("all white"). Federica does the same and both girls laugh and giggle at their creation. The children then go on to talk about going shopping as they continue to rub their rocks against the stone. Several minutes later four other girls (Viola, Bianca, Giovanna, and Flora) arrive and sit near Carla and Federica. These girls pretend they are riding on a bus, and at one point Bianca asks Carla if she wants to join their play. Carla says no, but then tells Bianca: "Guarda che ho tutta la mano tutta bianca" (Look, I have my hand all white"). Bianca and the other girls then ask to have their hands white. Carla says "OK", but makes them line up and then, one at a time, whitens one of their hands by placing it on the large stone. After finishing the hand of the last girl, Flora, Carla turns away, but Flora reaches from behind and places her other hand on the stone attempting to get it white as well. Carla pushes Flora's hand away saying.

*1. C–F: Basta! 'E coperto. La prendi tutta! Basta!
            (Enough! It is covered. You're taking it all! Enough!)
 2. V: 'E coperto
            (It is covered.)
((B now returns near C and reaches her hand out toward the stone.))
 3. B–C: Voglio così coperto in tutte e due le mani.
            (I want it covered all over like this and on both hands.)
 4. V–B: Anch'io!
            (Me too!)
 5. C–BV: Basta! Andate via!
            ((Waves Bianca and Viola away with her hand.))
            (Enough! Go away)

In this example the dispute ensues when one of the newly included children in the play (Flora) violates two rules regarding the nature of play as defined by Carla (one of the original participants). First, Flora reaches over and tries to whiten her own hand rather than submitting totally to Carla's control, and, secondly, she attempts to whiten both of her hands rather than just one. Carla opposes this move arguing that Flora's hand is already covered and that if Flora does not stop she will use up all of the powder. At this point, Bianca having noted Carla's restriction of Flora asks for more powder. She argues that her hand should be covered all over ("così") and so should her second hand as well (3). Bianca is thus attempting to counter Carla's opposition to Flora. Viola now also asks to have both of her hands covered. Carla dismisses both Bianca and Viola with an imperative ("Andate via"), and at this point Bianca, Viola, Giovanna and Flora were no longer allowed to play with Carla and Federica, who guarded their activity closely until they decided to leave the area about fifteen minutes later.

In this dispute Carla is attempting to maintain control over the play routine ("making white powder") she has created with Federica. This desire on the part of the children to maintain control of events they generate and share is a consistent feature of the peer culture of the American and Italian nursery school children (see Corsaro, 1985; 1986; 1988). Thus, disputes over the nature of play are often a reflection of peer concerns and values and the children's dispute strategies can be seen as important resources in the production and maintenance of peer culture.

Before moving on to consider other types of disputes it is useful to examine how real versus pretend elements of children's play often complicate the generation and maintenance of on-going activities. As we saw earlier in example 4 from the American data, the real/pretend distinction often creates a need for delicate negotiations (see Aüwarter, 1986), some of which are oppositional in nature. Consider example 11:

Example 11

Later in the episode described in example 9 ("Il capo"), a boy (Alberto) not originally involved in the play begins hitting the ants on the wall with a plastic bat. Giovanni, the boss' assistant, notices this and informs "il capo" (Matteo). "Martedini" is our pseudonym for Alberto's last name. Alberto's last name is used because he and several other children in the school have the same first name.

   1. G–M: Martedini vuole ammazzare le formiche. Martedini vuole ammazzare le formiche, Generale.
        (Martedini wants to kill the ants. Martedini wants to kill the ants, General.)
*2. M–G: Ma, non sono le formiche ( ) ammazzate.
        (But, the ants have not been killed.)
((Matteo is looking in a bucket instead of at the wall.))
   3. G–M: Quelle sul muro vuole ammazzare. Guarda. Guarda, sul muro. Guarda!
        (He wishes to kill those on the wall. Look. Look, on the wall. Look!)
   4. M–A: Martedini!
((Alberto stops hitting the ants and moves away from the play area.))

In this example a simple dispute involving the sanctioning of inappropriate activity becomes more complex because of the children's attempts to deal with the problem *within the established play frame*. Since Alberto was not officially one of the workers in the role play, Giovanni could have merely told him to stop killing the ants. But, Giovanni decides to maintain the pretend frame and instead reports Alberto's infraction to "il capo" who he addresses as "generale." Matteo ("il capo") was attending to other matters and did not notice Alberto's inappropriate behavior. Upon hearing Giovanni's report, Matteo looks into the bucket of ants brought to him by the workers and sees that they are not dead. He then denies Giovanni's claim (2). There is now a misunderstanding regarding which ants Alberto wishes to kill. Giovanni clarifies this ambiguity by noting he means the ants on the wall and then directs Matteo to look at the wall. Matteo does so and then immediately sanctions Alberto's behavior by calling out his name in a highly authoritative style (4). Alberto then ceases hitting the ants and moves away from the play area.

The above sequence is quite similar to example 4 from the American data in that it illustrates how the children's attempts to maintain the pretend frame in play can result in additional problems in the ongoing flow of discourse (in example 11, referential ambiguity) which in turn demands negotiation often involving oppositional exchanges or disputes. The example also again reminds us of the importance of studying children's discourse strategies within the speech activities making up children's social worlds.

Object and access disputes   In the *scuola materna* Italian children must learn to share a wide range of play materials in common by means of temporary possession. As was the case in the American nursery school, the Italian children's negotiations over temporary possession occasionally turned into object disputes. Although there were fewer object disputes in the Italian data (12% of the total disputes as compared to 22.7% in the American data), the nature and structure of these disputes were very similar to those which occurred among the American children. In the Italian data, 14 of the 19 object disputes were simple in structure and involved opposition to a child's claim (verbal or nonverbal) to an object and reactions to the opposition. In the disputes, oppositions and reactions typically involved personal claims (e.g., "that's mine") or temporal justifications (e.g., "I had that first"). Consider the following example:

Example 12

Several children are at a table drawing with magic markers. A boy (Nino) announces that the child who gives him a brown marker is his friend. This is a common verbal routine during this activity. A girl (Giovanna) immediately grabs a brown marker and then a dispute ensues between her and another boy (Luigi).

  1. N: Chi mi da il marrone è il mio amico.

      (Who gives me brown is my friend.)

((Giovanna grabs a brown marker from Luigi's grasp, Luigi reaches for it and Giovanna offers him a yellow marker instead, saying:))

*2. G–L: L'ho avuto prima.
      (I had it first.)
 3. L–G: No, non è vero.
      (No, it is not true.)
 4. G–L: Si.
      (Yes.)
 5. L–G: Va bene.
      (OK.)
((Luigi takes the yellow marker and begins working with it and Giovanna hands the brown marker to Nino.))

Other object disputes in the Italian data were not settled so easily. Some (relatively few, 5 of 19) object disputes involved multiple participants and in two instances the entry of an outside party. The addition of participants tended to increase the complexity of the unfolding disputes. Consider example 13:

Example 13

Three girls (Rosa, Grazia, and Clara) are playing with some plastic building materials. Another girl (Sara) brings a basket and sits near Rosa. After a few minutes Sara reaches for and takes one of the plastic pieces Rosa is using.
*1. R–S: No, te lo ruba – Dammelo!
      (No, she is stealing it – Give it to me!)
((Rosa struggles with Sara and takes back the plastic piece. Sara then takes another piece and hides it behind her back.))
 2. R–S: No!
((Rosa now pinches Sara's hand.))
 3. S–R: Ahh! ((Sara inspects her pinched hand and continues to hold the second piece behind her back.))
 4. R–S: Mettilo – lì dentro.
      (Put it – inside there.)
((Points to basket.))
((Sara refuses, continuing to hold the piece behind her back.))
 5. R–G: Grazia, vallo a prendere.
      (Grazia, go and get it.)
((Grazia tries to take piece from Sara but is not successful.))
 6. R–G: Grazia, te lo lascio – vallo a prendere – vallo a prendere – io tengo fermo.
      (Grazia, I'll let you have it – go and get it – go and get it – I'll hold tight.)
((Grazia again tries to get piece from Sara and is again unsuccessful. Rosa again pinches Sara, who now begins to cry. At this point a boy (Matteo) enters.))

7. M: Voglio la mia cassetta.

(I want my basket.)

((Matteo takes basket that is near R and then grabs the plastic piece from Sara and puts it in the basket.))

8. S–M: Non è la tua!

(It's not yours!)

9. M–S: Si ( )!

((Matteo now hits Sara and then Rosa hits Matteo and Sara. Sara cries again and Matteo leaves with the basket. Shortly thereafter a teacher enters to settle the dispute.))

In this example Rosa first tries to handle the situation alone. However, Sara is persistent so Rosa tries to keep her occupied while she directs Grazia to take the disputed object from Sara. Finally, another child (Matteo, who was not initially involved) enters and makes a claim on another object (the basket), takes it and the disputed object, and, after a bit of physical aggression, leaves the area. Although physical aggression of this type was rare in the Italian data, it occurred most often in disputes over objects. What is of most interest in this example, however, is the attempt by two of the children to work as a team in defending their possessions and the entry of the third party. The party in this instance (Matteo) literally thrust himself into the dispute which he had originally observed as he approached the play area. Third-party entry into disputes occurred with some regularity in the Italian data, especially during claim disputes as we shall see below. Such entry of an initially non-involved child never occurred in the American data.

As we noted earlier when discussing the American data (also see Corsaro, 1981a; 1981b; 1985; Rizzo, 1988) disputes over access to ongoing play frequently involve the protection of interactive space. The defense of interactive space builds solidarity among defenders (see example 7) and often results in references to and the children's reflection on "friends" and "friendship." This tendency on the part of children to articulate developing conceptions of friendship in access attempts and the protection of interactive space was also evident in the Italian data as we can see in example 14.

Example 14

Two boys (Matteo and Luigi) are playing with building materials making spaceships and other objects. A third boy (Nino) comes over and sits near them. They ignore his presence at first and Nino shows something he has built to the researcher (Bill) who is sitting nearby. Finally, Nino attempts to be a part of Matteo and Luigi's play.

1. N–LM: Anch'io posso?

(I can also?)

2. L–N: Si, puoi giocare.

(Yes, you can play.)

*3. M–L: No, io sono il capo.
(No, I am the boss.)

4. N–ML: Si, è vero.
(Yes, it's true.)

5. L–M: Lui – può giocare?
(He – can he play?)

((Nino now reaches over near Matteo and picks up some building materials. Matteo tries to stop him saying:))

6. M–N: No, non puoi – Ma, non puoi!
(No, you can't – But, you can't!)

((Nino holds materials he had picked up away from Matteo's reach.))

7. L–N: Non darcelo!
(Don't give it to him!)

8. M–L: Non può giocare!
(He can't play!)

((Nino now stands up, throws the materials he has on the floor near Matteo, and runs off to tell the teacher about Matteo's behavior.))

9. B–ML: Perché?
(Why?)

10. L–B: Perché non vuole Matteo – non vuole – solo ai suoi amici fa giocare.
(Because Matteo does not want – does not want – he only lets his friends play.)

11. M–B: Eh, ma lui è non – un mio amico.
(Eh, but he is not – my friend.)

Example 14 is similar to typical access attempts in the American data which frequently involved initial resistance, protection of interactive space, and references to friendship. However, in this instance the access dispute is complicated by the Italian children's perception of the role of "il capo." Earlier in examples 9 and 11, we saw the position of "il capo" embedded in the nature of the play itself, role play with a boss and workers. Here the designation of "il capo" is more general. It refers to the leader of a particular group during a specific period of play. In such instances the leader (or "il capo") is seen as having the most say regarding the choice of play activities, lines of action within the play frame, and who can and can not participate. However, one can not simply proclaim oneself "il capo." It is necessary to gain legitimation and to work constantly to maintain authority. Thus we have, in example 14, a multi-layered dispute which on the surface involves resistance to Nino's entry bid. But there are, embedded at a deeper level, subtle negotiations between Matteo and Luigi regarding the position and authority of "il capo."

The sequence begins with Nino's request to participate, which is quickly accepted by Luigi. Matteo then challenges Luigi's action implying that it is he, "il capo," who is to make such a decision (3). Nino in turn endorses Matteo's claim, possibly anticipating that such support will benefit his entry attempt. Luigi, having been set straight by "il capo," now asks the chief if Nino can indeed play (5). At this point Nino tries to enter the play more discreetly by attaining needed materials for participation (plastic objects for making spaceships). Matteo rejects this move as well as Luigi's request on Nino's behalf. Things now become more complex as Nino resists Matteo's opposition while Luigi urges Nino not to give in (7). In fact, it now appears that Luigi is using Nino's entry bid as leverage to dispute Matteo's authority as "il capo." Nino, however, decides not to play along and runs off to get a teacher.

Although the central access dispute in this example has a relatively simple sociolinguistic structure (a request for access – a denial of the request), the dynamics of the oppositional process take on extraordinary complexity reflective of Simmel's (see Wolf, 1950) classic theorems regarding the interactional consequences of the movement from a dyad to a triad. The example also again shows how disputes are embedded in the contexts of peer culture. The nature of the dispute is tied directly to the children's concerns to gain entry into play, to protect the play space, and to establish power and dominance within ongoing play activities.

While the entry attempt of a third party into dyadic play can have such complex interactive effects, the intrusion of non-involved children into a multi-party peer activity in the Italian nursery school often leads to a virtual chain reaction dispute in which oppositions, reactions to oppositions, and comments on the ongoing scene occur in rapid-fire succession. Consider example 15:

Example 15

Two girls (Luisa and Emilia) and two boys (Franco and Stefano) are playing around a table with building materials. They have constructed a city with each child adding new buildings as the play progresses. The researcher (Bill) is sitting with them and has placed a microphone on the table. They talk briefly about the microphone and how it records what they are saying. After a while another boy (Matteo) enters and points at the microphone and asks:

  1. M: Che cos'è quello?
           (What's that?)
  2. F–M: 'E per registrare.
           (It's for recording.)
  3. S–M: Che basta che parli qui, che si sente tutto –
           (It suffices that you speak here, that hears everything –)
((Stefano points to the microphone and then to the microphone wire as he speaks.))

4. M: Parla!
          (Speak!)
((Matteo leans foward pointing to the microphone and bumps against the
building Luisa and Franco are working on.))
*5. L–M: Ma che fai?
          (But, what are you doing?)
((Franco now reaches over and breaks off a piece of the spaceship Matteo
is holding in his hand.))
6. F–M: Se te non te vai, ti spacco questo qui sulla testa.
          (If you do not go away, I'll crack this here on your head.)
((Franco holds up the piece of Matteo's spaceship in his hand. Matteo
reaches for it and they struggle, bumping against the table and knocking
over several buildings.))
7. L: 'E crollato tutto! 'E crollato tutto!
          (It is all fallen down. It is all fallen down.)
8. E–L: | Tutto è colpa di Matteo. – Matteo!
          (It's all Matteo's fault.)
9. L–E: Aggustassi!
          (Nonsense word that rhymes with M's last name.)
((Luisa and Emilia begin repairing the city. Meanwhile Franco and
Matteo continue to struggle and Franco strikes Matteo inadvertently.))
10. F–M: Scusa, ma questo –
          (Excuse me, but this –)
((Matteo now runs over and knocks down nearly all the buildings of the
city, saying:))
11. M: Adesso, così!
          (Now, like this!)
12. L–M: No!
13. E–M: No!
((Matteo now runs off.))
14. E: Io ce lo vado a dire.
          (I am going to tell it to her.)
((Emilia is referring to telling the teacher and she runs off to do so followed
by Franco and Stefano. Luisa remains alone at the table.))
15. L: Abbiamo distrutto tutto. Adesso l'abbiamo rifatto e tu ce l'hai
          distrutto!
          (We destroyed it all. Now we have rebuilt it, and you have
          destroyed it!)

In this example Matteo's entry into the play space of the other children
begins innocently enough as he questions them about the researcher's
microphone. Two of the children (Franco and Stefano) do not see this
question as inappropriate or threatening. In fact, they respond informatively

with Stefano providing quite a bit of detail in his theory of how the microphone works. Matteo wears out his welcome, however, by leaning across the table, knocking against a building under construction, and demanding that someone speak directly into the microphone (4). Given that the imperative is marked syntactically in Italian (here Matteo uses the informal, singular imperative, "Parla") as well as through intonation, there can be no mistake that Mateo is telling the other children what they should do in their own play activity.

At line 5 we get the first opposition to Matteo's access by Luisa who uses a very typical Italian expression of displeasure ("Ma che fai?"). The use of the question "che fai?" is in this instance indirect and stylistic in that it is not a true question, Luisa can see what Matteo is doing. It is rather a negative reaction to his behavior. The use of "Ma che fai?" (rather than simply "Che fai?") adds emphasis to the oppositional move. The use of "Ma" to emphasize opposition occurred frequently in the Italian data, especially during claim disputes.[3] In fact, we have observed Italian children as young as two years old often responding "Ma no" rather than simply "no" to express displeasure. As we noted earlier when discussing example 6 the use of indirect oppositional forms (see M.H. Goodwin, 1983) was rare among the American children. This highly stylistic form of disputes was common among the Italian children. In this example we see that with Luisa's initial opposition the main focus of the activity becomes *discussione* with all the participants becoming involved.

In support of Luisa's opposition, Franco resists and threatens Matteo using a complex "if – then" construction (6). Franco's verbal warnings is impressively reinforced, in that he breaks Matteo's spaceship and then threatens to crack him on the head with it. Matteo then tries to grab back the fragment of his spaceship and a tussle ensues, leading to the destruction of several buildings on the table. Luisa laments this misfortune (7) and Emilia begins to help repair the damage, placing all the blame squarely on Matteo (8). Emilia's utterance is especially interesting in regard to her contrastive stress of Matteo's first and last names. She first says "it is all the fault of Matteo" using his first name for identification, then pauses and pronounces his last name in a disgusted tone of voice. We are somewhat restricted here because we can not use Matteo's real last name, but the message of an expression like "it's all Bill's fault – Corsaro!" is unmistakably interpreted as something on the order of "that Corsaro what a jerk." Luisa immediately reinforces Emilia's mocking comment by producing a nonsense word which rhymes with Matteo's last name using the same disgusted intonation.

At this point the struggle between Matteo and Franco escalates with Franco inadvertently striking Matteo. Franco attempts to excuse himself for this excess (10), but he is cut short by Matteo who runs over and, while saying: "Adesso, così", knocks over nearly all the buildings of the city (11). Luisa and Emilia loudly shout "no" and then Emilia reports her intention to tell the teacher. She runs off to do so and is joined by Franco and Stefano. Luisa, meanwhile, is left alone with the remains of the devastated city. She sums up the incident, apparently directing her speech to Matteo who has run off expecting the worst when the teacher arrives. Luisa's comment is interesting because she implies that Matteo's misconduct is all the worse given that the city was previously destroyed and rebuilt. In any case, her summary brings the sequence to a close.

As we noted earlier this dispute over access escalates into a highly stylistic *discussione* or what M.H. Goodwin (1983) has termed an aggravated disagreement which the children work to achieve in its own right. Such aggravated disagreements are very much a part of the peer culture of the Italian nursery school, and they occurred most frequently within claim disputes and dispute routines.

Claim disputes   As we noted earlier claim disputes occurred much more frequently in the Italian than in the American data. The Italian children's claim disputes emerged spontaneously in the course of a wide variety of peer activities. These disputes frequently involved multiple participants (as opposed to being strictly dyadic) and in several instances included the entry of initially non-involved children. The claim disputes in the Italian data were highly stylistic and complex containing a number of sociolinguistic strategies: (1) to gain the floor; (2) to express opposition; and (3) to give emphasis to specific points and counterpoints. Claim disputes occurred a bit more frequently and were clearly more complex (in terms of length and sociolinguistic structure) among the older children in the *scuola materna*. We begin our discussion by looking at some of the stylistic elements of claim disputes among older children. We then go on to look at an example produced by younger children, and end with an analysis of a multi-party claim dispute involving some of the older and younger children in the *scuola materna*.

Claim disputes among the older children were frequently about the nature of social relations among peers. Discussions and disagreements about the choice of play activities, participants, and expertise or knowledge related to a particular activity were common. These disputes reflected the older children's developing awareness of the importance of play and interaction for making and keeping friends. The following example aptly illustrates these concerns and also contains several important stylistic elements of claim disputes.

Example 16

Three boys (Mario, Enzo, and Dante) are all about three months shy of being six years old. The three are frequent playmates, but there is history of competition between Enzo and Dante over Mario's friendship. In this sequence the boys have been playing for some time with a board game and are now considering other play alternatives. Dante has suggested that they play with building materials called "clipo" (grooved plastic objects that clip together) which he likes to use to make spaceships. Enzo resists Dante's proposal.

*1. E: Ma perché doviam fare tutte le cose che fai te Dante?
(But why do we always have to do what you do, Dante?)

2. D: Ma no, non è giusto Enzo! (Io un giorno ho saputo una cosa) dal Mario che tu voi costruire le cose più belle e poi ci fai sempre mandare via.
(But no, it is not right, Enzo! (One day I heard something) from Mario that you wish to construct the best things and then you always exclude us.)

3. M: Invece, non è vero perché io non l'ho detto che lui ci vuole sempre mandare via.
(On the contrary, it is not true. I did not say that he always wants to exclude us.)

4. E: Al clipo che mi costruivo quello che mi veniva, e tu poi, dopo, un giorno sei stato a reclamare che io mi sono construito una cosa più bella. Io me lo ricordo se tu non te lo ricordi, io me lo ricordo, capito Dante?
(With clipo I always build what came to me, and then afterwards one day you started claiming that I built something better. I remember it, if you don't, I do. do you understand Dante?)

5. D: Ascolta Enzo, si ma però ti ho detto una cosa detta da Mario. Io non ci ho voluto credere –
(Listen Enzo, I told you something that Mario said.
I didn't want to believe it –)

6. E: Ma scusa, Mario non l'ha detto perché c'ero in quel giorno.
(But excuse me, Mario didn't say it because I was there that day.)

7. D: Lo so, però tu eri da un'altra parte. Mario me l'ha detto di nascosto, e tu non hai potuto–
(I know it, but you were somewhere else. Mario told me secretly, and you couldn't–)

8. E: No, lui non te l'ha detto di nascosto, perché se me l'avesse detto di nascosto, io a Mario non gli sarei più amico.
(No, he didn't tell it secretly, because if he told it secretly, I wouldn't be his friend anymore.)

9. D: Però tu c'eri, però tu eri da un'altra parte.
(But you were there, but you were somewhere else.)

10. E: Ma dove parte?
(But where was I?)

11. D: Eri della – hai presente quel giardino che c'è li giù, tu eri là da quella piscina piccolina a giocare con gli altri mentre M era là

diviso dall'albero a dirmi così: "e perché lui ti voleva mandare via dal gioco per ottenere"–

(You were – do you know that garden down there, you were there on the other side of the little swimming pool playing with the others while Mario was behind the tree there and told me that: "we're back here because he wanted to exclude you from the game to obtain"–

12. E: Come!//
    (What!)
13. M: //Io non// ti ho detto così.
    (I did not say that.)
14. E: Io non ti volevo mandare via dal gioco.
    (I did not want to exclude you from the game.)
15. M: Io ti ho detto–
    (I told you that–)
16. D: Come, mi hai detto? Dimmi!
    (What did you tell me? Tell me.)
17. M: Io non ci ho detto–
    (I did not say–)
18. D: No, non è vero [M's last name].
    (No, it isn't true [M's last name].
19. M: Enzo, avrai capito male soltanto.
    (Enzo, it is probably only a misunderstanding.)

The sequence in example 16 is drawn from a much longer claim dispute which has been analyzed in detail in another paper (Corsaro and Rizzo, 1988). Our purpose here is to focus on several strategies the children consistently employed in this sequence to initiate and develop the claim dispute. Enzo initiates the dispute by opposing Dante's proposal (i.e., to play with the "clipo"). His oppositional move is composed of a preface or predisagreement ("Ma") and an interrogative with an implicit claim (i.e., Dante always tries to control choice of activities within this group). Enzo's use of an interrogative not only challenges Dante's proposal, it also *creates an arena* for talk about the nature of the social relationship among the three children. Dante immediately denies Enzo's claim, emphasizing his disagreement by using "Ma", repetition and direct address (2).

After his denial Dante adds that Mario told him that Enzo said that he can make or construct better things and that he does not want to play with Dante. Mario denies this at (3) employing a predisagreement ("Invece, non è vero," "On the contrary it is not true") and the disagreement "I did not say it." Enzo now responds (4) with an accusation that evokes a past event in which Dante supposedly criticized him for building (or trying to build) something better than his peers. The implication is that this "something better" is a result of Enzo's copying from a model rather than creatively building what comes to him spontaneously. This is a highly complex oppositional move with the accusation internally embedded ("I remember it, if you don't, I do") and the use of "capito" plus direct address at the end of the utterance for emphasis. Dante then denies that he criticized Enzo (5), claiming instead that he was simply repeating something Mario told him though he "didn't want to believe it." Dante's utterance here is also interesting because of his use of "Ascolta" along with direct address prior to his denial. Italian speakers frequently use "Ascolta" or "Senti" positioned prior to disagreements in *discussione* of this type. It is clear that this form can be seen to be in line with M.H. Goodwin's (1983) notion of predisagreement. It is a predisagreement in that it signals and calls attention to the disagreement which follows.

At this point the dispute becomes what M.H. Goodwin (1980, also see Goodwin and Goodwin, 1987) in her work with adolescent girls has termed a "he-said-she-said confrontation." By referring to Mario's statement at another point in time, Dante attempts to account for his past action by denying responsibility, and in the process Dante thrusts Mario into the dispute. In addition, Dante greatly complicates the dispute because now the participants must argue across two time frames (i.e., what was said and happened in the past to support present claims, oppositions, points, and counterpoints).

At line 6, Enzo gains the floor by using a common Italian interruption device ("Ma scusa"). Enzo's use of the device is impressive in that he displays a sensitivity to subtle rules for turn-taking. He does not interrupt Dante at random, but rather waits until Dante makes his point about what Mario said and then interrupts with "Ma scusa" as Dante goes on to embellish the report ("I didn't want to believe it"). Enzo's use of "Ma scusa" is also interesting because in disputes of this type interruption devices can serve multiple functions. First, "Ma scusa" or simply "Scusa" and other variants (e.g., "Scusami," or the formal "Scusi") most visibly seek pardon for an interruption. However, in claim disputes and other types of *discussione* they also signal or preface the opposition which follows. In line 6 the opposition itself is introduced by *repetition* of elements of Dante's prior turn ("Mario didn't say it") which is an excellent example of Goodwin and Goodwin's (this volume, 1987) notion of format tying. Finally, Enzo's turn at line 6 moves the dispute back to the past in that he does not accept Dante's recollection, claiming that since he was present at the time he would know if Mario had indeed made such a statement.

Dante then agrees with Enzo, but immediately qualifies this agreement ("però") and adds new information ("Mario me l'ha detto di nascosto" – "Mario told me secretly"). At line 8, Enzo denies this new information and again uses repetition both to tie back to Dante's claim and to set up his opposition which is, in this case, an implicit threat aimed at Mario. The syntactic structure of the threat is highly impressive for several reasons. First, *embedded* in the threat is the same phrase first produced by Dante ("detto di nascosto") and then repeated by Enzo in his denial. This use of repetition and embedding creates a strong coherence linking the present talk back to Dante's original claim regarding something Mario said in the past (line 5). Second, the threat itself is a complex "if-then" construction, with Enzo using the proper sequence of tenses: the pluperfect subjunctive ("avesse detto") in the if-clause and the conditional ("sarei") in the result clause. But Enzo's construction is impressive not simply because of his correct use of Italian grammar. More importantly, the correct use of this sequence of tenses at this point enables Enzo: (1) to challenge Dante's present claim about a past event; and (2) to threaten Mario about their present relationship if Dante's report regarding secrecy is indeed true. In fact, we see, after further discussion about where Enzo was when the supposed past event occurred (9–11), that Mario must now enter the dispute. Once in the dispute Mario first denies that he said he wanted to exclude Enzo (13) and then goes on to tell Enzo that there must have been a misunderstanding. As it turns out, Mario did indeed say something about Enzo to Dante. However, the exact nature of what exactly was said is never cleared up in this dispute.

This sequence is just the opening phase of a highly complex dispute which we can not examine in detail here (but see Corsaro and Rizzo, 1988). Although this particular claim dispute was the most complex one recorded in the Italian data, many of the strategies the boys employed here (e.g., interruption devices, predisagreements, emphasis markers, and format tying) appeared consistently in the claim disputes of other of the older children and with some regularity among the younger children (see below) in the *scuola materna*. As we noted above, such highly complex dispute styles were rarely employed by the American nursery-school children.

Although the claim disputes of the younger Italian children were not as complex structurally as those of the older children, the three- and four-year-olds did produce a high proportion of claim disputes. An interesting feature of the young children's claim disputes was their tendency not "to give in" when their claims were challenged. The children would hold their ground even if it meant "making up" evidence for their position as the disputes developed. Consider example 17:

Example 17

Two girls (Franca and Carla) who are both around 4.6 years old are playing in the outside yard of the *scuola materna*. They have been rubbing small rocks against a large stone and in the process are producing a fine white powder. Franca shows some concern about a need for new rocks when the present ones are used up. This concern leads to a debate about who will buy the new rocks and where she will buy them.

1. F: E quando si consuma – quando si consuma – tutt'e due – lo compriamo, tutt'e due, va bene?
   (And when it's used up – when it's used up, both of us – we buy it, both of us, OK?)

*2. C: No, quando si – si – domani le compro tutto io.
   (No, when it – it – tomorrow I will buy them all.)

3. F: Noo, tu ne compri tre e io tre, non tutte quelle del negozio.
   (Noo, you buy three of them and I buy three, not all of them that are in the store.)

4. C: Ma va'che non l'ho comprate nel negozio – l'ho comprato nel 'nanen'. L'ho comprato nella banca.
   (Oh come on! I didn't buy them at the store – I bought it at the 'bad'. I bought it at the bank.)

5. F: Be'ma la banca non vende.
   (Well, but the bank does not sell them.)

6. C: Io l'ho comprato alla banca. Io l'ho comprato alla banca.
   (I bought it at the bank. I bought it at the bank.)

7. F: Be'alla banca – ci da i soldi. Non si vendono le cose alla banca.
   (Well, at the bank – we get money there. They do not sell things at the bank.)

8. C: Si, si vendono! Ci danno anche questo – hai visto che a me – me l'hanno dati. Si sta consumando – fai piano. Mettilo qua.
   (Yes, they do sell things! They gave us even this – did you see that – they gave them to me. It is getting worn out – go easy. Put it here.)

((Carla holds up her rock when she says "they gave us even this."))

The above sequence is an earlier phase of an event which we first discussed in example 10. The two girls have spontaneously created a game of making white powder. This sequence begins when Franca shows some concern about what they will do when their rocks are used up (i.e., her use of the impersonal construction "si consuma"). She, therefore, proposes that she and Carla can buy new ones (rocks) together (1). Carla, however, rejects this idea, saying that she will buy the rocks alone. Franca is insistent in her attempt to get Carla to agree to her proposal of joint action (3), and in the process claims that they will buy some but not all of the items at the store ("non tutte quelle del negozio"). At this point, the claim dispute emerges as Carla challenges Franca's claim that the items (again it appears they are talking about rocks) can be bought at the store. Carla's turn at 4 is interesting for several reasons. First, she introduces her opposition to Franca's claim with the slang expression "Ma va'che" ("Oh, come on") which is, in this case, a predisagreement marking the coming challenge of Franca's claim. The last part of the challenge itself (beginning with "l'ho comprato–") is produced in a sing-song cadence which in Italian is known as "la cantilena." The cantilena is a verbal routine which often signifies opposition (see below). In this instance, Carla's use of the cantilena involves: (1) the denial of Franca's claim about the store; (2) a temporary nonsense claim that she bought things at the "nanen" (general expression meaning "bad"); and (3) a final claim that she bought it at the bank. What is occurring here is that Carla wants to challenge Franca and produces the cantilena. But once into the rhythm of the cantilena, Carla seems to become unsure regarding where exactly you might buy rocks if not at the store. So she says she bought them at the "bad", which, of course, does not make sense. Such a claim is like an American child saying she bought them at the "yucky." Carla then continues with the rhythm of the cantilena repeating the phrase "l'ho comprato–" and eventually comes up with the more acceptable (but still quite implausible) place of purchase, the bank. Without using the cantilena, Franca counters Carla's challenge, pointing out correctly that the bank doesn't sell these things ("rocks"). Carla again responds in the cantilena, repeating the phrase twice. At 7 Franca tries to come up with an argument about what does go on at banks ("you get money there"), and then she again denies that rocks are sold there. Franca's position here nicely demonstrates the children's use of developing conceptions of social knowledge during the course of a peer dispute.[4] Finally Carla pushes the dispute to an end by claiming that she bought the rock in her hand at the bank. This is, of course, an obvious untruth. But before Franca can challenge this claim, Carla goes on to shift the topic by suggesting to Franca that she "fai piano" ("go easy") so that the rocks are not used up.

Although the dispute in this sequence involving younger children is less complex than example 16 with the older boys, it does demonstrate that the younger children understand the basic nature of claim disputes. That is, the children clearly display knowledge of the importance of making points and counterpoints. Secondly, it is clear that in claims disputes the children are forced to attempt to go beyond their existing conceptualizations of social knowledge and in the process further develop their grasp of the social world. Finally, we see that claim disputes sometimes induce the emergence of dispute routines such as the cantilena which we discuss in more detail in the next section.

The cantilena also appears in the last claim dispute we will consider. In example 18 below, a mixed age group of children are drawing pictures while they sit around a work table. During this type of activity children often talk about their drawings as well as past activities and shared information of the peer culture. Claim disputes often emerge in these discussions.

Example 18

Several children (Sara, a girl about 6 years old; Franco, a boy about 6
years old; Luigi, a boy about 5 years old; Giovanna, a girl about 5 years
old; and Nino, a boy about 4 years old) are sitting around a table drawing
pictures. There has been a great deal of discussion at the table before the
following claim disputes emerge. A boy (Giovanni, around five years old)
has been painting at another table in the room. He overhears the dispute,
goes to the table and actively joins the discussion (see line 6 below).

1. S: I lupi non esistono.
        (Wolves do not exist.)
*2. Ga: Si, esistono i lupi.
        (Yes, wolves exist.)
3. S: Non esistono – solo gli ossi.
        (They don't exist – only their bones.)
4. F: Non è vero, esistono i lupi.
        (It's not true, wolves do exist.)
5. L: Si.
6. F: Ma, non esistono solo sulle montagne.
        (But, they do not exist only in the mountains.)

((Giovanni, Gi, now enters scene and stands near the table where Sara
and Franco are sitting.))

7. Gi: 'E vero, esistono!
        (It's true, they exist!)

((Sara waves Gi away with her hand as she says:))

8. S: Te non c'entri.
        (You're not in this.)
9. F: Te non c'entri. Perche–
        (You're not in this. Because–)

((Franco pokes his finger at Sara's chest.))

10. S: Te–
        (You–)
11. F: Tu dici che non'centro. Esistono i lupi!
        (You say that I'm not in this. Wolves exist!)
12. S: No, non è vero.
        (No, it's not true.)
13. Gi: Neanche i fantasmi.
        (Not even ghosts.)
14. F: 'E vero.
        (It's true.)
15. L: I fantasmi–
        (The ghosts–)
16. F: Yah! Non esistono.
        (Yah! They don't exist.)

17. S: No. No. Quelle, no.
   (No. No. Those, no.)
18. F: Si. Si, esistono. I fantasmi però esistono–
   (Yes. Yes, they exist. Ghosts however exist–)
19. N: Sono nei boschi.
   (They are in the woods.)
20. F: Eh, non è vero. I fantasmi esistono sotto il mare nelle case–
   (Eh, it's not true. Ghosts exist under the sea in houses–)
21. L: ( ).
22. F: No.
23. Gi: Nelle – nelle case abbandonate.
   (In – in abandoned houses.)
24. F: 'E vero, sottomarine.
   (It's true, underwater houses.)
25. S: Nelle – le case buie. Stanno nelle buie–( ).
   (In the – the dark houses. They stay in the dark – ( ).)
((This turn is produced in sing-song cadence as are the next seven turns.))
26. Gi: Eh, è vero.
   (Yes, it's true.)
27. F: E sotto mare – è buio!
   (And under the sea – it's dark.)
28. N: Eh, è vero.
   (Yes, it's true.)
29. S: E sotto – ci vanno loro.
   (And under – they go there.)
30. L: No, ci vanno anche i granchi.
   (No, also crabs go there.)
31. F: Ci vanno i sommergibli.
   (Submarines go there.)
32. N: E anche i pescecani.
   (And also sharks.)

In this sequence several children of various ages participate in a series of claim disputes about the existence of supernatural phenomena (wolves or werewolves and ghosts) which are of much interest to young children. The dispute begins with Sara's claim that "i lupi" do not exist. Although we can not be sure here, it is almost certainly the case that the children are talking about werewolves or perhaps "bad" wolves. Giovanna challenges Sara, claiming that wolves do indeed exist. Sara, then, gives in a bit by saying that only their bones exist. At this point several other children join the dispute including a child (Giovanni) who was not originally involved in the main activity. Giovanni was painting nearby when he overheard the claim dispute. He comes over, paint brush in hand, to stand next to Sara and argue: "'E vero, esistono" ("It's true, they do exist").

Third-party entry of this type is interesting because although it was common among the Italian children, it never occurred in peer disputes in the American nursery school. In this sequence, Sara tries to exclude Giovanni ("You're not in this"), but Franco immediately challenges her action as inappropriate by throwing Sara's same phrase back at her. In this way Franco is implicitly challenging Sara's attempt to be the boss. After Sara's attempted rebuttal (10), Franco say in essence "who are you to say I'm (or anyone) is not in this," and then he goes on to argue again that wolves do exist (11).

Giovanni, now a full participant in the discusson, adds a new element arguing that ghosts do not exist (13). Franco first agrees with this claim (14), but then changes his mind (18). At this point there is a general discussion with different children adding (and often arguing about) new information regarding where ghosts live if they do exist (in the woods, in abandoned houses, and finally in abandoned houses under the sea). At line 25, S begins chanting in the cantilena, stringing together several elements from the earlier discussion. Her chant sets off a series of turns by four other children (Giovanni, Franco, Nino and Luigi) which are all produced in the cantilena. Each turn either adds new information (30, 31, 32), refines previously mentioned information (27, 29), or signals agreement (26, 28) or disagreement (30). In all of these turns the children rely on the repetition of key phrases for both format tying and to maintain the basic sing-song cadence and rhythm of the cantilena. It is clear at this point that the original claim dispute has been transformed into a dispute routine involving the cantilena (see below).

In closing this section we wish to make several points about this particular example and claim disputes in general. First, claim disputes are important for children's confronting a wide range of ambiguities or confusions they may have about the social world. The challenging of claims of peers is a common activity among Italian children. In the process they are forced to think more carefully about and articulate their knowledge of the social world. The end result of such activity may be a better grasp of such knowledge and the expansion of its base. Second, claim disputes like the one in example 18 are generative in nature in that, rather than being focused on a central issue which can be settled, new, but semantically related, elements are added on with almost every additional turn at talk. As a result the children are becoming aware of and actually experimenting with the very devices which give conversation its coherence and structure. Finally, claim disputes provide an arena for participation in and sharing of peer culture. The children debate things that are important to them (e.g., friendship, play activities, ghosts, werewolves, etc.), and in the process develop a shared sense of control over their social world.

Dispute routines   In examples 17 and 18 we saw that the "cantilena" emerged within the course of claim disputes. As we noted in our analysis of these examples the cantilena is a verbal routine in which the children produce a sing-song chant during their speaking turns of what is usually a mock dispute. The chant is often accompanied rhythmically with nonverbal gestures such as hitting one's fists or the sides of one's open hands together. As we saw in the previous examples, the cantilena is a routine in which form is stressed over substance. Although the sing-song cadence and rhythmic gestures usually signal the oppositional nature of the routine, we saw in example 18 (lines 25–32) that the cantilena is also used to mark agreement and communal sharing of an aesthetic production. In this instance the communal nature of the routine was marked by frequent repetition of key words and combinations of lexical items which reverberate the cadence and rhythm of particular turns in the routine.

Of the ten routine disputes which occurred in the Italian data, six were lengthy versions of the cantilena. These occurrences were not simply one or two exchanges of the chanting routine in claim disputes or role play, but rather sequences of multiple exchanges with the routine itself being the main focus of the activity. These routine disputes occurred during two activities: meals and snacks, and drawing (*disegno*). While engaged in these activities in the *scuola materna*, the children are left to sit at tables without adult direction or close supervision. Engaged in these parallel activities (having lunch or a snack or drawing), the children occasionally launch into sustained productions of the cantilena, with generally four or more children participating.

An important feature of the cantilena is that the routine is a consciously shared element of peer culture beyond its actual production. That is, the children not only produce the routine, but refer to and talk about it using the term "cantilena." Additionally, the term was also known by the teachers at the *scuola materna* and the children's parents. In fact, the routine is often irritating to parents who reported that they restricted its usage in the home with the command "Non far la cantilena!" ("Don't do the cantilena!"). Interestingly, in family role play in the *scuola materna* children in superordinate roles (mother, father, and older siblings) often used this same command when disciplining peers in subordinate roles (babies, and younger children) who produced the cantilena in pretend quarrels. Here the children have taken the adults' disapproving reactions to their peer routine and embedded them into their shared peer culture in role play. Such embeddings nicely display what we have termed the underlife of the nursery school (see Corsaro, 1985).

A final note on the cantilena is in order. In addition to the teachers and parents, we talked to a number of young adults in Bologna who recognized the cantilena routine and who reported enacting it as children. Some of these informants reported falling into the routine when arguing with adult friends as a way of relieving tension or to mark the pettiness of the arguments themselves.

In addition to the six extended enactments of the cantilena, there were four other dispute routines. These occurrences were all, with minor variations, replications of a routine that we first observed during participant observation in the *scuola materna*. In early field notes we had referred to this activity as a group dispute over art and craft materials. However, after witnessing several repetitions of the event, it became clear that our original categorization was incorrect. The activity was really not an object dispute, but rather a mock dispute and a basic routine in the peer culture of the Italian children.

Let us further explore this element of the peer culture, which we shall call "Ci hanno rubato" ("They robbed us"), by starting with a narrative description of the routine.

During the late afternoon at the *scuola materna* the teachers are often in need of a brief respite before they give the children a snack and put things in order for the arrival of parents and the end of the school day. To keep the children occupied during this transition period the teachers frequently rely on "il desegno libero" ("free drawing"). The tables in the back room are covered with oil cloth, and cans of magic markers and sheets of paper are set out. The children come and in groups of five or six sit at each of three or four tables amidst loud chattering as they discuss previous activities and plans for their drawings. "Disegno libero" seems to be a good activity for this time of day. The children usually relish the opportunity to have full control over the themes of their drawings, and since the activity requires minimal supervision the teachers have a chance to talk and relax.

Things generally proceed smoothly at first. The volume of noise around the tables is high, but the activity is ordered. The children work on and talk about their drawings while the teachers converse around a table in the far side of the room near the kitchen. Frequently, however, the loud but consistent hum of activity is disrupted by a dispute. The dispute is normally nondescript at first, a few children arguing over a particular magic marker. But these disputes tend to grow. More children become involved, the noise increases dramatically, and soon all the children are gathered around one table shouting loudly and gesturing. The fighting bothers the teachers. Somewhat reluctantly they go to intervene, maintaining that there are plenty of markers of all colors for everyone. Order is restored. The children begin to draw again and the teachers resume their conversation.

But the dispute will emerge again. In fact, its re-emergence is in the early stages right now as Roberto looks for a red magic marker that does not "write badly" ("scrive male"). Roberto finds a red marker, tries it, but dissatisfied, tosses it aside. He then finds another, but is again displeased. At this point Roberto leaves his work table, approaches another, and without the children at that table noticing (or pretending not to notice), he takes a red marker. Roberto then returns to his table and begins drawing with the marker. Meanwhile back at the second table, Antonia looks through the can of markers and asks, "Dov'è rosso?" ("Where's red?"). Maria hands her a red marker, but Antonia waves the offer aside, saying: "Quello scrive male" ("That one writes badly"). Two other children now help Antonia and they find several red markers, but they all "scrivono male." At this point, Antonia slaps her forehead with the palm of her right hand and shouts: "Ci hanno rubato!" ("They robbed us!").[5]

This exclamation sets several things in motion simultaneously. Roberto looks up from his work and smiles at the other children at his table. They all catch his eye and smile back, signaling that they know what is about to happen. At the same time, several of the children at the third table look over to Antonia's table and then quickly over to Roberto's. Finally, at Antonia's table Maria jumps up, points to Roberto and shouts: "'E stato Roberto!" ("It was Roberto!"). Immediately Antonia, Maria and several other children march over to Roberto's table. Just as they arrive, a girl at the table, Luisa, grabs seven or eight markers (including the one Roberto took) and hides them in her lap under the table. Once at the table Antonia accuses Roberto of stealing the red marker. He denies it, challenging Antonia and the others to find the stolen marker. As Antonia and Maria began to look for the red marker, Bruna backed by several other children from the third table enters the dispute, claiming that Roberto did indeed steal the marker and that Luisa is hiding it. Lusia shouts, "No, non è vero!" But, Antonia reaches under the table and grabs the markers that Luisa is hiding. At this point there is a great deal of shouting, gesturing, pushing and shoving and the teachers must once again intervene and settle the dispute.

We witnessed and recorded many re-occurrences of the above event in field notes. In fact, this type of dispute occurred on average about three times a week in the *scuola materna*, and in all but a few instances it erupted in the afternoon during "disegno libero." Later we recorded several additional occurrences on audio or videotape. From the transcription and micro-analysis of the tapes we concluded that "ci hanno rubato" is not really a dispute over objects, but is rather a dispute routine. It is not that there are too few red, green, or whatever color markers that write well, but rather that this feigned scarcity allows for the emergence and enactment of the mock dispute. At this time of the day when the teachers are trying to get the children to engage in a quiet activity until snack time, the children would, in simple terms, rather argue than draw.

We see "ci hanno rubato" as a consistent feature of peer culture in that it is a routine the children consistently employ to *challenge adult control* (i.e., the requirement that the children draw to fill time before snacktime) and to *share a sense of control with each other* while they do something they want to do (i.e., engage in a dispute routine). In this sense, the Italian children's production of this dispute routine is clearly in line with the major themes of control and communal sharing we identified in earlier work on the peer culture of American nursery-school children (see Corsaro, 1985).

5. Conclusion

We have in this chapter examined the nature and the functions of disputes in the peer culture of American and Italian nursery-school children. In our analysis we noted a number of similarities between the disputes of American and Italian children as well as several important differences. First, in terms of similarities the same general types of dispute (with the exception of dispute routines) appeared in both data sets. Further, the general nature of disputes was similar. That is, disputes were directly tied to features of ongoing interaction and peer culture and were seldom context-independent factual or moral questions which could be clearly answered. For this reason the majority of the disputes in both data sets were not resolved. The fact that disputes are embedded in peer play and culture is also reflected in the large number of disputes over the nature of play which appeared in both nursery schools. Such disputes were the most frequent type of oppositional exchanges for both the American and Italian children. As we noted earlier, disputes over the nature of play most often involved the children's attempts to reach shared agreement regarding play frames, especially real/pretend distinctions. The oppositional nature of disputes during such negotiations should be seen in terms of their positive contributions to discourse. Rather than simply accepting or ignoring pretend frame signals offered by a co-interactant, young children often seek to reach mutual understanding regarding the nature and significance of ongoing activities. Children are not always successful in reaching shared agreement, but disputes are an important element in children's development of the cognitive and communicative abilities necessary to organize and construct play events.

As we have seen throughout the analysis, a major difference between the American and Italian data is the overall pervasiveness and importance of language and verbal routines in the peer culture of the Italian children. It is not simply that there were more disputes in the Italian as compared to the American data that is important here. It is rather that disputes are a central feature of peer culture among the Italian children. Italian children produce and enjoy *discussione* as an end in itself. Artful, creative participation in *discussione* is a valued skill. It is for this reason that we believe the Italian children produced dispute routines and such a high proportion of claim disputes. But there is, in addition, running through the production of all disputes among the Italian children, *an emphasis on style*. It is not simply that the children want to make a point, to be persuasive, to win an argument. Rather the children want to participate to the fullest. For the Italian children the doing, the participation, the absorption in *discussione* is the thing.

Finally, it is clear in the findings for both the Italian and the American children that disputes and argumentation serve positive functions in terms of children's development of communicative competence and social knowledge. As Goodwin and Goodwin (1987, this volume) have noted, adults too often evaluate children's arguments negatively, seeing them as something to stop or sanction. They note that "when arguments are looked at as natural phenomena it is found that, rather than being disorderly, argumentation gives children an opportunity to actively explore through productive use the structural resources of their language" (Goodwin and Goodwin, 1987: 27). We agree and argue further that disputes and argumentation like other forms of communication and discourse enable children to reproduce the adult society of which they are developing members through their own creation of and participation in a shared peer culture.

Notes

We wish to thank Allen Grimshaw for his comments on an earlier version of this paper. We are also grateful to Giovanna Wedel, Manuela Gieri and Pier Paolo Giglioli for their help with the transcription, translation, and analysis of the Italian data.

1   The use of the first person in this introductory section and later in the methods section refers to the first author (Corsaro) who carried out the ethnographic research in nursery schools in the United States and Italy.

2   In the transcript presented in examples throughout the text the following notational devices are employed:
  *   Marks the initial opposition
  –   Marks self-interruption and interruption by others as in: "Non è vero che sono scuse, perché lui–perché lui–siccome lui–ne sa più di me di astronavi se la costruisce più belle, capito?" and "Io non ci ho detto–"
  ( )   Notes probable transcription when words are enclosed in parenthesis. Blank parentheses denote unintelligible speech.
  //   Marks overlapping speech. When placed at the beginning and ending of overlapping speech as in:
  E: Come!//
  M: //Io non// ti ho detto così.

3   Although one could argue that "Ma" is, in this case, a predisagreement (see M.H. Goodwin, 1983), native speakers of Italian argue against this interpretation. Paolo Giglioli (personal communication) stresses that "Ma" in phrases like "Ma che fai?" ("What are you doing?"), "Ma scusa," or "Ma no", is generally heard as being part of the whole phrase. That is, speakers do not say "Ma", hesitate briefly (or even very briefly) and then say the rest of the phrase. Upon listening to the intonational pattern in the present case, it was clear that "Ma che fai" was said as an entire phrase with the "Ma" serving to emphasize or stress the "che fai." However, as we shall see below there are other instances in the data (see example 16) where "Ma" clearly functions as a predisagreement.

4   In an initial transcription of line 7 we thought Franca had said "Ci va gli uomini" ("men go there"). This phrase is interesting because it not only shows some confusion about what goes on at banks, but also implies that

the development of knowledge of occupational and gender roles may be intertwined. Later, however, I asked several of the Italian children to view segments of the videotapes to check our transcriptions and interpretations. Franca could not do so because she had left the *scuola materna* and now attended first grade. Carla, however, was still at the school, and she and another girl, Luisa, viewed this sequence. Both children responded that Franca said: "ci da i soldi" and not "ci va gli uomini." Later upon listening to the phrase several more times, we were convinced that the children were correct.

5   Until a recent conversation with Paolo Giglioli I (Corsaro) was unaware that the correct translation of "Ci hanno rubato!" is not "They robbed us!" In fact, the literal (and correct) translation of the phrase is "They stole us!" which is, of course, ungrammatical. Giglioli had felt that I knew this, but just translated what the children meant. I must be honest and admit that such was not the case. In Italian the word for "to steal" is "rubare", and, as is the case in English, one can steal money, pens, etc.; but you "rob" people, banks etc. of these possessions. In Italian the word for "to rob" is "dirubare" which is very similar to "rubare." It is for this reason that both the children and the senior author of this paper were confused.

3 Serious and playful disputes: variation in conflict talk among female adolescents

DONNA EDER

1. Introduction

The ways in which children use and deal with conflict among peers has been the subject of considerable research. Some of the earliest research on children's conflict was based on role-play episodes rather than naturally occurring interaction (Brenneis and Lein, 1977). This research has been criticized by Eisenberg and Garvey (1981) who found that pre-school children used more complicated strategies than those used by elementary school children in the role-play study. Subsequently, the focus of research has been on conflict exchanges during normal peer interaction.

Early research also focused primarily on conflict resolution. Eisenberg and Garvey (1981) found that adaptive strategies, i.e. those which show awareness of the other person and/or the constraints of the interaction, were more likely to lead to resolution. For example, compromising, suggesting alternative solutions, and providing reasons were strategies which were more likely to lead to a resolution of the conflict than were ignoring, aggravating, and insistence. While many of the conflict exchanges among these pre-school children were not resolved, certain adaptive strategies, such as providing reasons, were frequently used.

While it might seem that older children would be more likely to resolve conflicts, studies of older male children have found that most conflict exchanges are not resolved and, furthermore, resolution is often not even an important goal. Instead, conflict exchanges may be used to meet other goals, such as displaying verbal skills and maintaining status hierarchies within groups (M.H. Goodwin, 1982b; W. Labov, 1972b; Kochman, 1983).

Conflict which is not aimed at resolution has sometimes been referred to as ritual conflict. The most common example is that of ritual insulting which has been studied primarily among pre-adolescent and adolescent males. It typically involves the exchange of insults between two peers, often in the presence of other peers who serve as an audience. This activity is usually competitive in nature, in that each male tries to top the previous insult with one that is more clever, outrageous, or elaborate. The audience may also actively evaluate the insults as being particularly strong or weak responses.

There has been some debate over the nature of the insults themselves. While Labov's (1972b) research suggested that it was important that insults not be considered by either party to be true, Kochman (1983) found that the black males in his study often used insults that were or might be considered true accusations. In the latter case, the important factor was the response to an insult, so that even insults that had some truth were not to be taken seriously.

While there has been considerable research on conflict exchanges, and especially ritual conflict exchanges among males, we have much less information about the nature of conflict among adolescent females. M.H. Goodwin (1980a) found that much of the conflict among the black female children in her study was expressed indirectly in the form of gossip. Most of the direct exchanges which occurred were confrontations about previous episodes of gossip in which a girl was informed that someone had been talking about her and was often encouraged to then confront the alleged gossiper. While competing for status did not appear to be important to these girls, the exchanges did point to the importance of being able to stand up to people who talk about you behind your back.

The extent to which girls also learn self-defense strategies through insult exchanges is less clear. The few studies which have examined ritual conflict among adolescent females have reported conflicting results. While M.H. Goodwin (1980b) found that black girls seldom engaged in insulting each other, she did find that they competed successfully in ritual insult exchanges with boys. Folb (1980), on the other hand, found that the black females in her study exchanged insults with their girlfriends, but that they seldom engaged in ritual insulting when males were present. This difference may be due in part to the fact that Goodwin studied younger girls and Folb studied older adolescents. Abrahams (1970) found that as black females got older they became increasingly concerned with being respectable and stopped using the vernacular. Mitchell-Kernan (1973) also found that black women engaged in ritual insulting, but not in the context of verbal dueling since social norms did not allow them as much license in speech as successful dueling required. Likewise, while Heath (1983) found that the black girls in her study did not routinely engage in insulting, their playsongs and cheers incorporated several aspects of insulting, such as its assertive and mocking tone.

Most of the studies which have examined conflict or insulting skills among females have looked only at black females. S.B. Heath (1983), who did study white as well as black females, found that white females did not sing assertive and mocking playsongs. Nor did they perform the more assertive and mocking cheers which were found among the older black females. Likewise Schofield (1982) found that the white females in her study were often intimidated by the more aggressive style of their black peers. This has led to the impression that insulting and insult-related skills are only found among black females. There is some evidence which suggests this may not be the case. In a study based on interviews in which most white girls denied knowing how to use ritual insults, a black girl claimed that white girls knew how to use them, but were reluctant to admit it (Ayoub and Barnett, 1961). This suggests that white females who engage in ritual insulting may view this behavior as less appropriate than do black females and may therefore not report knowing these skills.

It is clear that more information is needed about the nature of playful as well as other forms of conflict exchanges among adolescent females, especially white females. Since females are concerned with developing shared norms and maintaining a high degree of cohesion within their groups (Eder and Sandford, 1988), it is likely that they will also be concerned with conflict resolution. On the other hand, since girls are less concerned than boys with establishing status hierarchies within groups (M.H. Goodwin, 1980b; Schofield, 1982), they are less likely to use conflict exchanges to display and maintain status differences. They could, however, engage in ritual conflict for other reasons, and there is evidence which suggests that black females and perhaps some white females do participate in ritual insulting.

This chapter will examine various types of conflict exchanges among white adolescent females from a range of social backgrounds. It will focus specifically on the different types of communication skills that are being learned through different types of conflict exchanges. While serious and playful conflicts will be discussed separately, the considerable overlap between playful and nonplayful exchanges will be demonstrated. At the same time, playful and nonplayful exchanges emphasize different communication skills and, to the extent that certain groups engage in some types of conflict and not in others, girls are likely to develop different verbal skills. This provides more evidence of diversity in the speech of females, challenging the notion that there is a single feminine style of speech.

This chapter is part of a larger study of peer relations and interaction in a middle-school setting. The school enrolled students from a range of socio-economic backgrounds, including students from working-class and lower-class families. The school was located in a medium-sized midwestern community and enrolled approximately 250 students per grade. Some of the students came from surrounding rural areas. While most of the students were white, a small number of black students was also enrolled.

Three female researchers observed peer-group interaction during lunch periods on a regular basis over a three-year period. The students in the groups we observed were predominantly female, between ten and fourteen years old, and came from a variety of social backgrounds, ranging from middle class to lower class. While one of the groups included a black female for part of the year, the rest of the students were white. Once rapport was established, we audiotaped approximately eight lunch-time conversations in each of eight groups and videotaped three additional conversations in one of the groups. Altogether we have recorded data on fifty-nine students.

This chapter will focus only on direct conflict exchanges and will not include various indirect expressions of conflict such as gossip, complaining about and ridiculing someone who is not present. While a considerable amount of conflict among girls is expressed indirectly (M.H. Goodwin, 1980a; Eder and Sanford, 1988), I am interested here in the degree to which girls participate in direct exchanges and in the types of skills that are acquired through these exchanges.

Transcripts of recorded conversations serve as the primary source of data for the analyses. In addition, ethnographic information from field notes will be used to help interpret the meaning of certain acts and strengthen the sociolinguistic analyses. Without such background information, it is hard to make accurate interpretations since meanings and social functions of speech acts are often context specific (Corsaro, 1982).

2. Use of resolution strategies during normative conflict

There has been suggestion that girls are less successful at resolving peer conflicts than are boys. Lever (1976) found that while boys were able to resolve conflicts during games, girls could not. She reported that when conflicts arose, girls made no attempts to settle them, causing the play group to disintegrate.

In contrast, the girls in this study often made attempts to resolve interpersonal conflicts between themselves. In some of the groups we observed, girls used a range of different strategies to attempt to clarify and resolve normatives debates. Though it is not always possible to identify the extent to which a resolution has been reached, in many cases the girls appeared to have resolved the tension between them, if not also the actual debate.

Most conflict exchanges among these adolescent females began with an accusation about another girl's inappropriate behavior or attitude. A common response to such an accusation among the younger girls was a simple denial. From there the exchange might consist of repeated accusation–denial sequences as in the following conflict between two best friends, Tami and Heidi:[1]

Example 1, sixth grade

1. Tami: Why were you combing Peggy's hair yesterday?
2. Heidi: I didn't.
3. Tami: Yes you were!
4. Heidi: I was not.
5. Tami: You were feathering it back.

4.   Heidi: I was not.
7.   Tami: You were *too*.
8.   Heidi: I was *not*. You can go ask Peggy. ((Peggy walks by.))
9.   Peggy, was I combing your hair yesterday? ((Peggy shakes
10.   her head no.))
11. Heidi: See! What did I tell you?
12. Tami: Whose hair were you combing?
13. Heidi: I wasn't combing anybody's hair.
14. Tami: Who was combing Peggy's hair?
15. Heidi: I don't know. ((Pause)) And the, well, um, Jane and Sally
16.   are married. ((Continues to tell me about her family.))

Here, Tami accuses Heidi of violating a best-friend norm by engaging in behavior that she feels should be limited to their relationship.[2] Heidi repeatedly denies that she engaged in this behavior. Her denials, however, do not lead to a resolution of their conflict. Finally, in line 9 she makes an appeal to a third party, asking Peggy if she did indeed comb her hair. Peggy's denial is then used as evidence to substantiate her position, and, after a few additional questions, the conflict is resolved and Heidi returns to the previous topic.

In this example, the first strategy other than a denial was successful in resolving the conflict. In other cases, numerous strategies were tried before the conflict was resolved. For example in the next episode Bonnie makes several attempts to resolve a conflict with her best friend, Irene.

Example 2, eighth grade

1.   Irene: You told me you was gonna have me spend the night with
2.   you, during that week. So I already asked my mom. Every
3.   week, every day, she'd say, "When you gonna spend the
4.   night with Bonnie?" and I kept saying, "( )."
5.   Bonnie: I asked my mon at the very beginning of the week and she
6.   said no that day. She said because Karla was gonna ask
7.   Sandy and Sam was gonna ask Jim and that was just, we
8.   already had two teenagers running around the house.
9.   Irene: You told me she said *yes*.
10. Bonnie: I said I'd have to ask her first. Remember? We said that
11.   when we were getting off the bus.
12. Irene: I don't remember, all I heard. . ."I'm gonna have you spend
13.   the week this week."
14. Bonnie: ( ) the day I stayed home.
15. Irene: Yeah that's how my mom got ( ), staying home with
            Bonnie.
16. Bonnie: You stayed home anyway, so why are you crying?!
17. Irene: I wasn't with you.

18. (?):   ( )
19. Irene: Neither did I 'cause one time we lied to my mom and told her
20.   we were going to bake a cake.
21. Bonnie: We did.

Irene begins by accusing Bonnie of failing to come through with an invitation to spend the night at her house. Bonnie first offers a long explanation for her failure which Irene contradicts. Bonnie then tries to appeal to Irene's memory in line 10, but Irene denies hearing Bonnie's remark. Finally, in line 16, Bonnie calls Irene's initial accusation into question by asking, "You stayed home anyway, so why are you crying?!" Irene then expresses the importance to her of spending time with Bonnie.

In this episode, Bonnie demonstrates considerable skill in conflict resolution. She tries several different strategies for resolving the conflict until she is successful. The final strategy is one that Irene cannot simply contradict as she could the first two and leads Irene to express the real issue behind the conflict, i.e. Irene's desire to spend more time with Bonnie. Once this is out in the open, the girls discuss an activity they did together, allowing them to reinforce their closeness and thus alleviate Irene's underlying concern about not spending enough time together.

In some cases, conflict exchanges involved several group members. This was more common in seventh and eighth grade when relatively stable peer groups had formed. In the next example, which occurred in a seventh-grade group, a conflict between Betty and Carol is the topic of a discussion which also includes Mary, Linda and Nancy.

Example 3, seventh grade

1. Mary: Ted came up to Carol and said she – that he loved her.
2. Linda: Who?
3. Betty: *Carol!*
4. Carol: What?
5. Betty: I don't like you no more.
6. Carol: What'd I do?
7. Linda: Taking Betty's boyfriend.
8. Carol: I didn't either! ((Pounds table as she half laughs.))
9. Mary: It wasn't Carol's *fault* though.
10. Betty: *Yes it was!* She *flirts!*
11. Carol: I was just walking there // (   ).
12. Betty: You *flirt*, You *flirt*. Yes you //.
13. Carol: I didn't even do nothing. ((Laughter.))
14. Betty: You *flirt* Carol! You're mean! I don't like you no more.
15. Carol: You won't (mind me) after I get done talking # *if* you still

16.   want me to.
17. Betty: Huh?
18. Carol: If you – do you want me to still talk to him? // ((Betty
19.   nods.)) Alright shut up. God.
20. Nancy: Hell she called me up she goes, "Nancy call Ted and talk to
21.   him."
22. Betty: (I sank you) ((Silly voice.))

Although these girls did not date boys yet, they were beginning to identify boys they liked and refer to them as their boyfriends. In some cases, the relationship was one of mutual liking and frequently the couple was then considered to be "going with" each other. They, might, however still only spend a minimal amount of time together, such as walking around or sitting together for part of the lunch period. In this example, Betty is using the term "boyfriend" to refer to a boy that she likes, but not someone that she is considered to be "going with."

While this conflict primarily concerns Betty and Carol, several of their friends participate in the exchange. In fact, Linda makes the accusation of inappropriate behavior in line 7 and Mary defends Carol's behavior in line 9, saying "it wasn't Carol's fault though." This defense, however, leads to a second accusation made by Betty herself, i.e. that Carol flirts. Carol tries to explain her behavior and then simply denies it, saying "I didn't even do nothing." She finally offers to talk to Ted for Betty. Friends often talked to the boys their friends liked, typically conveying some indication of their liking to them. By offering to do this, Carol shows that she is aware of Betty's underlying concern that she might be losing a boyfriend. When this concern is directly addressed through Carol's offer to help strengthen Betty's relationship with her boyfriend, the conflict is resolved.

It is important to note that while this conflict exchange is a serious one from Betty's point of view, Carol initially tries to treat it more lightly. Both of her denials (lines 8 and 13) are accompanied by laughter. Children as young as six years of age have been found to attempt to transfer serious disputes into lighter ones through various keying mechanisms such as smiles, laughter, and joking (Maynard, 1985a). However, in this exchange Carol is unsuccessful in her attempts to lighten the dispute and eventually treats it as a serious one, while expressing some exasperation (line 19). Participants in a dispute, thus, may differ in how seriously they regard the dispute. Until a shared perspective is reached, it is unlikely that the dispute will be resolved.

3. Ritual insulting

Unlike the exchanges discussed above, ritual insulting seldom results in resolution (M.H. Goodwin, 1982b; W. Labov, 1972b) and thus does not develop conflict–resolution skills. However, other important skills are needed to participate successfully in this type of conflict exchange and these are developed through frequent participation. To begin with, children need to learn how to interpret and respond to insults in a playful manner. According to Kochman (1983), the ability to respond to even personal insults in a nonserious manner is a critical skill needed for successful participation in ritual insulting. Also, the competitive nature of this activity and the fact that certain types of insults are evaluated more highly than others means that children who participate in this activity are likely to learn how to respond with more clever and elaborate insults. Successful learning of such skills would make it possible for individuals to be better able to defend themselves from real and potential insults from others, insuring greater self-confidence in social interaction in adulthood as well as in childhood.

While ritual insulting did not occur frequently in all of the groups we studied, it was a common activity in certain groups of girls who came from working- or lower-class backgrounds. These girls placed a higher value on "toughness" and being able to defend yourself than did girls from middle-class backgrounds. One important way of learning self-defense was to learn how to respond to insults. In the following example, a girl who is relatively unpopular and often the target of insults successfully defends herself from a verbal attack by another girl, although not in the most skillful manner:

Example 4, eighth grade

1. Dana: You act like you're hot stuff. You're ugly Helen.
2. Helen: You *are* ugly, aren't ya?
3. Dana: Just cool your ass down a little before I//
4. Helen: Cool your ass off, Dana. Put it in some cool water; maybe
5.   it'll cool.
6. Dana: Aw shut up.
7. Helen: Why don't you make me?
8. Dana: I don't//
9. Helen: Kiss my grits![3]

Girls who engaged in ritual insulting on a regular basis tended to engage in fewer disputes aimed at the resolution of normative conflicts. Instead they relied on ritual insulting to communicate interpersonal norms and particularly norms regarding male – female relationships. In the following example, Tricia, Natalie, and Peggy all accuse Ellen of having a dirty mind. While Tricia's accusation is direct, Natalie's is more subtle, implying that the boys who are watching their group should look at Ellen because she represents the general deterioration of social values (see lines 8–9). Peggy's insertion of the phrase, "Yeah, the gutter" in line 10 makes this view more explicit while also providing support for it.

Example 5, eighth grade

1. Natalie: Kerry # Williams! Why did you guys look at me?
2. Boys: ((Respond in background.))
3. Ellen: Cause they # wanted ta # they wanted to look at somethin'
4. that they # no (   ).
5. Tricia: Ellen, you've got a dirty mind.
6. Ellen: I'm not (dirty) ((Squealing, then breaks down in laughs and
7. coughs before she can complete sentence.))
8. Natalie: Look at # look at Ellen. ((To boys.)) Give you somethin' to
9. think about, # what's goin' /1/ on in this /2/ world.
10. Peggy: /1/ Yeah, the gutter.
11. Boy: /2/ No. ((To suggestion he look at Ellen.))
12. Natalie: The gutter. ((Giggles.)) That was a good one.
13. Boys: Who is it?
14. Ellen: It's better than what *you* were, which is a piece of # #
15. shit.
16. Tricia: ((Finishing with her.)) shit.
17. Natalie: Okay you guys.
18. Ellen: ((Squeals.))
19. Tricia I was I was just helping her. I wasn't really sayin' // it.
20. Natalie: You guys # ((pleading() – now shut up // (Kick out.) you
21. *know* we will. He likes to kick us out.

Ellen first responds to the accusation that she has a dirty mind with a denial accompanied with laughter, showing she is not taking the accusation seriously. Her ability to respond in a nonserious manner is an important skill and is necessary for the continuation of the activity. Natalie and Peggy then jointly insult Ellen, with Peggy adding the phrase "Yeah, the gutter." The competitive nature of this activity is evident in Natalie's positive evaluation of the phrase. She both repeats it and explicitly evaluates it, saying "That was a good one." This time Ellen responds with a counter-insult which Tricia joins in finishing. The fact that Tricia switches sides during the course of this exchange, first accusing Ellen and then joining with her, indicates again its playful nature. Also, the fact that the exchange is not restricted to two participants as it often is with males (M.H. Goodwin, 1982b; W. Labov, 1972b; Kochman, 1983), suggests that girls may be less likely to use ritual insulting to establish and maintain status differences within groups.

This is not to say that girls do not view ritual insulting as a competitive activity. Since they value self-defense, it is important that they learn how to respond to the insults. In the process they continually challenge each other to come up with a better, more clever response to an accusation or insult. In another example involving the same girls, Natalie responds to Ellen's insult with a counter-insult. When Ellen fails to respond she repeats her counter-insult, challenging her to top it.

Example 6, eighth grade

1. Natalie: ((Screaming suddenly, perhaps due to being hit.))
2. Peggy: Boy, Natalie – today's the day for you to get beat, isn't
3.   it?
4. Ellen: Everybody beats Natalie. Natalie –
5. (?):   Hi, Peggy! ((Someone from outside group.))
6. Natalie: At least people *want* // to beat me – At least people want to
7.   beat me – nobody wants to touch *you* with a ten-foot # ten-
8.   foot pole! ((Laughing.))
9. (?)   ((to Peggy)): What did we do in Health yesterday?
10. Hannah: Make it twenty.
11. (Natalie): Huh?
12. Hannah   Make it twenty.
13. (?):   Peggy
14. Peggy: What?
15. Hannah   Make it twenty.
16. (?):   What did we do in Health?
17. Peggy: Nothin'. ((This conversation continues a little while in
18.   background.))
19. Natalie: At least every – at least everybody wants to beat me.
20.   Nobody wants to touch *you* with a // ten-foot pole.
21. Ellen: Yeah, whoever beat me was Robin Anders.
22. Natalie: Well, *you* went with him too!! ((shouting))
23. Ellen: I never touched // him!
24. Natalie: And *you* knew who he was! *I* went with him over the
               phone!
25.   ((Screaming.)) // And I was forced!
26. Ellen: Yeah, but you sure enjoyed him that May first though, //
27.   didn't you?
28. Natalie: I was *forced.* ((Quietly.))
29. Ellen: You were not. ((Quietly.))
30. Natalie: The hell if I wasn't. We wouldn't 'ave had (   )
31.   ((Tape cuts off for 7 seconds.))
32. Ellen: You (didn't) have very much fun with him. Not me!
33. Natalie   ((Angrily)): When I *met* him he didn't have his glasses on.
34.   And he looked # okay without his glasses. // He didn't look
35.   that bad. And whenever I see him with his glasses on I
36.   (started barfin') at the door, man.
37. (Peggy):   Is Robin Anders sittin' around here anywhere?
38. (Boy):   (Bull!)
39. Natalie: ((Shrieks in response.))

When Ellen fails to respond to Natalie's insult, Natalie repeats it (line 19). Ellen provides a fairly weak response at this point which simply makes reference to Robin Anders. However, even this reference to Robin appears to imply the accusation of Natalie having gone with him since Natalie responds with a counter-accusation saying, "Well, *you* went with him, too!!" As this exchange continues, it becomes more heated and somewhat more serious. Natalie's last comment is a more serious explanation of why she had been tricked into going with an unattractive male, i.e. she had agreed to go with him during a phone conversation and did not realize how unattractive he was until she later saw him wearing his glasses. She finishes by indicating that she now shares the same negative view of him.

It is interesting to note that Hannah attempts to expand on Natalie's initial insult when she says "Make it twenty," i.e. a twenty-foot pole (see line 10). Even though she repeats this comment several times, no one picks up on it or responds to it. Instead, in this instance Natalie is more concerned with getting a response from Ellen, perhaps because the insult exchange is a way to release some of the underlying conflict between them. The fact that the exchange does become more heated and more serious suggests that it is serving more purposes for these girls than do disputes which remain more playful.

Just as more serious forms of conflict often involved a lighter side, this example indicates that ritual insulting often involves a more serious side. This is even more evident in the next example where the normative issue is more salient. This exchange took place during an in-depth interview with the same group of girls on the topic of relationships with boys. They have been discussing whether or not you can have several boyfriends at one time. The researcher has just asked Tricia how important boys are to her. After Tricia answers, Natalie attempts to clarify her view by saying, "See, we may be friends with them, but we're not sluts." Both Hannah and Ellen assume that Natalie is referring to them and respond seriously rather than jokingly.

Example 7, eighth grade

1.	Tricia:	I feel the same way that Peg does, especially now when
2.		we're just about to go into high-school our grades are
3.		more important than // boys.
4.	Natalie:	See, we may be friends // with them, but we're not sluts.
5.	Researcher:	Um hum. ((To Tricia.))
6.	Hannah:	Will you repeat that please? ((Angry, controlled voice.))
7.	Tricia:	No, /1/ you /2/ don't qualify.
8.	Natalie:	/1/ I know, but we're not sluts.
9.	Ellen:	/2/ ( ) fuck you (you guys)! ((Ellen stomps off
10.		angry and upset.))
11.	Natalie:	Well *look* at that! // She does that every time!

12. Hannah:	She's pissed at *me*. She's pissed at me because I want to
13.	fight her and she doesn't – and she won't fight me.
14. Ellen	((Calling from another part of the room)): What did *you*
15.	do the last time (remember that) Natalie!?
16. Natalie:	I stayed *around* ta fight ya! ((Laughs.))
17. Researcher:	Are her // feelings really hurt or is she just pretending?
18. Hannah:	( ) around when *I* wanted to fight. I told her to call
19.	me when she wants // to fight.
20. Natalie:	She – *every* time, every time I – we call her a name she
21.	takes it *seriously* and *goes* off and *pouts*. ((Angry tone.))
22. Peggy:	She calls *us* names all the // time. ((Angry tone.))
23. Natalie:	And she calls *us* names *every* // (day).
24. Tricia	((whispering)): She'll *call* ya a *bitch* for no reason.
25.	She'll come in // and say ( ).

During the previous year the terms "slut" and "bitch" were frequently used by these girls and were usually responded to in a joking manner. This year, however, they were beginning to develop different attitudes about relationships with boys. While some girls now thought you should only have one relationship at a time, other girls still felt it was acceptable to have several relationships at once. As a result, the term "slut" was sometimes used in reference to the latter group and had a more serious connotation.

Despite the serious connotation, the rules of ritual insulting require Ellen to respond in a playful manner. Indeed, several of the girls are upset that she failed to especially since she insults them all the time. Also, Natalie's comment in line 19 implies that this is not the first time that Ellen has taken a joking comment too seriously.

The failure to respond in a playful manner has several important implications. For one thing, it causes the exchange to break down. If one of the participants does not respond in a playful manner to an insult, the conflict becomes a serious one, requiring other types of skills. The inability of these group members to deal with more serious conflict exchanges is evident in Ellen's immediate decision to leave the group once she defines the insult as a serious one. Since this group relies extensively on ritual insulting to communicate interpersonal norms, it is particularly important that members be able to participate in such exchanges without taking the insults or accusations seriously. Otherwise they may be left, as they are in this example, with no further way to communicate their views on this conflicting issue.

Girls who engaged in ritual insulting on a regular basis with other girls were able to participate successfully in insult exchanges with boys. If a boy should insult them in some way, the girls were able to not only defend themselves, but often responded with an insult that the boy was unable to top, as in the following examples:

Example 8, eighth grade

1. Boy: We found another book here you might be interested in –
     Teenage Alcoholism.
2. Natalie: You might be interested in teenage faggism.

Example 9, eighth grade

1. Boy: All these girls are dogs!
2. Tricia: Oh, but you're a real fox.

In both cases the girls' counter-insults were not responded to by the boys who initiated the conflict exchange. In the latter case, Tricia's sarcastic response is particularly effective in that it is a compliment, although one which is not meant seriously. M.H. Goodwin (1980b) also found the black, working-class girls were able to successfully compete with boys in insult exchanges.

This same degree of skill was not evident in other girls at the school. In general, the less frequently girls engaged in insult exchanges, the weaker their insulting skills. Some girls hardly ever exchanged insults and were clearly less competent on the few occasions when they did. For example, one day Ginny jokingly remarked that Julie looked funny in the leotards that she had to wear for a school skit:

Example 10, eighth grade

1. Ginny: Julie. You look – you look funny in those leotards.
2. Julie: So do you!
3. (Nancy): For what?
4. Ginny: I didn't wear one.
5. Julie: You wore your dress!
6. (Nancy): For what?
7. Ginny: You know that play they're doing. Julie has to wear this
8.   brown leotard thing and she looks like ( ).

Not only did Julie take the insult seriously, she responded in a way that did not make sense, since Ginny did not wear leotards for the skit. Julie's second response does not make much sense either since it is not clear what is funny or unusual about wearing a dress.

While this particular group did not engage in insult exchanges, they did engage in other forms of playful conflict. In the following episode a girl accuses another girl of violating an interpersonal norm, but does so in a joking manner:

Example 11, eighth grade

1. Irene: *Hey* did you tell Bonnie that # Did you tell Bonnie that #
2.   Did you tell Bonnie that ((Laughter begins.)) Did you tell
3.   Bonnie that you told me that I knew that you ((More
4.   laughter.)) Did you tell *her*, that you told me, that you
5.   told her what she got her for her birthday? Did
6.   you tell me that, what, I got for my birthday from her?
7.   Then you told her ((More laughter.))
8. Karen: Cook ((Julie's last name)), you're not a very good liar are
           ya?
9. Irene: Did ya?
10. Julie: Yah.
11. Irene: Do # you told me that? Well you didn't tell me.
12. (Penny): Yes she did.
13. Irene: (   ), you didn't tell me what she got me for my birthday, did
14.   ya?
15. Julie: Yah.
16. (Penny): Yah she did.
17. Irene: No she didn't!
18. Julie: Yes I did! I told you – what'd I tell you?
19. Penny: She doesn't know what she told ya now.
20. (?):   She said // me.
21. Julie: Yes I did.
22. Irene: No you didn't. No you didn't. And now he doesn't even
23.   trust me cause I promised that she, that you, didn't tell me
24.   and now you said, "Yes I did tell you." And you did not!
25. Julie: Yes I *did*. ((Half-scream)) Yes I did.
26. Irene: She didn't.
27. Bonnie: Maybe you were so drunk that you didn't remember.
28. Julie: I don't think; maybe you weren't with me.
29. (?):   Lemme go to the car!

It is clear that Irene is accusing Julie in a joking way as she pretends to have trouble phrasing by starting it over several times. That and the complex nature of her question, i.e. "Did you tell Bonnie that you told me that I knew that you," produces considerable laughter from other group members. Julie goes along with the joke by claiming she did something she really did not do. She adds her own humorous remark in line 18 when she says, "I told you – what'd I tell you?"

The structure of this exchange is relatively complex, in that Irene puts her accusation in the form of a question rather than a statement. Furthermore, it is a question that she herself has an answer to, so that the actual conflict occurs when Julie provides a different answer, which Irene then contradicts (see line 11). This exchange is then repeated several times with Julie claiming that she told Irene and Irene denying it.

The participation of several other group members further contributes to the complexity of the exchange. One girl collaborates with Julie on the falsehood by saying, "Yes she did." Other members also comment on the exchange at several points, emphasizing the joking nature (see lines 8 and 19). Finally, Bonnie provides a possible resolution for the conflict saying, "Maybe you were so drunk that you didn't remember."

All of the girls appeared to participate competently in this exchange. Not only were they able to interpret its nonserious nature, they built on the humour in several different ways. Even Julie, who in the previous example did not appear to be very skilled verbally, responds in appropriate ways to the joking accusation, despite its complex form. This suggests, that even though these girls are not as skilled in the exchange of ritual insults, they have other forms of playful conflict which they perform quite competently.

4. Discussion

Our findings indicate that white adolescent girls do engage in direct confrontations of various types. In some groups, serious disputes were relatively common and girls in these groups gained considerable skill in conflict resolution. While many different strategies were used, those strategies which addressed the real issues behind the conflict were most successful. In other groups, ritual insulting was relatively common and girls in these groups gained more competitive and self-defense-related skills. They also learned to respond to insults playfuly and to communicate normative information in an indirect manner. Finally, other types of playful conflict were identified which developed different, yet equally complex verbal skills.

While conflict exchanges were found at all grade levels, more incidences occurred among eighth graders. Eighth graders also demonstrated both better conflict-resolution skills and better insulting skills than did younger students, suggesting that these skills are being developed during the early adolescent years. Eighth graders also tended to be members of more stable peer groups (Eder, 1985). It may be that girls are more likely to engage in direct conflict with girls they know well, which would indicate the importance of being in a stable peer group for the developing of conflict-related skills.

These findings indicate that some females may get more practice in conflict resolution than do males, who seldom attempt to resolve conflict (M.H. Goodwin, 1982b; Kochman, 1983). Previous research which found that girls did not attempt to resolve conflicts focused primarily on conflicts arising during sports and other games (Lever, 1976). These conflicts may be less salient to girls than the interpersonal conflicts which were examined in this study. Other research has shown that adolescent females rely on direct discussions as the main means for resolving problems with close friends. Adolescent males were much less likely to talk over problems and instead tended to either simply accept the problem and forget about it or to not resolve the problem at all (Youniss and Smoller, 1985).

Also, it is now clear that some white as well as black females engage in ritual insulting and develop competitive and self-defense skills through this activity. Insulting skills would not only allow these females to assert and defend their rights, but might also contribute to an impression of greater intelligence and wit, since quick and clever responses are often viewed as an indicator of general cleverness and intelligence. On the other hand, those females who fail to learn such skills may not only be less successful in asserting themselves, they may also be perceived as less intelligent or clever than females or males who have learned to respond with quick and clever insults.

While our sample is limited, it appears that ritual insulting is more common among girls from working- and lower-class backgrounds where "toughness" is more highly valued and there is less concern about "politeness." However, more research is needed to determine the extent of this activity among females from different social class backgrounds. It is important that this research be based on in-depth observational and discourse studies, since self-reports of insulting practices may differ from actual behavior (Ayoub and Barnett, 1961).

While girls participated in ritual insulting, they did not appear to use it primarily to maintain status hierarchies within groups as has been found in previous studies of males (M.H. Goodwin, 1982b; W. Labov, 1972b; Kochman, 1983). This was most evident in the fact that disputes were not restricted to the two participants who were vying for status, as is often the case for males. Instead, other group members joined in and even switched sides during the course of the dispute. This indicates the importance of examining the social functions or functions that an activity serves for a group rather than making assumptions about the functions *a priori*.

One of the functions that both playful and more serious conflict exchanges served for the girls in this study was to communicate normative information. It is interesting that this was an important aspect of both types of conflict exchange. Also, it is interesting that certain groups seemed to rely on one type of conflict more than the other for meeting this function. Thus, girls who relied on ritual insulting to communicate normative information were much less likely to engage in more serious disputes and when the disputes did become more serious they were less successful at resolving them.

While both serious and playful disputes were identified, there was also considerable overlap between them. On the one hand, girls attempted to lighten the tone of more serious disputes with laughter and other playful acts. On the other hand, playful insults were sometimes taken seriously. The latter is always a possibility with ritual insulting, especially if the insults tend to be more personal in nature, as is the case among certain groups of black males. In such cases, considerable skill is needed by the responder in order to maintain a playful attitude (Kochman, 1983). To the extent that girls rely on insulting to communicate normative information, the insults are also likely to be more personal and thus also require considerable skill on the part of the responder.

More research is needed to determine the extent to which girls from different social-class backgrounds engage in different types of conflict. However, these results indicate that there is considerable diversity in female speech and that this diversity is not simply a result of ethnic differences in speech style. In particular, the view that female speech is polite and submissive (Lakoff, 1975) needs to be reconsidered. This perception of female speech is likely to reflect a middle-class bias, since both black and white females from working- and lower-class backgrounds have been found to talk in ways that might be considered both rude and assertive.

The fact that females do not share a single style of speech has important implications for cross-group interaction, particularly between females from different social-class and/or ethnic backgrounds. Schofield (1982) found that the middle-class white females in her study were intimidated by the working-class black females. Since they were unfamiliar with the rules of ritual insulting, they tended to interpret insults by black females seriously. Also, since the white females did not know how to defend themselves, they were easy targets for black females.

In general, if females differ in their tendency to engage in serious as compared to more playful forms of conflict, misunderstandings are likely to occur when females from different backgrounds interact. As we have seen from some of the disputes examined here, when a shared perception regarding the seriousness of a dispute is lacking the dispute is unlikely to be resolved or continued in a playful form. Since disputes are an important way for females to resolve and communicate normative concerns, the inability to carry on disputes would also affect the ability of females to develop other shared perceptions and norms.

Notes

I would like to thank Cathy Evans and Stephanie Sanford for their assistance in collecting the data used in this paper and the following people for their help in data transcription: Cathy Evans, Angela Marato, Cynthia Murphy, Joyce Owens, and Stephanie Sanford. This research was supported by NIMH Grant No. 36680.

1   All names are pseudonyms. The following notations are used in the examples from transcripts: ( ) refers to an uncertain or unclear utterance or speaker, (( )) refers to nonverbal behavior and other contextual

      information, // refers to the point at which the next speaker begins talking during someone else's turn, # refers to a brief pause.

2   Girls occasionally combed each other's hair, even if they were not best friends. However, here Tami is attempting to establish this behavior as an exclusive one which would be limited to their relationship.

3   "Grits" is a derogatory name referring to people from lower-class backgrounds or lower-status peer groups. It originates from the fact that grits are more commonly eaten by lower-class families.

4 Interstitial argument

CHARLES GOODWIN AND MARJORIE
HARNESS GOODWIN

Recent research into the organization of argument has begun to reveal much about its intrinsic structure. For example, there has been detailed study of phenomena such as how arguments begin (Adger, 1984; Maynard, 1985b) and end (Adger, 1984: 137–143, 149–174; M.H. Goodwin, 1978: 288–334, 1982b: 87–88; Vuchinich this volume), the sequencing of actions within such exchanges (Adger, 1984; Brenneis and Lein, 1977; Boggs, 1978; Eisenberg and Garvey, 1981; Genishi and di Paolo, 1982; Haviland,1982b; Lein and Brenneis, 1978), the internal organization of oppositional moves (M.H. Goodwin, 1983; M.H. Goodwin and C. Goodwin, 1987), and how argument is tied to both other activities and larger social processes (M.H. Goodwin, 1980b, M.H. Goodwin, 1980a; Maynard, 1985a). From a slightly different perspective, recent research has also begun to reveal that participants pay very close attention to their local environment, for example the exact words spoken in the immediately prior talk, and use that knowledge to build appropriate subsequent talk.[1] Such phenomena become inaccessible to study when analysis takes as its point of departure a gloss of a turn's talk as an instance of a particular type of speech act. Finally, research that pays close attention to the details of what participants are attending to as they move from utterance to utterance has demonstrated that, despite the way in which argument is frequently treated as disruptive behavior, it is in fact accomplished through a process of very intricate coordination between the parties who are opposing each other (M.H. Goodwin and C. Goodwin, 1987).

One feature of oppositional exchanges that has so far been largely neglected is analysis of the way in which the talk of the moment constitutes those who are present to it (i.e., how what is said in a given turn can make relevant particular social identities). A participant building an appropriate oppositional move must attend not only to the action that is being opposed, but also to proposals in prior talk about how those present are being positioned vis-à-vis each other.[2] Attributes of participants that can become relevant for the organization of particular moves encompass a wide variety of phenomena, including the types of social personae that have traditionally been discussed as components of status and role (and which will here, following Goodenough (1965), be referred to as identity relationships),[3] occasion-specific social identities (e.g., accuser and defendant in a gossip confrontation), differential rights to participate in the talk of the moment, and affect displays tied to particular moves (for example, "righteous indignation"). Our approach to the analysis of such phenomena differs from that found in most sociological analysis. Rather than assuming the presence and relevance of social categories we will focus on how such events are constituted by participants in the production of their talk. Central to such phenomena is the way in which they are intimately tied to the visible activities that the participants are currently engaged in, and are locally invoked within the talk of the moment. Such attributes constitute both a constraint on the actions of the participants, something that they may be required to attend to for the organization of their subsequent action, and a resource that can be exploited; for example, by using talk that reshapes how those present are aligned to each other a speaker can attempt to strategically alter the social organization of the moment. Research into how such phenomena are organized has a clear relevance to an important question in the analysis of social processes: the issue of how actors constitute themselves as particular types of social entities.

Using as data an audiotape of talk ocurring between urban black children at play on the street, this chapter will use such issues as a point of departure to investigate a range of phenomena relevant to the organization of argument including:

The **dyadic** organization of an argumentative exchange.

How **third parties** can participate in the exchange by slotting actions of their own in the interstices of the actions between the principals.

How actions in these different sequential positions make alternative proposals about the **participation status** of the party performing the action.

The way in which a participant can utilize such interstitial structures to **build a single utterance that simultaneously constructs two different types of action to two different recipients**, and which receives two simultaneous responses.

How such processes can make visible **larger social activities** within local talk including

changes in relevant **social identities**, and

the **interactive constitution of hierarchy**.

The **interactive, reflexive organization of context** and the way in which the emerging structure of talk *reorganizes* context.

Analysis of such phenomena will permit us to investigate in detail how participants in the midst of argument dynamically exploit sequential organization, participation frameworks, and contextual organization as creative resources for the organization of the activities they are engaged in.

1. Data and transcription

For over a year and a half one of us (M.H. Goodwin) audiotaped a group of urban black children as they played on the street.[4] The current study is part of a larger project investigating a range of speech activities, including gossip, argument, stories, directives, etc., found in the talk of the Maple Street children (as they will be referred to here). Our study of argument is based on analysis of over 175 oppositional exchanges from a corpus of over 200 hours of transcribed conversation. Analysis of the children's activities and social organization, including a range of phenomena relevant to the organization of their arguments, are reported in detail elsewhere (M.H. Goodwin, 1980b, 1980a, 1982b, 1982c, M.H. Goodwin and C. Goodwin, 1987).[5]

Data are transcribed using the Jefferson transcription system (Sacks, Schegloff and Jefferson, 1974: 731–733). For purposes of the analysis to be developed in this chapter, the following transcription conventions are the most relevant:

Punctuation symbols are used to mark intonation changes rather than as grammatical symbols:
A period indicates a falling contour.
A question mark indicates a rising contour.
A comma indicates a falling–rising contour.
Bold italics indicate some form of emphasis, which may be signaled by changes in pitch and/or amplitude.
A bracket joining the talk of separate speakers marks the point at which overlapping talk begins.
A dash marks a sudden cut-off of the current sound.
An equals sign indicates that talk attached by the equal sign follows prior talk without any gap whatsoever.
Colons indicate that the sound just before the colon has been noticeably lengthened.
Numbers within parentheses (e.g "(0.5)"), mark silences in seconds and tenths of seconds.
Arrows pointing to particular lines are used to locate for the reader specific events within a longer transcript.
Round brackets around a strip of talk indicate that the transcriber is not sure of what was being said there. Blank space within the brackets means that the transcriber heard talk there but could not recover it. Empty round brackets in the speaker column indicate that the transcriber could not identify the speaker.

In the following, a number of the boys on Maple Street are preparing for a sling-shot fight. They have divided themselves spatially into two separate groups that are cutting and shaping wire coat hangers into projectiles that will serve as ammunition during the fight. Huey (age 14)[6] and his younger brother Michael (age 13) have emerged as the leaders of the two groups. Preparations for the fight are taking place in Michael and Huey's back yard.

Though who will be on each team is still the subject of considerable negotiation, one group of boys – Chopper, Poochie and Tokay – is working with Michael in a lower stairwell. Another group – Bruce, Robbie and Nate – is working with Huey on a platform several steps above Michael's group.

Example 1

1. Michael: All right who's on your *side* Huey.
2. Chopper: Pick-pick four *people*.
3. Huey: It's quarter after four and I'm not
4. ⁻   ready to *go* yet.
5. Bruce: Me neither.
6. Huey: I'm not going till four thirty.
7. Michael: Well get in there and get them papers
8.   off that couch before–
9. Huey: ⌊I did already
10. Chopper: Get your four *guys*,
11. Michael: You get *three* guys.
12. Huey: ⌐I only get three guys?
13. Chopper: ⌈⌈I mean three guys.
14. Michael: That's right.

2. Invoking activity domains within local talk

In the data being examined, four different parties speak. However, the core skeleton of the sequence is provided by a series of exchanges between Michael and Huey. For clarity we will begin by looking in some detail at the organization of these exchanges, omitting for the moment the talk of Chopper and Bruce. We will start with the talk between Michael and Huey that occurs in lines 1–6:

Example 1

1. Michael: All right who's on your *side* Huey.
3. Huey: It's quarter after four and I'm not
4.   ready to *go* yet.
6.   I'm not going till four thirty.

Here Michael asks Huey to do something and Huey refuses to do it. The sequence thus provides a prototypical example of an oppositional exchange. However, simply classifying the exchange in this fashion misses the complexity of what the participants are doing in this talk. For example, what is it that Huey refuses to do? In line 1 Michael asks Huey to specify who is on his side. In his answer, Huey never directly addresses this issue but instead notes the current time and says that he is "not ready to go yet." To be more explicit about what is happening here, and the phenomena that the participants are paying attention to in the organization of their talk, requires that we investigate how this sequence is embedded within specific activities being performed within the current interaction.

Michael and Huey are in the midst of preparations for a sling-shot battle. This activity is relevant to the organization of their talk in at least two related ways:

1. The talk invokes features of the activity (such as "sides" and the sequencing of stages within the sling-shot battle) for its proper understanding.
2. Through what they say, the participants constitute and shape the activity in progress, including the positions of those present within it.

The talk is thus informed by the activity while simultaneously it helps shape its future progress.

3. Organizing a sling-shot battle

In example 1 Michael asks Huey to pick his side for the upcoming battle. The question of how sides are to be formed has been debated extensively throughout the afternoon in the events leading up to example 1. Since that discussion also focused on a range of other phenomena that participants attend to within this sequence (for example, team size), some of the ways in which these issues have been dealt with in prior talk will be briefly noted.

3.1 Preparing for the fight

Before the boys can actually have their battle with each other they have to make their weapons. Their sling shots are made from wire coat hangers and powered by rubber bands. However, the rubber bands lack a pocket to hold projectiles such as stones. Instead the boys use as ammunition small U-shaped bits of wire which can be placed around the rubber band like the notch in an arrow. Such details of the technology they employ have consequences for the larger organization of their activity. For example, since ammunition cannot be picked up from the surrounding environment, but instead must be specially manufactured, the actual fight is preceded by a period of preparing for it in which the necessary sling shots and ammunition are made. The talk currently being examined occurred during this preparation stage.

3.2 Team size and membership

Both the actual play with the sling shots, and the manufacturing process that precedes it, could be organized in a range of different ways – for example, as a group activity or with each person working in isolation. Instead of choosing either of these alternatives the boys have begun to divide themselves into two sides or teams, one under the leadership of Michael and the other under his older brother Huey. Such patterning is visible in the details of their talk and contrasts quite markedly with the group-centered, egalitarian structures used by Maple Street girls to organize their task activities (M.H. Goodwin, 1980b).

The division into teams has emerged as an issue of some importance in the talk of the boys that precedes example 1. Two related questions about this division have been repeatedly raised:

1.   Who will be allowed to play.
2.   Who will be on each team.

For example, shortly after Bruce arrives the following exchange occurs. Here Michael interprets a question from Bruce about a prior game (i.e., a comparison of the present activity with a similar one in the past in which Bruce participated) as a request to join Michael's team:

Example 2

(Simplified
transcript)
1.→ Bruce: Hey Michael.
2.→   *They do*in what we did down in the park?
3.   (1.5)
4.→ Michael: You ain't on our *si*de.
5.   You ain't *play*in *ne*ither!
6. Bruce: Who.
7. Michael: *You.*
8. Bruce: Why.
9. Michael: Cu:z. We already got too many–
10.   We got enough people *no*w.
11. Bruce: What you talking bout?
12. Michael: We fightin war.
13. Bruce: (   )
14. (Tokay): I'm on his side?
15. ():   No.
16. Michael: Me and Chuckie and Poochie
17. Jack: ₍And Tokay.
                 [[
18. ():   And Tokay.
19. Michael: And Tokay, Tokey.

Bruce is not only told that he can't be on Michael's team but also that he can't play. The reason given is that there are already too many players (lines 9–10), and this is followed by a listing of four people who are on Michael's team (lines 16–19).

An exchange such as this does not, however, definitively establish either who will be allowed to play, or team membership. Rather these issues remain open for considerable subsequent negotiation. For example, shortly after example 2, Bruce asked if he could be on one side if Robert went to the other. Once again Michael argued that there were already too many players:

Example 3

1.	Bruce:	Can me and Robert play if Robert be on
2.		Huey's tea:m,
3.→	Michael:	It's already too *many* of us.
4.→		It should only be *four* of us.
5.	Chopper:	⌈Eight
6.	Michael:	Two on– one– one–
7.	Bruce:	⌈Five on each side.
8.	Michael:	I got somebody on *my* side and Huey got=
9.	Chopper:	⌈You on Huey side.
10.	Michael:	=somebody on his side.
11.		Like we played last time.
12.		Remember our private game?
13.		(1.5)
14.	Michael:	Instead of all this– instead of all
15.	.	this block party ( ).
16.	Chopper:	⌈Who gonna be on your side then.
17.	Michael:	I can't stand block party games.

Note how *team size* (which sets limits on how many of those present will actually be allowed to play) is attended to as a key issue in this talk. Thus after stating that "it's already too *many* of us" Michael proposes that "It should only be *four* of us," a situation that would leave room for only two players in addition to Michael and Huey (note lines 6, 8, 10). Chopper, however, in line 5 has proposed that there should be *eight* players (i.e. four on each side), an argument that is quite consistent with Michael's earlier listing of four players on his side. However, Bruce, who was not included in that earlier listing proposes that there should be "Five on each side" (line 7).

The way in which Michael has changed from allowing four men on his team to now proposing that there should only be two both demonstrates just how much in flux this issue is, and suddenly calls into question the positions of even those who have already been listed on a team. These issues, and especially the question of who is and is not playing, become the focus of subsequent talk. Shortly after Michael proposes that the game should be restricted to four players, like their former "private game," Chopper asks, "Who gonna be your side then" (line 16) and quickly advances reasons why he rather than Poochie should be chosen (lines 19, 20, 23):

Example 3

14. Michael:	Instead of all this– instead of all
15.	this block party ( ).
	[
16. Chopper:	Who gonna be on your side then.
17. Michael:	I can't stand block party =
18. Michael:	= games.
	[
19.→ Chopper:	I was on there before Poochie.
20.→	= I'll tell you *that*.
21. Bruce:	Hey Huey.
22. Huey:	( )And bend it over like that.
	[
23.→ Chopper:	I know I'm playing. When I win.
	[
24. Bruce:	Huey.
25. Bruce:	Huey.
26. Michael:	Poochie playin.
27. Bruce:	Huey
28.→ Chopper:	I'm playin *too*.
29. Bruce:	Can I be on your *si*:de,
30. Huey:	Yeah.
31. Robert:	May I be on your side?
32. Nate:	(Huey)
33. Michael:	You wasn't on *my* side, baby.
34. Bruce:	I'm on Huey side.
35. Huey:	[[If you got slings you could be on
36.	my side.
37. Robert:	I do!
38.	(1.2)
39. Robert:	But I'm *mak*in my slings *n*ow.

Michael responds to Chopper's arguments by saying that *Poochie* is playing (line 26) – a move that does not explicitly deal with Chopper's status – and this leads to further claims from Chopper (line 28). Meanwhile Bruce has been trying to get Huey's attention (lines 24, 25, 27) in order to ask to be on his side (line 29). When this request is granted Robert (line 31) makes a similar bid to join Michael's team, a move that is emphatically rejected with Michael's "You wasn't on *my* side, baby" (line 33). Huey then offers to let Robert be on his side if he has slings (lines 35–36), a proposal that is enthusiastically accepted by Robert (line 37).

What happens in these data demonstrates first, how important the issue of team membership is in the organization of the boys' activities; second, that team size is crucial to decisions about team membership; and third, how proposed resolutions of this issue are constantly being called into question and re-negotiated

It has been frequently argued that one of the things that differentiates girls' groups from boys' is a concern in girls' groups with processes of exclusion (Douvan and Adelson, 1966; Eder and Hallinan, 1978; Feshbach and Sones, 1971; Lever, 1976; Savasta and Sutton-Smith, 1979; Savin-Williams, 1980) In the present data we find however that the question of exclusion is a major issue for a group of boys engaged in an activity (choosing sides for competitive interaction) that has been treated in the literature as distinctively male. As we have argued elsewhere (M.H. Goodwin and C. Goodwin, 1987; see also West and Zimmerman, 1985), analyzing gender differences in terms of such global distinctions, instead of within the detailed organization of specific activities, may lead to serious problems.

Some time later team size is defined in yet another way when Michael states that all those currently working with him are on his team:

Example 4

→ Michael: Everybody down here right now is on *my* side.
    Poochie: I'm *down* here.
    Chopper: Us– us *four.*
    Michael: So you better *p*ick four *p*eople Huey.

Chopper uses this definition to propose that four people are on the team and Michael then tells Huey to pick four people. This same demand is made collaboratively by Michael and Chopper some time later in the sequence that will be the principal focus of this chapter.

4. Indexing an encompassing activity within local talk

Returning now to example 1, we find that issues of team membership are quite relevant to what happens there:

Example 1

1. Michael: All right who's on your *side* Huey.
3. Huey: It's quarter after four and I'm not
4.   ready to *g*o yet.
6.   I'm not going till four thirty.

The talk that occurs here both indexes the activity in progress, and makes proposals about the positions that those present occupy within it. Thus in line 1 Michael treats Huey as someone who occupies a special position in the sling-shot activity, i.e., he is the party who is entitled to pick the team that will oppose Michael's. In essence Michael's talk proposes that Huey occupies the activity-relevant identity of *team leader*. Moreover, while the talk is explicitly addressed to only Huey, the action that Huey is being asked to perform, choosing a side, has consequences for others present as well, especially those working with Huey, who are not yet recognized as belonging to a team. For example, if Bruce is not chosen by Huey he will not be able to participate in the actual battle. Thus, though the scope of address in Michael's talk encompasses only a single individual, Huey, it nonetheless has very clear relevance to other participants as well.[7]

In replying to Michael, Huey attends to not only what he has been explicitly asked to perform, but rather analyzes Michael's talk by bringing to bear on it the larger structure of the sling-shot activity. Thus, in saying that he is "not ready to *go* yet," Huey treats what Michael has said as a proposal calling for immediate movement to the actual fight. With his reply, he not only refuses to perfom the action requested by Michael but also argues that control over when the activity will move from one stage to another is under his control, not Michael's.

5. Selectively interpreting prior talk

Of central importance to this process is the way in which Huey's talk formulates what Michael has said in a particular way. Michael asks Huey to pick his side. While this *may* imply a proposal that the boys should now move to the fight itself,[8] that issue is not raised explicitly in Michael's talk. However, by organizing his reply in the way that he does Huey focuses on that possible reading of the talk to the exclusion of others. Indeed he effectively removes that issue from the latent position it occupies in Michael's talk and topicalizes it.

Casting what is happening in such terms has a range of consequences. Thus Huey formulates Michael as someone attempting to control a basic parameter of the activity in progress – when it will move from the current preparation stage to the fight itself – but now exhibits that *he*, not Michael, has control over this parameter.

5.1 Accounting for a refusal

In the midst of a task situation a range of accounts for not doing something are available to participants (M.H. Goodwin, 1980b). For example, Huey could have argued that they had not yet made enough ammunition to have a good fight, and thus accounted for his refusal to do what Michael asked by pointing to demands imposed on him by the activity itself (Pomerantz, 1978). Instead he emphasizes the way in which he is acting purely in terms of his own desires, (e.g., "I'm not ready to *go* yet"). Other research (M.H. Goodwin, 1980b, 1988) has demonstrated that accounts of this type are frequently used by boys attempting to display their relative power or status *vis-à-vis* each other. Such accounts differ quite noticeably from those found in the task activities of girls which rely on legitimate demands of the activity in progress, rather than status claims of participants. By organizing his talk in the way that he does Huey is able to undercut claims being attributed to Michael, while simultaneously arguing that he has the power to determine the very issues that Michael cannot enforce.

When considered in light of the activity in progress, Huey provides a complex, multi-faceted response to Michael's action. While demanding that Huey do something, Michael's request also treats Huey as someone in a privileged position: a team leader who has the power to determine which of the others present will get an opportunity to play. In his reply Huey affirms that identity and moreover accepts the relevance of what Michael has asked him to do. However, he refuses to do it immediately. By formulating his refusal in the way that he does, Huey calls into question Michael's claims about being able to control a basic parameter of the activity, while simultaneously arguing that that parameter is under his own control. Huey thus builds a return that ratifies some of the proposals made in the talk being answered, while opposing other aspects of that talk.

6. Maintaining opposition

Analysis has so far focused on the way in which the talk that occurs here is embedded within the larger activity that the participants are engaged in. It is, however, also possible to look at this sequence in more abstract terms. In line 1 Michael tells Huey to do something, and this can be noted without going into detail about precisely what the recipient of the demand is being asked to do. Indeed, much analysis in pragmatics has proceeded precisely on this level of abstraction. For example, the way in which directives include as one of their core components the proposal that recipients should perform some action has long been noted in speech act theory (see, for example, Labov and Fanshel, 1977).

Such phenomena can also be looked at from a sequential perspective. Conversation analysts have noted that a first pair part, such as the talk in line 1, creates a field of relevance that will be used to interpret whatever happens next (Sacks, 1970; Schegloff, 1968, Schegloff and Sacks, 1973). Michael is thus able to not only formulate a request to Huey, but to also build within the interaction of the moment a specific place where the issue of whether or not Huey will acquiesce to demands from him can be publicly established. Quite independently of whether or not Huey considers the moment a proper one to pick his team, he might be strongly motivated to not act in a way that could be interpreted as giving in to the demand contained in Michael's talk.

This suggests that in the actions being produced here participants may be attending to (1) the particulars of the activity they are engaged in, and (2) more abstract social proposals about their relative standing *vis-à-vis* each other, these social proposals being negotiated through the detailed sequential organization of the talk in progress.

Do participants in fact attend to these different types of phenomena in producing their talk? The sequence that follows provides some evidence that they do:

Example 1

1. Michael:	All right who's on your *side* Huey.
3. Huey:	It's quarter after four and I'm not
4.	ready to *go* yet.
6. Huey:	I'm not going till four thirty.
7.→ Michael:	Well get in there and get them papers
8.→	off that couch before–
9.→ Huey:	⌈I did already.

Here Michael moves the subject matter of the talk to a completely different domain of activity, household chores, but makes another demand, which Huey again rejects. Though the conversation has moved to different subject matter, the talk in lines 7–9 maintains the underlying oppositional format of the prior exchange. This provides some evidence that rather than attending only to the details of the events being talked about at the moment, participants in argument also actively orient to the underlying structure of opposition moves, and can preserve that structure as the issues being disputed change.

Looking at what happens here in more detail, it can be observed that the switch to household chores in line 7 is not formulated as an action that is disjunctive with what was said in line 6. The "Well" that prefaces Michael's turn explicitly ties it to the talk that has just been heard, and proposes that that talk is being taken into account in the production of the current turn. Moreover the talk in line 7 is an appropriate next move in the opposition sequence that is unfolding. Huey has rejected Michael's prior demand by stating that he will perform the requested action at some time in the future rather than immediately. Rather than letting this rejection terminate the oppositional exchange, Michael demands that something else be done immediately. In addition to being a coherent counter to Huey's put-off of Michael's initial request, it, as well as Huey's answer to it, repeats the actions that were performed in the prior exchange.

	Lines	Speaker	Action
Pick team	1	Michael	**Demand** (Subject Matter X)
	3–4	Huey:	**Refusal**
Pick up papers	7–8	Michael:	**Demand** (Subject Matter Y)
	9	Huey:	**Refusal**

Thus in both cases Michael tells Huey to do something and Huey refuses by providing a reason for why the action requested won't be performed. The coherence that exists between the first exchange and the second, is provided not by ties in content, but rather through (1) the sequential organization that links exchanges to each other, and (2) the structural continuity of the oppositional format that is used to organize the material found in each exchange.

7. Content shift within argument

The beginning of the sequence in example 1 deals with the current sling-shot activity. However, in lines 7–9 the talk turns to household chores. On the level of content a noticeable shift thus occurs in the talk at this point. Such changes in content are frequently talked about in terms of *topic shifting*. There are, however, problems with such terminology. The notion of what precisely constitutes a topic, and how that phenomenon is oriented to by participants, has turned out to be a very intricate issue in the analysis of discourse (Button and Casey, 1984; Chafe, 1972; Jefferson, 1984; Keenan and Schieffelin, 1983; Li, 1976; Schegloff and Sacks, 1973). We will therefore call what happens here a *content shift* rather than a topic shift. One of the reasons we want to make this distinction is that, despite changes in subject matter, the two demand-refusal exchanges are not disjunctive with each other, but rather have a common, underlying coherence by virtue of their continuity in action structure. Such underlying coherence across separate turns (or sentences) within a strip of discourse seems to be one of the core concepts that the notion of "topic" attempts to capture; e.g., on the level of action it would be quite wrong to describe Michael and Huey as moving from one type of talk to another. This suggests that rather than being a monolithic whole, topic is constituted through participants' attention to a range of phenomena. It is therefore crucial that topic not be approached as a global phenomenon, but rather that studies of topic distinguish analytically different types of processes relevant to its organization.

The way in which content shifts and underlying structure interact with each other constitutes an important organizational feature of argument. One very interesting feature of argument is the way in which a single oppositional exchange can encompass talk about a range of different subjects.[10] Argument begun about one issue can escalate to include many points of contention between the parties.[11] The present data provide some insight into why this might be the case.

First, it would appear that the organization of argument and the organization of topic (in the sense of content domains) interact with each other. By virtue of the way in which the sequential structure of an oppositional exchange frames the turns occurring within it as parts of a single activity (a cohesion that might be provided elsewhere by continuity in content), talk about diverse subject matter can nonetheless be organized as a coherent whole.

Second, argument would be severely constricted if it had to come to an abrupt halt every time someone made a statement that could not be disputed. Instead, by shifting topic participants are able to continue an opposition sequence without denying the validity of what the other has just said. Indeed, specialized machinery seems to be available for just such a contingency. For example, turn prefaces such as "well" and "so" (M.H. Goodwin, 1982b: 85, Haviland, 1986b), which occur frequently in argument sequences, function to signal both that the validity of the immediately prior talk will not be challenged, and that opposition will be continued.

Third, previous research (Adger, 1984: 104, 184; Corsaro and Rizzo, this volume; Genishi and di Paolo, 1982: 65; M.H. Goodwin 1982b: 87–88; Maynard, 1985a; Vuchinich, this volume) has revealed that, despite the way in which academic research has traditionally studied dispute within the framework of "conflict resolution," arguments frequently terminate without resolution of the issues being argued about. An argument's ability to encompass a succession of topics raises the possibility that even in cases where termination does include resolution, the issue that is resolved may not be the issue that began the argument.

8. Constituting context within argument

These phenomena are relevant to another issue as well, that of how sequential organization and other aspects of social context are related to each other. Like "topic", the notion of what constitutes "context" poses important definitional questions, and indeed can become a highly charged question in debates between competing schools of discourse analysis. A common approach to the study of social context argues that to investigate language in actual social settings it is necessary to provide an ethnographic description of those settings, what Hymes (1964) has called an "ethnography of speaking." The situation encompassing the speech is described in terms of features such as the setting, the types of participants present, the speech events that occur in that setting, speech genres, the keying of speech, etc. In essence it is argued that the organization of the talk is constrained and organized by its ethnographic context. A rather different approach to context is found in the work on the sequential organization of conversation initiated by Sacks and his colleagues. Here it is argued that a key resource that participants use to build and understand talk is the precise positioning of an utterance within an environment of other talk (or other action).

That sequential environment constitutes a core aspect of the context that participants utilize to make sense out of the talk they are hearing and to engage in the activities they are performing. As noted by Heritage and Atkinson (1984: 11):

in examining talk the analyst is immediately confronted with an organization which is implemented on a turn-by-turn basis, and through which a context of publicly displayed and continuously updated intersubjective understandings is systematically sustained.

Sacks and his colleagues have argued that one cannot assume the relevance of particular contextual features, for example specific categorizations of participants or events, unless it can be demonstrated *within* the talk being examined that the participants themselves are orienting to such phenomena as a constitutive feature of the activities they are engaged in.

The activities indexed within the sequence being examined in the present paper, such as the sling-shot fight and the identities for participants it provides (e.g, team leader), are clearly relevant to the kinds of issues that are addressed when context is studied from an ethnographic perspective. However, in the present data we find that a subsequent utterance can quite rapidly change the activities and participant identities that constitute the relevant context of the moment.[12] When content shifts from the sling-shot fight to duties in the household that Michael and Huey share with each other, the talk then indexes a different set of activities, and in so doing provides new social identities for those implicated in these activities. Instead of formulating Huey as a team leader, Michael is now addressing him as a brother, and events within their household have replaced the sling-shot encounter as the world of relevance constituted through their talk.[13]

Subject matter	Relevant "context"	
	Activity domain	*Participant identities*
Pick team	Sling-shot battle	Team leader–team leader
Papers on couch	Household chores	Brother–brother

Rather than constituting a frame that shapes the speech within it, such activity structures stand in a reflexive relationship to the talk; they are invoked within the talk while simultaneously providing resources for its appropriate understanding. Moreover, the precise way in which such activity structures are made relevant is shaped by the emerging sequential organization of the talk. For example, the shift to talk about household duties, and the new social identities for participants thus invoked, provides a way for Michael to construct an appropriate next move within the emerging opposition sequence. Even within a single activity participants do not deal with context in a global way, but rather select features of it that attend to the sequential tasks they face at the moment. Thus when Huey is faced with the task of building a next utterance to Michael's initial demand, he focuses on one particular aspect of the activity, its time structure, while not addressing other features of it, such as team size and membership, that are equally salient in Michael's talk. The "external context" is thus invoked and shaped within the details of the very talk that it is context to, and because of its ties to the emerging sequential organization of the talk, such context is not fixed and static but rather fluid and dynamic.[14] In brief, the sequential organization of talk provides a key locus for the analysis of context.

9. Multi-party argument

Analysis has so far focused largely on the talk of Michael and Huey. However Chopper and Bruce also participate in this sequence. The exchange is thus a multi-party one, in that it encompasses more than the minimum number of participants (two) sufficient to constitute an argumentative exchange. Some definitional issues arise here. We will use the expression "multi-party" to describe sequences of interaction constituted through the actions of three or more participants. However, two-party exchanges are also *multi-party* in the sense that they are built through the actions of multiple participants. Moreover, there are perfectly good ways in which the term "multi-party" could be applied to two-party exchanges in the analysis of language and interaction, for example, to distinguish approaches to language that focus on isolated speakers from others that study such processes in the midst of interaction. Thus it would be appropriate to say that C. Goodwin (1981) analyzes the construction of the turn at talk as a multi-party event even though quite frequently the only parties being talked about are speaker and hearer. Using the term "multi-party" to distinguish two-party exchanges from those in which there are more than two participants is thus somewhat clumsy. However, a clear term to separate the three-party case from situations with less than three parties does not seem to be available. Moreover, the term "multi-party" has been used to make precisely this distinction in previous research (Maynard, 1986). Thus, while we are not completely happy with this way of describing exchanges with more than two participants, we will continue to use the term in the way in which it has been used in previous research.

There are, however, good reasons to avoid use of the term "dyadic" to describe the two-party case. First, jargon-free alternatives to this term (for example, "two-party") are readily available. Second, this term carries with it a great deal of baggage that might not always be appropriate to the phenomena being examined. For example, in some previous research this term has been used to suggest that the two-party case has its own intrinsic structure, without, however, investigating whether the phenomena being investigated are indeed unique to the dyadic situation, or whether they might be examples of more general structures that would be found as well in n-party interaction. In addition, the way in which so much experimental research has focused almost exclusively on the "dyad" seems to suggest not only that this situation is easier for the researcher to manipulate, but also an implicit belief that research should work up from the dyad to the study of multi-party interaction. There are, however, good reasons to propose instead that the structures being utilized by human beings to organize interaction are in fact general structures, that are easily able to adapt to variations in number of participants present, so that the two-party case does not in any way constitute a privileged locus for analysis. Claims about research into the organization of dyadic interaction might thus be more rhetorical than substantive, at least with respect to the issue of treating dyadic interaction as a domain of action with its own intrinsic properties. From a slightly different perspective it may well be the case that some structures (for example, simultaneous address to structurally different kinds of recipients [C. Goodwin, 1979, 1981; Holmes, 1984], fission of a conversation into separate subconversations (Sacks, Schegloff and Jefferson 1974), etc.) are most clearly visible in multi-party talk. If this is correct, then it is a serious mistake to focus research exclusively on the dyad (a point also made by Haviland (1986a)).

While most previous research has focused on two-party arguments both M.H. Goodwin (1980a, 1982b, 1982a) and Maynard (1986) have analyzed dispute processes as intrinsically multi-party. Their research has a clear relevance to the analysis of the current sequence. Both M.H. Goodwin (1982b) and Maynard (1986) investigate how parties who are initially outsiders to a two-party dispute can display alignment to particular positions within the dispute. Maynard distinguishes a range of alignment patterns that are possible within multi-party disputes. He notes that outside parties can differentially align either with a position or with a counterposition with the effect that "parties can dispute a particular position for different reasons and by different means" (Maynard, 1986: 264). Maynard uses the term *alignment structure* to refer to a participant's position with respect to a particular perspective within a dispute. Following Goffman (1981) we will use this term in a broader way to include not only alignment to a position being disputed, but also a participant's orientation to the talk in progress (for example, treating what is being said as a laughable) and alignment to other participants.

10. Piggybacking

The contributions of Chopper and Bruce to the sequence in example 1 might initially appear far less substantive than those of Michael and Huey. However, analysis of their actions in fact provides an opportunity to considerably expand our study of the types of alignment structures and social organization that can be invoked within an oppositional sequence. In line 2 Chopper elaborates Michael's demand that Huey pick his team, and in line 5 Bruce states that just as Huey is not yet ready neither is he.

Example 1

1. Michael: All right who's on your *side* Huey.
2.→ Chopper: Pick– pick four *people.*

3. Huey: It's quarter after four and I'm not
4.   ready to *go* yet.
5.→ Bruce: Me neither.
6. Huey: I'm not going till four thirty.

The talk produced by Chopper and Bruce has a somewhat special sequential organization. Though the utterances of each build upon immediately prior talk, the parties speaking are not the addressees of that prior talk, and what they say does not reply to it. Thus though Chopper's talk occurs immediately after Michael's, unlike Huey's talk a moment later it does not constitute an answer to what Michael has said. Rather it reiterates the action just performed by Michael. Sequentially Chopper's talk has a far more optional status as a subsequent move to Michael's talk than Huey's does. More precisely, the action that Michael directs to Huey creates a situation in which an answer from Huey becomes relevant. Were Huey not to reply, the absence of his response could be not only seen but dealt with as a noticeable event.[15] Chopper's talk is neither tied to, nor projected by, Michael's talk in this way. If Chopper had not spoken, the action sequence initiated by line 1 would not be disrupted in any way: i.e. a response to Michael's talk would not in any relevant sense be lacking. Similarly, Bruce's talk does not reply to what Huey just said, but rather uses Huey's talk to create a second refusal to the demand that teams now be chosen.

In brief, though the actions of Chopper and Bruce are strongly tied to the actions they follow, the sequences they create do not have the characteristic features of many paired actions found in conversation, for example the structural organization analyzed by Schegloff and Sacks (1973) as constitutive of adjacency pairs. Instead of being projected by the prior action, the paired utterances found here emerge when a subsequent speaker uses the resources provided by the prior talk to create another utterance closely tied to it;[16] the pair thus comes into existence with the second action, not the first. Moreover, at least in the types of utterances we are now examining, the subsequent speaker, rather than producing a reply to the talk being tied to, seconds in some fashion the action embodied by the prior talk. The utterances of Chopper and Bruce thus have a distinctively parasitic structure.

One important consequence of the parasitic organization of these utterances, and in particular of the way in which they second the action of prior speaker, is that the subsequent speaker affiliates himself to the position being taken by the party whose talk is being followed. Maynard (1986: 267) notes that parties outside an original conflict can offer to collaborate with one of its protagonists by taking "a stance that is parallel or consistent with that of a principal party." In the present data. Chopper aligns himself with Michael's position in the oppositional exchange, and Bruce with Huey's.[17] Principal parties within the dispute can reject as well as accept such offers of collaboration.

Affiliation in argument is frequently analyzed in terms of *agreement* (or disagreement) with another's position. It is therefore important to note that the alignments made visible in the present data do not take the form of agreement with what another had said but rather are done when the affiliating party takes up an equivalent position himself. Thus Bruce does not "agree" with the proposition that Huey is not yet ready to go, but rather performs an equivalent action to the one done by Huey, saying that he, Bruce, is not ready to go. Similarly Chopper does not "agree" with what Michael has just said, but rather performs his own challenge to Huey. The affiliating parties thus state, and become responsible for, positions of their own.

Looking at such phenomena from a slightly different perspective, it can be observed that the talk between Michael and Huey creates a sequential environment with a distinctive structure that Chopper and Bruce then exploit for their own purposes. The issues involved are well illustrated by Chopper's talk in line 2. In line 1 Michael addresses an action to Huey, a request that he pick his team. However before Huey has an opportunity to reply Chopper directs an action of his own to Huey. Chopper's action thus occurs in a particular sequential environment:

> **After** an action by A calling for a response from B,
> but **before** B has the opportunity to provide that response.

Chopper's talk thus occurs in the *midst* of an exchange between other participants.

The exchange between Michael and Huey is an example of what Sacks and his colleagues have termed an "adjacency pair" (Sacks 1972b; Schegloff and Sacks, 1973; Sacks, Schegloff and Jefferson, 1974). Adjacency pairs, such as questions and answers, greetings and return greetings, offers followed by acceptances or refusals, etc., constitute a pervasive type of organization found within conversation. By assigning to separate participants different moves within a single coherent structure of action, they provide a prototypical example of how sequential organization provides resources for the achievement of social organization within conversation.

A key feature of adjacency pairs is the fact that the turns comprising the pair are positioned adjacent to each other. In the present data, Chopper's turn is placed *between* a first-pair part and its response, with the effect that the turns of Michael and Huey are each placed adjacent to the talk of Chopper rather than to each other.

Michael:	Pick your side.	*First-pair part*
Chopper:	Pick four people.	*Piggyback*
Huey:	I'm not ready to go yet.	*Second-pair part*

Talk placed between a first-pair part and its answer has received extensive study within the field of conversation analysis. Most of such research has focused on the properties of *insertion sequences* (see Schegloff, 1972 for detailed analysis of their structure). The following provides an example:

Example 5

1. A: Can I borrow your car? *Question₁*
2. B: When?   *Question₂*
3. A: This afternoon.   *Answer₂*
4. B: Okay.   *Answer₂*

Here an initial question is followed by a second question as one adjacency pair (lines 2–3) is inserted in the midst of another (lines 1 and 4). Despite the fact that elements of the initial pair are now displaced from each other, the structure of such a sequence in fact provides strong support for the argument that participants are attending to adjacency-pair organization. Thus the second question (line 2) deals with issues to be resolved before an answer to the first will be provided. It is asked by the recipient of the initial request and addressed to prior speaker, the party who made that request. Once the issues raised in the insertion sequence have been resolved, the initial first-pair part (line 1) is answered by its original addressee.

Chopper's talk in line 3 occurs in the same sequential environment as an insertion sequence, e.g., between a first-pair part and its answer. However it does not have any of the properties of insertion sequences:

1   It is not a sequence but a single action.
2   It is not spoken by an addressee of the original action but rather by someone who has not been located as a participant in the exchange by the prior action.
3   In so far as Chopper's action expands the participation framework beyond the two parties implicated in the original action it, unlike insertion sequences, requires at least three participants in the exchange for its occurrence, i.e., this action has intrinsic multi-party properties.
4   It is not directed to the party who provided the original first-pair part but rather to the addressee of that action.
5   The issues it deals with are not prerequisites to the performance of the action requested in the initial first-pair part.

In brief, while Chopper's talk is inserted between the actions of Michael and Huey it does not have the properties of an insertion sequence, the prototypical type of action which is placed in this particular environment.

The placement of Chopper's talk in the midst of the exchange between Michael and Huey has a range of consequences. For example, in that Huey's talk will now occur immediately after Chopper's challenge to him, it might be seen to constitute an answer not only to Michael, but also to what Chopper has said. Moreover, by performing his action where he does, Chopper is able to voice a strong demand at a very safe place, i.e., at a point where another is publicly committed to the same position. By piggy-backing his talk on top of Michael's, Chopper is thus able to hitch something of a free ride on both the action initiated by Michael and its sequential implicitiveness.[18]

Before looking further at the social proposals made by Chopper's talk let us briefly examine Bruce's action in line 5. This talk does not occur between a first-pair part and its answer. Nonetheless it has strong structural analogs to Chopper's action in line 2.

1. It seconds the action in the prior talk by echoing Huey's refusal to Michael.
2. It is spoken before Michael has an opportunity to respond to Huey.

The placement of Bruce's action enables him to tap into the sequential organization of the exchange between Huey and Michael in much the same way that Chopper did. It therefore seems appropriate to extend the notion of where a piggyback can occur beyond the specific sequential environment of adjacency pairs. What is crucial is placement after a prior action visibly directed to another party. Such expanded placement makes it possible for both actions in an adjacency pair to be piggybacked, a point nicely demonstrated in the matching piggybacks that occur here.

Despite the apparent simplicity of Bruce's "Me neither", by saying what he says in the precise place that he says it Bruce manages to make proposals of some importance about his participation in the activity in progress. Thus, in arguing that the fight cannot begin since he is not yet ready, Bruce talks as someone who will be a participant in that fight. By not topicalizing or in any other way focusing explicit attention on this issue Bruce treats his continuing membership in the activity as something that can be taken for granted. However, as was seen earlier, many of the proposals about team membership that have been advanced so far in the boys' talk exclude Bruce from participation, and indeed when sides are eventually chosen he is not allowed to play.

The actions of Chopper and Bruce have so far been discussed as though they were essentially equivalent to each other. There are, however, significant differences in the way in which each of these parties ties their talk to that of the party they are affiliating with.

Example 1

1. Michael: All right who's on your *side* Huey.
2.→ Chopper: Pick– pick four *p*eople.

3. Huey: It's quarter after four and I'm not
4.   ready to go yet.
5.→ Bruce: Me neither.
6. Huey: I'm not going till four thirty.

With his "Me neither" Bruce explicitly formulates what he is saying as an echo of what Huey just said. However, while Chopper reiterates the action just performed by Michael this reiteration does not take the form of an exact repeat of what Michael just said. Instead Chopper displays an analysis of the underlying sense of Michael's talk by using quite different words to produce an action of analogous import. The fact that Chopper substantially changes the words used to perform the action has a number of consequences.

1.   Chopper adds new information, the number of people Huey is allowed to pick, to Michael's original demand that the choice of players be made now. While the number chosen is the same as one proposed by Michael earlier (see example 4) Chopper is nonetheless now able to portray himself as someone who can tell Huey how many players he can have on his side.
2.   By virtue of the way it differs in both form and substance from Michael's talk Chopper's talk is formulated as an independent demand that Huey pick his team, rather than as simply a repetition of what Michael just said. In this it differs quite noticeably from Bruce's "Me neither."

In brief, though both Chopper and Bruce construct similar types of parasitic utterances, repeating in some form the action of the party who has just spoken, through the details of the way in which they build their talk they are able to make quite different types of displays about phenomena such as their relative status as independent actors.

By speaking in the way in which they do Chopper and Bruce are able to make a variety of claims about their standing in, first, the current sequence and, second, the larger activity that that sequence is embedded within. Chopper is claiming that he has the status to tell Huey what to do and when to do it, and Bruce is proposing that if he is not ready the activity should not proceed to its next stage, and in so doing acting as someone who is to be a participant in that subsequent activity. However, the status of such proposals, whether or not these claims will be honored, is not up to them alone but rather something to be worked out through interaction with their coparticipants.[19]

When we look at actions of others in the sequence, however, we find that none of these claims are ratified: what Chopper and Bruce say is completely ignored by Michael and Huey. However, if their proposals are not ratified neither are they explicitly challenged, as indeed they could be. For example, when Bruce earlier made what was interpreted as a bid to join the activity Michael answered him as follows:

Example 2

    Bruce: Hey Michael.
               *Th*ey *d*oin what we did down in the park?
               (1.5)
→ Michael: You ain't on our *s*ide.
               You ain't *play*in *n*either!

In the present data the claims being made by Chopper and Bruce stand as proposals that have been put forth but neither ratified nor explicitly challenged. On the one hand the sequential treatment that these actions get may be a systematic consequence of their placement in the midst of exchanges between Michael and Huey; if Michael or Huey were to address Chopper or Bruce they would in effect be putting on hold their exchange with each other. Piggybacking thus provides an opportunity to make claims in a sequential environment in which it will take special work to challenge them. However, on the other hand, the liability of making such claims without having them acknowledged is that Chopper and Bruce are essentially treated as nonparticipants in the sequence, i.e., what they say is not taken into account by the others present as consequential for their action.

11. Interstitial participation

Despite the way in which four people manage to participate in this exchange, the structure of the sequence itself shows that the positions of each within it are not equal. Thus the actions between Michael and Huey provide the exchange with its basic structure and core skeleton. Chopper and Bruce tap into that sequential structure by slotting their actions at the interstices of the actions between Michael and Huey; rather than defining an alternative framework for action they adapt what they do to what Michael and Huey are already doing. Moreover they use the positions taken by Michael and Huey as guides for the positions they will take and the actions they will perform. Indeed they use the structure of the talk produced by Michael and Huey as a template for the organization of their own talk. For their part Michael and Huey never officially acknowledge the contributions made by Bruce and Chopper or treat them as ratified participants in the sequence. Michael and Huey thus emerge as the principal protagonists in the sequence, the parties who define its basic parameters and whose actions are used as models for the actions of others, while Chopper and Bruce, despite the energy with which they advance their positions, define themselves as interstitial players.

Such organization has a number of consequences for how those speaking display themselves as aligned toward each other. First, the way in which multiple parties address equivalent actions to the same addressees (i.e. the pair of directives to Huey in lines 1 and 2 and the dual responses that they receive in lines 3–5) portrays what is happening as something more than one individual directing talk at another. Larger corporate entities, incipient teams or sides challenging and answering each other, become visible through the detailed organization of the talk of the individuals positioning themselves for membership on particular sides. Moreover, those on each side of the exchange differentiate themselves from each other through the way in which they speak. Michael and Huey are the only ones whose standing is officially acknowledged in the primary sequence; Chopper and Bruce shape their actions to fit those of Michael and Huey, and indeed echo what they say. For each side there is thus both a primary spokesman and another who does the activity of following that spokesman by using that party's behavior as a guide for the organization of his own behavior. It is thus possible to see some of the participants in this talk proposing an alignment of themselves into something like two teams, each of which is composed of a "leader" and a "subordinate." Of course, as the situation of Bruce makes clear, these are only proposals which can be, and indeed are, called into question in subsequent interaction. Moreover, the proposals being made by separate participants are not treated equivalently. The talk of Bruce and Chopper claims alignment with the positions of Huey and Michael but these claims are never recognized by Michael and Huey. Finally the patterns of alignment made visible within the talk are intimately tied to the larger sling-shot activity that the participants are engaged in, and indeed constitute part of the process through which that activity is being shaped.

12. Multiple participation frameworks

Line 11, and the sequence that follows from it, provides an opportunity to investigate how a single utterance invokes multiple participation frameworks (C. Goodwin, 1981; Goffman, 1981; Heath, 1986) that constitute different recipients to it in alternative ways. It was noted above that, unlike Bruce, Chopper did not just echo Michael but added new information, the number of parties on Huey's team, when he reiterated Michael's action. When Chopper first said this in line 2, it was not challenged. Indeed, because of the way in which Chopper's talk was embedded into the sequence between Michael and Huey, there was no slot after it for Michael to immediately comment on it, the place after Chopper' talk being occupied by Huey's answer to Michael. However, when Chopper in line 10 switches topic away from the discussion of Michael and Huey's household chores, and back to the choosing of teams by again calling on Huey to pick his four guys, Michael tells Huey that he gets only three guys.

Example 1

1. Michael: All right who's on your *side* Huey.
2. Chopper: Pick– pick four *p*eople.
3. Huey: It's quarter after four and I'm not
4. ready to *g*o yet.
5. Bruce: Me neither.
6. Huey: I'm not going till four thirty.
7. Michael: Well get in there and get them papers
8. off that couch before–
9. Huey: [I did already.
10. Chopper: Get your four *g*uys,
11.→ Michael: You get *three* guys.
12.→ Huey: [[I only get three guys?
13.→ Chopper: I mean three guys.
14. Michael: That's right.

Michael's talk in line 11 constructs two separate actions to two different recipients simultaneously.[20] What Michael says is officially addressed to Huey.[21] However, it also constitutes an action directed to Chopper in that it contradicts what Chopper just said (i.e. Michael tells Huey that he gets **three** guys, not the four just stated by Chopper).[22] In view of the differential relevance this utterance has for alternative recipients, it is not surprising that it recieves two simultaneous responses (lines 12 and 13), each attending to what Michael has said in a different way.

Before looking in more detail at the participation frameworks invoked here, it can be briefly noted that these data provide yet a further demonstration of the fact that in analyzing what a strip of talk is doing it is not sufficient to investigate that utterance in isolation, i.e. it is inadequate to simply gloss the talk as instancing a particular type of speech act.[23] On the one hand, as has long been demonstrated in the work of Sacks and his colleagues (see, for example, Schegloff and Sacks, 1973), one must attend to the sequential organization of the talk. For example, in the present data line 11 emerges as a contradiction in large part through its placement after, and contrast with, line 10. On the other hand analysis must also include the participation framework invoked by the utterance, a structure that encompasses, among other phenomena,[24] the addressee of the talk as well as its speaker. Vološinov (Bahktin?) noted long ago that a

word is a two-sided act. It is determined equally by *whose* word it is and *for whom* it is meant. As word, it is precisely *the product of the reciprocal relationship between speaker and listener, addresser and addressee.* Each and every word expresses the "one" in relation to the "other." (Vološinov, 1973: 86, emphasis in the original)

In the present data, Michael's talk in line 11 gets it two-edged implicativeness from the way in which it encompasses two separate (though linked) speaker-hearer relationships; by virtue of the way in which an implicit action to Chopper is piggybacked on top of an action explicitly addressed to Huey this single strip of talk constructs separate but simultaneous actions to each of its recipients.[25]

The two participation frameworks found within this utterance are not simply copresent but organized relative to each other. Huey is Michael's explicit addressee, while Chopper's talk is responded to but not officially acknowledged. The action to Chopper is thus embedded within the talk to Huey, but not dealt with explicitly. Such patterning encapsulates within a single utterance the alignment structures, discussed above, that Michael is occupying toward both Huey and Chopper. Just as Chopper piggybacked his initial directive to Huey within an action already being addressed to Huey by Michael, here Michael piggybacks his answer to Chopper within another utterance that continues to treat Huey as the only other official protagonist in the emerging sequence (i.e. the only party that Michael has explicitly addressed or responded to) and the only other party who occupies a position equivalent to Michael's, that of team leader. Moreover, just as Chopper earlier showed himself willing to use what Michael did as a guide for his own behavior, here Michael performs the obverse of that activity by treating independent action performed by Chopper as something that he can call into question and modify at will.

13. Participation status

The way in which Michael deals with what Chopper has said sheds light on some of the subtlety with which participation status can be formulated within talk. On the one hand the talk that Chopper produced has been taken into account by Michael in the production of his talk: what Chopper says is consequential for the organization of subsequent action within the sequence. In this sense Chopper's talk constitutes something more than an "outloud", and is recognized in ways that his earlier talk was not. However, Chopper himself is not treated as a ratified participant in the sequence; indeed he is actively ignored as the address of Michael's utterance remains focused on Huey. If Michael had explicitly ratified Chopper's participation he might be seen as granting him the type of status that Chopper was claiming and Michael was denying. These data thus provide an example of how someone might produce talk that is attended to within a sequence, without, however, being ratified as a full-fledged participant in that sequence.

From a slightly different perspective it can be noted that one of the key issues in the current dispute centers on who will establish the parameters of the activity in progress (for example, team size and when the activity will move from stage to stage). With his talk in line 11 Michael not only makes

such claims toward Huey; in addition, by changing the parameters established by Chopper's talk Michael proposes that it is something that he, not
Chopper, has ultimate control over, and thus treats what Chopper has said
as an echo or expansion of talk that is properly his own.

The way in which Michael establishes his control over parameters that
Chopper has attempted to control has the flavor of treating what Chopper
has said as competitive with his own position in the activity. This suggests
two other phenomena that might be relevant to the organization of the
sequence. First, while analysis of the argumentative structure of this sequence has so far focused on opposition between Michael (and Chopper)
versus Huey (and Bruce), the possibility emerges that a second, quite
separate, axis of opposition exists *within* one of these sides, with Michael and
Chopper competing with each other. The sequence thus contains two quite
distinct oppositional frameworks, both of which are addressed simultaneously in Michael's utterance in line 11.

Second, the proposal in line 10 that Chopper is explicitly sanctioned for
(i.e. that Huey's team should consist of four guys) was first stated in line 2
("Pick– pick four people"). Michael's talk in line 11 can thus also indicate
retrospectively that Chopper was talking out of turn in line 2 as well. It is
thus possible that Chopper's earlier talk might also have been seen as
competitive not only with Huey but also with Michael's status (i.e. Chopper
was proposing that he could act in a way that was equivalent to Michael and
indeed state parameters that Michael had failed to set).

13.1 Topic-invoked participation frameworks

These possibilities shed additional light on the content shift that occurs in
line 7 right after Chopper first tells Huey to "pick four people." In addition to
setting a new task for Huey, picking up the papers off the couch, this change
in content indexes a new activity that does not include Chopper in the way
that the sling-shot activity did. Instead of speaking within the realm of the
sling-shot fight, a domain of activity in which Chopper is also a participant,
Michael is now talking to Huey as one household member to another. Since
the duties being talked about are restricted to members of a particular
household, and Chopper does not belong to that household,[26] such a shift
can signal to Chopper that the current talk does not include him in the way
in which the earlier talk did. The content shift that occurs in line 7 might
thus not only provide Michael with resources for continuing to make
demands on Huey, but also be a way of restricting the focus of the dispute to
issues that do not involve the participation of Chopper.

Traditionally topic has been defined largely in terms of the *content* of what
is being talked about. The present data suggest that an equally important
constituent of topic is the participation framework invoked by it. The talk in
lines 1–6 is situated within an activity system, the sling-shot fight, that

provides situated identities, such as team-leader and potential team-member, for all who are present. However, when talk is shifted to duties in a particular household an activity is invoked that provides relevant positions within it for only two of the present parties, Michael and Huey. In essence talk has moved from one world, with its relevant set of characters, to another with a different situated identity structure that maps onto those present in a very different way, and indeed does not provide positions for all who are present in the way that the first did.[27] In brief, by virtue of its ability to invoke alternative situated activity systems, topic provides parties to a conversation with resources for rapidly changing how they are aligned to each other, and the activities that are relevant at the moment.

Crucial to the organization of such a participation framework is the way in which it is invoked by topic and thus can change as the topic of the moment changes. In this sense it is different from distinctions such as that between ratified participants (whether addressees or not) and overhearers; i.e. rather than separating those within the conversation from those outside it, and being a stable property of the conversation as a whole, *topic-invoked participation frameworks* apply to those within a specific conversational encounter and dynamically rearrange them and their standing toward each other as the talk in progress unfolds.

14. Displaying social organization through sequential organization

We will now look more closely at Chopper's reply to this talk. In line 13 Chopper not only changes what he had said in line 10 (now saying "three guys" instead of his original "four") but also claims that the original statement was wrong by preceding the modification with a correction preface: "I mean." His action provides an example of one of the clearest procedures that can be used to terminate a dispute: in a situation where there are two discrepant positions one party modifies their position so that it is brought into agreement with that of the other party (i.e., here Chopper changes his position so that it coincides with the one that has just been stated by Michael). Since discrepant positions are no longer being held by different parties the dispute is effectively terminated.

The preface "I mean" also characterizes what is happening as a version of a correction sequence, a formulation that further highlights the way in which Chopper grants Michael ultimate rights to determine the issues being discussed here. By modifying his position in this way Chopper thus publicly displays that he is withdrawing from any competitiveness that his activities might have exhibited.

Taken together the actions of Michael and Chopper not only constitute a small dispute that is quickly resolved, but also make visible a hierarchy. Thus, in much the way that one animal can display dominance over another by forcing the subordinate animal to move, in these data Michael challenges a position that has been taken by Chopper, and Chopper immediately backs away from that position to one that is compatible with Michael's. Note that this display of hierarchy is an interactive event that could not have been constructed by the actions of either party alone. While the talk in line 11 proposes that Michael is able to contradict Chopper, such an action could well be challenged by its recipient. A hierarchy is only definitively visible when Chopper acquiesces to Michael. It is thus a collaborative achievement, accomplished as much through the actions of the subordinate party (who actively demonstrates his willingness to change his behavior at the suggestion of the other) as through those of the dominant party. From such a perspective a hierarchy is an activity, a phenomenon accomplished by participants through a range of specific interactive work (and thus something to be explicated through concrete analysis of the details of their talk), rather than a description of a static feature of the social organization of a group.

The hierarchical relationship between Michael and Chopper that is made manifest in the present data can be found at other points in the sling-shot encounter as well. Thus, while the social organization accomplished through argument may characteristically be indigenous to the argument itself and capable of change as issues change,[28] the structures used to negotiate opposition can also provide participants with resources for reproducing forms of social organization that have a life that is greater than that of the argument itself.

15. Piggybacking revisited

Our earlier discussion of how Chopper and Bruce piggybacked their talk into the exchange between Michael and Huey might have seemed to suggest that positioning talk in this way is an inherently weak action; i.e., by sequencing their talk as they did Chopper and Bruce constituted themselves as subordinate, interstitial players in an exchange that was being given its primary shape by the actions of others. However, Michael's "You get *three* guys" in line 11 is structurally analogous to the earlier actions of Bruce and Chopper in a number of ways: first, it is also placed between a first-pair part (Chopper's "Get your four guys") and its projected answer; second, it uses what was said in the prior turn as a resource for the organization of its own talk, and, third, unlike an insertion sequence, it is addressed (at least explicitly) to the addressee of the original first-pair part. Michael's utterance thus provides a third example in this sequence of a turn that is piggybacked into an exchange between others. The patterning that becomes visible when Chopper attaches his talk to Michael's action thus becomes a structural resource for the subsequent organization of the sequence as it is picked up and utilized first by Bruce in line 5 and then again by Michael in line 11.

Michael's action is, however, treated very differently from the earlier actions of Chopper and Bruce. Instead of remaining an appendage to a primary sequence that is not explicitly ratified in the talk of others, Michael's action reshapes the emerging sequence and becomes the talk that others respond to.

In their piggybacks Chopper and Bruce echoed or seconded the action of the speaker who preceded them. It was thus quite possible for others to ignore their talk. However, Michael challenges Chopper by contradicting him. By way of contrast, Chopper's piggyback did not direct an action to Michael. Michael thus constructs an action that is sequentially implicative for prior speaker as well as its official addressee. Indeed, when Chopper formulates his next action as a repair of his prior talk we find the structure of insertion sequences and organization of piggybacking interacting with each other. Moreover, because of the way in which Michael challenges what prior speaker said, the addressee of the initial first-pair part is not in the position of responding to a pair of roughly equivalent actions (the action of initial speaker and its second) but is instead dealing with a set of *contradictory claims* and is being invited to focus his response on the specific issue that has been called into question by the challenge. Huey is thus made answerable to a very different action than the one proposed by Chopper a moment earlier. The effect of all this is that Michael is able to utilize the piggyback environment to construct an utterance that transforms the sequence in progress by making others answerable to *it*, rather than to the talk that precedes it.

16. Conclusion

It is sometimes argued that the actual events of people's lives, for example the talk they produce in their mundane dealings with one another, are so disorderly that they do not provide appropriate data for the study of social or linguistic phenomena (see for example Chomsky, 1965: 3–4); to be scientific, a researcher must instead work with hypothetical, idealized versions of the phenomena being studied (as is frequently done, for example, in contemporary linguistics), or carefully control behavior through experimental manipulation (e.g. much research in social psychology). Here, however, we find anything but disorder. The participants themselves, within the space of a very few turns, produce a range of systematic permutations on a basic structure with a precision that would tax the ingenuity of even the most inventive experimental design to replicate. For example, Chopper abandons the surface structure of Michael's utterance in line 1 but builds an equivalent action; Michael, by way of contrast, *retains* with minimal transformations the surface structure of Chopper's utterance, reusing many of the exact same words, but constructs a very different type of action. In much the way that a collection of sonnets can demonstrate the diversity and creativity possible within the constraints of a particular pattern, here we find how participants can reuse the structural frameworks and sequential possibilities provided by each other's talk to not only build a range of different products, but to radically transform the emerging structure of the events they are engaged in. Moreover, though such *bricolage* uses as its raw materials structure provided by the *talk* of the participants, its field of relevance is not confined to that talk but instead encompasses a range of social and interactive phenomena, as well as having consequences for the organization of the activity in progress. Though Chopper, Bruce, and Michael all make use of the same resources to tie to prior talk, through the way in which each uses these resources they constitute themselves and each other as very different types of social entities.

Notes

We are greatly indebted to Douglas Maynard, William Hanks, John Haviland, Allen Grimshaw and Alessandro Duranti for detailed comments on an earlier version of this analysis.

1 See for example the discussion of format tying in M.H. Goodwin and C. Goodwin (1987).

2 For some analysis of how the structure of talk is utilized to align participants toward each other within argument see M.H. Goodwin (1980a, 1982c), M.H. Goodwin and C. Goodwin (1987) and Maynard (1986).

3 In his analysis of status and role Goodenough (1965) draws attention to the very important point that social actors cannot be defined in isolation from each other (hence the term "identity relationship" which encompasses a reciprocal pair of actors). While we find it necessary to expand such a framework in a number of directions (for example, tying identity relationships to the activities that are made relevant at the moment and not restricting them to only two parties) the importance of Goodenough's framing of these issues is clearly recognized.

   Analysis of how participants constitute themselves through talk has been an issue of major analytic concern in conversation analysis (indeed it was the subject of the first published work of Harvey Sacks (1963, 1972a), the perspective that the present analysis takes as its point of departure.

4 For discussion of the relevance of examining argumentative sequences within the natural activities that participants typically engage in, rather than using data from experimental settings, see Corsaro and Rizzo (this volume).

5 For a description of how the boys organized the sling-shot session that the present data is drawn from see M.H. Goodwin (1980b). For a more complete description of the ethnographic research on which this analysis is based see M.H. Goodwin (forthcoming).

6 Huey is not only older but also bigger and more physically powerful than any of the others present.

7 For more detailed analysis of implicit address within conversation see Holmes (1984).

8 One feature of Michael's action that is consistent with the possibility that it is calling for a transition from one stage of the activity to another is the use

of "All right" to preface the turn. Terms such as "well", "okay" and "all right" are frequently used to propose that one stage of an activity can be terminated and another begun. For analysis of the use of "okay" to bound topics and initiate closings see Schegloff and Sacks (1973).

9   With respect to the organization of directives Mitchell-Kernan and Kernan (1977) have argued that children may be more concerned with manipulating social face than with the specific outcomes of their actions.

10   See Coleman (1957) for other analysis of escalation and diffusion in argument.

11   Indeed many formal dispute frameworks, such as the British–American legal system, embody special procedural rules to restrict debate to the issues that are the official focus of the current litigation.

12   For other analysis of how features of talk can invoke alternative contextual domains see Gumperz (1982a), Duranti (1988), and Grimshaw (1974).

13   For other analysis of how larger social identities can be invoked through the detailed organization of local talk see C. Goodwin (1987) and Maynard and Zimmerman (1984).

14   For more detailed analysis of the relationship between conversational organization and context see Garfinkel (1967), Garfinkel and Sacks (1970) and Heritage (1984).

15   For more detailed exposition of the way in which an action such as that produced by Michael in line 1 makes a response to it relevant see Schegloff (1968) and Schegloff and Sacks (1973).

16   The way in which Chopper and Huey's talk uses the details of prior talk to construct a subsequent move to it, even though no action on their part was projected by that talk, is in fact a general characteristic of many self-initiated subsequent moves (see, for example, the discussion of action chains by Pomerantz (1978: 109–110). Indeed in many exchanges adjacency pairs and pairs that emerge through structural cohesion created by the tying operations of subsequent speaker work hand in hand with each other to give the sequence its larger shape. One particularly clear example of this within the domain of argument can be found in ritual insult sequences in which participants use adjacency pairs to provide insults, and returns to them, and then move to a subsequent round of such exchanges by tying a new first action to the structure of a prior closing action. Other features of the moves performed by Chopper and Huey, for example, the way in which they reiterate the action being tied to, are not, however, as common.

17   Maynard (1985a) has noted the importance of such alignment displays in constructing social organization within dispute sequences, and he argues that creating alignments constitutes a basic form of political activity for children.

18   For other research examining the distinctive types of action that can be accomplished by exploiting the sequential organization of an existing exchange in this fashion see Haviland's (1987) analysis of "piling on" in Tzotzil discourse.

19   Thus with respect to the issue of alignment to positions within argument Maynard (1986: 273) notes that "collaboration between an outsider and a

principal is an achieved outcome, not an automatic consequence of an outsider exhibiting a stance that is sympathetic with a principal party's position."

20 For detailed analysis of how utterances can simultaneously address different participants in alternative ways see Duranti (1986); C. Goodwin (1981: chapter 5), and Holmes (1984).

21 Indeed others present are specifically excluded from the scope of its official address by both the social identity invoked through the talk (i.e. Huey, as Michael's opposite team leader is the only party present who is in a position to "get" a certain number of guys) and by the personal pronoun which Michael uses to begin his talk.

22 The activity of contradicting Chopper is explicitly marked within Michael's utterance by the contrast-class emphasis he places on *"three."* The talk is thus visibly directed toward Chopper as well as Huey. For more detailed analysis of contrast-class replacement within opposition sequences see M.H. Goodwin and C. Goodwin (1987).

23 For an early but insightful statement of this position see Vološinov (1973: 98, emphasis in the original) who argues that *"The structure of the utterance is a purely sociological structure. The utterance, as such, obtains between speakers. The individual speech act (in the strict sense of the word "individual")* is *contradictio in adjecto."*

24 For detailed analysis of other aspects of the interactive organization of participation frameworks see Erickson (1979), C. Goodwin (1981, 1984); M.H. Goodwin (1980a)); Heath (1984, 1986); Dore and McDermott (1982) and Shultz, Florio and Erickson (1983).

25 See C. Goodwin (1981, chapter 5) for other analysis of how talk can be designed for the simultaneous listening of mutually exclusive types of recipients, and of how the emerging structure of that talk can be modified as the speaker moves from one recipient to another. For analysis of multiple recipients within the framework of speech-act theory see Clark and Carlson (1982). For analysis of how the internal structure of a story can change as its recipients change see M.H. Goodwin (1982c).

26 For more detailed analysis of how ties between particular types of activities and categories of person entitled to perform those activities are utilized in the understanding and interpretation of talk see the discussion by Sacks (1972a) of membership-categorization devices and category-bound activites.

27 For more detailed analysis of how the categories in a particular membership device can be applied to a population see Sacks' (1972a: 334) discussion of *duplicative organization*. For analysis of how talk that marks shared access to a common domain of activity can invoke particular social relationships (for example that speaker and addressee are spouses) see C. Goodwin (1987).

28 See also M.H. Goodwin (1982b), Maynard (1985a) for analysis of social organization that is indigenous to argument.

5   The sequential organization of closing in verbal family conflict

SAMUEL VUCHINICH

Sooner or later episodes of verbal conflict come to an end. Some end with resolution, consensus, and joking. Others end with overt hostility, physical violence, or withdrawal from interaction. And some conflicts subtly shade into other speech activities with the conflict being dropped. Verbal conflicts are arenas for displays of power and affect. Recurrent patterns in conflict endings can influence the relationships between members of groups. In small groups, such as families and work groups, patterns of conflict management develop which can promote or inhibit the effectiveness of the group (Simmel, 1908; Homans, 1950; Barry, 1970). Despite the importance of conflict terminations, there are no studies which focus on how participants close episodes of verbal conflict. Studies of verbal conflict have tangentially noted some interesting aspects of conflict terminations (M.H. Goodwin, 1982b; 1983; Schiffrin, 1984; Eisenberg and Garvey, 1981; Genishi and di Paolo, 1982; Adger, 1984; Turner, 1970; Vuchinich, 1984). But there have been no sustained treatments of the phenomenon since Simmel (1950 [1908]: 110ff.). This paper describes two aspects of verbal conflicts which occur in normal American family dinners. First, the sequential organization of verbal conflict closings is described. Five recurrent termination formats are analyzed. Second, the frequency of occurrence of the termination formats is examined. Some implications of the discourse structure of the formats and their frequency of occurrence are developed.

1. Theory

Verbal conflict is recognized as a distinctive speech activity (Gumperz, 1982a: 166) by participants and observers. In verbal conflict, participants oppose the utterances, actions, or selves of one another in successive turns at talk. Linguistic, paralinguistic, or kinesic devices can be used to express opposition directly or indirectly. Verbal conflict ends when the oppositional turns cease and other activities are taken up. This paper is concerned with the sequential organization of conversational turns involved in bringing episodes of verbal conflict to a close. Verbal conflict may include two or more participants. The focus here will be on two-person conflicts, with some concern with ways third parties become involved. Generic differences between dyadic and multi-person conflicts will not be addressed here.

1.1 Conflict and consensus

Verbal conflict is unique among speech activities because participants overtly display and focus upon the fact that consensus on a matter worth talking about has broken down. Verbal conflict is one way such interactional troubles are managed. Trouble often exists under such circumstances because consensus on many matters is a necessary prerequisite for successful verbal interaction. When consensus breaks down, stable interaction can be in jeopardy. But this is not inevitable as the conflict form can be used as an expression of sociability (Schiffrin, 1984).

Two kinds of consensus are closely related to the termination of verbal conflicts. First is consensus on features of the social world. This includes agreement on matters of fact, judgment, obligation, rights, attitude, feeling and so on. Participants usually agree on such things as the meaning of words, the truth of certain facts (e.g. "Today is Tuesday."), the existence of certain rights (e.g. "I have the right to get a drink of water."), the existence of feelings (e.g. "Jacks likes Jill.") and so on. Disagreement on such matters can provide a basis for conflict. The second kind of consensus is agreement on the speech activity that is to be pursued by the participants. Participants require a sense of "what we are doing here" in order to construct appropriate turns in talk. The speech activity in which participants are engaged is usually not overtly labelled. Participants rarely state "we are having a verbal conflict."[1] Instead, assorted contextualization cues are used by participants to co-ordinate the speech activity (Gumperz, 1982a). During verbal conflict, participants have consensus on the speech activity they are engaged in. It takes two to tangle.[2] But there is a displayed lack of consensus on some feature of the social world. The agreement on the speech activity makes it possible to continue interaction while the lack of consensus on other matters is addressed.

Verbal conflict can continue only as long as the participants tacitly agree to engage in the conflict. Participants may terminate the conflict-speech activity without achieving a consensus on the feature of the social world which is the source of the trouble. Consensus on the speech activity can occur independently of consensus on features of the social world. Participants can tacitly agree to disagree and move on to other speech activities.

The two kinds of consensus can be linked together. The verbal conflict may lead to consensus on the troubling feature of the social world. Once such a consensus is established, the conflict-speech activity is usually terminated. While the management of consensus is central to the organization of conflict terminations, such conflicts carry another layer of meaning which is equally important. That is the logic of winning and losing.

1.2 Submission and dominance

In verbal conflict participants verbally place themselves in symbolic positions that are opposed to one another. Oppositional turns can take many forms, which range from stating opposing positions in a rational debate format, to the irrational trading of vicious insults or threats. Whatever specific form it takes, this oppositional positioning establishes preconditions for the display of dominance and submission. Once the oppositional positions have been taken up, one of the participants may give in, or submit to the other. Submission by one party marks the dominance of the opposing party (Simmel, 1950 [1908]: 113). In terms of game theory the dominant participant is the winner and the submissive participant is the loser. This creation of dominant and submissive participants provides a basis for terminating verbal conflicts (Simmel, 1950 [1908]: 113). By submitting, a person tacitly accepts the position maintained by the other party. This acceptance dismantles the oppositional discourse structure and usually marks the termination of a conflict episode. The submissive party may not privately agree with the other's position but accepts that person's dominance on that issue for the time being. The submission stands not only as a signal of consensus on some feature of the social world but also as a signal to change the speech activity to something other than conflict. Dominant participants usually accept their victory and are willing to move to a new speech activity.

Gumperz notes that speech activities can have expected outcomes (1982a: 166). Once a conflict is under way, the participants know that winners and losers may be established. In fact, participants usually strive to win conflicts and avoid losing them. Social standing as well as self esteem are at stake in verbal conflicts so there is much to be gained by winning. Goffman described the win/lose logic of "character contests" – verbal conflicts where character is at stake (1967). While the establishment of winners and losers is a possible ending for conflict it is by no means inevitable. Conflicts can end in a stand-off in which the conflict dissipates (Vuchinich, 1984; Adger, 1984).

The termination of verbal-conflict episodes requires at least a consensus on shifting the speech activity. This consensus may be accomplished by establishing dominance or by negotiating consensus on contested issues. But there are other ways of closing off verbal conflicts. For a more complete analysis we turn now to the conversational mechanisms used to close episodes of verbal conflict.

1.3 The terminal exchange

For this analysis we will assume that verbal conflict is one kind of speech activity. We further assume that the speech activity is a discourse unit which can be recognized by participants and observers. The problem of how verbal conflicts are closed is related to the problem of how discourse units in general are closed. We will show how a two-slot sequential mechanism used in closing other discourse units is important for closing verbal conflicts as well. This mechanism functions to organize the consensus and dominance which is important in many conflict closings.

Schegloff and Sacks examined the "closing problem" for the single conversation discourse unit (1973). They point out that the organization of closing is an issue for other discourse units as well (1973: 292). We will apply aspects of their analysis to the closing of the verbal-conflict discourse unit. One key to the solution of the closing problem for a conversation is a *terminal exchange*, such as an exchange of good-byes (Schegloff and Sacks, 1973: 295). In the terminal exchange, the first slot of the adjacency pair implicitly proposes that the conversation end. In the second slot the other speaker shows "that he understood what a prior [speaker] aimed at, and that he is willing to go along with that." (Schegloff and Sacks, 1973: 297). Through the terminal exchange, consensus regarding termination is displayed and silence as well as leave-taking can occur without untoward interpretation.

The closing problem in verbal conflict is how to organize the arrival of the opponents at a point where one speaker's oppositional turn will not elicit an oppositional turn from the other. There are special difficulties in arranging this because verbal conflict puts participants in jeopardy of losing face and esteem as well as more concrete benefits that may be at issue in a dispute. And it is at the end of the conflict episode where these matters are settled. The terminal exchange is used by participants to coordinate the closing of verbal conflicts.

The terminal exchange takes two basic forms in verbal conflict. Both forms have a fundamental two-slot structure. Both forms can close a verbal conflict immediately when they are applied. Both forms occur after at least one oppositional turn has occurred. One displays a dominant/submissive relationship between participants. The other displays consensus on a compromise.

One form of terminal exchange is the *submission terminal exchange*. The first slot is an oppositional move. The second slot is assent. The term assent will be used here to refer to either agreement or compliance. Assent placed after the opponent's oppositional turn signals submission. The assent marks acceptance of the validity of the oppositional attack. The assentor also accepts a subordinate position regarding the dispute. The submission terminal exchange has some of the characteristics of an "other correction" which follows disagreement (M.H. Goodwin, 1983; Adger, 1984; Schegloff, Jefferson, and Sacks, 1977). This pattern is also related to the primitive attack-submit patterns found in other species (Chase, 1980).

The second form of terminal exchange employed in verbal conflict is the *compromise terminal exchange.* The first slot is a concession offering. The second slot is acceptance of the offering. This two-slot sequence displays a consensus on the terms specified by the concession. The basic two-slot form can be extended to include multiple concession offerings. Concessions offered may not be accepted immediately. In such cases a concession can still serve as a "pre-closing" which signals that a participant is ready to begin closing a conflict (Schegloff and Sacks, 1973; Levinson, 1983: 325).

The remainder of this paper focuses on how these terminal exchanges are employed in closing verbal-conflict episodes. The basic two-slot structure may be used in a variety of systematic ways. For example, we will see that avoiding the performance of the second slot in the submission terminal exchange leads to the most frequently used format for conflict termination – the stand-off. Five distinct termination formats involving the two terminal exchanges will be examined. Before pursuing the analysis with examples, the nature of the data will be described.

2. Data

The data was taken from video and audio field recordings of sixty-four normal family dinners taped in the homes of the families. Fifty-two different families from five states (South Carolina, Pennsylvania, Indiana, Illinois and Georgia) were taped. Lower, middle and upper-class families were represented. Forty-eight of the tapes involve white families, sixteen involve black families. Fifty of the recordings include audio and video while fourteen are audio only. The taping procedure was designed to acquire the most naturalistic family dinners possible. Researchers were not present during the dinners and no camera lights were used. In most cases family members, or close friends of the family, did the actual taping. Participants were fully aware of the taping and its academic purposes. Signed permission/release forms were obtained. Families were given the option of viewing their tape with the author. These sessions provided useful information for the analysis. Members of the author's extended family were involved in thirteen of the dinners. This circumstance provided useful ethnographic background information for those dinners. Before examining the operation of the terminal exchanges some general features of the verbal conflicts in the data will be reviewed. This review will clarify some aspects of the data examples presented.

Verbal conflict is a discourse unit that can be constructed in a variety of ways. Speech activities known to participants as spats, arguments, disputes, fights, squabbles, run-ins and so on are variations of the basic verbal conflict discourse unit. Because conflict is a primary framework for organizing interaction it is subject to transformation into different keys (Goffman, 1974: 40ff.; Schiffrin, 1984). This makes mock conflict and other variations possible. This gives participants the option of shifting keys in the midst of a conflict episode – eg. from serious conflict to mock conflict.

American English provides many different illocutionary structures for accomplishing oppositional turns at talk. These include disagreement, challenge, denial, accusation, threat, insult (M.H. Goodwin, 1982b; Adger, 1984; Schiffrin, 1984). These oppositional turns can be performed in a mitigated or aggravated manner (M.H. Goodwin, 1983; Labov and Fanshel, 1977) using direct or indirect constructions (M.H. Goodwin, 1982b; Vuchinich, 1984). Paralinguistic and kinesic cues can be important in conveying the oppositional character of a turn and its level of intensity. Such cues include "increased volume, rapid tempo, contrastive stress and exaggerated intonation contours" (Schiffrin, 1984: 318).

Turn taking becomes more competitive during verbal conflict. Overlaps and interruptions are frequent. In multi-party conflicts teamwork (Goffman, 1959b) is common. Two or more parties can "gang up" on one party. Verbal conflicts, as other discourse units, can be interrupted by side sequences (Jefferson, 1972) after which the conflict is resumed. Topic shifting occurs within conflicts as participants maneuver for tactical advantage.

The data examples provided below include occurrences of many of these phenomena. Detailed treatment of them is beyond the scope of this report. The alert reader will recognize them when they appear. Our focus is on the sequential organization of conflict closings. We turn now to a description of five conflict termination formats observed in the data – submission, dominant third-party intervention, compromise, stand-off and withdrawal.

3. Analysis

3.1 Submission

As described above, a conflict may be terminated when one participant "gives in" and accepts the opponent's position. The submission terminal exchange accomplishes this kind of closing. The second-slot assent which signals the submission may be verbal. In example 1 three teenage sisters disagree over a matter of history.

Example 1[3]

1. Jane: Well see King Henry the Eighth is the one that started Protestantism.
2. Alice: UH UH. Calvinists did that.
3. Jane: No they didn't. King Henry the Eighth did. He wanted to divorce his wife.
4. Alice: He was the first King to revert re– (1.4) Protestantism.
5. Jane: He declared (   )
6. Alice: Lutheranism and Calvinist happened before that. It was just that Henry was the first one to proclaim that as the Church of England.

7. Jane: Yeah. (1.0) Whatever.
            (6.5)
8. Mary: What you all doin' besides read?
In turn 7 Jane submits to Alice with the assenting "Yeah." and the conflict
terminates. A 6.5-second silence and topic shift (turn 8) follow.

Verbal submission may be indirect rather than overt. In the following
minor run-in between two teenage sisters indirect submission occurs.

Example 2

9.   Marie: Ah you left the window down on the car. (2.7) Just thought I'd
            remind you.
10. Jill: Uh uh.
11. Marie: Yes it was.
12. Jill: I–I I opened the door and rolled it up and the reason I thought
            it was shut was it squeaked when I rolled it up and it squeaked.
13. Marie: Really hard to do idn't it?
14. Jill: Yeah.

The issue in example 2 is whether or not Jill left the car window open. In
turn 10 Jill denies that she did. But in turn 12 she gives an excuse for why
she "thought it was shut." This construction presupposes that she had, in
fact, left the window open. In this presupposition Jill is giving in or assenting
to Marie's oppositional accusation. Thus Jill indirectly submits.
    The submission signal may also be given nonverbally. In the following
example a father (age 28) and son (age 6) disagree on whether or not the son
should eat his beans.

Example 3

15. Father: Chow down on them beans. They're good.
16. Son: Uh uh.
17. Father: Yes.
18. Son: I just don't like 'em. That's why.
19. Father: Well they're there. You eat 'em.
20. Mother: Has he eat alot of 'em?
21. Father: No. He hasn't eat but maybe one of 'em.
22. Son: Uh uhm.
23. Father: EAT. (6.1) Or you'll go back to your room when you get
            done.
            (10.5)
(Son begins eating food and cutting meat.)

24. Father: Cut it right.
(The family dog out in the yard barks.)
25. Mother: Think he'll learn after today to stay off peoples' trees?
26. Father: What's he barkin' at?

By eating after the father's directive and threat (turn 23) the son submits nonverbally.

3.2 Dominant third-party intervention

One particular pattern of submission warrants separate treatment. An on-going conflict involving two or more participants can be "broken up" by a third party. Usually this third party has some power over the participants. In this termination format neither of the original opponents submits to the other. Instead both submit to the third party. Often the third party's turn is a directive which opposes the conflict activity. In the family setting the intervening third party is usually a parent. In the following example the mother breaks up a dispute between her son (age 17) and daughter (age 20). The daughter's name is Melissa and the father's name is Duke.

Example 4

27. Mother: Would it be ill manners if I smoked in front a y'all.
28. Father: Yeah. While we're eatin'.
                  (2.6)
29. Son: You know how I feel about that.
                  (4.0)
30. Daughter [to Mother]: Wull he's got alot a room to talk.
                  (1.2)
31. Mother: He just dudn't like people smokin' around him.
32. Son   [to daughter]: WHAT ARE YOU TALKIN' ABOUT? (1.7)
                  What are you talkin' about?
33. Daughter: Huh?
34. Son: What are you talkin' about?
35. Daughter: All your friends and everything.
36. Son: They don't smoke around me.
37. Mother: MELISSA.   Y'ALL. (2.0) Duke would you bring
                  home some strawberry shortcake tomorrow?
38. Father: If they got any.

In turn 37 the mother overlaps the son's turn (36) by loudly saying the daughter's name then "Y'ALL" which refers to the son and daughter. Ellipsis is involved in the mother's turn. Her loudness and intonation contour convey to the children the message, "Y' ALL STOP SQUABBLING" or an equivalent. The mother pauses for two secconds, the children are silent and the mother begins a new topic. The children submitted to the mother's oppositional directive – to stop the conflict.

The intervention mechanism can be used in various ways. Individuals without much power may attempt to break up conflicts with directives. And such attempts may well fail. Participants with relatively low status may invite dominant individuals to break up a conflict if there is a tactical advantage for them. In the following example a daughter (age 17) and son (age 14) disagree on whether the son will help the daughter dump the family trash.

Example 5

39. Daughter: (You're gonna) work on the trash with me.
40. Son: No.
41. Daughter: Yes he is idn't he daddy?
42. Son: Tom can. I got to work.
43. Daughter: Tom won't be able to.
44. Father: EMPTY THE TRASH WITH HER.
              (1.2)
45. Son: I get to drive then.

In turn 41 the daughter invites the father into the conflict. In turn 44 the father ends the dispute in favor of the daughter. The son's turn 45 indicates that he will help the daughter with the trash and wants to drive the pick-up truck in the trash-dumping task.

The submission of multiple subordinates in this intervention format is an important pattern for defining and maintaining the dominance hierarchy in baboon troops (Kaufmann, 1967: 79). Later we will consider its relative frequency of occurrence and significance in the family-dinner data.

3.3 Compromise

In the submission format one type of consensus is achieved through dominance. Another mechanism for accomplishing consensus which closes off conflict is the negotiation of a compromise. The critical move in this kind of negotiation is the concession. In a concession a participant offers a position that is *between* the opposing positions that define the dispute. A concession does not give in to the other position but rather establishes a middle ground which moves toward the other position but still opposes it. A concession proposes a compromise position between the two opposing positions. If the concesssion offered is accepted by the opponent the conflict can terminate. The most basic compromise terminal exchange has two slots:

(1) concession offering and (2) assent, which accepts the offering. This basic two-slot structure may be expanded to include multiple concessions and acceptance may be tacit.

An important feature of compromise terminations is that none of the participants must lose face. This is especially apparent when both opponents make concessions. But even when only one participant makes a concession it is self-initiated, not externally imposed. It is analogous to the difference between self-correction and other-correction (Schegloff, Jefferson, and Sacks, 1977). The self loses face when corrections or concessions are imposed by others. When these moves are self-initiated, face loss is minimized. Compromise termination formats have been observed in children's conflict (Eisenberg and Garvey, 1981; M.H. Goodwin, 1983), though close analysis of the compromise process in adult conversation has not been undertaken since Simmel (1955 [1908]: 114).

In many cases a concession functions as a pre-closing (Schegloff and Sacks, 1973; Levinson, 1983) which signals that one participant is ready to close the conflict but is unwilling to submit. The opponent may accept the concession, reject the concession, or offer a counter-concession. The conflict is closed off when a concession, or set of concessions, is accepted through assent. The acceptance may be verbal or nonverbal and can be tacit under some circumstances.

The following example shows a simple concession offering. The husband is explaining to the dinner guests why they might not be able to watch a certain television channel after dinner. His wife disputes his explanation.

Example 6

46. Husband:	And what happened was channel 4 and channel 6 were both playin' the same cartoon and they just totally obliterated channel 5 because that ah– that ah– frequency ( )
47. Wife:	You– They weren't playin' the same cartoon.
48. Husband:	They were.
49. Wife:	Not according to the TV Guide.
50. Husband:	For awhile For awhile. But then it went off. (1.0) I don't know we might be able to watch it or we might not.
51. Husband's sister:	Where did you take the TV to?

The wife disputes the husband's claim that the same cartoon was on at the same time on the two channels. In turn 50 the husband offers a concession – that they were on at the same time only "for awhile" and then "went off." This turn does not submit to the wife's position but does soften the husband's position and moves it toward the wife's. The wife does not overtly accept the concession but does not oppose the husband after turn 50. Given that she opposed him twice before (turns 47 and 49) and given the husband's concession in turn 50, and given that she does not oppose him after the concession, we assume that she accepted the concession as a basis for closing the conflict. This example shows that a concession can be much more than a pre-closing (Levinson, 1983: 325). Here the concession itself is the only overt move needed to close the conflict. Concession acceptances can be assumed just as greeting or leave-taking second-slot responses can be assumed under certain circumstances (Goffman, 1971: 151).

The negotiation of a compromise can be more extended with multiple concessions and the involvement of third parties. Concessions can be indirect. In the following example a mother and daughter disagree on whether the meat they are eating is "dry" or "delicious." The daughters are Ann (age 10) and Joyce (age 12).

Example 7

52. Ann: The meat is dry.
53. Mother: No. I think it's delicious.
54. Joyce: It's not dry it's just (   )
55. Mother: Put some mushroom sauce on it.
56. Joyce: I didn't say it was–
57. Ann: It's not dry it's just hard.
58. Joyce: It's good though.
             (6.0)
59. Mother   [to Father]: Uh Duane hollered at me today. (2.1) That man's name is Virgil Long.

The oppositional positions are established by the mother and Ann in turns 52 and 53. The third party (Joyce) begins offering a compromise position in turn 54. The mother interrupts this turn with an indirect concession in turn 55. Her mushroom-sauce suggestion leaves open the possibility that the meat could be dry without the sauce. In turn 57 Ann concedes that the meat is not dry but does not submit to the mother's position by adding that "it's just hard." At this point both initial opponents have made concessions, though neither has overtly accepted the other's position. The third party (Joyce) fills the concession acceptance slot with turn 58. The "It's good though." accepts the mother's position with the assessment down-graded (Pomerantz, 1978) from delicious to good. The use of "though" allows turn 58 to accept Ann's assessment of the meat as hard while simultaneously accepting the mother's down-graded assessment – the meat is good even though it is hard.

In example 7 the mother and Ann did not arrive at a total consensus about the meat. But by both offering concessions and with the third party mediating they use the compromise format to end the dispute. In the next example, multiple concessions are followed by overt assent moves which seal the compromise.

In example 8 the participants are siblings (Carl, Sue and Ray) in their thirties. They are discussing their parents, who are not present. Jack is their father. Faye is their mother.

Example 8

60. Carl: I think Jack is basically happy. I don't think it takes that much for him.
61. Sue: Just something to bitch about.
62. Carl: Oh GOD. He– he really is not that bad.
63. Ray: AH-H O-O-OOOHH.
64. Sue [to Ray]: That's what I tried to tell him. He didn't–
65. Ray [to Carl]: When you must, you must, they must calm down when you were there or something.
66. Sue: I said I–I–
67. Carl: NO. NO! That's– that's just the way they talked over the years and it wasn't really any different when we were growing up.
68. Ray: OH NO! OH NO!
69. Carl: It was the same old thing. It's just the way they talk.
70. Ray: Its a little– Its not as bad really now.
71. Carl: They don't have the energy they used to have. They don't do it as much.
72. Ray: Hhhhh Heh.
73. Carl: They don't do it as much.
74. Ray: I– I've noticed that the past ten years that mom has started to play a more active part.
75. Carl: Yeah right. She likes–
76. Ray: She gets her digs in.

This conflict begins on the topic of how bad the father's complaining is and then shifts to how serious the conflict between the parents (Faye and Jack) has been. The episode starts in turn 61 when Sue impugns the father's character by implying that he is happy as long as he has "something to bitch about." Carl opposes this insult claiming that their father is "not that bad." Ray's loud, extended reaction with falling intonation (turn 63) challenges Carl's claim and aligns Ray with Sue. In turn 65 Ray proposes a compromise position – that the parents "must calm down" when Carl visits them. This compromise position allows both opposing positions to be correct. Jack is bad when Ray or Sue visit but is not bad when Carl visits. This compromise is flatly rejected by Carl in turn 67 and he adds elaboration of his position that the parents' conflict was not that bad. Ray rejects this in turn 68. But in turn 70 Ray makes a concession that "it's not as bad really now." This marks a concession on how bad the parents' situation is with the "now" indicating that there has been change over time. This turn also carries an opposition to Carl's claim that the parent's conflict "wasn't really any different when we were growing up." Turns with more than one layer of meaning are common in verbal conflict. The oppositional layer of turn 70 signals that while Ray is making a concession he is by no means giving in.

In turn 71 Carl provides the acceptance slot for the compromise terminal exchange by agreeing with Ray's claim that the parental conflict is "not as bad now." At the same time Carl is conceding his earlier claim that the conflict has been the same over time. This turn 71 also includes an element of humor with the ironic joke that the parents are too old to have enough energy to fight much any more. Ray shows acceptance and solidarity by laughing at the joke in turn 72. Ray adds another observation in turn 74 which Carl agrees with in turn 75. Carl's concession and assent in turn 71 marks the last turn in the conflict. The agreements which follow that solidify the consensus through a supportive interchange (Goffman, 1971).

Example 8 shows some of the complexity which can be involved in the compromise format. Within this complexity the basic concession offering/acceptance terminal exchange still functions to organize the closing of conflict. The compromise terminal exchange allows conflict to be closed without loss of face. But it requires that one or more participants be willing to alter positions they had previously taken. It also requires a certain level of trust that the opponent will not exploit a concession that is made. The delicacy of concession negotiations as well as the requirement that one alter a previously stated position makes compromise a difficult termination to achieve. The relatively low frequency of compromise closings will be discussed later.

3.4 Stand-off

Participants can close a verbal conflict avoiding the second slot in a terminal exchange. In those cases oppositional turns continue until the topic is changed or until the opponents withdraw from participation. Third parties may be involved in shifting the topic and speech activity. When a conflict terminates with participants continuing to maintain opposing positions, with neither submitting, we call it a stand-off.

In a stand-off participants change the speech activity and drop the conflict form. The social meaning of a stand-off is susceptible to multiple interpretations because a terminal exchange is not present to resolve the opposing positions. When conflict is sociable in nature there is little concern or need for interpretation of an outcome (Schiffrin, 1984: 329). In terms of game theory, a stand-off is a draw where there is no winner or loser.

In a stand-off any efforts to induce the opponent into submission or to work out a compromise fail. A crucial feature of the terminal exchange is that it requires the participation of at least two parties. There is not unilateral terminal exchange. Most oppositional turns are constructed so that the next turn can be an assent marking submission. Because of this, participants become adept at avoiding a submissive response to oppositional turns. Conflicts can proceed with participants trying to "get in the last word." Oppositional moves can become redundant, more aggravated or mitigated, as a conflict develops. At some point the participants realize that the opponent is not going to submit and that compromise is not possible. Unless the hostility is intense and the conflict is effectively expressing it, participants seek an opportunity to get out of a conflict that is not getting anywhere. But at the same time each party does not want to make a submission move. Third parties may provide an opportunity to change the speech activity or an opponent may construct a turn that changes the activity but does not submit.

In the following example a husband and wife bicker about what the husband previously told the wife about which direction is east. There are two adult dinner guests – a female and a male named Charlie. The family dog, Mercury, is sitting near the table.

Example 9

77. Wife:	Now you told me that this was east.
78. Husband:	I never did. That's west.
79. Wife:	Yes you did.
80. Husband:	No I never.
81. Wife:	Last week.
82. Husband	[to guests]: She has a terrible sense of direction.
83. Wife:	I asked you whether the trains went– ran north and south or east and west.
84. Husband:	Okay and what did I say?
85. Wife:	East-west.
86. Husband:	Right, very good.
87. Wife:	Then I said I was tryin' to figure out if ( ) was right and then I asked you what direction that was and we finally decided the sun comes up over here so this was east.
88. Husband:	No no no no.
89. Wife:	'Cuz I– its west and you said the sun comes up over here.
90. Husband:	No.
91. Wife:	Yeah, I remember that very clearly.
92. Female dinner guest	[to dog in the room]: Hi Mercury dog. I eat all my crust. Sorry. Charlie ate his crust too.
93. Wife:	It was good crust.
94. Female dinner guest:	Uh huh.

In turns 83–87 the opponents attempt clarification of the disputed points. These efforts break down and the conflict overtly restarts in turn 88. Note that the assents included in turns 84 and 86 do not follow an oppositional turn and are thus not second slots in the submission terminal exchange. In turn 92 the dinner guest provides an opportunity to change the speech activity which the wife takes advantage of in turn 93. The conflict closes with no submission or compromise.

3.5 Withdrawal

Conflict termination may occur if one opponent withdraws from conversational activity or physically leaves the area. This action leaves the conflict in a stand-off with no terminal exchange. Withdrawal may occur when an opponent becomes too distraught to continue the conflict. But withdrawal can also be used as a strategic move to discredit one's opponent.

In example 10 a husband and wife argue about where to move their place of residence.

Example 10

95. Husband:	Why go out there and pay twenty-two dollars a square foot to build one when I can buy it for less than eighteen already built and not have that trouble?
96. Wife:	Cause it ain't big enough is what. We– what am I supposed to do, give away my furniture?
97. Husband:	Dat house is almost as big as this house right here.
98. Wife:	JOHN IT DON'T GOT NO DEN IN IT and a dinin' room neither.
99. Husband:	Now that ain't really ah no– no trouble to put up a ( )
100. Wife:	That's alot a trouble to me. I ain't arguin'.
101. Husband:	No it ain't. It ain't no damn trouble to you cause you ain't gonna drive ner nail in it. (2.0) Now, how can it be trouble for you? It'll be there when you move in it. (4.0)
102. Wife:	If that's the only way you can talk to me is cussin' then ( )
103. Husband:	NOOO:O– ahh– just statin' the facts.
104. Wife:	I don't (even wanna) talk about it. (6.0)
105. Daughter:	It looks like it's gonna rain. (12.5)
106. Daughter:	Mom, what time is it?
107. Wife:	Four fifty-four. (27.5)

The wife first moves to close the conflict in turn 100 ("I ain't arguin'."). The husband takes another oppositional turn (101) so the wife retaliates by justifying her withdrawal on the basis of the husband's "cussin." The husband opposes that move so the wife makes another withdrawal statement (turn 104). This time the husband does not continue the attack and the conflict closes. The wife here insures that her withdrawal is not interpreted as submission by insisting on getting in the last word and by justifying the withdrawal on the basis of the husband's uncivilized profanity.

Withdrawal may not be so clearly set up or justified in advance. In the following example the mother withdraws by not answering a question addressed to her. This run-in is about putting pepper on corn plants in the family garden to keep wild animals from eating the corn.

Example 11

108. Father: Did you put that there ah pepper on the corn?
109. Mother: Nope. I didn't have time since I got home.
110. Father: Didn't have time. I didn't think you would.
111. Mother: Well when did you expect me to have time?
112. Father: Well hell you coulda done it last evening.
113. Mother: I'd a been up til about midnight.
114. Father: Huh?
             (12.0)
115. Son: Sun tried to come out for awhile.

The mother had said she would pepper the corn. She didn't do it and the spat is about whether or not she had time to do it. The mother makes her withdrawal noticeable by ignoring the father's question directed to her in turn 114. The twelve-second pause marks the end of a discourse unit as the terminal pauses in earlier examples do. The silence after a withdrawal, however, is strategically induced by one participant.

These examples show how terminal exchanges can serve as mechanisms for displaying dominance and consensus. Such displays provide a social and ritual basis for terminating conflict. The use of the stand-off and withdrawal formats shows that conflicts can be closed without completed terminal exchanges. But the terminal exchange structure is still involved in such formats because submission slots are systematically avoided. Getting in the "last word" does not win a conflict but it does show that you haven't given in or submitted.

Table 5.1 gives a summary of the basic sequential structure of each of the termination formats. A, B and C represent different participants. The use of these formats leads to a new speech activity or to no speech activity. These basic structures are subject to expansion, elision, side sequences, and other sequential variations (Goffman, 1971; 1976).

Table 5.1 *Basic conflict termination formats*

| | Dominant third-party | | | |
Submission	intervention	Compromise	Stand-off	Withdrawal
A: Oppositional turn	A: Oppositional turn	A: Oppositional turn	A: Oppositional turn	A: Oppositional turn
B: Oppositional turn	B: Oppositional turn	B: Oppositional turn	B: Oppositional turn	B: Oppositional turn
A: Assent	C: Oppositional turn	A: Concession offering	C: Topic shift	A: Withdraws
	A: Assent	B: Concession acceptance		
	B: Assent			

3.6 Frequency of occurrence of the termination formats

The various termination formats are not all used with the same frequency. Table 5.2 shows how frequently each termination format was used in closing the conflicts observed in the data described above. Perhaps the most striking finding in this table is that the stand-off terminated 66% of the conflicts that occurred. Furthermore adults as well as children were involved in stand-offs more frequently than any other termination format. Resolution by submission or compromise occurred in 26% of the conflicts.

Why do so many of these conflicts end in a stand-off? In a stand-off no one must lose face through submission. In addition, opponents do not have to make concessions or engage in the delicate negotiation of a compromise position. In general, the stand-off is the "easiest" way to end a conflict since it does not require the level of coordination, consensus, or self-sacrifice associated with compromise or dominance. Studies of children's conflict have found low frequencies of resolved conflict (M.H. Goodwin, 1982b; 1983, Adger, 1984). Avoidance of face-loss has been proposed as an explanation for so many unresolved conflicts among children (Adger, 1984). In addition, Maynard found compromise to be rare in misdemeanor-plea bargaining disputes in a municipal court setting (Maynard, 1984a), though the legal process precluded frequent stand-offs.

The absence of resolution in most verbal conflicts does not mean that senseless verbal aggression prevails. Verbal conflicts perform important social functions even when resolution by dominance or compromise does not occur. Important information about social boundaries (involving rights, obligations, and relationships) is transferred during conflict (Vuchinich. 1984). Conflict can also serve as a form for indirect expression of solidarity and intimacy (Schiffrin, 1984). In addition, verbal conflict provides an organized arena for the expression of negative affect. Such expression can be cathartic. But even when it's not it allows a person to make negative feelings

Table 5.2 *Number of conflicts closed by each termination format*

	Submission to opponent	Dominant third-party intervention	Compromise	Stand-off	Withdrawal
Across generation	13	9	7	62	2
Within younger generation	7	1	1	14	0
Within older generation	8	0	8	35	2
Total	28 (17%)	10 (6%)	16 (9%)	111 (66%)	4 (2%)

known to other family members, feelings the other family members may want to consider in guiding their action.

Stand-offs occur when submission or compromise do not develop. Hypothetically stand-offs could continue indefinitely with opponents trying to get in the last word. This doesn't happen. Participants sometimes perceive that a conflict "isn't getting anywhere." The projected utility of successive oppositional moves decreases as the conflict lengthens. Participants may seek a way out of the conflict-speech activity without the costs of submission or compromise. The stand-off termination is thus based on considerations of utility while submission and compromise terminations are based on the reestablishment of a "ritual equilibrium" (Goffman, 1967: 19).

Table 5.2 shows that only 9% of the conflicts observed ended in compromise. Not only is negotiation required for compromise but opponents must also be willing to make and accept concessions which alter previously held positions. The drive to defend and maintain the self, and the positions it espouses, is strong, so concessions do not come easily. Table 5.2 shows that compromise is very rare in the younger generation but more frequent when adults are involved. The skills and inclinations for compromise may be acquired in the socialization process.

Withdrawal is the most socially disruptive termination format because it halts communication and prevents a smooth transition to a new speech activity. It is the least frequently used format, occurring in only 2% of the conflicts observed. This low frequency shows that in the family-dinner settings opponents usually participate in the conflict until it runs its course.

Table 5.2 provides information on conflicts in only one setting – the family dinner. Data from other settings would be needed to determine if the frequencies in table 5.2 depend on the setting. It is possible that the presence of taping equipment influenced the frequency distribution of termination formats. Observations of family dinners when no taping equipment was present suggested that taping did not influence how often the various termination formats were used.

3.7 Power displays in verbal family conflict

About one in four conflicts in the data ended with some form of submission. Some aspects of the power relations in the sampled families can be inferred from a closer look at the submission frequencies. Almost half (46%) of the submissions that occurred took place in across-generation conflicts. In 85% of these across-generation submissions it was the younger generation member submitting to the older generation member. Mean age for younger generation members was 18.4 years. Younger-generation submission is not surprising since parents usually wield power in families. But what is somewhat surprising is that parents did not choose to – or were not able to – use their power to win most conflicts with their children. Parent–child conflicts ended in a stand-off three times more often (62 cases) than they ended in submission (21 cases). Parents did not usually "put their children in their place" in conflict closings. This does not mean that parental power can not be exercised in a stand-off. Power can be maintained through other mechanisms besides inducing submission. These mechanisms include defining the terms and boundaries involved in a conflict and controlling the flow of negative affect (Vuchinich, 1984). In addition, some of the parent–child stand-offs are sociable conflicts where power display is less prominent (Schiffrin, 1984).

4. Discussion

Some of the most influential work on interpersonal conflict has been based on game theory (Schelling, 1963; Rapoport, 1960). In game theory the focus is on outcomes. Outcomes are defined in terms of winning and losing. A calculus of reward quantifies an amount won or lost. While theoretically appealing, game theory has been dogged by the problem of mapping the calculus of reward onto social actions outside of artificial laboratory experiments. In the case of verbal conflict the question becomes, how many units of what are won or lost as the outcome of a conflict? No adequate answer for this question has ever been found.

Goffman's analysis of the ritual organization of verbal conflict (i.e. character contests) included elements of game theory, but "not necessarily with zero-sum restrictions" (Goffman, 1967: 244). Goffman noted that such conflicts can end with one winner and one loser, two winners or two losers (1967: 245). But what is more revealing is Goffman's observation that the outcomes of a verbal conflict may be interpreted differently by different participants as well as observers (1967: 247). That is, there may be no consensus on whether there was a winner or a loser. Furthermore, if there is consensus that somebody won, there may not be consensus on which opponent it was. This is a critical point, because game theory rests entirely on the assumption that the opponents agree on the interpretation of outcomes – e.g. who won. This is an incorrect assumption for verbal family conflict. In verbal conflict such agreement must be accomplished by participants – it cannot be assumed (Schegloff and Sacks, 1973: 324).

This chapter describes sequential mechanisms used by participants to accomplish consensus regarding the outcome of episodes of verbal conflict. The submission and compromise terminal exchanges function to accomplish this kind of agreement. However, the high frequency of stand-off terminations shows that, for the data studied here, agreement on a resolved outcome was usually not attained. Participants avoid submission to save face. Compromise is interactionally more difficult to achieve and is relatively infrequent. The stand-off, however, requires neither the face-loss of submission nor concession negotiations. Conflicts can end because consensus is attained through submission or compromise. But when such consensus is not established the conflicts end in a stand-off which allows participants to at least save face and move on to another speech activity.

Verbal family conflict exhibits some of the properties of a game (e.g., there can be a winner). But such game-like properties are embedded within the discourse structure of the conflict-speech activity. An understanding of how verbal conflicts terminate requires a focus on the way the conflict-speech activity organizes sequential structures to produce consensus, dominance and closure.

Notes

This research was facilitated by funding from the Office of Research, University of South Carolina and the Rose-Hulman Institute of Technology. I would like to thank Charles Goodwin and Douglas Maynard who made helpful comments on drafts of this paper.

1   When participants do verbalize reference to the on-going speech activity it is known as "formulation" (Garfinkel and Sacks, 1970).
2   There may be competition over what kind of conflict is being done. Furthermore there can be conflict over whether a conflict is to be done at all – the "contest contest" (Goffman, 1967: 248). But even in such cases there has to be sufficient consensus on doing some kind of conflict in order for it to occur.
3   The following transcript conventions apply for all examples:

Number within parentheses, e.g. (2.5).
     The number refers to the number of seconds of silence which occurred at that point in the transcript.

Empty parentheses, e.g. (   ).

An utterance that could not be transcribed because it was not clearly audible.

All capitals, eg. WHAT?.

A very loud utterance.

Comments included in square brackets, e.g. [to Mother].

Nonverbal details about an utterance available only from videotape.

Spaces within a turn at talk, e.g. Mother: Tommy.   Stop it.

The speaker is silent while the previous speaker continues to talk.

6 Ideological themes in reports of interracial conflict

TERESA LABOV

The classic statement of the "American dilemma" points to a disjunction between the acceptance of an egalitarian ideology and individual behavior reflecting bigotry (Myrdal, 1944). Several recent studies have explored the relation of bias to ideology (Carlton, 1984; Headley, 1986; See, 1986; Kluegel and Smith, 1982; Tuch, 1981; Wacker, 1981). Smith examined the cognitive inconsistencies observed by Myrdal as they appeared in questionnaire data. He found evidence of conflict between tolerance for the principle of racial equality and hostility to desegregation of schools and concluded that "there is no internal dilemma, because individuals predetermine a set of conditions under which they will adhere to their principles" (1981: 569). There remains, however, an objective contradiction in the results of peoples' actions and the way that they talk of their beliefs and actions.

This chapter focuses on a series of incidents illustrating that dilemma, and especially on the ideological themes which recur in reports by liberal whites of conflicts with blacks. The conflicts took place in a food co-operative established by residents in a neighborhood of Philadelphia with mixed housing to provide food at low prices.[1] The food co-operative operated as an alternative institution (Rothschild-Witt, 1979: 509),[2] over a period of seven years in the 1970s, attracting few black participants, despite the hopes expressed by many of its founders. The question to be examined is why, when contact with blacks did occur, was the outcome more likely to be exclusion, rather than inclusion. The answer will be found through an analysis of reports of conflicts made by Co-op people to each other and to me.[3]

The activities of the Co-op people as they ordered, collected, and distributed food, exchanged information and views at meetings, formed a collective style which was pragmatic and informal as well as co-operative. These characteristics can also be viewed as themes in an ideology, outlining the behavior expected of Co-op people, and hence what was currently considered good Co-op practice.[4] A "Co-op ideology" was constructed from a study of peoples' talk and actions over several years. It can be expressed as a series

139

of propositions that capture both the practical goals and the underlying values of the Co-op.

1. *Co-operation.* Co-operative labor is a better way of satisfying community needs than competition among individuals.
2. *Commitment.* Commitment to the interests of the group is preferable to action that maximizes the interest of each individual.
3. *Harmony.* An atmosphere of peace and harmony (e.g., "good vibes") is preferable to one in which individuals express themselves violently in speech or action.
4. *Openness.* Participation should be open to all in the community who subscribe to the above values.

Changes were observed over time in the translation of this ideology into practice. But these ideological themes persisted in the behavior and talk of the Co-op participants.

1. Three incidents of conflict

In the course of several years' observation of the Co-op, I recorded reports of a number of incidents that involved conflict between white Co-op people and black residents. I shall focus on three of these incidents. They do not provide a profile of black/white relations as a whole in this mixed neighborhood, but they do share features with other incidents observed.

My summaries of these incidents draw on reports and discussions at meetings and during interviews. Since the antagonists' names were not used at meetings, and indeed their names were not generally known to most Co-op people, they will be referred to here as the *man*, the *woman*, and the *youths*.[5] The full transcriptions of the relevant portions of the meetings and interviews are given in the appendix.[6] Each incident is represented by more than one account.

1.1 The angry man

On an early February morning, two Co-op workers – Ben and Sheldon – returned from buying produce at the food distribution center. They found a car blocking the driveway leading to the Co-op. They recognized the car as having been illegally parked there on other occasions, but this time they pushed it out of their way. The car belonged to a man who lived across the street. He appeared, and a scuffle followed, but the Co-op people did not actually fight. Ben attended the next meeting with his arm in a sling and explained that charges had been pressed against the man.

At the meeting, details of the incident were given which highlighted the seriousness of the encounter. A neighbor reported that the man had tried to borrow a gun that morning. It also became apparent that the incident had racial overtones. Glen, a participant at the meeting who had no previous knowledge of the incident, asked Ben:

Glen: . . .what does he look like, for one thing, so I can avoid him.
    [Laughter]
Ben: He's about 5'11", he's black with pretty short hair—
Glen: He's black?
Ben: Yeah, he's got a little mustache, pretty thin, he's slim, and his car is
    the green one . . . (from A2 in appendix)

Glen's interruption showed that the second of these six characteristics was salient for him. In the following discussion Glen suggested that the Co-op people take the black/white issue into account, and have an informal talk with the man instead of taking him to court; this suggestion found no support.

Instead, a second theme surfaced, that the man was not a reasonable person, but "insane." As one outcome of the incident, the meeting passed a motion to allocate funds (if they should be needed) to obtain a "No Parking" sign to mark more clearly the loading zone outside the Co-op. Subsequently the city painted the words "No Parking" on the sidewalk at the curb.

1.2 The indignant woman

On a fall distribution day, a neighborhood woman was asked to leave the Co-op, because it was alleged she had been taking food without paying for it. The account was given by Joel at the same meeting as the incident with the man, during the same agenda point. The incident of the woman had occurred several months earlier: it does not seem likely that it would have been brought up if the talker had not seen it as relevant to the report on the man.

The organization of the Co-op distribution day was extremely informal at the time. Users filled their own orders, sometimes even calculated their own bills. Those who were not fully committed to the Co-op, even some long-standing participants, sometimes strayed from strict accountability. This incident might have been viewed as an extreme case of the same behavior, but it was not. Joel gave a full account of the event in his interview with me:

. . . she just walked right past the cashier, and was about ready to leave the door,
and ah, I said:
    "You're not leaving without paying,"
and ah, you know, indignant black woman shouted:
    "Racist, I'm going to get my people in here,"
and that type of thing. [Oh wow] And I just got up on one, on top of one of the
tables, and said – there were about thirty people present in the Co-op at the time, it
was very crowded – and I said:
    "I need your cooperative help in this situation, I need support here. This

woman is not – has not paid for her groceries, and I'm not going to let her leave
without paying for it . . ." (from A9 in appendix)

Joel's action reflected his active participation in the Society of Friends, where
public calls for co-operative support are an accepted way of dealing with
difficult courses of action. The woman left without taking any produce and
never came back.

An interview with another Co-op participant, Caren, affirmed this account, and emphasized the view that the black/white issue was being used
by the woman for her personal ends. No one proposed alternatives to the
action of throwing the woman out.

1.3 The neighborhood youths

In its early days, neighborhood youths were variously encouraged and
discouraged by different Co-op people from "hanging out" at the Co-op. Six
weeks after the meeting discussed above, two youths were asked to leave the
Co-op. They refused. Martin recounted the incident at the next regular
meeting, saying that he "pushed them out a little bit."

Later in that meeting, Martin gave a more detailed account of the
incident:

> . . . and you know, I said,
> "The rule is that we don't want people hanging around when we're cleaning
> up and finishing up and getting the stuff out of here, because we want to go
> home,"
> so I kind of opened the door, and I kind of moved and I kind of very gently I
> thought, kind of guided them out, showing them the light . . . they were still
> swinging their spikes, and one threw, one threw a spike at me . . . they threatened
> they were going to kill me, which I didn't really think they were going to do . . .
> (from A12 in appendix)

Sheldon, who had also been present, commented that Martin's use of force
was warranted. Though Martin's reference to a "rule" was a more formal
construction than the Co-op structure warranted, it reflected the long
history of Co-op contact with neighborhood teenagers. A year before, one
very active Co-op person, Linda, had encouraged neighborhood teenagers to
use the Co-op as a hangout. For several months it was fairly common to see
young black teenagers, usually, but not always, males, in the Co-op. At
times they helped set up the food or clean up afterwards. Some Co-op people
objected to the noise and confusion that generally ensued, some to the
occasional consumption of oranges or other fruit.

A meeting had been held to consider ways to preserve an atmosphere of
peace and harmony, and it was decided to institute a policy of excluding the
youths. Linda quit the Co-op in protest, but her point of view was not
forgotten. It was mentioned in this context by James, another participant at

the meeting. The reference to Linda and to "that kind of problem" may have been the first indication for some of those at the meeting that the youths being discussed were black, like those she had sponsored. It was Joel, however, the main participant in the earlier conflict with the woman, who made the black issue explicit.

Sheldon proposed that in the future the youths be removed promptly. No vote was taken, but there are reports in subsequent meetings that Co-op people did ask teenagers to leave.

2. Presenting ideology in talk

A study of these accounts of conflicts requires an understanding of how ideological themes are presented in talk. Talk has been studied as the medium by which events are reported to others (Sacks, 1970; Cicourel, 1974; Grimshaw, 1981b), but not as a means by which ideology is presented in on-going interaction. The Co-op participants did not preach or deal in ways that could be glossed as moralistic. Informally, people gossiped about incidents and people that harmed the Co-op. Even during meetings participants expressed indignation or ridicule at actions which were not seen as consistent with Co-op ideals. But the question of what would be an ideal Co-op, or what ideological principles should guide specific Co-op actions, were not meeting topics. Time was more likely to be spent on questions of which hours the Co-op should be open, how to get more members, and who had the extra keys to the walk-in refrigerator.

Yet morality or ideology clearly played a part in the reports of incidents that had taken place during food distribution days. In order to study the operation of Co-op principles in Co-op operation, means of identifying sources of ideological matters are needed. In order then to locate the bases of ideological themes, I shall need to consider more generally the way people spoke as individuals in a variety of collections of people, including especially "Co-op people" and "blacks."

The notion of "collections of people" (T. Labov, 1980: 126) will be introduced here as a more general concept than group, class, collectivity, or race, since the propositions that make up the core of an ideological position apply without regard to these distinctions. A study of talk showed that people introduced such collections to support a position without regard to the degree of interaction, membership status, or any other characteristics which conventionally distinguish social units. Whether the unit is "couple identity" (Giles and Fitzpatrick, 1984: 258), or marriage (Berger and Kellner, 1975: 36), or any momentary or long-established interactional social bond considered as "social identity" (Tajfel and Turner, 1979: 40; Tajfel, 1978: 64), each instance counts as a collection of people.

A collection of people is readily represented as characteristic of feature(s) plus people, such as in "Co-op people" or "black people," or in "black, Co-op people." Any collection of people can be indicated with a simple "we" (cf. A1 in appendix) or "they" (A15), though a variety of other means are used here, such as "the Co-op" (A3); "all white people" (A7); "troublemakers" (A8); "neighborhood kids" (A11). In the following passage, which is excerpted from an account of the conflict with the woman, the Co-op and many other collections of people are present and will be illustrated.

Example 1

Caren: . . . there was one woman who went in there and consistently filled up her whole cart and then paid for like one dozen eggs or something . . . she was just trying to use her color to rip off the Co-op . . . (from A10 in appendix)

Some of the collections of people are people who "went in there" [the Co-op], and people who "filled up her [their] whole cart," as well as people who "rip off the Co-op." Caren's talk locates the woman in all of these collections. One would expect Co-op people to be present in the first two, but not in the third. In conversational space and time, information is not always present to distinguish which of these or other collections are classes, or groups, which fleeting, and which long standing.

The second "there" in example 1 refers to the Co-op as a place, and less directly to the Co-op people who physically were the Co-op (T. Labov, 1980: 220). The term "there" further shows the value of the notion of collections of people as a means of blurring a distinction between the organization and the people who make up the organization. Such ambiguity is not always resolvable by listeners at the speed that talk takes place.

The people participating in the Co-op were necessarily involved in collections of workers or co-ordinators, as well as the collection of people picking up their orders. Most Co-op people were potential members of two or more such collections of people each week, since they both put in a share of labor and obtained food from the Co-op. Any and all of these collections of people would be included in the larger collection of "Co-op people."

The term "Co-op people" and the notion of collections of people are also useful here, since some of the expected features of formal organizations were missing from the Co-op. The notion of membership was not emphasized and some participants never paid an initial fee. Thus individuals are better characterized by the fact of participation, rather than membership (or degree of commitment, Merton, 1966: 1059), and I include here as "Co-op people" any who shared in Co-op activities, either by putting in hours working, or by paying for produce they had pre-ordered.

Co-op people were also likely to talk about the Co-op to each other, both at the produce distribution sessions and at meetings, as well as on the phone or on the street. Ideological themes appeared at times. To locate ideology in talk it will be useful to distinguish what people say as they "speak of" and "speak for" the Co-op.

2.1 Speaking of the Co-op

The first issue concerns the means by which people show that what they are saying can be attributed to their position as Co-op participants, and not to other statuses, such as persons who live in a commune or who have children. Two ways of "speaking of" the Co-op are particularly important in these materials: knowledge display and formulation.

Knowledge display When a person speaks as a member of a collection of people, he or she makes use of knowledge or perspectives gained from participation in that collection which show that he or she is part of that collection. By speaking as a Co-op person or displaying any such location, the individual gives confidence (credibility) to what is said, perhaps adding colour or affect by touching on shared experiences. For instance, in example 1 above, "there" is used instead of "Co-op." It is also the case that special vocabulary developed, and these Co-op people used the term "extras" for produce bought beyond the amount needed to fill orders, whereas for example, a Co-op in Boston used the term "overs."

Whether individuals have "monopolistic or privileged access" (Merton, 1972: 12) to knowledge, or even no legitimated access, they are able to sound like insiders or experts. Mehan's explanation for the differential acceptance of professional and lay reports in institutional decision-making situations, is relevant here as he points to individuals in roles which "gain their authority from the mastery and use of technical language that others do not understand and do not question" (1983b: 209). In terms of the Co-op, being a participant (or even being present) during a distribution session acquainted individuals with vocabulary and knowledge of procedures and ideology which made it possible for them to speak as a Co-op person about those activities.

Formulation In speaking as Co-op people, speakers were able to evaluate the seriousness of actions with reference to the collection of people, by the choice they made in how they mentioned, named, or made reference to events, as in characterizing a situation as "a problem" or "trouble." The term "formulation" (Garfinkel and Sacks, 1970: 346) will be useful for such choices, a term roughly equivalent to Thomas' "definition of the situation," although here formulation will include characterizations of persons. These are not "accounts" (Scott and Lyman, 1968: 47) in that they are immediately neither excuses nor justifications, although they readily become the basis for either. Rather, such formulations show the talker as able to recognize and evaluate a situation with reference to the ideology of the collection of people. For example, one account of the conflict concerning the youths is as follows:

Example 2

Sheldon: . . . in this kind of situation I think . . . when anybody gives you that kind of trouble in the streets . . . (from A5 in appendix)

Sheldon is speaking as a Co-op person in example 2 as he formulates a situation as not only "trouble" but a particular variant, "that kind of trouble." This evaluation is negative, referring to previous unpleasant encounters with unspecified persons. A formulation of "trouble" reflects knowledge of what constitutes problems for Co-op people.[7] These problems may also have been problems for other residents who feared "the street." But warrant for talking about the situation during a Co-op meeting is that it entails the Co-op in some way participants see as important.

In the course of interaction, individuals speak as persons in particular collections of people, using both knowledge display and formulation. The selection of a particular collection and the techniques used are relevant to the potential conflict of ideologies. To understand how such conflicts can be resolved, it is necessary to understand the interactional structures which lead individuals to speak as persons in collections of people in the first place. Although Co-op people readily spoke as Co-op people, few were heard speaking for the Co-op.

2.2 Speaking for the Co-op

More is at stake when a person "speaks for" a collection of people, since his or her statements are then attributable to, and interpretable as, relevant to the collection as a whole, rather than to the individuals who make up the collection of people. The perspective and ideology of the collection of people is the basis used by a speaker to interpret situations with reference to the goals of the collection and to formulate situations *vis-à-vis* the collection. But beyond that are the actions, including especially words, used to implement policies explicitly in the name of the collection.

In "speaking for" a collection of people, the talker claims to represent it. This sort of behavior is expected of officials of an organization, those having a "representative role" (Parsons, 1951: 100), and is characteristic of persons who are official spokesmen or spokeswomen for businesses, voluntary organizations, sports teams, etc.[8] Those who are elected or appointed to serve in such a capacity include both corporation presidents and "mouth pieces" of groups outside the law.

This study presents a broader focus by considering those individuals who take it upon themselves to serve as spokesmen or spokeswomen to others for various collections of people. In the Co-op, individuals by and large selected themselves to speak for the Co-op. Such unofficial spokesmen or spokeswomen may be recognized as speaking for a collection of people either by representation or enforcement.

Representation Speakers show themselves as representing what the collection of people ought or ought not to be or do. Individuals make use of plural references terms which include the self, such as "we," along with linguistic forms such as modals (ought, must, etc.) (Conein, unpublished; Spiegelberg, 1973) to express the underlying morality of that collection of people, such as when Joel commented on the importance of the image of the Co-op:

Example 3

Joel: . . . for the interests of the Co-op developing as a community institution, we've got to keep clean in all senses of the word. (from A14 in appendix)

Joel speaks as a Co-op person in example 3 as he displays knowledge of goals of the Co-op. But more than this knowledge display is present, for Joel takes on a representative role in stating what the Co-op ought to be like, doing this by using both "we" and the colloquial modal form ("we got to keep clean"), reflecting what "ought to" be rather than what just might happen to be the case. Thus Joel shows acceptance of the ideology of the collection of people as he displays himself as representing that collection of people.

Enforcement. Speakers show themselves as taking actions for the collection of people, as in enforcing rules or customs. For instance, Martin's second account of getting the youths to leave recounts this interchange with the youths:

Example 4

Martin: . . . I said:
  "Look, you know the Co-op isn't open, we got to take care of all this stuff,"
and you know, I said:
  "The rule is that we don't want people hanging around when we're cleaning up and finishing up and getting the stuff out of here . . ." (from A12 in appendix)

Martin cited Co-op policy: "The rule is," which he followed by acting directly in performing the act implicit in the rule as he "pushed them out." The same phrase appears in both versions of the story, that given at the start of the meeting (A11) and that given further along (A12), although the first instance is mitigated ("I kind of pushed them out a little bit") and the second, lengthier report gives additional details which show more of the actions which Martin made. But in both cases Martin shows himself speaking (and also acting) for the Co-op as he took on the representative role.

The possibility of enforcement by an individual or individuals in a collection of people is implicit in a threat or promise, for it assumes the individual occupies a representative role within a collection of people, and is in some way entitled to implicate others to take action. An example of a threat appears in these materials, but it is once removed, in that the speaker reports another to have made a threat, "I'm going to bring my people in here" (from A8) and will be discussed further along.

During food distribution sessions, some individuals were more likely than others to speak for the Co-op. Those who did were the main channel for spreading information about meeting decisions or happenings at distribution sessions. They were the ones likely to correct violations or enforce Co-op regulations. Other Co-op people retreated from a representative role, and preferred to emphasize the individual self as the person participating in the Co-op, rather than the collectivity (cf. Goffman's discussions on modes of presenting self (1959), and also 1967: 31–33; 1974: 519–521 and 1981: 145).

The conditions which lead specific individuals to take on a representative role and speak for a collection of people may be only incidentally linked to the internal structure of interaction, and more a matter of power relations or the strength of ideological commitment. Both internal and external factors may then govern whether representation alone or a more active enforcement is employed to put into effect the ideology of the relevant collection of people. These questions need to be explored generally, but in the following pages, they will be examined in the context of the Co-op ideology.

3. Presenting Co-op ideology

The analysis which follows examines the reports of conflicts described above, in order to show how elements of the Co-op ideology appear in what the Co-op people said as they told of these conflicts. Two principles from the ideology sketched above (p.140), cooperative behavior (Principle 1) and commitment to the Co-op (Principle 2), were minor issues in these incidents. The other two – the overall preference for peace and harmony (Principle 3) and for openness in encouraging participation in the Co-op (Principle 4) – proved to be major themes. First I shall focus on what the Co-op people reported they did, and then on how the others are said to have responded. Of primary concern are the formulations made of situations and of people, as these provide evidence of Co-op ideology. Amongst the instances of speaking as Co-op people are some in which people assumed a representative role. These are especially important for locating ideological themes.

3.1 The reports of the Co-op peoples' actions

In the accounts of the conflict, Co-op people were led to explain why they took the man to court, told the woman to leave, and pushed the youths out. The reports contain information about what the Co-op people did in the immediate face-to-face situation as they spoke as Co-op people either in the meetings or to me in the interviews. The people at the meetings relied on what was said and what they knew of other situations in order to understand what was reported, i.e., they employed their knowledge as Co-op people in interpreting the reports. Importantly, this included knowledge of Co-op ideology.

In the conflict over the man's parked car, Ben began by speaking as a participant in a small collection of people – himself and Sheldon – the ones who were attacked. His initial formulation of the event was neutral: "As far as the incident went on the 18th" (A1). As he continued in the same utterance, he assumed a representative role: "we've got a court hearing" (A1). But he introduced ambiguity, in whether he was continuing to speak for the small collection of people or whether his referent was now the Co-op. As Ben and Sheldon presented more information, it became evident they were worried about further involvements, not only of individuals, but of the Co-op, and of confrontations for the Co-op people which might result.

In their action of pushing the man's car out of the driveway area, Ben and Sheldon were acting in a representative role for the Co-op, making possible the delivery of the produce for Co-op distribution later that day. As Ben explained, "his car was in the way and we pushed it" (A4). They were concerned about Co-op operation that day and other days. Although on that day it was Ben and Sheldon who had been to the city market, on other days others went. Their action was an instance of enforcement, and was justified in terms of keeping the Co-op open and operating.

Joel formulated the woman's actions as one "who came in the Co-op week in and week out to steal from the Co-op" (A8). Throughout he showed himself acting for the Co-op in telling the woman to leave. He explained the action at the meeting as "when we threw her out one day" (A8) and in the interview he reported that he had stood on a table and told those in the Co-op that day: "I'm not going to let her leave without paying" (A9). He added that he "got support from the people there," (A9) showing that others were accepting his activities in his assumed representative role. Caren, too, referred to this act of enforcement, but did not specify the agent who assumed the representative role and accused the woman of stealing: "throw[ing] an absolute fit whenever she was accused." (A10) The minor differences in the meeting and interview reports which Joel gave and in the meeting report which Caren made, do not change the fact that the woman left and did not return.

The youths were also defined as a problem in terms of the Co-op operation. Martin spoke for the Co-op in his account to the meeting. He began by formulating their actions as "they refused to leave the place" (A11), then pointed to the particular fact that they were "kind of hanging around the money table" (A11). He told them to go.

In the second and longer version of the conflict, told later in the meeting, Martin referred to a "rule" (A12) that outsiders shall not be present, and made efforts to apply that rule, acting in a representative role. Since his talk did not succeed, he admitted to pushing them out of the door, acting for the Co-op in removing the youths from the Co-op. Sheldon at the meeting described such action more colloquially as "someone deliberately comes along and kicks them out" (A15).

In each instance, the response of the Co-op people in speaking for the Co-op was based on Co-op operational needs. Yet violence or the threat of force appeared, in each case, to be a contradiction to the Co-op ideology of harmony (Principle 3). The man's attack on the Co-op people was provoked by their laying hands (some would say violently) on the man's car, although it is also true that Co-op people reacted non-violently to his attack. In the case of the woman, the call for "support" was in the context of about thirty people using the Co-op, and presumably the threat of force was a factor in achieving the results desired. She left. In the incident of the youths, violence was resorted to after words alone had not produced the desired results.

Those at the meeting were able to recognize and monitor the appropriateness of what was said whenever someone reported speaking or acting for the Co-op. Each time someone was excluded, it was a contradiction to the ideology of openness (Principle 4). Someone might have suggested that such actions were in opposition to the Co-op ideology. No one, however, suggested that these people should not have assumed representative roles, and taken the actions they did.

The Co-op people at the meeting were also called upon to evaluate the reports they heard of the words and actions of the others involved in the conflicts. And, each time, the others were blacks and also lived in the neighborhood.

3.2 The reports of the others' actions

The fact that these were interracial conflicts specifically appeared in the reports of the others' response to the Co-op actions. In each incident, the Co-op people who were involved knew that the other(s) were black, and the people at the meeting either knew this from the start, suspected this, or at some point during the discussion at the meeting learned this fact, as was shown in the summaries of the incidents given above. The extent to which the black/white issues was relevant for each individual present at the meeting is not the issue. What is important is its presence in the discussion at the meeting as an element of the response of the Co-op people.

According to the Co-op people, the others responded not only as individuals, but also as members of a collection of people – blacks. In each instance, the reports by the Co-op people of the others' actions included something that the outsiders were reported to have said to the Co-op people. The black/white issue surfaced in each of these reported replies. The black verbal response, as reported by whites, was to see the Co-op as white.

In the case of the man, Ben reported that the man had rejected an appeal to the community as coming from whites:

> And as he so bluntly put it:
> "Fuck the community,"
> and it seemed like he generally sort of identified the Co-op as being pretty white . . .
> (from A3 in appendix)

Caren, in mentioning that he was black, at the same time denied its relevance to the conflict.

> . . . and it has nothing to do with his being black, and if he wants to bring that up as an issue, that's his business (from A6 in appendix)

Sheldon commented on the man's attitude in his interview, viewing the man's attitude as simply opposed to all whites:

> . . . and he had these very confused spread-out grudges that were basically against all white people in general . . . (from A7 in appendix)

Here, and in Caren's comment, it is still possible to see the man as being presented as speaking for blacks. But this role was much clearer in the case of the woman.

The woman was quoted directly by Joel at the meeting as claiming to speak for blacks as she threatened a racial confrontation after being told to leave:

> . . . when we threw her out one day she said:
> "I'm going to bring my people in here . . ." (from A8 in appendix)

As noted above, in the interview the same quotation appeared with the epithet "Racist" added (cf. A9). In her interview, Caren quoted the woman also as making a direct reference to the interracial issue:

> . . . this woman would stand up and say:
> "But you're discriminating against me, or saying this because I'm black."
> And she was just trying to use her color to rip off the Co-op . . . (from A10 in appendix)

In the meeting, Sheldon viewed the youths as trying to annoy the Co-op people. According to Sheldon:

> ... they were staying to hassle and harass, you know, ... to see how far they could go, to see how far they could push you . . . (from A12 in appendix)

Both colloquial formulations used by Sheldon suggest the youths' actions were in terms of individual goals of the youths in opposition to the collective Co-op enterprise.

Although Martin gave two reports of the incident at the meeting, both included threats by the youths.

> ... they kept threatening us, in fact, one of them threw a bolt at me ... (from A11 in appendix)
> ... they were still swinging their spikes, and one threw, one threw a spike at me ... they threatened they were going to kill me, which I didn't really think they were going to do . . . (from A12 in appendix)

The youths' words were not reported by Martin in the first account, and as the second continued, a quotation was given, but immediately glossed by Martin as nonsense.[9]

> ... the kids simply refused to go ... and they gave the same old shit that they have before, which is,
> "Why do I have to leave?"
> and duh duh di duh and dah, and it doesn't really matter what they said ... (from A12 in appendix)

But in Caren's interview, she was more explicit and reported that the youths had charged discrimination.

> The kids that have come in and stuff, have argued that they're being discriminated against . . . (from A13 in appendix)

In each conflict, the issue of black/white relations appeared. Blacks were reported as assuming representative roles, and emphasizing their (status) identity as blacks. And, in each case, it was a report by a white individual that preserved this information, and represented the others as viewing the Co-op as non-egalitarian.

4. Egalitarian ideology and the conflicts

The Co-op people showed awareness that these were interracial conflicts. The presence of the black/white issue added a special significance to the actions they took. In none of the accounts of the three situations did Co-op people suggest that the actions they took were desirable. In each instance a central figure in the incident saw that there were aspects of the situation which they formulated as "unfortunate." In doing this, they showed themselves as liberals who supported an egalitarian ideology.

> ... it was really unfortunate, because it was a black/white kind of thing ... (Ben, from A4 in appendix)

... and it was a bogus threat ... and it's an unfortunate situation, you know, that we don't have a larger black representation in the Co-op . . . (Joel, from A8 in appendix)

It was an unfortunate incident at the Co-op last week too, involving two of the neighborhood kids . . . (Martin, from A11 in appendix)

The conflicts were formulated as "unfortunate" by individuals who also were part of a collection of egalitarian people. Some of these same Co-op people showed insight that the lack of blacks in the Co-op was a relevant issue, and expressed that as Ben did:

So, anyway, from my point of view the whole scene sort of like brought home to me the basic fact that generally speaking, there's practically no black participation in the Co-op . . . (from A3 in appendix)

Although this statement begins by claiming the viewpoint as his own, this formulation of "no black participation in the Co-op" was said in a Co-op meeting,[10] with other Co-op people present. No one objected.

In one sense, the whole account of the woman in the meeting was itself a commentary on the black/white theme in the incident with the man. In the meeting at which the account of the conflict with the youth was given, the black/white issue surfaced again, with Joel saying:

...we're not going to attract any black people down to the Co-op ... any more than we're going to get an increase in white members . . . (from A14 in appendix)

How did the Co-op people justify taking actions which had racial overtones? The basic mechanism was that all these actions were shown as essential for maintaining the Co-op as an institution. The factual basis for this position was established by people speaking as Co-op people. The fact that these actions were seen as essential to maintain the Co-op does not complete the argument for their justification. It was possible that someone could have said that if the maintenance of the Co-op required exclusion of black people, it would have been better not to have had a Co-op. It follows that for the Co-op people quoted here who reported their actions (or gave their consensus to the actions reported) the maintenance of the Co-op was a source of value which justified their actions. In other words, they were able to present themselves as good Co-op people, even though they had taken actions which they would describe as unfortunate actions, and which might result in their being considered racist.

The initial justification for the actions occurred as the conflicts were formulated as problems. At the meeting the incident with the man was labelled "trouble" (A5), the woman was a "troublemaker" (A8), and the youths were there to "hassle and harass" (A12), and in the interview they were seen as "making trouble" (A13, cf. note 7 on page 159).

Further justification of Co-op actions was accomplished as Co-op people presented additional information on the combatants. These formulations were briefly that the man was crazy, the woman a thief, and the youths were a danger. These seem at first glance to be reported as facts. Yet there are alternative ways of formulating these reported actions, such as the Man was hot-tempered, the woman was careless, and the youths were unruly. But given the formulation of the man as crazy, the woman a thief, and the youths a danger, the Co-op people could then turn again to the ideology and could invoke principles in the Co-op ideology which made certain exclusions permissible, if not mandatory:

1. People who are unreasonable, like the man, and can not reasonably engage in cooperative activity. (Principle 1, co-operation.)
2. People who steal, like the woman, and are not committed to group interests. (Principle 2, commitment)
3. People who annoy or threaten Co-op people, like the youths, and destroy the atmosphere of peace and harmony. (Principle 3, harmony)

Thus a consequence of these actions was that the Co-op was not able to serve the whole community (Principle 4, openness), since it was used by only a subset, namely those who were white. Although it was repeated several times at this and other meetings that the Co-op people wanted greater participation of blacks, blacks did not generally participate. In their commentaries, Co-op people showed not only that they recognized this, but also that they regretted it.

5. Conclusion

During this period, despite the expressed desire of Co-op people to increase the level of black participation, that level remained minimal. In the reports of the conflicts, it might seem that such a result was inevitable. Yet an effort might have been made to reach the man directly (as Glen indeed suggested) rather than pushing his car out of the way; the woman might have been approached privately instead of by a public confrontation; and the youths might have been persuaded verbally, rather than pushed. One can not rule out the possibility that alternative ways of handling the situations could have contributed to a reputation for the Co-op as a place at which blacks were welcome.

The ways of handling the situation were a consequence of the fact that Co-op people took a representative role in performing Co-op activities, and implementing Co-op ideology. Ideological themes were reflected by the formulations made of the situations. In each case, the actions of Co-op people were shown as necessary for the operation of the Co-op. At the same time, these actions were inconsistent with another ideological theme endorsed by the same persons, an egalitarian ideology of respecting if not furthering black/white integration.

On the other hand, the black people are not described in these incidents as expressing surprise at the actions of the Co-op people. The Co-op people show them as almost expecting the Co-op to be discriminatory, and even labeling Co-op people as racists. It is not argued here that the black perception reported was characteristic of the neighborhood, but rather that the whites presented a uniform view of black feelings. It is an interesting question as to why holders of an egalitarian ideology should expect to be seen by others as bigots.

An ideological conflict would seem to involve a competition between simultaneously held but conflicting beliefs. Such a conflict would be resolved on the basis of which ideals were more strongly held, or perhaps even which were considered more expedient at a particular moment. The ideological conflict examined here suggests another and perhaps more common basis for understanding the resolution of such conflict. Here the formulation of the situation as "trouble" led to actions taken to support this belief which ran counter to the behavior demanded by other beliefs. In speaking (and acting) for a particular collection of people, individuals as they participated in the Co-op were able to ignore the fact that few if any of their black neighbors participated in the Co-op. Co-op people accepted a Co-op which was white, despite their support of a liberal ideology which would have preferred greater black participation.

The preference for one ideology over another, while not necessarily a conscious choice, was a legitimated option once the individuals defined themselves as committed to the institutional needs of the Co-op. They displayed themselves as committed to that collection of people by speaking for it. A more diffuse collection of people to which they were also committed – those who held egalitarian views – did not prevent the interracial conflicts from occurring. But in reports of the conflicts, egalitarian themes also surfaced. The crucial issue for social action then becomes the discovery of when and how ideological themes, which do not appear relevant in one situation, can come to become defined as relevant. Then a deliberate choice can be made between ideologies, rather than an automatic commitment to the ideology of one collection of people.

Appendix

1. The angry man

A1 Ben: As far as the incident went on the 18th, I guess he must be mentioned; we've got a court hearing and everything on the
Sheldon: Yeah.
Ben: fifth, and he's going to be summoned, and if he doesn't show up, there'll be a warrant put on him.   (Meeting, 1/29/73, 001–007)
A2 Ben: . . . here was something we would have to deal with on an on-going basis, you know, and any sort of like ah, brute warfare, that we, you know, undertake

him in, it's going to be sort of like drawn out and just exacerbated, so–
Glen: What I'm interested in, outside of the fact that I'm really sorry that you
got hurt is, that if we do have to–, what does he look like, for one thing, so I can
avoid him. [Laughter]
Ben: He's about 5'11", he's black with pretty short hair–
Glen: He's black?
Ben: Yeah, he's got a little mustache, pretty thin, he's slim, and his car is the
green one . . .   (Meeting, 1/29/73, 034–050)

A3   Ben: So, anyway, from my point of view the whole scene sort of like brought
home to me the basic fact that generally speaking, there's practically no black
participation in the Co-op.
Glen: Uuhuh.
Ben: And as he so bluntly put it:
"Fuck the community,"
and it seemed like he generally sort of identified the Co-op as being pretty white,
and you know . . . I really felt like if we had some sort of, some kind of
showdown, you know, it would have been, you know, a real bad scene for a lot
of other reasons . . .   (Meeting, 1/29/73, 080–091)

A4   Ben: . . . his car was in the way and we pushed it, and he came out and got really
pissed off, you know, and came out swinging eventually, you know, and it was
really unfortunate, because it was a black/white kind of thing . . .
                                                            (Interview, 5/16/73)

A5   Sheldon: I'd like to say in this kind of situation I think that is exactly the thing
you do, I think, when anybody gives you that kind of trouble in the streets . . .
                                                            (Meeting, 1/29/73, 127–130)

A6   Caren: There's no reason why he's that way, because – except he's crazy, and it
has nothing to do with his being black, and if he wants to bring that up as an
issue, that's his business.   (Meeting, 1/29/73, 146–150)

A7   Sheldon: . . . entirely insane, he was just crazy . . . he had these very confused
spread-out grudges that were basically against all white people, because he's a
black guy who stated he hated white people in general . . .
                                                            (Interview, 6/29/74)

2.   *The indignant woman*

A8   Joel: Troublemakers in the Co-op who are, who have been black have always
thrown this up into our faces. There's a woman who came in the Co-op week in
and week out to steal from the Co-op, and when we threw her out one day, she
said:
"I'm going to bring my people in here."
and it was a bogus threat,
Caren: Yeah, she hasn't done it yet.
Joel: And it's an unfortunate situation, you know, that we don't have a larger
black representation in the Co-op, but I don't think we should be cowed into a
corner by that fact.   (Meeting 1/29/73 151–165)

A9   Joel: The most difficult day I ever had there was at the peak of the Co-op buying,
ah, when people were coming in and picking out their own orders. There was a
black woman came in, and I was told as a co-ordinator that day, that this

woman was stealing, ah food, that she was coming in, filling her basket and just walking out without paying, and she had done this two weeks in a row and nobody ever stopped her. Well, I checked her out [Mmmmmm], I watched her, and ah, determined that was the case, and she was about ready to – she just walked right past the cashier, and was about ready to leave the door, and ah, I said:

"You're not leaving without paying,"

and ah, you know, indignant black woman shouted:

"Racist, I'm going to get my people in here,"

and that type of thing. [Oh wow] And I just got up on one, on top of one of the tables, and said – there were about thirty people present in the Co-op at the time, it was very crowded – and I said:

"I need your co-operative help in this situation, I need support here. This woman is not – has not paid for her groceries, and I'm not going to let her leave without paying for it. [Unhuh] I want your support in this. She says that she will, she'll bring her people down here. Uh, I don't care what she does, but she's not going to rip off the Co-op."

And I got support from the people there, ah, and she left without the produce. I didn't know whether she unloaded her basket or just what, but I do remember that the Co-op supported me, and the woman never came back [Unhuh] and the situation was rectified. It was a very emotional situation and very [Yeah] racially – racial things are always difficult, and we've always wanted to see a larger black participation in the Co-op.   (Interview, 5/20/74)

A10 Caren: . . . There was one woman who went in there and consistently filled up her whole cart and then paid for like one dozen eggs or something – I forget what her name was, Mrs. White or Mrs. Brown or something – and throw an absolute fit whenever she was accused . . . a lot of people have used – this woman was black — like a lot of people have used this race as a way of living off the Co-op, because this woman would stand up and say:

"But you're discriminating against me, or saying this because I'm black."

And she was just trying to use her color to rip off the Co-op, and she's not the only one who's done it, I mean, the kids that have come in . . .
                    (Interview, 5/6/73)

3. *The neighborhood youths*

A11 Martin: It was an unfortunate incident at the Co-op last week too, involving two of the neighborhood kids . . . at 7:30 when the place closed up, they refused to leave the place, and they were kind of hanging around the money table. So somehow I, perhaps I– I made a little mistake which is I kind of pushed them out a little bit, which may have been a mistake on my part, but I don't think they were going any other way, so they kept threatening us, in fact, one of them threw a bolt at me, and finally I called the police.

                    (Meeting, 3/19/73, first account)

A12 Sheldon: . . . And it sounded to me like they were staying to hassle and harass, you know, to see how far they could go, to see how far they could push you, and if they're not going to go, then you do have to use physical force.

Martin: Yeah, well that's what I eventually did, I pushed them out. They came

back in when I pushed them out . . . the kids simply refused to go . . . and they gave the same old shit that they have before, which is:
"Why do I have to leave?"
and duh duh di duh and dah, and it doesn't really matter what they said, so I simply said, I said:
"Look, you know the Co-op isn't open, we got to take care of all this stuff," and you know, I said:
"The rule is that we don't want people hanging around when we're cleaning up and finishing up and getting the stuff out of here, because we want to go home,"
so I kind of opened the door, and I kind of moved and I kind of very gently I thought, kind of guided them out, showing them the light . . . they were still swinging their spikes, and one threw, one threw a spike at me . . . they threatened they were going to kill me, which I didn't really think they were going to do . . .   (Meeting, 3/19/73, second account)

A13 Caren: The kids that have come in and stuff, have argued that they're being discriminated against and stuff, well, there's been similar incidents that I've heard about, about kids coming in and making trouble for people and stealing food . . .   (Interview, 5/6/73, follows A10)

A14 Joel: . . . we're not going to attract any black people down to the Co-op if they're going to get ripped off, or feel that it's a tense situation, like it's where the corner gang could go, any more than we're going to get an increase in white members. So, for the interests of the Co-op developing as a community institution, we've got to keep clean in all senses of the word.   (Meeting, 3/19/73)

A15 Sheldon: . . . an awful lot of people are really hesitant about doing anything about the kids and therefore sometimes they're there for half an hour or an hour before someone deliberately comes along and kicks them out, and that's not a good situation . . .   (Meeting, 3/19/73)

Notes

I would like to thank Allen Grimshaw and William Labov for their comments on earlier drafts of this chapter.

1   The Carverton (pseudonym) Co-op was a weekly pre-ordered food cooperative which operated successfully in Philadelphia in the 1970s, with weekly sales ranging from $100 to $1,500. Co-op people lived principally in Census Tract 90 (3,993 residents in 1970, 28% black) and to a lesser degree in Tract 91 (61.8% black of 2,814). Population of the area declined about 5% (city loss was 25%) by 1980, mostly due to loss of blacks in Tract 90. Data for 1975, which would be relevant here, do not exist, according to both the Philadelphia Planning Board and to U.S. Census Information Office.

2   For Rothschild-Witt, "alternative institutions may be defined in terms of their members' resolve to build organizations which are parallel to, but outside established institutions, and which fulfill social needs (for education, food, medical aid, etc.)"

3   Data include records of thirty-six meetings, retrospective interviews of

thirty-two people, a users' census, records of the Co-op and the neighborhood, as well as observer's notes. Meetings were generally held twice a month, open to all, although attendance never exceeded twenty, and was usually five or six people. Participant observation extended over three years.

4   A leaflet prepared by the Co-op as part of a campaign to get new members suggests some of the Co-op ideology. It begins: "Although the prevailing incentive for belonging to the Carverton Co-op is to get food cheap, its actual worth and purpose goes beyond money. The Co-op's real potential lies in its presence in the community as a place for people to meet and talk, exchange ideals and feelings."

5   The presentation of people in talk entails a list of features, such as race or a name, some of which are supplied, others presumably retrievable, since all people have them. Here gender was shown in the pronouns used in all three accounts. Age was a factor for the youths. During the meeting a name was supplied for the man but it was not used, nor were names used for the woman or the youths. The absence of, or emphasis given to a feature is a clue to the relevance of that characteristic for the situation.

6   For reasons of space, I give quotations without the context needed for a complete evaluation and understanding (cf. T. Labov, 1980, for full presentations). The excerpts used here have been "smoothed," i.e., specifically conversational features removed for the most part so as to make them more readable.

7   In my interviews I formulated situations in terms of "problems" or "troubles" which the answers reflected. Since I consulted people as experts, they often "spoke for" the Co-op. Of the fifteen excerpts in the appendix, five (A4, A7, A9, A10, A13) are from interviews and are so labeled.

8   Parsons, in his discussion of the internal differentiation of roles within collectivities, identifies a "representative role" as a leadership role whose "special concern is with relations of the collectivity and its members outside itself" (1951: 100).

9   Martin showed he was not interested in what the youth said by using nonsense words and denying that what was said mattered.

10   In an interview nearly eighteen months later, Joel said much the same thing, ". . . and we've always wanted to see a larger black participation in the Co-op" (from A9 in appendix).

7 Oracular reasoning in a psychiatric exam: the resolution of conflict in language

HUGH MEHAN

Men define situations as real and they are real in their consequences.

W.I. Thomas[1]

The two major purposes of this chapter are (1) to show how competing definitions of the situation are constructed and revealed in ongoing interaction within an institutionalized setting (a mental hospital), and (2) to show how institutionalized power is displayed and used to resolve disputes over conflicting definitions of the situation. In so doing, I will be commenting on the famous "Thomas Theorem." Parts of what I say will provide support for Thomas's idea that people define situations as real in and through their interaction. Other parts will stretch the limits of the theorem. Not all definitions of situations have equal authority. Competing definitions are resolved by imposing institutional definitions on lay persons' definitions. This "ironicizing of experience" (Pollner, 1975) requires a modification in Thomas's consensual world view, which I have reformulated as follows:

All people define situations as real; but when powerful people define situations as real, then they are real *for everybody involved* in their consequences.

My presentation will take a circuitous route. Before showing how institutionalized power is used to impose a certain definition on the situation, I will place the discussion in the context of debates about the thinking of "primitive" and "advanced" peoples. After introducing the notion of "oracular reasoning" (a concept which is central to the understanding of the events which follow), I will examine closely the interaction between a board of examining psychiatrists and a mental patient.

1. The thinking of primitive and advanced peoples

The reasoning of "primitives" (pre-literate people) has long been disparaged for not being logical. The lineage of the disparagement has been traced through enlightenment thinkers by Shweder (1984). It continues today in Hallpike (1979). Pre-literate people show a propensity to be closed minded (Horton, 1967), do not draw accurate conclusions from well-formulated premises (Luria, 1976), make less elaborate categorizations (Maccoby and Modiano, 1966) and do not transfer their knowledge from one situation to another (Lave, 1983).

More recently, developmental and comparative cognitive scientists have begun to look critically at these conclusions. Spurred on by ethnographic observations which show that pre-literates perform sophisticated cognitive operations in some (often naturally occurring) situations but not in other (often experimental) situations (Cole *et al.*, 1971; Serpell, 1976; Scribner and Cole, 1975; Goody, 1977; M. Donaldson, 1978; Gelman, 1978; Lave, 1983), they have begun to examine the research conditions which gave rise to conclusions about a depressed cognitive capacity among pre-literates. A new interpretation has been forthcoming, one that suggests that pre-literates are every bit as logical as literate people, if researchers take care to examine cognitive activities within the meaningful contexts of native life (Scribner and Cole 1975; Goody, 1977; Hutchins, 1980; Berland, 1982; Ginsberg, 1983).

This line of thinking has the consequence of equalizing the thinking of pre-literate and literate people by placing them both on the higher plane of sophisticated thinking. Pre-literate and literate people are equally logical and rational from this point of view.

Entering this discussion about human cognition obliquely, I, too, will draw parallels between the thinking of pre-literate and literate people. But instead of rescuing formal logic and rational thinking by demonstrating that schooled and unschooled people think alike and equally abstractly, I will, like Shweder (1977, 1984) make a different suggestion: poorly educated and well-educated people think alike, but their thinking is not as rational, not as formal as suggested by the recent wave of critical ethnographers. Instead, both well-educated and poorly educated people give extensive evidence of "oracular reasoning." Oracular reasoning, as I am using the term here, is a process of arguing from and defending a basic belief. People maintain the truth or efficacy of a belief by denying or repelling evidence which is contrary to or opposes the belief.

Before describing how the practices of oracular reasoning are worked out in the discourse of a psychiatric exam, I will locate its origins in "primitive thought," and point out studies which suggest that similar devices operate in a variety of other, modern, domains.

1.1 Oracular reasoning in a "primitive" society

The quintessential example of oracular reasoning is found in Evans-Pritchard's (1973) account of the Azande of Africa. When the Azande are faced with important decisions – decisions about where to build their homes, or whom to marry, or whether the sick will live, for example – they consult an oracle. They prepare for these consultations by following a strictly prescribed ritual. First, a substance is gathered from the bark of a certain type of tree. Then this substance is prepared in a special way in a séance-like ceremony. The Azande then poses a question to the oracle in a way that permits a simple yes or no answer and feeds the substance to a small chicken. The person consulting the oracle decides before hand whether the death of the chicken will signal an affirmative or negative response, and so they always receive an unequivocal answer to their questions.

For monumental decisions, the Azande add a second step. They feed the substance to a second chicken, asking the same question, but reversing the importance of the chicken's death. If in the first consultation sparing the chicken's life meant the oracle said "yes," in the second reading, the oracle must now kill the chicken to once more reply in the affirmative and be consistent with the first response.

Seemingly, insuperable difficulties accrue to people who hold such beliefs, because the oracle could contradict itself. What if, for example, the first consultation of the oracle produces a positive answer and then the second produces a negative reply? Or, suppose that someone else consults the oracle about the same question, and contradictory answers occur? What if the oracle is contradicted by later events – the house site approved by the oracle, for example, is promptly flooded; or the wife the oracle selected dies or turns out to be infertile? How is it possible for the Azande to continue to believe in their oracle in the face of so many evident contradictions of their faith?

The answers to these questions are both simple and complex. Simple, because the Azande do not see the events just listed as contradictions, as threats to the oracle. Complex, because of the reasoning practices that are invoked to keep the efficacy of the oracle intact. The Azande know that an oracle exists. That is their beginning premise. All that subsequently happens is interpreted in terms of that "incorrigible proposition" – a proposition that one never admits to be false whatever happens; one that is compatible with any and every conceivable state of affairs (Gasking, 1955: 432 as quoted in Pollner, 1975). The Azande employ what Evans-Pritchard (1973: 330) calls "secondary elaborations of belief," practices which explain the failure of the oracle by retaining the unquestioned faith in oracles.

The culture provides the Azande with a number of ready-made explanations of the oracle's seeming contradictions. The secondary elaborations of belief that explain the failure of the oracle attribute the failure to other circumstances, some of this world, some of the spirit world – the wrong variety of poison being gathered, breach of taboo, witchcraft, the anger of the owners of the place where the poison plants grow, the age of the poison, the anger of ghosts, or sorcery.

By explaining away contradictions through these secondary elaborations of the belief in oracles, the reality of a world in which oracles are a basic feature is reaffirmed. Failures do not challenge the oracle. They are elaborated in such a way that they provide evidence for the constant success, the marvel, of oracles. Beginning with the incorrigible belief in oracles, all events reflexively become evidence for that belief.

Recent research suggests that maintaining belief by denying or repelling contradictory evidence is not limited to so-called primitives. Well-educated "modern" people also give evidence of oracular reasoning.

1.2 Oracular reasoning in modern form

Everyday reasoning.   Wason (1977) reviewed a set of delightful experiments that he and Johnson-Laird have conducted, with the same problems presented to subjects alternatively in abstract and concrete form. Again and again, the subjects of these ingenious experiments seemed to be influenced by the context and the content of the problems. When information was presented in semantically coherent form, such as stories, or with real-life manifestations, subjects performed consistently better than when information was presented in algebraic or symbolic form. When the totality of these studies is considered, we find that people do not employ problem-solving procedures that would challenge or falsify the hypothesis being tested nearly as often as they employ problem-solving procedures that confirm the hypothesis under consideration.

Pollner and McDonald-Wikler (1985) examined the routine transactions of a family with their severely mentally retarded child. They reported that the family employed practices which sustained the family's belief in the competence of the child in the face of overwhelming evidence to the contrary, i.e., a team of medical practitioners had diagnosed the child as severely mentally retarded. The authors' observations of videotaped family interaction revealed that family members pre-structured the child's environment to maximize the likelihood that whatever the child did could be seen as meaningful, intentional activity. The child's family would establish a definition of the situation and use it as a frame of reference for interpreting and describing any and all of the child's subsequent behavior. They also tracked the child's ongoing behavior and developed physical or verbal contexts that could render the behavior intelligent and interactionally responsive.

Religious reasoning.   Millennial groups are organized around the prediction of some future events, for example, the second coming of Christ and the beginning of Christ's reign on earth, the destruction of the earth through a cataclysm – usually with a select group, the believers, slated for rescue from the disaster. Festinger *et al.* (1956) identify Montanists, Anabaptists, the followers of Sabbatai Zevi, as examples of millennial groups. (Festinger's account should be compared to Lofland's (1977) description of the "Divine Precepts" group.)

No millennial group is more fascinating than the Millerites. William Miller was a New England farmer who believed in literal fulfillment of biblical prophecy. In 1818, after a two-year study of the Bible, Miller reached the conclusion that the end of the world would occur in 1843. He slowly developed a following. The faithful took all the necessary precautions – including dissolving relationships, settling debts, selling possessions – and waited together for the second coming of Christ. When the fateful day came – and went – the faithful were confronted with a devastating contradiction to their belief (and lives which were in total disrepair). Their response to this devastation was amazing: instead of turning away from their religious beliefs and spiritual leaders, they used the failure of prophecy as further proof of the wonder and mystery of God. The leaders, far from doubting their basic belief in the second coming, elaborated their belief by citing errors in calculation and weakness in faith as reasons why God did not reveal Himself at the time they predicted. Group leaders retreated to their texts and emerged some time later with new calculations. The number of believers increased – as if conviction was deepened by evidence which contradicted their beliefs. Alas, after three more specific predictions failed, the group disbanded in disbelief.

Scientific reasoning. Oracular reasoning appears among scientists as well as among religious zealots, as Gould's (1981) chronicle of a long history of research conducted in defense of Caucasian racial superiority shows. Morton's craniology, Lombroso's criminal anthropology, and Burt's intelligence testing start from the premise that whites are superior to blacks, native Americans and other racial or ethnic groups. Gould describes the methodological errors and outright fraud which arose, often unintentionally, when researchers held too dearly to that basic belief. For example, Gould's meticulous re-analysis of Morton's data uncovered a systematic pattern of distortion in the direction of the preferred hypothesis. Statistics were summed inappropriately across groups and groups which seemed to counter the argument were excluded from statistical analysis. The overall effect of these practices was the production of data that confirmed the hypothesis of racial superiority, but did so by systematically manipulating or excluding potentially contradictory evidence

Gould says that the recurrence of racist uses of IQ tests and other measurement techniques is aided by "unconscious bias." This concept liberates us from the suspicion that all racists are cynical plotters against the truth and it implies the existence of a coherent structure of expectations about the phenomena of the world which guides the thoughts of scientists and nonscientists alike. But "unconscious bias" is too limited an idea for such a pervasive intellectual practice (Greenwood, 1984: 21). To the extent that unconscious biases are shared widely and perpetuated despite the use of empirical data and sound analytical procedures, they are not biases at all; they are collective conceptions about the structures and operation of the natural world.

2. Oracular reasoning in a psychiatric exam

These discussions have identified oracular reasoning in general terms. I want to show its practice concretely, in the detail of on-going discourse. To do so, I will discuss a "gatekeeping encounter" (Erickson, 1975) between a board of psychiatrists and a mental patient. Unlike most gatekeeping encounters (in which the gatekeeper is judging whether the applicant is worthy of *entering* an institution – a place of business, a college, a medical care center) in this encounter the gatekeepers are deciding whether the applicant can *leave* the institution (the mental hospital).

The materials used in this analysis come from an unusual source, which requires some comment. During the course of making his documentary film on a mental hospital in the State of Massachusetts, *Titicut Follies*, Frederick Wiseman filmed a "psychiatric out-take interview." The edited version of this interview appearing in the film is the one I use for the analysis which follows. The use of edited documentary film for discourse analysis, of course, places me at a disadvantage: I neither have the background knowledge of the setting normally available to ethnographers nor am I privy to the film-editing process. Nevertheless, the language in the interview is so provocative that I can not resist analyzing it. It is my hope that readers of the analysis will forgive problems associated with the data in exchange for the heuristics with the analysis.

I approached the analysis of this film as I have others: I have watched the film numerous times – both in private viewings and in courses I teach. I constructed a transcript of the interview (see appendix). The transcript and my memory of the audio and visual record served as the basis of my interpretation. After I completed the analysis which follows, I watched the film again, and made minor modifications – mostly concerning seating arrangements and the physical movements of the participants.

2.1 The basis of the conflict

The interview starts with the patient, Vladimir, being led into the examining room. He stands before a table, behind which are seated four members of the examining board. The head psychiatrist begins questioning the patient, but the interrogation quickly breaks down into an argument about the quantity and quality of the patient's treatment. After a number of exchanges, the head psychiatrist abruptly orders the patient to be taken away.

At this point, the film is edited; we see the members of the examining board give their interpretation of the case, and reach a conclusion about the patient's status.

The status of a patient's "career" in a hospital (Goffman, 1959a), indeed, about the patient's life, was established during the course of this gatekeeping encounter. He will remain in the hospital, diagnosed as a paranoid schizophrenic, and receive increased dosages of medicine.

At the outset, it is important to comment on the *social* nature of the outcome. The state of the patient's mental health was not the automatic result of a machine or a meter reading; the patient's mental state was determined by people, who participated in the assembly of an outcome. Here then we have a quintessential example of social construction (Berger, 1968; Garfinkel, 1967; Scheff, 1966; Cicourel, 1973; Mehan, 1983a, 1983b): the medical fact of mental illness is constructed in social circumstances.

While this event is social in that a medical fact is assembled in interaction, it is not social in another sense. The event is not social in the sense that the participants failed to reach a mutually agreed-upon definition of the situation. Here we have a set of circumstances in which people, a group of doctors and a patient, have interacted with each other for a stretch of time; each has arrived at a definition of the situation, but the definitions are considerably different, indeed, in conflict with each other.

By looking at the interaction which takes place among the participants in this meeting closely, I will try to determine how it is that the doctors and the patient come to conflicting definitions of the situation. Putting the punch line up front, I will try to demonstrate that both the doctors and the patient were engaged in "oracular reasoning." Normally associated with the procedures used by so-called primitive, or poorly educated peoples when making decisions about life, both the psychiatrists (a presumably well-educated group of people in an "advanced" Western society) and a mental patient (not as well educated, nonetheless a member of an industrialized society) are engaged in this mode of discourse.

The practices of oracular reasoning which are visible in the out-take interview include the following:

A basic premise or a fundamental proposition is presented which forms the basis of an argument.

When confronted with evidence which is potentially contradictory to a basic position, the evidence is ignored, repelled, or denied.

The presence of evidence which opposes a basic position is used reflexively as further support of the efficacy of the basic position.

I will now go through the transcript of the out-patient interview and show the presence of these features in both the doctors' *and* the patient's discourse. Doing so will enable us to understand how multiple and conflicting definitions of the situation were arrived at. The location of these features in the doctors' and not just the patient's discourse will illustrate the further point that oracular reasoning practices are not limited or confined to primitives or the uneducated; they make their appearance in the reasoning of highly educated thinkers. The persistent presence of oracular reasoning in a wide variety of domains recommends that we consider the possibility that oracular reasoning is a more widespread practice than often acknowledged.

2.2 The basic propositions

The basic premise or proposition which underlies the psychiatrists' definition of the situation concerns the health or rather, ill-health of the patient. From the doctors' point of view, the patient is mentally ill. The conclusion about this particular case is founded in even a more basic premise about a physician's expertise: the psychiatrist has access to a body of knowledge which is inaccessible to lay people. This premise gains ready empirical support: the patient is, after all, in a mental hospital. People who are in mental hospitals are presumed to be mentally ill (Scheff, 1966). The psychiatrists' commitment to this assumption is voiced by the head psychiatrist, who begins the hearing by saying:

> okay, now Vladimir, as I've promised you before, if I see enough improvement in you . . . (1)[2]

Although the patient, Vladimir, interrupts the psychiatrist before he finishes his introductory statement, the syntax of the psychiatrist's utterance enables us to infer the concluding phrase: (if you show improvement, then we will release you). The "need to show improvement" presupposes a prior mental state which is in need of improvment, i.e., mental illness. The fact of incarceration presupposes that same damaged mental state.

The psychiatrists' commitment to this assumption is reinforced throughout the hearing, especially as the head psychiatrist challenges the patient's arguments. He parries the patient's assertions of his mental health with questions about how he came to be a patient in the hospital ("what got you down here?"[3]) and his strange beliefs ("you felt the coffee was poison . . . you felt that people were mixing you up in your thinking" [7]).

The patient also has a basic premise from which he argues his definition of the situation. It is the exact opposite of the psychiatrists' definition: he is mentally healthy and does not deserve to be hospitalized. The patient's assertion of his mental health, argued in the face of underlying belief in psychiatric expertise, is to be found in virtually every one of his utterances during the hearing. Here are some quotes which give a sense of belief in his health and the depth of his commitment to this belief:

> my mind's perfect . . . I'm obviously logical, I know what I'm talking about. (2)
> . . . everytime I come in here you call me I am crazy. Now, what's, if, if its something you don't like about my face, that's I mean, that's another story. But that has nothing to do with my mental stability. (2)

2.3 The incorrigibility of the propositions

The reasoning of the psychiatrists and of the patient share another feature: they both retain their belief in their basic premises and do so despite evidence which is presented to the contrary. The psychiatrists and the patient maintain the incorrigibility of their propositions by deflecting, ignoring, or reinterpreting evidence which is contrary to their basic beliefs.

The incorrigibility feature of oracular reasoning is present in virtually every exchange between the psychiatrists and the patient. I include some of these exchanges here to show how each uses the evidence presented by the other to retain their commitment to their original belief.

The head psychiatrist asks the patient about his participation in hospital activities, including work, sports, and therapy. The assumption underlying the doctor's line of questioning is that affirmative answers to these questions indicate a positive approach on the part of the patient – a patient who is making an effort to improve himself. The following exchanges indicate that the patient has a different attitude about these issues:[3]

9. HP: Are you working here Vladimir?
10. Pt: No, there is no suitable work for me here. All I've got is, all I got is the kitchen and all they do is throw cup cups around. In fact, they got two television sets which are blaring, machines which are going, everything which is against the mind. There is one thing uh uh uh that a patient does need, and this is what I do know, absolutely, is is quiet, if I have a mental problem or even an emotional problem. I'm thrown in with over a hundred of them and all they do is yell, walk around, televisions are blaring, so that's doing my mind harm!
11. HP: Are you involved in any sports here?
12. Pt: There are no sports here. All I've got is a baseball and—and–a a glove, and that's it! There's nothing else. Hum. There's nothing else . . .
13. HP: Are you in any group therapy here?
14. Pt: No! There is no group, obviously I do not need group therapy, I need peace and quiet. See me. This place is disturbing me! Its harming me. . . I'm losing weight. Every, everything that's been happening to me is bad. And all I got, all I get is: "well, why don't you take medication?" Medication is disagreeable to me. There are people to whom you may not give medication. Obviously, and the medication that I got is hurting me, its harming me!

The doctor has phrased his questions (9, 11, 13) in such a way that a "yes" or "no" is the expected reply. Instead of providing the canonical yes or no response to the doctor's questions about work, sports, and therapy, the patient denies the premise underlying the doctor's questioning (and by extension his professional expertise). There *is no* work, there *are no* sports, there *is no* therapy:

> I was supposed to only come down here for observation. What observation did I get? You called me up a couple of times. (2)

In denying the doctor's fundamental assumption, the patient articulates his commitment to his own belief – his health:

> I do not need group therapy, I need peace and quiet . . . This place is disturbing me. (14)

The doctors do not respond immediately to the patient. We must wait until the patient is removed from the room to hear them articulate their reaction to his position. In general, they do not accept the patient's assertion of his health; in fact, they maintain the opposite - that "he's now falling apart" (25), "reverting" (30), "So he's not looking ready to be able to make it back to prison" (25). The patient's assertions on his behalf contribute to the doctors' conclusion. By his own admission, he doesn't participate in hospital activities, sports, work, and therapy. These are the very activities which have been established to help rehabilitate the patient. The patient's calculated avoidance of these rehabilitative activites becomes further proof of his recalcitrance and contribute to hs regression to a prior, unhealthy state of mind.

The attitude that the doctors and patient adopt toward medicine is a particularly telling example of how the same evidence can be used to support diametrically opposed positions. For the patient, medicine is for sick people; since he is healthy, he doesn't need it. In fact, to take medicine would be to admit that he *is* sick. Since he is healthy, he doesn't need the medicine. For the doctors, medicine is a part of a rehabilitation process; the patient's admitted reticence to take medicine is taken as a sign that the patient is both sick and unwilling to help in his own rehabilitation:

> Well I think what we have to do with him is, uh, put him on a higher dose of tranquilizers and see if we can bring the paranoid element under a little bit better control and see if we can get him back on medication. If he's taking it now, and I'm not even sure that he is. (36)

Coulter (1979: 101) discusses how psychiatrists may engage in "strategic contextualization" to make sense out of what is manifestly disorderly or contradictory. In this instance, we seem to have the opposite set of circumstances: a strategic contextualization which undermines the ostensive rationality or logic of the patient's presentation. The patient's very logic becomes an expression of disorder. This strategic decontextualization (cf. Molotch and Boden, 1985, who report on a similar process in the Watergate hearings), through the selective invocation of background knowledge and the demand for literal (yes/no) answers to questions, simultaneously frames and undercuts the speaker and the power of his discourse. From the psychiatrists' point of view, even the patient's expressed emotion is symptomatic of his disorder (cf. Rosenhan, 1973):

> the louder he shouts about going back the more frightened he indicates that he probably is. (32)

The patient has presented himself to the doctors as agitated and unreasonable, which is further proof that he is mentally ill.

Of course, there is another perspective on the patient's presentation of himself. He feels unjustly treated, confined against his will. Given this one, brief opportunity to present his case, he does so forcefully, energetically. Anticipating the prospect of leaving the hospital, he is excited, which is an understandable emotion for a person who sees himself languishing in a cell:

> I have a perfect right to be excited. I've been here for a year and a half, hum, and this place is doing me harm. (2)

With the patient's presentation of himself, as with the medicine and hospital activities, then, we have an instance in which the same state of affairs is interpreted differently from different perspectives (Gurwitsch, 1962; Schutz, 1962). This perspectivally induced perception contributes to the maintenance of belief on the part of the physicians and on the part of the patient. Both cling to their basic assertions, denying the information presented which has the potential of undermining those basic beliefs.

One member of the board of examiners makes this belief-validating process visible for us during her contribution to the board's interpretation of the case:

26. DR2: He argues in a perfectly paranoid pattern. If you accept his basic premise the rest of it is logical. But, the basic premise is not true.

She admits to the possibility of the patient's interpretation ("If you accept his basic premise"), entertains the viability of the patient's conclusions and the evidence he has presented in defense of his conclusions ("the rest is logical"), yet she does not change her opinion. She rejects the patient's line of reasoning and remains committed to her belief that the patient is mentally ill.

2.4 Competing languages of expression: the medical and the sociological

Two competing languages about the nature of mental illness have developed in the recent history of medicine. One, called the "medical model," treats the issue in biological terms. Because the body is an organism, its various parts are subject to pathologies. Mental illness has developed as an extension of this way of thinking. The mind is treated by analogy to an organ of the body; it, like the heart, liver or pancreas, is subject to disease. As an organ, it can be treated in the same way as disease to other organs, i.e., by medicine, confinement, operations to remove diseased tissues. The cause and the cure of mental illness, like physical illness, is to be found in the biological realm, a state or trait of the individual person.

The second, called the "sociological" or "deviance" model, treats the issue of mental illness in social and contextual terms. Denying the analogy between the mind and organs of the body, mental illness is talked about in terms of actions and rules. Mental illness is the label attached to people who break a certain set of society's rules. Its origins are to be found, therefore, not in biological pathologies, but in the social context of relationships between people, people who identify rule breakers, people who apply labels and in extreme cases, institutionalize the rule breakers (Scheff, 1966; Kitsuse, 1963; Becker, 1963; Goffman, 1959a; Laing, 1967; Szasz and Hollender, 1956). Mental illness is eliminated by rearranging social contexts such that bizarre behaviour is no longer necessary.

The participants in the meeting use these two languages during the course of their interaction. The medical language appears in most pronounced form during the discussion among the doctors after the patient was removed from the room. The cause of the patient's difficulties are talked about in terms of the patient's personal states. He is "paranoid," "schizophrenic", "depressed" (25, 38, 39). That is, the cause of the problem is located within the patient. Increased doses of medicine are prescribed in order to gain better control of his paranoid state (37).

The patient voices the sociological model in virtually every one of his pronouncements. He blames the circumstances, focusing particular attention on the hospital and the treatment he has been getting (or rather, has not been getting) but *not* his mental state for his problems:

> I've been trying to tell you, I can tell you, day by day, I'm getting worse, because of the circumstances, because of the situation. (2)

> So, its obviously the treatment I'm getting or its the situation or the place or or or the patients or the inmates or either of them. I don't know which. (2)

His denial of the equation of mind to body, internal causes of illness, and the proposition that medicine can cure the mind, could have come from any of Thomas Szasz's or R. D. Laing's books:

> You say "well, take some medication." Medication for the mind? I am supposed to take medication for, if I have some bodily injury. Not for the mind. My mind's perfect. (2)

A crucial exchange between the head psychiatrist and the patient highlights the patient's articulation of the sociological theory of mental illness with its emphasis on contextual causes:

18. Pt: if you leave me here, that means that YOU want me to get harmed. Which is an absolute fact. That's plain logic. That goes without saying. Obviously.

19. HP: That's interesting logic.

20. Pt: Yes. It's absolutely perfect, because if I am, if I am at a point, it's as if I were in some kind of a hole or something, right, and if you keep me there, obviously you intend to do me harm.

By blaming the hospital and the doctors, the patient gives us a perfect rendition of the iatrogenic theory of illness; the locus of the patient's trouble is in the social context, not his own mental state.

3. Conclusions

We can draw the following conclusions from the doctor-patient exchange:

The psychiatrists and the patient differ in their definitions of the situation.

These differences are assembled because an array of behavioral particulars are bestowed with different meaning by participants operating from different theoretical perspectives and in different common sense systems of belief.

Within each system of belief, the participants marshal evidence to support a basic proposition and deflect evidence which has the potential to challenge the basic proposition.

If left here, the conclusion would be a (potentially interesting) demonstration of the Thomas theorem and would point to relativism played out in face-to-face interaction, i.e., that each perspective – that of doctor and patient – is equivalent.

While we can see that differences in perspective were visible in the interaction and maintained by a belief-validating process, there is another, important, dimension to the interaction that can not be overlooked. That dimension has to do with conflict and its resolution in language.

3.1 Conflict resolution in language: the politics of experience

While the physicians and the patient have conflicting definitions of the situation, these definitions are not equal. The patient's definitions of his sanity is not on a par with the psychiatrists' definition of his insanity. The doctors' definition prevails. Despite the vehemence of his protestations and the admitted logic of his presentation, at the end of the meeting the patient is led from the examining room and returned to his lodgings, still convinced that he is healthy, there to await the decision and subsequent treatment recommended by the examining board.[4]

So, although there is evidence of the socially negotiated construction of a medical fact here, the constituent negotiation is not evenly balanced. Instead, we have an example of what R.D. Laing (1967) has called "the politics of experience" (cf. Pollner, 1975; Mehan and Wood, 1975: 215–218; Mehan, 1983b). Some persons, by virtue of their institutional authority, have the power to impose their definitions of the situation on others, thereby negating the others' experience. Speaking with the authority of the medical profession, in particular psychiatry, and, by extension, the legal institution, the definition voiced by members of the board is imposed on the definition voiced by the patient. The conflict between the patient and the psychiatrists is resolved by the imposition of an institutional definition of the situation on top of an everyday or lay definition of the situation. This imposition negates the patient's definition, relegating his experience to an inferior status.

The process by which the patient's experience is ironicized demonstrates how institutionalized power is manifested in language, making it necessary to fashion the corollary of the Thomas theorem that I proposed at the outset of this chapter.

All people define situations as real; but when powerful people define situations as real, then they are real *for everybody involved* in their consequences.

3.2 The logical status of oracular reasoning

In closing, I'd like to make some final comments on the status of the logic of oracular reasoning. These comments are admittedly speculative, requiring further specification.

The parties in the conflict that I examined each operated within a certain frame of knowledge. They adhered to statements about the world whose validity could neither be confirmed nor disconfirmed (Shweder, 1984: 39–40). The doctors maintained the absoluteness of their belief in the patient's mental illness by denying, repelling, and transforming evidence which was contrary to their basic belief. The patient, too, used evidence presented in opposition to his argument as further support for the efficacy of his position. Thus, both a poorly educated, hospitalized patient and professionally educated physicians engaged in similar reasoning process. They admit to no universal standard (i.e., one that is outside both frames or in some frame acceptable by the people in the two frames) for judging the adequacy of ideas. As a result, no evidence or experience was allowed to count as disproof by either party.

Shweder has found evidence of what I am calling oracular reasoning in kinship classification, friendship concepts, concepts of personhood, principles of justice, and ideas about the meaning of dreams. This doctor–patient exchange suggests that oracular reasoning can operate in medical settings (cf. Scheff, 1968; Elstein *et al.*, 1978). Other commentators have found a similar process operating in science (Kuhn, 1962; Goodman, 1978; Gould, 1981). Belief-preserving practices have long been recognized in religion (Frazer, 1890; Festinger *et al.*, 1956; Jules-Rosette, 1976; Ryno, 1985). Also found in courtroom arguments over legal facts (Pollner, 1975; Maroules, 1985), they certainly pervade the everyday reasoning of contemporary peoples (Pollner and McDonald-Wikler, 1985; Wason and Johnson-Laird, 1972).

The widespread appearance of belief validating practices should lead us to realize that oracular reasoning is not limited to primitives, ancients, children, or the uneducated, and to consider the possibility that it is a more extensive feature of reasoning. Since the appearance of oracular reasoning is not universal but variable, a productive next step would be to investigate *how* belief-validating practices operate in detail. If such practices can be found in any group, in any belief system, then it becomes important to determine when protection against discrediting evidence becomes so extensive that disconfirmation becomes virtually impossible and how potentially contradictory evidence is sufficient to change the structure and practice of belief.

Appendix: transcript of out-take interview

Key: Pt   Patient (Vladimir)
     HP   Head psychiatrist
     Dr2 Second doctor
     Dr3 Third doctor

1. HP: Okay, now Vladimir as I've promised you before, if I see enough improvement in you.
2. Pt: How can I improve if I'm getting worse? I've been trying to tell you, I can tell you, day by day, I'm getting worse, because of the circumstances, because of the situation. Now you're telling me uh uh how can I until you see an improvement each time, I get worse. So, its obviously the treatment I'm getting or its the situation or the place or or or the patients or the inmates or either of them. I don't know which. I want to go back to the prison where I belong. I was supposed to only come down here for observation. What observation did I get? You called me up a couple of times. You say "well take some medication." Medication for the mind? I am supposed to take medication for, if I have some bodily injury. Not for the mind. My mind's perfect. Cause I'm obviously logical, I know what I'm talking about. There's noth— and I am excited. Yes, that's the only fault you might find with me. I have a perfect right to be excited. I've been here for a year and a half, hum, and this place is doing me harm. I come in here, I, I, uh, everytime I come in here you call me I am crazy. Now, what's, if, if it's something you don't like about my face, that's I mean, that's another

story. But that has nothing to do with my mental stability. I have an emotional problem now, yes, which I did not have.

3. HP: What got you down here?

4. Pt: They sent me down here for observation.

5. HP: Why?

6. Pt: They, they thought, I, I, went to see a social worker, and I saw a psychiatrist, they said that, well why don't you go down there. Because I had an old problem.

7. HP: You felt the coffee was poison and you felt that people were mixing you up in your thinking, you were shaking.

8. Pt: Not so! The only part that's true is coffee. And what sort of treatment do I get now? There are a hundred patients going back and forth, who are, who are obviously doing me harm.

9. HP: Are you working here Vladimir?

10. Pt: No, there is no suitable work for me here. All I've got is, all I got is the kitchen and all they do is throw cup cups around. In fact, they got two television sets which are blaring, machines which are going, everything which is against the mind. There is one thing uh uh uh that a patient does need, and this is what I do know, absolutely, is is quiet, if I have a mental problem or even an emotional problem. I'm thrown in with over a hundred of them and all they do is yell, walk around, televisions are blaring, so that's doing my mind harm!

11. HP: Are you involved in any sports here?

12. Pt: There are no sports here. All I've got is a baseball, and—and–a a glove, and that's it! There's nothing else. Hum. There's nothing else. Back at the other place, I had I had all the facilities to improve myself. I had the gym, I had the school, I had all kinds of uh uh anything I want.

13. HP: Are you in any group therapy here?

14. Pt: No! There is no group, obviously, I do not need group therapy, I need peace and quiet. See me. This place is disturbing me! Its harming me. I'm losing weight. I'm losing weight. Every, everything that's been happening to me is bad. And all I get, all I get is "well why don't you take medication?" Medication is disagreeable to me. There are people to whom you may not give medication. Obviously, and the medication that I got is hurting me, its harming me!

15. HP: ? Well Vladimir, you should

16. Pt: In fact to be specific it harmed my thorax, I do know that much, what it harmed. And if it harmed

17. HP: The thorax?

18. Pt: Yes, right here. Yes, and it has harmed me. And it has harmed me in every way possible. Like my, my, my. Obviously, if you leave me here, that means that YOU want me to get harmed. Which is an absolute fact. That's plain logic. That goes without saying. Obviously.

19. HP: That's interesting logic.

20. Pt: Yes. It's absolutely perfect, because if I am, if I am at a point, it's as if I were in some kind of a hole or something, right, and if you keep me there, obviously you intend to do me harm. Isn't that perfect logic?

21. HP: No it isn't, Vladimir.
22. Pt: It's absolutely perfect. I am getting harmed. I say I am getting harmed.
You tell me that until I show some improvement, yet each time we say
until I show improvement, I have been getting worse. Medication has
harmed me. Hum.
23. HP: Thank you Vladimir.
24. Pt: No, no. (Patient is removed from room.)
25. HP: He's been much better than this, and he's now, he's now falling apart,
now whether this is some reaction to uh his medication, is certainly
something I'll have to look at. However, uh, he was looking a lot more
catonic and depressed before and sometimes we find that, I mean, uh,
antidepressants, you remove the depression and you uncover the paranoid stuff, and we may have to give him larger quantities of tranquilizers
just to tone this down. So he's not looking ready to be able to make it back
to prison.
26. DR2: He argues in a perfectly paranoid pattern. If you accept his basic premise
the rest of it is logical. But, the basic premise is not true.
27. HP: He was very much more closed off and mute before. He'd open up in a one
to one relationship, but never at a staff meeting. And he's opened up over
at medical rounds, some. And yet this is why we had him brought up to
staff to see what would happen and I think he's certainly showing that
um, that
28. DR3: At one time they sought executive clemency for him. And it is true, he did
learn English. Well now he was building up with a great deal of hope to get
out, and he did get to a, to the flow of water one time. And he was
29. DR2: When he came here he was?
30. DR3: Yeah, he is now talking about the same things, about his rehabilitation
from his incarceration up to a given point. So he's reverting in a way to
that kind of thinking.
31. DR2: But I think he's terrified of leaving.
32. HP: Um, the louder he shouts about going back the more frightened he
indicates that he probably is.
33. DR3: This is known as Ganzer Syndrome.
34. HP: Well not quite.
35. DR3: Almost. Close.
36. HP: Well I think what we have to do with him is, uh, put him on a higher dose
of tranquilizers and see if we can bring the paranoid element under a little
bit better control and see if we can get him back on medication. If he's
taking it now, and I'm not even sure that he is.
37. DR3: Apparently the psychological testing showed the paranoid it was the, the
thing that was going through it all
38. HP: Right. Uh, uh um (leafing through papers). Ah. Diagnosis: Schizophrenic
reaction chronic and undifferentiated type with um prominent paranoid
features.

Notes

This chapter was prepared for presentation at the Eleventh World Congress of the International Sociological Association, New Delhi, India, August 18–24, 1986.

A number of colleagues have commented on earlier drafts of the chapter. I wish to thank Dede Boden, Aaron Cicourel, Roy D'Andrade, Allen Grimshaw, Ed Hutchins, Jean Lave, Jim Levin, Tom Scheff, Ron Ryno, Alexandra Todd, Jim Wertsch – and especially Mell Pollner for penetrating criticisms and helpful suggestions.

Permission to quote from Frederick Wiseman's film, *Titicut Follies*, was kindly granted by *Zipporah Films*, Cambridge, Mass.

1 W.I. Thomas and D.S Thomas, *The Child in America*, New York: Alfred Knopf, 1928, page 81.
2 Numbers in brackets refer to the appendix.
3 – , — indicate pause length.
4 The institutional imposition of meaning is visible throughout the meeting, not just in its final stages when the definition of the patient's insanity is reaffirmed: the patient is led into the meeting and led out of it by minions of the institution while the members of the examining board are free to walk in and out at their own will; the psychiatrists sit while the patient stands; the psychiatrists are dressed in professional clothes (suits and ties for the men, dresses for the women), while the patient is in rumpled shirt and trousers; the psychiatrists control the flow of conversation in the meeting, asking the questions, setting the topics, deciding when the meeting itself is terminated. (For further discussions along these lines, see Frankel, 1983; Fisher and Todd, 1983; Mishler, 1985; West, 1985, Waitzkin, 1983.)

8 Rules versus relationships in small Claims disputes

JOHN M. CONLEY AND WILLIAM M. O'BARR

1. Introduction

In the past decade, linguistic inquiry has increasingly focused on discourse as an interesting and appropriate level of analysis. This shift has
occasioned two kinds of insights into language processes: the discovery of
previously overlooked phenomena that occur at levels of organization
higher than the sentence, and the understanding of discourse-level aspects
of phenomena previously studied only at the sentence or sub-sentence level.
Our research on language and law, guided since its beginnings in the mid
1970s by linguistic theory, has been affected by this shift in interest. As we
have moved from style to discourse in our own considerations, we have
discovered some new aspects of language in legal settings that previously
went unnoticed by us and other researchers working at the level of speech
styles. For example, by investigating the structure of litigant narratives in
small claims and more formal courts, we have begun to uncover differences
between lay and legal structures of argumentation, standards of proof, and
concepts of evidence (O'Barr and Conley, 1985).

In addition to discovering entirely new issues that arise at the level of
discourse, we have also been investigating the degree to which features of
legal language studied at one level are manifest at other analytic levels. In
our earlier research, we found that certain speech styles were characteristic
of speakers with particular social backgrounds, and that stylistic variations
appeared to influence a speaker's likelihood of succeeding in court (Conley *et
al.*, 1979; O'Barr, 1982). In this chapter we use data from small claims
courts to argue that elements of discourse structure may be correlated with
the speaker's social background and that these structural variations may
also affect a speaker's opportunity to succeed.[1]

2. Rule-oriented versus relational accounts

In our study of self-represented litigants in small claims courts, we have
discovered two contrasting modes of organizing and presenting accounts. A

178

relational account emphasizes status and relationships, and is organized around the litigant's efforts to introduce these issues into the trial. A *rule-oriented* account emphasizes rules and laws, and is tightly structured around these issues.[2] Relational and rule-oriented accounts are ideal constructs based on our study of almost a hundred litigants in the small-claims court of North Carolina and Colorado. Actual accounts usually contain some features of both types, although typically features characteristic of one or the other of these orientational principles will predominate.

Rule-oriented accounts mesh better with the logic of the law and the courts. These accounts lay out a theory of the case, describing the rules that are at issue and the violations of them that are alleged. They contain few extraneous facts, but instead concentrate on the issues that the court is likely to deem relevant to the case. For example, in a dispute involving a contract, a rule-oriented account contains a statement about the existence of a valid contract, interprets the meaning of the contract, and presents facts that bear on whether the parties met their obligations under the contract. It does not deal with motivations, feelings, or reasons why the contract should never have existed. Nor does it beg for understanding of contract violations on the basis of greater and more pressing problems than the need to meet contractual obligations.

By contrast, relational accounts are filled with background details that are presumably relevant to the litigant, but not necessarily the court, and emphasize the complex web of relationships between the litigants rather than legal rules or formal contracts. Even an event such as an automobile accident between strangers can be transformed into a history of encounters between the parties. The courts typically treat such accounts as filled with irrelevancies and inappropriate information, and litigants employing this mode of presenting their cases are frequently evaluated as imprecise, rambling, and straying from the central issues.[3]

2.1 The nature of relational accounts

The relational form of account is illustrated by the testimony of the unsuccessful plaintiff (Rawls) in a Denver, Colorado, small claims case,[4] who has sued her next-door neighbor (Bennett) for removing a hedge on her side of the property line, failing to control the growth of his shrubbery onto her property, and generally harassing her. In the excerpt of her testimony contained in example 1, she responds to the judge's questions about how the hedge was removed. Previously, he has asked a series of specific questions about the location of the property line, but she has been unable to provide any specific information about that issue.

Rawls' testimony typifies the tendency of relational account-givers to analyze and describe legal problems in terms of social relations rather than the precise rules courts refer to in deciding cases. She tends not to respond specifically to the issues raised in the judge's questions. Instead, his questions frequently evoke lengthy digressions about the history of her relationship with Bennett. These digressions meander through time and place, drawing the listener ever deeper into the speaker's social world, but providing little information about the specific issues that are of interest to the court. Her account contains references to personal status (e.g., "I'm getting crippled up;" "I only got one [trash] can"), items which are significant to her social situation but are irrelevant to the court's more limited and rule-centered agenda. Additionally, the account assumes that the listener shares her knowledge of background events and places. Although the assumption of shared knowledge is common and appropriate in familiar conversation, it creates difficulties for a stranger who is trying to extract a set of facts and to apply strict legal rules to them.

Example 1[5]

Q: You're alleging that these trees and the shrubs and apparently the hedge included were removed. When did this happen?

A: Oh, well now that happened this year. At uh

Q: And how did it happen?

A: Well I can, well, well I have to jump back because, uh, for three years when Mr. Bennett moved back, because he was there once before and then he moved and then he come back into that house, and all the time before, I have to say this though judge because all the time before everybody took care of that hedge and they wouldn't let me take care of it. They trimmed it and I went even to Mr. Bennett when he was there before

Q: Wait a moment. Now the question that I asked you, and I would like to have you answer it, and that is how did the hedge get removed?

A: Well, um, Mr. Bennett said he told me when he moved back in, uh, because I was taking care of my trees coming up through the hedge, I was cutting them off and he told me not to do that. He said, "Don't do it," he said, "I'm going to have, the church is going to pay to take them out of there, because my wife wants to put a fence and plant roses on the other side." He said, "Is that alright with you?" I said, "I don't care what you do with it," you know, and I said, "if you need, uh, money for tools, maybe I can rent a tool and help in that respect because I can't dig," you know. And I said, "If you need uh, a tool to help you remove the hedge," I said, "uh, I will," well it wasn't the hedge then it was all the stumps underneath because he wanted that removed because he, his wife wanted the fence and she wanted roses on it. And so then three years went by and they let these trees grow up like you see the picture there. I think you've got it. And they're so big and then when he told me to stop taking them out because he was gonna take out that hedge, uh, the stumps, why uh, in the meantime I called a man and I had them, because I'm getting crippled up and I can't bend down sir, and here I was still taking out those trees and he wasn't coming to help me like he said he was. So then I had a man come, here Jim give him this, and I paid forty-five dollars. There's the bill there and he cut it right off down level with the ground. Well, I knew that wouldn't take it but at least it would keep me for a little bit trying to get them tree things out of that shrubbery there. Well, um, Mr. Bennett, when he finally come out he said "You know that isn't going to do it," and that's when he told me, "My wife want to put a fence," and he said, "You know that isn't going to do it. Those stumps are going to have be taken out." And that's when I told him, and he said he would do it, "I and the church would take them out," and I that's when I told him, "If you need, uh, money for a tool or something to help you. I'll pay for the tool or whatever." And he told, didn't do it, and so then I just had a, the Milehigh, uh, Tree Service come uh, uh, and um, a, and Mr., I had his name here, Mr., uh, Cook come and he come in the house and sat down with me and he looked at that and he said well he surely should help in the shrubbery in the back because there's shrubbery in the back that was over on my line that I've got to take out and I've got pictures of that too sir. And he said he didn't know what the man or what the man was because the tree was dead why didn't he take it out? Well all he wants to do is harass me so he leaves it there so I have to keep taking the stuff out and bending over and using my trashcan, you know. This is something else. I only got one can. Why don't he pick up his own trash? And so I went ahead and paid it. He told me he would come if I need. He says, "I'll cut it when you need me." Yet I could never get this man. I tried to have him subpoenaed, yet I could never get him because I think Bennett got to him first. But anyway I got the Milehigh Tree Service here for 275, and I got his mess in the backyard, if you want the pictures here, that's what I took them for. Did you give him the ones with the trees?

2.2 The nature of rule-oriented accounts

Example 2 illustrates the alternative rule-oriented mode in which some small claims litigants relate their cases to the court. This witness (Hogan) is a sales executive who is appearing in court on behalf of her company, the successful defendant in the case. The plaintiff (Webb), a former sales representative of the company, is suing over the company's refusal to pay him a bonus commission on the sale of an expensive scientific instrument. In the excerpt of the case contained in example 2, Hogan presents the company's defense with respect to Webb's claim. She deals directly with the issue that the court must resolve to decide the case. She treats the dispute as a contractual problem between two parties and does not discuss personalities or social relationships. Her account is highly factual; names, dates, and the contents of conversations and documents are reported precisely. Unlike the relational account of Rawls in example 1, this account presumes no prior knowledge of people, places, or events on the part of the listener. It is related in chronological sequence and without the constant interjections of background information that typify relational accounts. The speaker presents the court with information relevant to the narrow principles of contract law on which the outcome depends in an efficient manner and with a minimum of extraneous matter.

Example 2

> Q: We'll come back to you in just a moment. Let's turn over to you ma'am. We do need your name, business address and connection with the uh, Instrument Supply Company.
> A: My name is Lynn Hogan. Uh, my address, do you want my business address or
> Q: Business address is fine.
> A: 1200 Cavanaugh Street, Denver, Colorado. I am the scientific sales manager for Instrument Supply, Denver.
> Q: As such of course you've heard everything that's been stated so far. We have several exhibits. I believe in this case you're probably familiar with all of them.
> A: Yes sir, I am.
> Q: But if not, you're certainly free to look them all over and your opportunity to react to what you've heard and to further develop whatever answer or defense you may have.
> A: Okay, thank you. Um, as uh Dan [the plaintiff] stated, uh, Instrument Supply is a scientific distributor. Uh, we represent over 1500 manufacturers and we sell over 60,000 products. Um, we are continuously being exposed to gimmicks from our manufacturers to boost the sale of their products. Uh, the only control that management has, um, over these prod–, over these promotions, is to pick and choose the ones that uh, best support our local selling programs, where we want the local emphasis to be. Um, then it is my responsibility, as well as the district manager, to assist the sales reps in focusing on these sanctioned programs. Uh, in order to keep track of what we have sanctioned, we have a calculation sheet that specifically shows the sales representative what we are sanctioning. This is one for the first half. I have highlighted that, that particular promotion for spectrometers was on the first half, from March until August of 1984, giving the particular payouts, and as you'll see there is a 200 dollar payout there for 1001 Spectrometer. In the, we, uh, usually will change some of the

programs on the second half uh, PIP program. Um, we also as sales managers, provide to the representatives, um, some sort of indication that we are bombarded, our plate is full. So I put out to them in September of 1984, a list of the sanctioned promotions. You will see on there that the Diller and Macy double payout is not on there. Uh, I was unaware that this, um, letter had gone out from D and M. Approximately October of 1984 they did send this out to the sales representatives. Uh, I received notification that it was out amongst the reps late October, early November, upon returning from vacation. My management told me of his conversation with Mr. Harper and the agreement was made between John Taylor, uh the Den–, the then district manager and Mr. Harper, that there had been a, uh, an advance notification put out of an unsanctioned program through Diller and Macy, not sanctioned by Instrument Supply. And uh, that Mr. Harper was more than uh, uh, uh, he was more than open to go ahead and pay his 200 dollars, but that we would not pay the matching 200 dollars.

Q: What is his basis for that? Which seems to be contrary to the flier that he put out.

A: Um, Mr. Harper in a, in a letter that Mr., I asked for Mr. Harper to write, which I believe you already have a copy but here is another copy. In there it states the events. It does say that he um, prematurely put the promotion out to the sales force without talking to local management. Um, in early, either late October, early November, I asked him, he told me at that point about um, what was going on with Mr. Webb and I asked him at that time, I said, "Would you please call Mr. Webb and tell him that you have prematurely put a promotion out that's not sanctioned and that you will honor your 200 dollars and that Instrument Supply will not." He told me that he had. Uh, it is true that I was semi-aware of this 1001 from um, uh, the sale at Lakeview. Mr. Webb did a quotation to Lakeview on November 15th of 1984, uh, stating on there that this particular quote was good until December 15th, 1984 to the customer. Um, it is my job to encourage the sales representative to close sales. At that time I was not aware of the fact that Dan did not know it was not 400 but only 200 through Diller and Macy. Upon his resignation, um, when he came into the office the end of December, he did at that time state the 400 dollars and I did at that time tell him that it was 200 dollars from Diller and Macy and not a matching 200 dollars from Instrument Supply. Um, at that point, um, Dan continued to pursue it and um, you know we, you see the answers that we have have uh put out. So we have paid, we did pay 200 dollars out for Diller and Macy. Diller and Macy is reimbursing us for that 200 dollars through the PIP program. And um, excuse me, if I could just present one other thing.

Q: Go right ahead.
A: For the second half, and this goes with that one other thing that I gave you, this is the second half PIP calculation sheet, and you will see on there there is no Diller and Macy payout for the second half.
Q: Anything else before we hear again from Mr. Webb?
A: No sir.

When relational and rule-oriented accounts are compared it becomes clear that only the latter articulate easily with the agenda of the law. Despite the fact that small claims courts allow considerable leeway to litigants as to both the evidence and the manner in which it can be presented, judges must nonetheless adjudicate disputes within the bounds of the law. And although their positions allow them to listen to a much broader range of issues than likely would be allowed in more formal courts, small claims judges in North Carolina and Colorado are not empowered to act as counsellors or social workers.

It is clear from even the excerpt of Rawls' testimony presented in example 1 that she and Bennett have had a series of disagreements prior to the dispute that has brought them to court. The particulars of this case represent only some of their difficulties in getting along. Such a "story behind the story" is by no means unique to this case; nearly every case we have studied has a broader context than the specific issues which eventually make their way to court. The fact is, however, that some litigants limit their accounts in court to issues that fit well within the framework of the law while others do not choose or manage to do so. One might wonder whether Rawls is less concerned about the dispute over the hedge than finding a means of getting back at Bennett for the several injustices she feels he has done to her over the years.

By contrast, the testimony of Hogan in example 2 is devoid of the details of her relationship with Webb, their respective relationships with the company, what Scientific Instruments is like as an employer, etc. She has limited her testimony to a specific issue – whether Scientific Instruments had a contractual obligation to pay a certain commisson to Webb – and the details she introduces into her testimony are for the most part directed specifically to this question. It is understandable why many small claims judges prefer witnesses like Hogan to those like Rawls. Hogan has presented a case that is relatively easy to examine within the limits of contract law, but Rawls has made a claim about expenses incurred in removing a hedge that is almost lost in a complex set of complaints against Bennett as a neighbor. With some effort, the court might sift through Rawls' account for the legal issues that may be involved, but what can it do about "neighborliness" and social relations gone sour? The structure of a small claims court may indeed allow Mrs. Rawls to "tell it to the judge," but what can he do about the larger issues that lie behind her specific claim?

These two accounts were selected because they are striking examples of the critical differences between the rule-oriented and relational approaches to giving small claims testimony. They were also selected to suggest that the distribution of these differences does not depend on a single discrete factor such as gender, age, ethnicity, or status as defendant or plaintiff. Rather, it is our impression at this point in our study that the distribution of the two modes of presentation depends on a complex set of social attributes. In particular, exposure to and experience with the linguistic conventions of business and the law may be an important determinant of the tendency of some self-represented litigants to present rule-oriented accounts. We also suspect that relational accounts may have similar distribution to the "powerless" style of testifying that we reported in earlier work (Conley *et al.*, 1979; O'Barr, 1982). If this is true, we would expect the relational approach to be more characteristic of persons who occupy positions of relatively little power and control in the society at large.[6]

3. Conflicting modes of presenting information: a case study

In the remainder of this chapter we examine a single case, a landlord–tenant dispute. The plaintiff (Broom) is a commercial landlord who owns a number of rental buildings; the defendant (Grumman) is a handyman and former tenant in one of the plaintiff's buildings. During the spring of 1983, Broom bought an industrial building in which Grumman had been renting a large room that he used both as shop and his living quarters. In May 1983, the two signed a one-year lease. By May 1984, Grumman was behind in his rent and Broom evicted him. In this case, Broom is suing for back rent, late charges, cleaning costs, and the expenses associated with replacing a heating system that Grumman installed during his tenancy (it is unclear whether Grumman installed it before or after Broom bought the building). Grumman's position is that he does not owe the allegedly overdue rent, that he and Broom reached an implicit agreement to give him credit for the value of the heating system he had installed, and that the space was in poor condition when he first occupied it.

Example 3 is an excerpt from the plaintiff's testimony near the beginning of the trial. Prior to this point, the judge has summarized the plaintiff's written complaint and the defendant's answer and has begun to ask the plaintiff a series of specific questions about his case. In example 3, Broom responds to the judge's questions concerning the calculation of damages and offers an explanation of his reasons for removing the furnace that the defendant had installed.

Example 3

Q: Alright. Now several other questions can be answered this way, what are the arithmetic parts of your 487? How did you get there and why?

A: May I submit this as a

Q: Come right ahead. Mark this likewise for the plaintiff. This being a letter of June 29, '84 addressed to the defendant and uh, citing certain statutes and uh, rental for May '84 and the 375 plus the fifty late charge. Is, does the lease contain a provision for a late charge in that amount?

A: Yes sir, your, your attention is directed to a

Q: A written-in portion about a third of the way down?

A: Yes sir. I said, "Postmarked after the fifth, add fifty dollars."

Q: Then you're looking for recouping those first four days of June.

A: Yes sir.

Q: At the rate of twelve-fifty and, without going through the arithmetic process, is that based on thirty-day month into 375?

A: Yes it is.

Q: The next is to clean up, and that turns into a $185 amount, including a dumpster for 125, broken glass, debris and uh, the labor.

A: Thirty-five for dog feces on the floor sir.

Q: Alright sir. So that added in brings you to 310.

A: Yes.

Q: Then we're just going over the arithmetic. We're gonna back up to the $185 item in just a moment. And labor costs to remove unauthorized gas service you had installed, labor, materials that he installed,[7] comes to 182. And then deducting the deposit brings you to a 487 figure. Then let's back up to, where's the furnace at this date?

A: It's, it's discarded, was put in the dumpster, sir. I had to remove the furnace because, uh, this is a, uh, I went over to the city of Parkwood and uh, did some further uh, leg work on this. I have found this is a garage, it has a garage door. This is a, a garage repair type of facility, and when Mr. uh Grumman moved in we had just installed prior, three months, ninety days prior to his taking uh, commune of that area, a new overhead hanging furnace which is about oh, six feet above the floor and this was a 90,000 BTU furnace which is adequate to heat this thousand square feet. Now he removed that furnace and threw it in the back and I subsequently installed it in another area of the same building. It's working fine today. He had a used house type furnace that he put into this area and he uh, cut some ducts and ran some ducts down through the ceiling of this, of the leased area and put this furnace back in the back area. Could I, could I show you some pictures perhaps?

[explanation of pictures]

A: You see, uh your honor, that type of furnace injects combustion air off the floor and
Q: The one that was installed by the defendant?
A: Mr. Grumman.
Q: Alright.
A: And if, if he had called me and said, you know, "Uh, Mr. Broom can I take out your furnace and, your heating unit and put this in, that I obviously got left over from a job?", I would have said, 'No, because I don't want that kind of a heating unit in my building because if you have gasoline or volatile fumes or anything of that nature in these areas, those fumes can lie on the floor and be sucked into this furnace." Now it might be one chance in a thousand, but I would rather have that furnace up in the air and it's my building and I certainly could decide what kind of heating I wanted. But instead without my permission, he took my heater out and installed this, this house type of furnace. Now I understand, I know that he's gonna say, "You know, I incurred a lot of expense and time and labor and such as that to put this in." But my rebuttal is, "I didn't want that furnace and I don't think that uh. . ." It cost me money then to, I had to go buy another heater. I hired some people to install the furnace. I had to first take his furnace out, all the ducting and all the grills and everything, I got rid of that and then I had to install this overhead furnace at my expense.

Like Hogan in example 2, this witness is oriented to the legal rules that he believes are at issue. Both Broom and Hogan treat written contracts as binding and minimize personal and social factors that might be claimed to mitigate the effects of the contract. Although Broom represents himself, as do most small claims litigants in the United States, the court can readily extract from the details he presents a case that can be examined in the light of applicable landlord–tenant laws.

In example 4, Grumman, the defendant, is given an opportunity to respond to the case presented by the plaintiff. His approach is markedly different. Instead of being oriented to the specifics of his written contract with the plaintiff, he presents a case that focuses on his own personal problems and the consequent reasons why he did not pay the rent that the plaintiff alleges is owed. The details of the lease are of relatively less concern to Grumman than are the details of his relationship with Broom and how these relations bear on the manner in which he behaved in this dispute.

Example 4

Q: Now as the defendant, of course, you have heard all the statements so far. We have two exhibits which I believe you're familiar with. The copy of the lease and then the copy of the June 29 letter and plaintiff had other exhibits which the court and you have both had the benefit of looking at, the photos that uh, were taken. Now of course this is your opportunity to tell me what you think I should know about this, and included in that, your reactions to what you've heard and then what is there about this settlement that you rely upon. Why do you believe that everything has been taken care of?[8]

A: Well, to start with, I didn't rent the building, lease the building on the date that he stated. American Builders uh, American Wood Products had the building leased and I don't know where he was at, at the time I was looking for a building. I leased the building from the other man at a cheaper rate and a cheaper deposit. Because the roof was leaking it had a dirt floor in the back and it had inadequate heat. It had a broken window and an another one cracked and the stool was leaking out the back of it and it had two big piles of trash in the back of the building. After I got it all cleaned up and everything, he comes back, raises the rent, raises the deposit, and "You can either take it or leave it."

Q: Who did you have a lease with at that time?

A: His pre–, uh previous tenant, which was supposed to have had a lease on it.

Q: Did that previous tenant assign it over to you or how did

A: Yes he did.

Q: Do you have a copy of that with you?

A: I don't, I can't find a copy, but I had one.

Q: How long did that lease run?

A: For about

Q: American Wood Products lease?

A: I don't know when his lease run out

Q: Do you remember the date that you took over?

A: But uh, according to Mr. Elrod, the man, that was there with Products, he was supposed to had authority from Mr. Broom to lease the building at what, at the same rate as what he had it for such and he rented it for 200, uh $200 a month, more than what he had been paying.

Q: Then first of May rolled around, of '83, and we have before us what appears to be a business lease form, which purports to have your signature on it. Did you then at that time lease from the, uh, plaintiff in this case, Mr. Broom?

A: Yes I did. Uh, I really had, I'd already moved into it and didn't really have too much choice. I'd spent two weeks plus fixing the roof.

Q: Well, it appears that whatever prior situation existed, that it all terminated by a new agreement signed up on May 1, '83 between yourself and the landlord and that would put the rest whatever happened in the past.

A: Right.

Q: Alright sir. Then carry forward from there, you uh, do you disagree about moving out on the fourth of June?

A: I'm not through yet sir.

Q: Well I, I realize that but uh, did you move out on the fourth of June?

A: Yes I did.

Q: And did you pay rent for the uh, month of May '84?

A: May, uh, no I did not. I used the deposit.

[. . .]

Q: Now then what else is there that I should know as to why you don't believe you're obligated?

A: Okay here's a, here's another deal from Mr. Broom, stating that, I took the hanging heater down and set it in the back and had it setting back there so that when I got ready to, to move out I could rehang it cause the only thing I moved was a piece of gas line. He was gonna sue me if I took that furnace out of there and he took pictures of it and every-thing. If I took it out of there he was gonna sue me. So then he finally decided to give me credit for it.

Q: Could I see that?[9]

Q: You certainly can. Uh, go right ahead uh, Mr., uh, Grumman, we're still with you.

A: Okay I, that, I have another slip signed here from Mr. Elrod.

Q: And what does this one, what does it do, say?

A: Well, what it conc–, that the windows were broken when I went into the building and the window was cracked, the stool was leaking and I also fixed the stool on the other side and ran a copper line to the other side, which I never charged nobody for. I fixed the roof on the building, I fixed the roof on the shed back behind and I hauled all the trash off that was back behind the building.

Q: Anything further sir?

A: Also my, at the time, he, when he served me the three-day notice, I went to my attorney because I couldn't be out of there in three days and my attorney contacted his attorney and asked his attorney for me to stay the additional four days right there.

Q: What was that deal?

A: That everything would be fine and use the deposit because he was doing nothing, he wasn't standing by and had men standing by. Tops right next door was empty and he wasn't doing anything with that building either.

Q: Was this deal uh, reduced to writing?

A: Beg your pardon?

Q: Was this reduced to writing, the deal to stay until the fourth of June? Did the lawyers put anything down on paper?

A: No, they, I don't think they did. They had an agreement between them. It cost me actually where I paid my attorney $200 for taking care of the matter, before this popped up.

Q: Anything else you want me to know? Do you understand the nature of the claim, the plaintiff is seeking rent for uh, the month of May, and uh, for the removal, installation, removal of the your furnace, the installation of the, a replacement and then the uh, clean up cost of 185 and the late charge.

A: I understand it. But I mean when he, when he offered to give me credit for that furnace and he took the other furnace that I took down, that I planned on reinstalling, at the time that I left.

Q: What happened after this memo, which states I will give you credit for the heater that you've installed as a fixture? What happened after that? Did anything get put down in writing, other than that lease?

A: I've got another, sir, I've got another letter that I cannot find where he was gonna sue me if I took the heater out of the building.

Q: Well this says as soon as possible. Let me hear from you since time is getting short. This sounds as though this memo was awaiting getting signed up on a lease. Is that correct?

A: I don't recall at this point.

In example 5, Broom, the plaintiff, responds to the defendant's testimony and the concerns expressed in it. He draws the court's attention to his interpretation of the dispute in terms of the lease and makes his case for the legal irrelevance of the defendant's understandings, motives, and explanations.

Example 5

Q: Come back to you in just a moment. Return at this time to you uh sir, Mr. Broom. You've heard those statements and the production of the letter from American Heating and Cooling, uh Herb Elrod that the defendant has talked about, that states that uh, yes we did rent it and this is always referred to as the cold room. Then secondly the memorandum that says that there will be a credit for the heater and I've inquired as to where it went from there and how much of a dollar amount was to be extended as credit and all of that. What else should I learn from you?

A: Well sir that was, was predicated on us for throwing out the lease. And, and as he installed the heater, I wasn't interested in it at that time. He didn't get back to me. Uh, everytime I call him he doesn't return my calls. I would like to just draw your attention sir to, uh I, I put this in lease because this has come up before in this business and I'm sure you've heard this about 400 times but uh, I said the 375 security deposit, not to be used as rent. And I try to point that out to people when they sign these leases. I say now this security deposit is an apple and rent is a banana and they, and you just, they don't mix. And then I put a disclaimer in this also this same lease that Mr. Grumman signed. I said this is an old building. It was built in 1947. I want to, I just want to get it so we're talking. This is an old building, no representations as to security, heating, cooling, etc., other than what is here and now as of 1 May 1983. I put that in the lease, when they sign that then that, I assume that they know the, I said, I tell these people, read your lease, read that thing. In other words I, I, what you see is what you get. This is a, and then later on when they discover that it's cold or it's uh, it uh, you know, it isn't exactly what they want, then they can't come back and say, "Well gee wiz, you know, I thought it was this and that." Well I want to emphasize that what you bought, it was a cheap lease at, at 375, it's a \$4.50 a square foot. It's 280,000 square feet of stuff available in Lakewood you could have leased any place and I would just say, "Did I use any coercion of any type when I, when I asked you to sign the lease on 1 May, 1983?" You you read it and signed it, I, I certainly didn't force it on you." And there's one other item that said that in the same Bradford Lease, which is a standard business lease that uh the uh, the tenant would not make any alterations or change in, upon or about such premises without first obtaining the written consent of the landlord and I found out that's very helpful to put because many times a tenant will cut a hole in the wall and put in a door and I've never seen a tenant yet that didn't put in the most expensive mill work, \$200 and \$300 door and he always put in Tiffany glass and they always, they do these things, then after a couple of months in becomes an obligation that they do, that the landlord should reward them for doing all these great things that they've done to the lease space and I it's a communications problem I, I recognize this, and I suppose the basis of this thing is that I inherited this gentleman because I was out of the country when he moved in and Herb Elrod had leased the whole building. Herb had no right, in the same Bradford Lease it said you can't sublease without permission of the landlord. Then I came back and discovered that I had inherited this gentleman and I said well let Herb Elrod, and I, points in his letter said you don't have a legal right to this property because Mr. Elrod did not have the right to lease this thing to you. But really that's not germane to what we're, we're discussing right now. We did have a valid business lease and it was a period of one year. I did not get the, the rent for May. Uh, I tried to follow the laws as much as I posted my three day, I uh received this letter from Howard saying that he was going to leave on the 31st, which he didn't quite make and he said he wasn't gonna pay his rent. And I've heard that before, your gonna use security for a rent, and they can't do that. That's an apple and the rent is a banana. [Long pause] Uh, I don't which I need to amplify it's my building. I should be able to decide what kind of rent, what kind of heating system I want in it and I want the kind that I feel is the safest for my, for my uh investment and here is the uniform build building code for Lakewood, which I have, if I could show you that this is the reason that I don't want that kind of heater in my building.

At the conclusion of Broom's rebuttal, the judge gave the defendant a brief opportunity to conclude, and then ruled in favor of the plaintiff, adopting his argument in its entirety.

Examples 3 to 5 reveal points of comparison between the relational and rule-oriented modes of presenting cases. An important distinction is the rule-oriented litigant's greater responsiveness to the judges specific questions. In example 3, Broom's precision with reference to the amount of damages suggests that he has anticipated such questions. He is able to itemize the damages and has brought pictures that he believes support his claim. He has also prepared a detailed explanation of why he removed the furnace the defendant had installed. His entire testimony has an aura of precision and authority: it contains many quantitative references ("ninety days," "six feet," "90,000 BTU"); it suggests that careful research preceeded the plaintiff's coming to court ("I went over to the city of Parkwood and uh, did some further uh, leg work on this"); and it contains numerous legal- and technical-sounding words and phrases ("city of Parkwood," "garage repair type of facility," "leased area," "volatile fumes or anything of that nature," "rebuttal").

In example 4, by contrast, Grumman seldom provides any direct or precise responses to the judge's questions. In response to an initial question about why he believes the matter has been settled, he relates a lengthy account of his relations with the prior landlord and the condition of the premises when he moved in. When the judge pursues the issue of the prior landlord, the defendant is unable to say when the lease expired; when asked about when he moved in, he discusses the amount of rent he was charged. Later, when the judge asks him to summarize the contents of the note from Mr. Elrod, he begins to do so ("Well, what it conc–"), but quickly digresses into a lengthy description of the work he performed. Note also that he lacks written evidence of either of the agreements on which he relies, the lease with the prior landlord ("I can't find a copy but I had one") and the "deal" arranged by his lawyer ("Was this deal uh, reduced to writing?" "Beg your pardon?" . . . "No . . .").

These differences in the parties' ability to anticipate and respond to the judge's questions appear to reflect fundamental differences in the way that each has conceived of the dispute. As his statements in example 5 make clear, Broom sees the dispute in purely commercial and contractual terms. He contends that the relationship between Grumman and himself is governed entirely by a commercial document, the May 1983 lease. As he argues in example 5, many lay persons try to invoke everyday rules of social relations in such situations, but from a legal perspective the document renders such consideration irrelevant ("But really that's not germane to what we're, we're discussing right now. We did have a valid business lease . . .").

Grumman, by contrast, sees the dispute as a problem in social relations. At the start of the second segment of example 4, he appears to acknowledge Broom's analysis of the dispute (". . .it all terminated by a new agreement signed up on May 1, '83 between yourself and the landlord and that would put the rest of what happened in the past." "Right."). Throughout example 4, however, his primary emphasis is on the work he did in cleaning up the premises, the inherent unfairness of Broom coming in and raising the rent when he had nowhere else to go, and the fact that he paid a lawyer $200 to straighten out the situation. His position seems to be that the court cannot take the side of the landlord against a person who not only is in a dependent status but has gone out of his way to behave responsibly. To him, perhaps, such an argument is coherent and adequate; he seems unaware that the law's conception of the dispute might render his own conception irrelevant.

Throughout his presentation, Broom strives to impose his conception of the case on the judge. For example, at the beginning of example 3, he directs the court's attention to specific provisions of the lease. When the judge asks narrow, businesslike questions about damages, he reinforces the court's approach by giving precise, businesslike answers. Finally, in example 5, he makes an explicit comparison between the competing outlooks on the case, and denigrates the defendant's approach. By contrast, Grumman is unable to respond to Broom's imposition of a structure on the facts of the case. When the judge seeks to engage him in the sort of focused dialogue that Broom has initiated, he fails to furnish appropriate answers. Then, when given open-ended opportunities to speak, he is unable to suggest an alternative structure of his own.

The law would have permitted the judge to evaluate the case in terms other than those suggested by Broom. For example, he could have considered whether Broom was unjustly enriched by Grumman's uncompensated work on the building, or whether an agreement to credit Grumman for some of the value he added to the premises could be inferred from the parties' conduct. Once Broom provides a familiar framework, however, the judge works entirely within it. Grumman's plea to probe the underlying social relations evokes no response. Thus, Broom seems to benefit from his approach to the court as a limited-purpose institution which deals most readily with those issues that are presented in a rule-oriented format; Grumman, conversely, seems disadvantaged by his implicit assumption that the court has the willingness and ability to impose solutions on broader social problems.

Grumman is unable to analyze or to speak about the dispute in a way that evokes understanding from the court. What is particularly interesting is that the way that each party deals with the dispute in court appears to mirror the way that he dealt with it as it occurred. Grumman ignored such technicalities as leases, he did what he thought was socially appropriate, and he relied on others to do the same. Broom, by contrast, ignored Grumman's social expectations, and instead took care to define all the terms of their relationship in writing. At trial, each presents an account that embodies his approach to the dispute.

4. Conclusion

By selecting a single case, which contains both relational and rule-oriented accounts, we emphasize that the distribution of the two approaches does not appear to be a function of the facts at issue in particular cases, but of the capabilities and proclivities of individual litigants. Our present belief is that use of the rule-oriented approach correlates with exposure to the sources of social power, in particular the literate and rule-based cultures of business and law. Such exposure is in turn differentially distributed between men and women and among the members of various classes and ethnic groups. The distribution of the rule-oriented and relational approaches may thus parallel that of the powerful and powerless speech styles we have previously described (O'Barr and Atkins, 1980; O'Barr, 1982; Conley *et al.*, 1979). Indeed, the rule-oriented relational continuum may be the discourse-level manifestation of the power/powerless stylistic continuum. In our future work, we will explore the relative frequency of the two modes of presentation and attempt to correlate the mode employed with various aspects of the social background of small claims litigants.[10]

Whatever our further research actually shows about the relation between modes of presenting cases and social power, the presently available data are sufficient to show that small claims litigants frame their cases in at least two different argumentative modes, and that rule-oriented accounts are decidedly easier for courts to handle than relational ones. Thus, in instances where alternative sides of a dispute are presented in different modes, it seems fair to say that the court is inherently biased in favor of the rule-oriented side.

Notes
The research reported here is a joint project. The authors alternate priority of authorship in their publications. The research was supported by grants from the National Institute for Dispute Resolution, the Research Council of Duke University, and the Law Center Foundation of the University of North Carolina. We acknowledge with appreciation the assistance of the officials of the small claims courts of Durham, North Carolina, and Denver, Colorado, and of the anonymous persons whose cases we studied.

1   Our data consists of over fifty small claims trials in Durham, North Carolina, and Denver, Colorado, which were observed and tape recorded. The cases are summarized in Conley and Childress (1985). We studied the tapes and transcripts prepared from the tapes to understand litigants' social and legal objectives and strategies. For a detailed discussion of our method and its antecedents, see O'Barr and Conley (1985: 673–676).

2   In describing the phenomena reported here, we have sought terminology that is both simple and descriptive, and we believe that the terms *relational* and *rule-oriented* accomplish these goals. It should be remembered, however, that both types of accounts are in fact oriented to rules, although the specific rules vary. In a relational mode, the account is oriented with respect to social rules. In a rule-oriented mode, the rules are specific and *legal*. We are indebted to Craig McEwen for reminding us that our terminology, although brief and descriptive, might convey to some readers the notion that *relational* accounts are not oriented with respect to any rules.

3   Interviews with both litigants and judges about small claims experiences suggest that such situations are unpleasant and frustrating for both the litigants and the legal decision makers.

4   Names, dates, and other identifying details have been changed to protect the anonymity of litigants and other witnesses in the cases we report.

5   The transcripts contain the data needed for the type of analysis we perform in this paper. We have not attempted to indicate such details as phonology, pauses, intonation, and so forth, because they are not required when considering attributes and structure of discourse at the level on which we are working. We take the position that no transcript can contain all possible information of potential interest to other researchers and have elected instead to provide transcripts that are readily accessible to readers without specialized knowledge of various transcribing procedures.

6   We are currently engaged in the investigation of these and related issues under a two-year grant from the Law and Social Science Program of the National Science Foundation to study the "Conceptualization and Presentation of Small Claims Cases." At this point in our research, we are not prepared to offer any statistics on the relative frequency of the two modes or to make the claim that small claims courts generally treat these modes in the manner we describe in the remainder of this paper. Our present objective is simply to describe the two modes of presentation and to illustrate what can happen when the two occur in the same case. We present only a single example of such a case, in large part because of our desire to provide readers with as much of the original text as possible, within the space allotted to this chapter, and to set out the hypothesis that litigants who can present rule-oriented accounts may have an important advantage over those who cannot.

7   The switch from "you had installed" to "he installed" is apparently a self-correction.

8   It might be expected that an invitation to respond of this sort invites a relational response. We have found throughout our data, however, that the form of litigant accounts bears little, if any, apparent relation to the form of magistrates' invitations to speak.

9   Asked by the plaintiff.
10   We also expect that the rule/relational differences when more fully expli-
     cated will shed additional light on such issues as differences in negotiating
     styles (see, for example, Fisher and Ury, 1981), and in approaches to moral
     reasoning (Gilligan, 1982), and other issues.

9 The judge as third party in American trial court conflict talk

SUSAN U. PHILIPS

1. Introduction

In the social-scientific literature that characterizes the management of conflict in Anglo-American trial courts, the discourse format for working through a case is typically characterized as one in which each of two sides presents its view of relevant events, and then fact finders, a jury or a judge, choose which of the two versions of reality they consider to be most plausible. This conflict between opposing views may characterize the trial as a whole (Bennett and Feldman, 1981), the contrast between direct examination and cross examination (Danet *et al.*, 1980; Woodbury, 1984), or a contrast between the reality proposed by the questioner and that offered by the witness responding to the questions (Atkinson and Drew, 1979).

In much of such characterization, the judge is either invisible, so that one is unaware of his having any role at all in the proceedings, or he, like the jury, is cast in the role of the person who must choose absolutely between two sides (Lind, Thibaut, and Walker, 1973; Nader, 1969). The purpose of this chapter is to examine more closely the interactional role of the American trial court judge in court proceedings, to make it more visible than it has been in social-scientific literatures, and to challenge both this characterization of the judge's role and the characterization of the sequential order in the structuring of conflict management in the American trial court as one in which each side presents a position, after which a judge (or jury) chooses which position will become a legal reality.

More specifically I will argue that during a jury trial, where matters of fact are being decided, the judge plays a relatively minor role in the structuring of courtroom speech, and enters in primarily to rule on motions and objections when called upon to do so by the lawyers on each side, minimizing and even concealing any active taking of positions on his part, in order to avoid biasing a jury. Where matters of law are being decided, however, and particularly where motions are ruled upon out of the presence of a jury, we find American trial court judges taking a far more active role in shaping the structure of talk. In deciding matters of law, they not only listen to each side and rule, but also mediate by proposing third positions, initiate positions when neither lawyer or only one lawyer has taken a position, and argue actively and sometimes heatedly against the position they intend to rule against. In all this, trial court judges are not unlike the justices of the U.S. Supreme Court and other appellate courts.

To develop this view of the judge as advocate, mediator, and adversary where matters of law are being argued in the American trial court, I will first highlight major features of the characterizations of Anglo-American trial court judges in the social-scientific literature to substantiate my claim that the portrayal has been one-sided and misleading. Then I will draw upon a data base of transcripts of court proceedings from an Arizona state court of general jurisdiction to illustrate the range of ways in which trial court judges are more activist in argumentation than they have been presented, and to illustrate the variability in the sequential structure of argument which has been neglected in characterizations of court procedures. Finally, I will consider the implications of these findings for our understanding of the nature of conflict talk in the American courtroom and more generally.

One major set of anthropological views of Anglo-American judges stems from Max Gluckman's (1955) characterization of Barotse jurisprudence. In his study of this African tribe's court activity, Gluckman contrasted Barotse courts with Western courts. He suggested that whereas in Western courts, and he had in mind his own experience with British courts, either one side or the other wins, and there is no compromise, in the Barotse courts he studied it was common for some sort of compromise to be worked out, so that each side went away feeling that they had neither entirely lost nor won. Gluckman also found that Barotse judges asked litigants questions not just about the incidents thought to be litigible. They also delved into the history of the relationship between the litigants in all its ramifications. He saw the judges' use of both compromise decision and broadly defined case histories as motivated by the nature of the relationship between the litigants, which typically was multi-stranded, involving strong links in a variety of institutional domains in Barotse daily life. He contrasted such relations to the more typically single-stranded relations of litigants in Western courts, who might have no relations outside, say, the contract in dispute brought to court. Unlike the Western litigants, who would lose little if their relation was shattered forever as a consequence of the dispute and its outcome, Barotse had a great deal to lose if the relationship between the litigants was not patched up and a way found to keep it functioning, hence the particular judicial style of Barotse judges.

Nader (1969) sets up a dichotomy quite similar to that of Gluckman, focusing on the contrast between zero-sum decisions and compromise decisions and relating them causally to litigants with single-stranded relations and multi-stranded relations respectively. Although Nader did not stress the Westerness of zero-sum decisions for litigants in single-stranded relations as Gluckman did, emphasizing rather the existence of two styles of conflict management which appear around the world, Gluckman's association of this pattern with Western judicial decision making has lingered in current discussions of Western courts. Thus in Abel's work (1973), typical Western courts characterized as more "formal" are thought by some to provide less justice than courts which are "informal", in part because the former can provide only zero-sum decisions while the latter, being introduced as a supplement to the more typical courts, can provide compromise decisions.

In the anthropological literature of conflict management, then, the Western judge, but not the non-Western judge, is seen as imposing zero-sum decisions on litigants, decisions in which one side or position is fully supported, and the other side or position totally denied, with efforts being made presently to change that characteristic role in the Western judge.

In a more recently burgeoning psychological literature focusing on procedural variation, procedural style is dichotomized to reveal the Anglo-American judge in a similar light, but the dichotomy itself is somewhat different. Most notably, Thibaut and Walker (1975) distinguish between legal procedure in the "adversarial" system of Anglo-American law and the "inquisitorial" system of European continental law. As they envision it, in British-derived adversarial courts the lawyers for each side present opposing views through questioning of witnesses, with the judge functioning as a referee to assure that procedural law is followed. In the courts of the European continent, in contrast, the lawyers for each side play a much less active role in marshalling evidence, while the judge assumes the role of inquisitor, questioning witnesses from each side, to yield a more integrated view of what actually occurred. The main purpose of Thibaut and Walker is to provide experimental evidence that the adversarial system produces fairer trials than the inquisitorial system, because the opposition of perspectives brings out the strengths and weaknesses of each. The main point of describing this contrast in styles here, however, is to show how once again a dichotomy casts the Anglo-American judge in a relatively passive role in the judicial process.

In a recent review of the literature on courts as forums for dispute processing, Yngvesson and Mather (1983) challenge such dichotomies, particularly those like Gluckman's (1955) laid down in the anthropological literature, contrasting "tribal" and "modern" modes of conflict resolution. In challenging some of the claims about Western/modern judges' roles which have just been noted, they point to several studies in which judges have been found in the more active roles of mediation and negotiation, yet the general thrust of their argument is to find mediation and negotiation outside the court in informal rather than formal proceedings.

In data to be considered here from the Arizona Pima County Superior Court, however, there is considerable evidence that, while on the bench, judges constrained by procedural law not imposed in more informal, noncourt, and lower court proceedings not only mediate and negotiate but also initiate positions and arguments, primarily in interaction with lawyers on motions on which judges must give rulings.

2. Data presentation and analysis

The data used below to illustrate the diversity of positions taken by judges, and their effect on the sequential structure of trial-court argument, come from two contexts in which judges were tape-recorded in 1978–1979 as they made procedural decisions: (1) A criminal trial in which the defendant was charged with possession of cocaine. Here our main data consists of pre-trial and during-trial motions to exclude evidence or to stipulate that evidence be presented in a certain way, and a motion for a directed verdict of acquittal following the presentation of evidence. (2) Initial appearances in which criminal defendants are brought before a judge for the first time and charged with a crime. Here our main data consists of argument around the decision the judge must make regarding conditions of release for each defendant. Must he stay in jail, or will he be released? If released, what bail will be set, if any, and what constraints imposed regarding where and with whom the defendant can engage in social activity?

To organize presentation of the variation in the judge's contribution to oral argument, I will conceptualize it as coming in first position, second position and third position. I have already indicated that the Anglo-American judge is typically conceptualized as entering into court debate in third position, when Position 1 is the first lawyer's presentation of a position or argument, Position 2 is the second lawyer's opposing position, and Position 3 is the judge's choice between those two positions.

In the Pima County Superior Court data base we consider here, this arrangement in which the judge is in Position 3 is illustrated in example 1:[1]

Example 1

Public
Defender: Your Honor, I, I– I realize these are serious charges. [2 secs]
            Correctional Volunteers,[2] uh, have recommended that, uh,
            he be released ROR. And, uh, based upon, uh long-standing
            community ties – lived here all his life, and uh, I think in view
            of that, uh, you can be pretty well assured that he will show
            up.
County
attorney: (Your Honor) I recommend that the uh, suggested bond be
            imposed. (To wit) fifty-five hundred.
Judge: Well [2 secs] he has a job [2 secs] he's got a family here, he's
            live in Tucson all his life. The charges are serious, but–

County
Attorney: He doesn't have a job anymore.
Public
defender: ₍/Yes he does/
Defendant: ⌐/(At the (   ))/ (2 secs) [2 secs]. At the movies.
Judge: I'm gonna release him on his own recognizance . . . . .

(IA-CB-10-#9)³

In this example, the judge listens to the public defender's view, then the county attorney's view, then goes along with the public defender. But even in this rare example of some approximation of the classic view of the judge's role in argument, things are more complex than the idealized view of such arguments. Each lawyer argues more than once, and the county attorney directly contradicts the judge. Even the defendant gets into it, which is rare, though most of what he says is inaudible to the tape recorder. The judge also argues, giving the reasons for his agreement with the public defender. This giving of reasons by the judge also appears in the only other example of this format in this data base:

Example 2

Defense
lawyer: Your Honor, at this time I'm gonna move for a directed acquittal. Uh, the state obviously is tryin' to get some type of constructive possession theory in this case to try to uh, convict Elliot sitting here and I would like to point out there has been absolutely no evidence uh presented by the state indicating Elliott Jenkens uz living at that residence, rented that residence or in in any way was occupying that particular residence on the date in question. They have Rosanna Jenkens living there. They have knowledge that she is married to Elliot. 'N' the fact that her baby is there. That is all they've presented. They have not shown that – that he lived there regularly, say, or the day before or uh, any other thing that he might have uh, just dropped by that particular morning to see his wife and his child . . . . .
Judge: What d' you say Dave? About that?
County
attorney: Your Honor, the evidence uh – I have not read the cases that uh, Mr. Paluso cited but uh, it occurs to me that uh, the (opinions) uh, is uh, the thing that stood out was that there was conflicting testimony at s–at various stages of the uh–of those proceedings in regards to the evidence. In this case there doesn't–so far there's absolutely *no* conflicting testimony whatsoever. They go to that address and the officer states why

>   (   ) that's particular time because (hard likelihood) of finding
>   people at home. The wife is found there with her child . . . . .
> Judge: C'mon not necessarily that *he's* living there, the – the child
>   may be livin' there an' she's livin' there. I mean cause she
>   gathers up children's clothes out of the house . . . . .
>
>   (Cocaine possession trial, 211–219)

Here the judge argues against the county attorney, and in favor of the
defense attorney, and ultimately rules in favor of the public defender, as in
example 1. Thus even when a judge takes Position 3, listening first to one
side and then to the other, and ultimately ruling as one side has requested,
he often argues against the side he disfavors, sometimes deliberately to
display to the lawyers why he rules as he does, but perhaps also because he
is, after all, a lawyer and an advocate first, in training and experience, and a
judge only later.

While judges do sometimes choose one or the other lawyer's positions as
their position, thus producing what can be called zero-sum decisions in
which there is a complete winner and a complete loser, they also often
respond to the positions offered by each lawyer with a third position different
from that of either lawyer. Example 3 illustrates the possibility of *compromise*
between the two lawyers' positions.

Example 3

County
attorney: I'd recommend that, un–fifteen thousand [7 secs]
Public
defender: Well, uh in view of the fact that he has a, uh, a probation hold, I
           would ask the court to, to follow the recommendation of the,
           uh, Correctional Volunteers.
Judge: Not for this type of an offense. Five thousand dollar bond,
           bond . . . . .

                                                        (IA 10, #10, p.54)

Often, however, the judge proposes a *different position* from that of either
lawyer, as in example 4:

Example 4

Defense
lawyer: . . . . . First of all, Your Honor, I'd like to motion to preclude the
           mentioning that uh, – to the jury that narcotics officers were
           over at that residence for purposes of serving a arrest warrant
           at that time – I think prejudice uh, involved in this instance

would uh, far outweigh any probative value that the state
could uh show (in this case) . . . . .

Judge: What d'you say about that, Dave?

County
attorney: Well the problem eh, with that, Your Honor, is uh, what
other–what–how do I tell the jury uh, what they were doing
there? Uh, I think i–it has to be allowed *in* or at least the fact
(we) –that they were there to serve the arrest warrant. Possibly
not to see–uh, I don't that the jury might–should be told why
the–what kind of warrant they were gonna arrest (   ) this pers
– who unh, uh, violate the marijuana–, uh, federal marijuana
whatever. I think uh /(   )/

Judge: [/Dave, wh–wh–wh–what/about if they were there for a lawful
purpose? . . . . .

(Cocaine possession trial, pp.18–19)

Here the defense lawyer wants to exclude the information that the federal
narcotics officers were at the defendant's house in order to serve an arrest
warrant. The county attorney wants to keep that information in, although
he is willing not to say what kind of charge the warrant was for. The judge
proposes that the jury simply be told the officers were there for a lawful
purpose. In fact, the judge postponed deciding until the next day what to let
the lawyers say, and at that time he ended up going along with the County
Attorney's position, but he could have opted for his own proposal rather
than either of theirs.

Example 5 illustrates an innovative position taken by the judge which is
in some ways also a compromise.

Example 5

Judge: Awright. Do you have any other motions?

Defense
attorney: Yes, Your Honor, uh there's–mirrors was uh,–been discussed
in pre-trial motions an' here today. Uh, on the surface of it uh,
paint the picture of what might be uh, considered the marijuana plant and uh, the lettering under there s–under it uh,
cannabis sativa which refers obviously to marijuana. Uh, I
would move to preclude the mirror from being introduced. I
will stipulate, or that–I have no objection to the testimony that
this particular mirror was found and that supposedly some
white residue was on top of the mirror and everything else like
that. I'm not gonna object that there's no mirror or that–that
there wasn't one at that particular instance or that time . . . . .

Judge: What d'ya say, Dave?

County
attorney: Your honor I (   ) that we uh take our evidence as we find it . . .
And eh, the mirror and the testimony that's gonna come
before this court uh, in terms of the role that a mirror plays in
cocaine use, flat surface (   ) surface un, razor blades, things of
that nature, are important to show knowledge and in the other
items. It's circumstantial evidence. Um, I agree with uh – with
counsel I that it's uh somewhat ironic what's uh, depicted on
the mirror but I can't help it . . . . .

Defense
lawyer: Your honor, m–my client's not on trial for marijuana
possesion . . . . .

Judge: Well is there any way you can tape that – tape the face of the
mirror over? 'N' they can, y'know, that it wasn't taped in the
condition in which they found it . . . . .

(Cocaine possession trial, 121–125)

The defense want to remove a mirror with a picture of marijuana on it from
the tray containing it, arguing that as evidence it will be prejudicial to the
client charged with cocaine possession, while the county attorney wants the
mirror left in as evidence because it is paraphernalia associated with cocaine
use. The judge's solution is to keep the mirror in, but have the picture of
marijuana taped over, and then tell the jury that when it was found, there
wasn't tape on it. This is in fact what was done.

Thus far we have considered the structure of arguments in which the two
lawyers present positions, and the judge then agrees with one position, offers
a compromise, or offers a third alternative. In addition, the judge sometimes
also takes a position after only *one* lawyer has taken a position, thus
occupying second rather than third position in an argument, as in the
following example:

Example 6

Defense
lawyer: . . . Uh, [2 sec] there's only one more matter, Your Honor, uh,
according to the uh, (scien–les–for) the report on the (   ) of
public safety un, [2 sec] allegedly three vials, glass vials, with
something, allegedly something in it, uh, two of which-one
was insufficient residue for analy–analysis and one was cocaine residue. Only one was alleged to've contained a usable
quantity. And I would move to preclude uh the analysis of the
other two un, vials or mention of the other two vials since *none*
of them contained uh, either–either enough to a–analyze or
enough to even be a usable–uh, a usable quantity. And hence,

since–since that's the uh, standard that we'll probably be
using in this case uh, I would move ( ) only–that only
mention of this one particular vial uh, be allowed into
evidence.

Judge: How 'bout the two vials together?

Defense
lawyer: Well–

Judge: I don't have any problem with the one that there was no
analysis.

Defense
lawyer: There's one was in–insufficient residue for analysis and one
just says residue. Uh–

County
attorney: ( ) it says cocaine residue.

(Cocaine possession trial, pp.29–30)

In this example, the defense attorney and the judge repeat the positions
presented here, with the county attorney essentially echoing the judge's
position afterward, and the judge finally rules later that only the one vial
with insufficient residue for analysis will be excluded, his original position.
This pattern, in which the second attorney either says nothing or reiterates
the judge's position, is fairly common in the data base addressed here.

In example 7, the defense lawyer and the judge *report* a similar two-party
exchange that they had earlier off the record, to get it into the record:

Example 7

Defense
Lawyer: Prior to lunch, Your Honor, uh, and uh, prior to uh, the
selection for the strikes being made at the *voir dire*, I had un not
put my (order) and forgot to ask the court to ask the question
uh, concerning uh, whether any of the individuals on the panel
were prejudiced because my client was black. This is a proper
uh, *voir dire* question and uh, inform the court first –(much) as I
inform the court uh, while we were in the processes of making
strikes an' then I came back 'n' informed Mr. Gonzalez that I 'ad
made that request to have the jury brought back in an' add that
question on *voir dire* and I not uh, consider if he'd already made
some strikes I would let him adjust those appropriately based on
whatever response was from the jury panel. Uh, an' I wanted to
make sure that–on the record that I made that request prior to
the final strikes being made of the jury panel–( ) panel. And it
was my understanding the court–from the court's uh conversation ( ) that you were gonna deny that request if I may

anticipate for a moment, with the same effect as if I had made it
uh, prior to the strikes being made uh ( ).

Judge: Uh, I think what I told you, Bob, was that if–if–if you'd a–asked
me to ask the panel that particular question, either in *voir dire*–
the written *voir dire* that you'd submitted to the court, or if you'd
asked me to ask that question at the time y–you approached the
bench while the full panel was still here 'n'–an' I asked you
what other questions you wanted to a–me to ask 'n' you told me
an' I denied those 'n' that wasn't *one* of the questions, then the
panel was excused an' after the panel w–was excused so–so uh,
the peremptory challenges could be made you they–then came
to my office an' ma–wanted me to call the panel back an'
inquire of 'em uh, that question an' I–I told you no I wasn't
gonna do it at that time. Is that a fair statement of what–what–
what happened?

(Cocaine possession trial, pp.86–88)

A final major variant of the sequential structure of argument in the
American trial court from the data base considered here is one in which the
judge takes a position on an issue before he has heard the position of either
lawyer. This does not occur in the trial motions, because these really must be
raised by lawyers. It does, however, occur in initial appearances, where the
judge must decide upon the conditions of release for each defendant who
comes before him charged with a crime serious enough to permit
incarceration.

Example 8

Judge: Okay, let me go ahead and set the bond here. I'm gonna go
ahead and set a secure bond [3 secs] un, in the amount of one
hundred thousand dollars. [6 seconds] And–you will be
brought, if you do not make the bond, sir, you'll be brought to
the Superior Court on August thirtieth at one o'clock at which
time you'll enter your plea at that time.

County
attorney: Sir, this one is screwed up. Apparently, my office doesn't want
a bond. Um, so I'm gonna recommend no bond.

Judge: You're gonna recommend no bond?

County
attorney: I mean–I–I–an I–I don't mean that. I don't mean no bond. I
mean OR. The–for–apparently for extradition reasons. That
uh, if we set a bond here it'll mess up the extraditions (I have).
[5 secs]

Defense
lawyer: I don't understand that uh. You're saying (release him out of
           the courtroom) . . . . .
County
attorney: There's a detainer on him . . . . .
Defense
lawyer: Well, I'd ask (for bond).
County
attorney: You wanna recommend a bond?
Defense
lawyer: Sure, I'll recommend a bond.
Clerk: We don't want–
Defense
lawyer: Eleven hundred dollars . . . . .
County
attorney: . . . . . C'mon Ed. Edward, you're not gonna recommend bond.
Defense
lawyer: /Alright/ ROR. (Laughs.)

                                        (IA 6, #5 and 9, 33–36)

In this case, the judge goes along with what the county attorney persuades
them all is right – to recommend the defendant be released on his own
recognizance.

In the final example, the county attorney tries to propose a condition of
release and is essentially not allowed to by the judge, who makes one himself
instead.

Example 9

County
attorney: I gotta ask for another condition.
Judge: I know.
County
attorney: You do?
Judge: Yeah . . . . . condition of your release you have no con-
             tact with your children. (2 sec) Pending this. That's a
             con/dition/
Defendant: [/But they/ said I can talk to her on the phone . . . . .
Public
defender: Well, uh [2 secs] can she call on the phone?
Judge: Nope. She's to have no contact with the kids. That's a
             condition–

                                        (IA 10, #26, pp.115–116)

3. Discussion

In the 1960s the domain of study for legal anthropologists gradually shifted from a focus on the exercise of legitimized authority in resolving conflicts to a focus on kinds of third-party intervenors or remedy agents, because this was argued to provide a more adequate basis for the cross-cultural comparative study of conflict management (Nader and Todd, 1978; Abel, 1973). Yet even as various kinds of third-party roles were distinguished, notably mediator, arbitrator and adjudicator, little evidence as to the actual nature of their contributions to conflict management was offered in published accounts of these roles, until researchers began to tape-record actual naturally occurring dispute resolution activity. As Yngvesson and Mather (1983) point out, it has been increasingly recognized that a single third-party intervenor may employ the strategies of more than one such kind of remedy agent, depending on the situation. I have argued here that while the concept of judge as adjudicator may to some extent characterize what a judge does in the presence of a jury, judges ruling on motions outside the presence of a jury, but still in open court, mediate by offering alternatives to lawyers' positions, and advocate and negotiate with individual lawyers, as well as adjudicating by choosing between positions offered by opposing lawyers, so that their verbal roles are functionally differentiated, depending in this case on whether a jury is present or not.

Recently Nader (1984) and Yngvesson and Mather (1983) have moved to a position advocating analysis of the contributions of *all* "users" of a dispute-resolution forum, not just those of the third party, while still recognizing that some users have more influence in shaping the course of a dispute than others. And certainly other contributions to this volume make it clear that much conflict is managed without the involvement or clear differentiation of "disinterested" third parties.

These developments and the data presented in this chapter invite re-examination of the concept of third party to a dispute. It is important to ask in what ways the contributions of a third party to conflict management are similar to and different from those of the parties identified as the actual disputants. What makes a third party different from others involved in a conflict?

In some kinds of courtroom procedures a judge's verbal contributions or interactional moves may be readily distinguished from those of the lawyers. Thus, when a criminal defendant offers a plea of guilty, it is the judge who informs the defendant of his criminal rights. And at a sentencing, the judge hands down the sentence. But in the more truly combative kinds of encounters I have considered here, the bulk of the judges' interactional moves are very much like those of the lawyers: they all *offer positions* on what evidence should be excluded, or what conditions of release should be imposed on a person charged with a crime. They all also vary in the sequential positions their proposals and rationales for them occupy in relation to each other. Judges' and lawyers' verbal contributions, then, are very similar in kind, so it cannot be said that what distinguishes the judge's role is the kinds of moves or uses of language he makes compared to the lawyers.

Instead, in these contexts, the same kinds of moves have different meanings and different consequences, depending on whether they are produced by the judge or the lawyers, because of the participants' shared understanding that it is the judge who has the authority to decide which of the offered and argued-for positions will be made to stick, will become the law of the case at hand.

I suggest, then, that there is a tendency in research or conflict management to assume that third-parties' verbal contributions will be functionally differentiated from those of disputants, when in fact, as the data here suggests, this cannot be assumed at all. Rather, to understand and compare third-party roles, we must ask more openly whether this is the case, and when, how, and why it is or is not the case.

Notes

1   Transcription notational devices include:

[2 sec]	Times in square brackets indicate length of pauses of two seconds. or more. Shorter pauses are not identified.
/Yes he does/	Slashes encompass talk that overlaps with that of another speaker.
[	A single large bracket links the speakers who overlap.
( )	Parentheses show where untranscribable speech occurs or where transcriber was uncertain.
. . . . .	Five dots indicate that the speaker continued speaking beyond what is quoted in the example.
–	A dash is used where there is repetition or reformation in the middle of a sentence or word, usually associated with what is perceived by the hearer as a slight hitch or pause in the flow of speech.

2   Correctional Volunteers are people who volunteer their time to obtain information from those arrested for crimes that is used by the judge in deciding what conditions of release to impose on those charged with crimes.

3   Notations in parentheses at the end of each example locate them in the larger data base.

10 Difference and dominance: how labor and management talk conflict

KATHERINE O'DONNELL

1. Introduction

Labov and Fanshel (1977) identify mitigation and aggravation as a fundamental interactive dimension. R. Brown and Gilman (1972) claim that power and solidarity semantics are universal aspects of social life. In this paper, I draw on these insights to investigate some grammatical and interactive dimensions of power and solidarity. I begin by briefly reviewing the literature in language and power. Next, I introduce Halliday's (1978, 1985) analytic framework on functional grammar and employ it to characterize the registers that labor and management use in doing organizational conflict, within a context where power asymmetry exceeds solidarity. Finally, I contrast labor/management conflict with a dispute between two managers and argue that their solidarity results in a very different form of conflict. Specifically, I address the following questions:

Do requests heard as challenges vary in form by speaker's status? By speaker's affiliation? By hearer's status? By hearer's affiliation?

How does the form that conflict takes vary with respect to differences in interactants' organizational and interpersonal relations of power and of affect?

In what ways does organizational conflict vary linguistically from interpersonal conflict?

Following Halliday (1973, 1978) and Fowler (1979), I contrast organizational (Episode 1) and interpersonal (Episode 2) conflict with respect to the grammatical features of pronominalization and modality, the pragmatic aspect of speech acts, and the dimensions of prosody and interactional sequencing (turn structure).

2. Language, power, and solidarity

Although many sociologists have traditionally viewed language as significant but as removed from fundamental social and material conditions, contemporary culture theorists like Williams (1977: 113) conceptualize language as a constitutive, productive social force. Utilizing Gramsci's

(1971) concept of hegemony, Williams sees power as a lived process, and discourse analysis as a way to "grasp the hegemonic in its active and formative but also transformative process."

With respect to the question of language and power, sociolinguists have identified both universal and context-sensitive differences in linguistic realizations of power and affect. Following Goffman's (1967) work on face, Brown and Levinson (1978) claim that universals in strategic verbal interaction exist and develop a model which accounts for cross-cultural politeness usage.

Bernstein (1971), Kochman (1981), Erickson and Shultz (1982) and Thorne, Kramarae, and Henley (1983), among others, investigate the macrostructural constraints on language along class, race, and gender lines respectively. These authors do not argue for universals, but rather that structural power differentials, linguistically realized, emerge from and perpetuate social inequities.

Given the context-sensitivity of talk, the bulk of recent studies examine the question of the linguistic realization of power and solidarity within specific institutional and organizational settings, including legal, medical, educational, and academic sites. These analysts predict that asymmetric relations of power and solidarity are recreated in non-reciprocal language use in multiple communication channels. At the prosodic level, tension and hesitation (Labov and Fanshel, 1977) and high, rising pitch (Brown and Levinson, 1978) have been associated with tentativeness and a desire to minimize imposition or threat. Uneven interactional rhythms are associated with cultural and power differentials (Erickson, 1982; Gumperz, 1977). Address terms (Brown and Gilman, 1972), speech acts (Grimshaw, 1980d; Brown and Levinson, 1978), and politeness formulae (Brown and Levinson, 1978) have all been analyzed as co-varying with interactants' power and social distance. Interactionally, greater power is correlated with floor holding, topic control, and interruptions. Friendly talk among equals is more likely to be characterized by utterance completions, latching, and casual overlaps.

In sum, speech analysts agree that the power semantic is realized in asymmetry in speech choices, while the solidarity semantic is characterized by greater linguistic reciprocity. Which specific linguistic features are associated with these semantic dimensions is explored by Halliday (1978) in his work on register.

3. Halliday's functional grammar and theory of register.

Halliday's (1978: 2–3) work on register is based on the assumption that the semiotic systems of culture are differentially accessible to various social groups. Halliday states:

> Variation in language is in a quite direct sense the expression of fundamental attributes of the social system; dialect variation expresses the diversity of social

structures (social hierarchies of all kinds), while register variation expresses the diversity of social *processes*. And since the two are interconnected – what we do is affected by who we are: in other words the division of labor is *social* – dialects become entangled with registers. The registers a person has access to are a function of his place in the social structure.

Registers, or different ways of saying things, are products of social structural, semantic, situational, and linguistic factors. As discussed above, social structural elements enter into language via social hierarchies and processes. Semantic features are realized in codes.

In Halliday's view, the adult semantic system is organized around three "macro-functions" of grammar: ideational, interpersonal, and textual. The ideational component serves the purpose of conveying information and ideas. The interpersonal function is used to express social and personal relations and the speaker's involvement in the speech situation. The creation of text and its relation to context is accomplished by the textual function. At the situational level, the category of

Field taps the ideational component and refers to the ongoing activity and the particular purposes that language is serving in a specific speech situation. It is realized linguistically primarily through tense and transitivity.

Tenor taps relations among interactants and is realized principally in choices of mood, modality, and tone or key.

Mode captures textual function and determines text via theme, voice, deixis, conjunction, and lexical choices.

Together, choices in field, tenor, and mode are the situational determinants of text, linking semantic patterns to concrete speech situations via register.

While the analyses following are informed by Halliday's (1978) perspective, my approach differs in three ways: (1) I concentrate my analysis on the category of tenor as revealing how relations of power and affect involved in organizational role relationships are linguistically realized; (2) unlike Halliday, I attend to interactional sequencing and turn structures as they reveal differences in interpersonal and organizational solidarity and power; (3) I employ Halliday's (1985, 1978) work on tone to analyze U.S. English, not British English. Although no comparison of U.S. and British English intonation differences presently exists, Labov and Fanshel (1977) and Brown and Levinson (1978) utilizing U.S. linguistic data have identified intonation contours similar to those that both Halliday and I discuss (i.e. fall–rise; high rising) and attribute to them similar interactional functions.[1]

4. Situational, interpersonal, and organizational contexts

4.1 Quality of Working Life in Midwestern City.

The Quality of Working Life Program (QWL) was initiated in 1979 by labor and management representatives with the general goals of "improving the quality of work and productivity" (Quality of Working Life, 1977). When QWL came to Midwestern City, it had become part of work programs across the U.S. and Europe. In Midwestern City, QWL was defined as "both a program to improve both the quality of the work environment of municipal employees and the services provided by the city government" (Handbook:5) as well as a "*method* for labor-management and supervisor-employee communication, cooperation and management" (QWL Memorandum, 1979:7).

The initial municipal QWL effort in Midwestern City was located in the city's Division of Sewage and Drainage; its success was sufficient to encourage the municipality and affected unions to expand the "experiment" into the Division of Water in 1978. In the spring of 1978 an organizational meeting of Division of Water representatives of labor and management was held and a chair and secretary chosen; between that meeting and the one studied, labor and management representatives caucused separately to discuss QWL goals and set their agenda priorities. Five management and five labor representatives and a QWL observer from the sponsoring university participated in the first "regular" meeting, held in the summer of 1978 in a conference room at a water treatment plant.[2] The labor representatives were members of the American Federation of State, County and Municipal Employees Union (AFSCME); management representatives worked in the city's public sector and were subject to civil service procedures. QWL administrators met separately with union stewards and with the superintendent, along with supervisors and managers, to select committee members; each group nominated individuals from both labor and management who they thought would be appropriate members of the divisional committee. Two criteria were followed in constituting the final committee, i.e.: (1) representation of major departments within the Division of Water and (2) equal numbers of labor and management representatives. As finally constituted, there were two union representatives from one sub-station, one each from the other two sub-stations, and a fifth from the central office of the Division. The management group included the City Superintendent and an additional person from the central office, managers from two of the sub-stations, and a manager from the Service Department. The QWL representative was a university project employee and had no affiliation with the Water Division of Midwestern City. Ned, a union representative from the Water Distribution Substation, was elected Chair at the first organizational meeting.

The choice of Sewage and Drainage as the site for the initial QWL "experiment" was a strategic one, reflecting a view of both labor and management that relations in the Division were poor – as one union person told me "in sewers and drains there was no communication at all." There were three reasons for choice of the Water Division for the next step in the program. First, an AFSCME leader had an interest in the Water Division

QWL program, as he had started out in that area himself. Secondly, the Water Division had low union membership, and the union felt that the QWL program might increase union membership (O' Donnell, field notes). Third, and most importantly, problems similar to those which existed in Sewage and Drains were also present in the Water Division, but they had not yet progressed to the same level of seriousness. Consequently, in the Water Division where people were "at least talking 'at' each other" (O'Donnell, field notes), it was felt that the QWL could help improve relations between and within both labor and management groups. While the QWL meetings were intended to bring management and union representatives together, they were also intended to differ in goals (shared rather than opposing), atmosphere (co-operative rather than conflictful and even confrontational) and format (informal and open rather than formal and constrained), from the more familiar bargaining and grievance sessions.

During the weeks between the organizational meeting and the session studied, management and labour representatives had caucused and had prepared lists of both general goals (i.e., harmony, co-operation) and specific objectives (i.e., mandatory overtime regulations, contract compliance). The principal agenda item for the meeting I have been investigating was to be a casual but serious discussion of these goals and objectives, both shared and potentially contradictory or contending, of labor and management. The QWL program is predicated on labor–management cooperation and an implicit hope of at least some participants was that participants would discover both common and complementary interests. As will be seen, there is disagreement both between labor and management and among managers both about appropriate objectives and how they can best be attained.

Interpersonal relationship   In addition to organization and department ties, these individuals are likewise involved in interpersonal relationships of varying types, durations, and intensity. The following discussion of interpersonal relations between the meeting's participants draws on information from interviews with Lyle, Hart, Georgia, Bonnie, and Allen, and field notes taken by myself and Allen.

The Water Distribution shop   Sam, Ned, and Lyle were Water Distribution shop representatives at the QWL meeting. Their relationships are analyzed with respect to work roles, union or management affiliation, and day-to-day interpersonal relations.

Sam and Lyle have a friendly working relationship. This is in part based on organization needs. Since Lyle has been unwilling to have an assistant manager at the shop, Sam, as shop foreman, has been given and has taken on additional job responsibilities. This relationship brings them into a closer and different type of contact than might generally exist between foreman and manager. Their successful working relationship also stems from the very different personalities and conversational styles which they possess. Lyle's aggressive style is tempered by Sam's calm and somewhat diffident manner.

In contrast, Ned, a union steward, both threatens and antagonizes Lyle. Their hostile relationship is documented in the numerous grievances that Ned has filed against Lyle in recent years. While Lyle is viewed as an aggressive individual by many people in the organization, management and university representatives alike agreed that Ned actively and consciously aggravated the situation.

Management relations. Lyle and Hart, the city's superintendent of water, have known each other for twenty-two years. While both characterize their relationship as a friendly one, both also agree that it has been stormy. Hart reported to me that at one point he symbolically conveyed his dissatisfaction with Lyle's behavior by awarding him a one-dollar yearly pay increase; each man is critical of the other.

The way that these men deal with work-related problems is reflective of their personalities; Lyle criticizes Hart's professional, logical style for being too idealistic and impractical and Hart finds Lyle's fiery, abrasive style to be irresponsible from a management point of view (O'Donnell, field interview notes).

Hart is in a position of greater power; over the years he has counselled and criticized Lyle and pushed him to change his ways. Like much of management's criticism of other managers, Hart reports that these objections were raised behind closed doors. Hart used the QWL program, and this meeting in particular, as the opportunity to make his criticisms open and to hold Lyle publicly accountable to the union and to the "semi-professional" (O'Donnell, field notes) university representative at the meeting.

The business at hand. The people at the summer Divisional meeting believed that they were participating in a program designed to promote social change in the workplace, and generally shared beliefs about the benefits that such a program could provide. Their charge was to develop guidelines that lower-level, workplace committees could utilize in developing specific and explicit policies.

Minutes from the meeting outlined this charge:

1. determine the effect of experiments on the Division as a whole and pave the way for implementation;
2. determine where, when, and how long experiments should last;
3. determine procedure for evaluation and review (Minutes, previous meeting).

At this second meeting, the guidelines for policy and evaluation procedures were to be discussed. The agenda reads:

Table 10.1 *Union and management goals and objectives*

	Union	Management
Goals	(1) Peace and harmony (2) Good working conditions better quality work (3) Good lines of communication (4) Good frame of mind for cooperation (5) Self examination (6) Realization of individual dignity (7) Accountability of *all* employees union and management	(1) Identify common concerns (2) Understand each other's attitudes (3) Improve cooperation and communication between labor and management
Objectives	(1) Consistency of uniforms throughout division (2) Abolish dual standards (3) Working out of classification (4) Ability to talk 1 to 1 in non-adversary roles (5) Promote job mobility (6) Stop anti-union activities (7) Union/management training in contract interpretation (8) Mandatory overtime regulations (9) Winter-work conditions (10) Definition of "emergency" condition; how it is determined and announced (11) Recognition of uses and requirements of new technology	(1) Uniform interpretation of work rules (2) Common concern about quality and quantity of work (3) Bring grievance procedures in compliance with contract (4) Understand the interrelationship among jobs in the division (5) Develop common concern for job appreciation

1. Minutes
2. Discusson of goals and objectives of union and management
3. Working-Level Committees (Agenda, summer meeting)

The meeting opens with discussion of minutes of the earlier meeting and some brief comments on organizational chores and routines by the chair. Ned then turns to introductory discussion of the two lists of goals (see table 10.1). Observing that there is much common ground between the two lists he comments that it is good to have co-operation in the beginning and continues by suggesting that it will be necessary to decide if goals are "expendable or expandable" (text not shown in transcript). Ned clarifies this last point by stating that the committee must decide whether the organization should conform to existing rules or create new ones. At this point, he turns to the list of goals and objectives attached to the agenda and jokes that "since the union has more goals, we'll start with their list."

The first union goal is peace and harmony. Ned asks for comments and calls on John, a union representative. Next he asks for a reaction from Hart, the Water Division's superintendent, and Hart observes that peace and harmony have to be goals. All agree that these two things are important. Hart then remarks that he is interested in getting a clarification of "better quality work," as mentioned in union goal number two, but then adds that his interest is out of the order of discussion. The university representative, Allen, intervenes at this point to clarify the meaning of peace and harmony asking whether the union intends an "active peace as opposed to a suspension of hostilities?" Discussion follows and Georgia, a union member, adds that she would like to see respect added to the goal of peace and harmony. The chair, Ned, next asks rhetorically, "if we are striving for peace and harmony, is there non-peace and disharmony running rampant?"

Hart and Jack, another management representative, note that other union goals, i.e.: (3) good lines of communication, (4) good frame of mind for cooperation, and (6) realization of individual dignity, are all parts of the peace-and-harmony goal. Once again the QWL facilitator intervenes and summarizes the discussion by saying that the group is working toward an active peace as opposed to a truce. Hart comments that discussion of differences should be approached rationally and calmly. The chair, Ned, concludes discussion of the peace-and-harmony goal by reiterating that the considerable overlap between the union and management goals is a good sign. Georgia joins in with the group's verbal agreement by saying, "Right." Hart, the superintendent, says he was pleased to see that communication was brought up by both sides. Ned concludes this initial round of talk by saying:

> in most communication problems, the first problem is to identify that there is a problem, and the solutions seems to fall into place after the (   )

The nature of meeting talk.   Participants in this meeting perceive two sides being represented. This view is reflected visually in the agenda for the meeting and is reiterated throughout the text in references to "sides" and "roles." Interactants recognize that most personal opinions in such talk have organizational implications; this recognition is displayed both through participants' references to organizational knowledge and their use of organizational ways of speaking.

In what follows, I look at two "episodes" (see next section) which followed the congenial talk with which the meeting begins. The talk in the two episodes is less congenial; the nature of the conflict talk in the two episodes also differs. When interactants are called on to make responses in episode 1 and at the beginning of episode 2, their talk emerges as chunks of uninterrupted talk which constitute "position turns." The extent to which these turn structures are embodiments of relations of power and solidarity will be explored in subsequent sections.

In episode 2, Lyle and Hart engage in a dispute which emerges in a quite different form from that of episode 1. I will argue that long-term relations between these two managers allow them to disagree in a far less formal way and with greater reciprocity. The solidarity semantic tempers power differentials.

Data and transcripts.   The principal data for my analysis are audiotaped conversations between labor and management representatives. The analysis begins at the point where the interactants begin to disagree, and continue through their struggle. Comparison across episodes 1 and 2 allows me to contrast the linguistic features which characterize organizational and interpersonal conflict.

For reference, transcripts and a list of transcription procedures are located in appendices 1, 3 and 4.

Mode of discourse.   Halliday (1985) analyzes ways of speaking or registers with respect to field, mode, and tenor patterns. As noted above, I concentrate on the category of tenor because it taps social relationships and realizes *interpersonal* meaning via amplification, reciprocity, and elaboration. Elaboration refers to the linguistic choices made by speakers and reflects the degree of involvement between interactants. The greater the shared knowledge and contact, the greater the range of choices available to speakers and the more condensed their form; with less contact, choices will be more limited and more fully and explicitly developed. Amplification involves the intensity of the linguistic exchange and includes degree of pitch movement, intensification, repetition, loudness, and intonational realizations of modality. Combined, these elements mark positive and negative affect of the speaker towards his listener or what she/he's talking about. Whether or not interactants have available to them the same linguistic options is captured by the category of reciprocity which reflects status, with interactants of unequal status speaking in ways different from those of equal status.

In this chapter, tenor will be discussed with respect to the grammatical categories of pronominalization and modality, the pragmatic dimension of strategy choice, and systems of prosody and interactional sequencing (turn structure).

4.2 Episode 1: organizational conflict

For the following discussion of organizational conflict, readers should refer to the text presented in appendix 3.

Pronominalization.   Lyle argues from the position of first person in developing his stance in episode 1. Out of forty-five instances of pronoun use, Lyle uses "I" thirty-six times, "my" twice, and "me" five times. "We" is used once in reference to people in attendance at the QWL meeting, and once when Lyle discusses his view of a proper union stance.

In responding to Lyle, Sam uses "I" twice, both times in the context of reporting a stance, not in actually taking one as Lyle had done throughout his turn. Instead, Sam uses "we", a pronoun of solidarity, fifteen times and does so only with reference to the union. He also refers to the union with the pronouns "us" and "our". "You" and "your" are used to refer to the management and specifically to Lyle.

In her response to Lyle, Georgia most frequently uses "we" and the impersonal "you" five times in reference to the union. She also uses "we" (once) to refer to both union and management. Georgia used the first person singular "I" twice, both times within the context of counter-challenging Lyle's claims and with tempered verbs of thought ("I think") or feeling ("I don't feel") as opposed to verbs of assertion or statement of fact.

While I have not presented an analysis of the noun–verb collocations in the text, it is important to note that Lyle makes particular reference only to a union. Sam refers to the union playing the role of a lawyer, while managers function as judges. In doing so he makes direct reference to the managers seated at the meeting and refers to them with formal address as "Mr. H.," "Mr—," a form of "negative politeness," indicating his assessment of his addressees' greater power.[3] Georgia used the terms "stewarts" and "members" when speaking of union people, and management and supervisors when referring to management representatives. Like Sam, she adopts the union as lawyer analogy and refers to the union as "acting like an attorney."

Modality and modulation.   Modality refers to the continuum of meanings that lie between the poles of yes and no (Halliday, 1985). For propositions (statements and questions), the positive and negative poles are realized through asserting and denying. In between these two poles lie degrees of indeterminacy involving probability: "possibly/probably/certainly/" and degrees of usuality "sometimes/usually/always." For proposals, the polar choices involve "do it" or "don't do it." In between these poles fall scales of obligation (allowed/supposed/required) and inclination (willing/anxious/determined) which are referred to as modulation.

Lyle seldom uses mitigation in episode 1. While he does use "just" twice to weaken the force of a statement, he more often uses metaphorical expressions of modality like "have been trying to kick out and kick around" or "would like to know why." He also uses reports ("as you say") and projections ("the fact that") to objectify his statements. By using a lawyer analogy, Sam distances himself from any personal challenge to Lyle. In stating the case that the union functions in a lawyer/client relation to its members, Sam avoids responding to Lyle's many individual questions and thus his turn lacks more tangible forms of mitigation. During his turn, Sam uses "only" twice and expresses tentativeness through use of the phrase "we think" as opposed to "we believe." While Sam overall is deferential in manner, his deference is not signalled as much by modality as by his speech-act choice and tone–issues which are examined below.

In contrast to Sam, Georgia remains "on-record" (Brown and Levinson, 1978) more often and utilizes a vast array of "negative politeness" strategies. Use of negative politeness indicates that the speaker (Georgia) sees herself as less powerful than her addressee (Lyle), and wishes not to offend him. Georgia uses two instances of strong modality, "always" and "totally," i.e., expressing certainty; "always" (line 53) when referring to and echoing Lyle's claim that the union stands up for its members even when members are in the wrong, and "totally" when referring to a union member who is considered guilty (line 62). Throughout the bulk of her turn, however, Georgia uses hedges including "necessarily" (three times), "probably," "sometimes" (three times), "just" (twice), "kinda think" (once), "not so much that" (once), and "depends on circumstances I think" (once). While these terms are scattered throughout her turn, they cluster in utterances surrounding her most direct challenges to Lyle (65, 75–76).

Strategy choice.   By referring to the text of episode 1 (appendix 1), the reader can note Lyle raising the topic of the union wearing two hats in lines 4–7 and questioning the union's motivations and ethics (lines, 7–10) as shown in the excerpt below.

4. Lyle: you said that you had to wear two hats or two cloaks which
5.   ever colloquial you u:sed on that (1) that uh *what you say te ME::*
        (1) eh eh
6.   over a bottle of beer may be different than what you say

                                                              ʊ
7.   in my ↑ OFFICE and ↑ I would like to know ↑ WHY (2) the union
8.   has (1) to have *two* you know it's it's either right or *it's* wrong (1)

                                                              Ω
9.   WHY do you have to: be on the side of WRONG (1) uh: if it's
        WRONG (1)
10.   WHY do you have ↑ WHY I th I the the reason I the reason I
        bring it

Lyle's string of questions functions as a challenge (Labov and Fanshel, 1977) to the status of the union. During the course of his turn, Lyle challenges the union eight times, four of which occur in a Wh- question form, with Lyle providing part of the answer (line 7, line 9). As Labov and Fanshel (1977: 172) suggest, Wh- questions in general presuppose the rest of the statement that is not questioned. In other words Lyle in saying "Why do you have to be on the side of WRONG" (line 9) presupposes "you are on the side of the wrong." The contrastive use of stress on "WRONG" (line 9) is further evidence for Lyle's challenge here, as it suggests that Lyle is contrasting his view of what the union is presently doing with his belief of what they *should* be doing and that is siding with the *right*.

Later in his turn, Lyle delivers the following ultimatum (line 25–26)

24. Lyle: who does the ↓ wrong, and I (I) and and I just don't think
((slowly, deliberately
that's right
))
25.   uh and and I I for that reason I'm not gonna answer any of
your questions until I get a
26.   REASONABLE ANSWER OUTA *THAT* because I don't I
((quickly   ))
I think that

which in combination with his further "bald-on-record" (Brown and Levinson: 1978) denunciations of the union reveal his hostility to the union and his perceived greater power *vis-à-vis* his union audience.

Even though Lyle has spoken from an individualistic point of view, personal comments become organizational positions in this context. That Lyle's comments are interpreted as management positions is reflected in the form that the union representatives' responses take. That other management representatives also interpreted Lyle's personalized attack as having implications for a management position is made clear in Hart's subsequent reprimand and repair work in episode 2.

In responding to Lyle's challenges, Sam and Georgia choose different routes. Sam characterizes the union position by drawing on a lawyer analogy. He does not directly challenge any of the assertions that Lyle made and distances himself from the position of personal accountability for his statement. As indicated by Lyle's subsequent remarks to Sam, Sam neither alienates himself from Lyle, his boss in the Water Distribution shop, nor the union, of which he is a loyal and trusted member. He manages to support the union's position by using both the lawyer analogy and conventional union rhetoric and defers to the power of management by acknowledging that the role of the union is merely to represent and that of management to judge and make final decisions.

Georgia neither works for nor regularly associates with Lyle, and thus is not in the same tight spot as Sam. Georgia is also freer to express her opinions, both because she has a higher organizational position than Sam and because she has once worked as a liaison officer between the union and management.

In her defense of the union, Georgia disagrees and counter-challenges (lines 54, 65, 71) restates the union's position (lines 60, 76, 77), and adds her personal opinions (line 65) but does so cautiously. Georgia removes herself as author from many of her critical comments to Lyle by employing the conventional union terminology as in (line 67) where she used the term "chronic" in a marked fashion to refer to labor and management people who have had long-term problems at the waterworks. Like Sam, she draws on the lawyer analogy (line 76), which allows her to go "on record" standing with the union, while not personally confronting Lyle. A final tactic used by Georgia is to make "existential statements" or general maxim-like remarks like "it's just one of those things you have to live with" (line 71) which permit her to go "off-record" (Brown and Levinson: 1978) in instances either where she wishes to escape *personal* responsibility for a claim or where she is being intentionally indirect in order to protect the sensitive information she is conveying (line 69–71). In such cases, she invites implicature (Grice, 1975).

Georgia makes explicit the two-sided nature of work-related issues in her comments by asserting that both union and management chastise workers (lines 55–59), stand behind their own members (lines 65–66) and share information (lines 68–69). By revealing organizational co-operation between labor and management, Georgia challenges Lyle's contention that she "says one thing in office and another over beer" (lines 5–7).

Prosody.   In this section, I discuss the recurrent prosodic features of the speakers' turns and of the episodes as a whole, attending to stress, pitch, intonation contours, and interactional rhythm. I will focus particularly on tone.

Halliday (1985: 401–403) suggests that the English tone system relates quite specifically to polarity, or the positive–negative opposition. Rising pitch means "polarity unknown" and conveys uncertainty while falling pitch means "polarity known" and conveys certainty. In everyday English, *tone 1*, or a statement delivered with falling tone, is the most common. *Tone 2*, a rising tone, is most commonly used with a yes–no question. A level tone, which neither falls nor rises, is *tone 3*, and basically means "is not yet decided whether known or unknown." *Tones 4 and 5* are combinations of rising and falling on a single tone contour. *Tone 4*, falling–rising, is associated with tentativeness or reservations. *Tone 5*, rising–falling, conveys a sense of initial uncertainty but turning into certainty and often carries the implication "you ought to know."

Lyle's long turn in episode 1 is marked by a great deal of pitch variation, strong emphasis through increased volume, and a marked use of tone 4 (falling–rising). Lyle heavily stresses the words "wrong" and "why" when speaking of the union. His challenges to the union's integrity frequently involve dramatic changes in pitch, and use of tone 4, conveying the message "there's a but about this." He concludes his turn with a definitive falling tone, which signals that he is not hesitant about what he had done.

The text immediately following displays Sam's response to Lyle. As can be seen, he emphasizes "we" and "represents" three times, "accept" (referring to the union), "made" (complaints), "judges," and "their" (referring to management) via vowel elongation, increased volume, and stress. He concludes his first turn with elevated, rising pitch, a pattern which has been identified cross-culturally with hesitation and tentativeness (Brown and Levinson, 1978: 177). In his second turn (lines 91–96, appendix 3), he repeatedly used tone 4, (fall–rise) as in (line 93) "there's nothin we can do we have to ac*cept* it," in this context conveying reservation.

42. Sam: The union is similar to the lawyer that goes and
43.　　　takes the case of a person, that uh in OUR MIND we are the way
　　　　　WE think we know that
44.　　　the person is guilty but that's not for us to decide that's
45.　　　for uh (2) whoever had (1) uh MADE the complaint and
　　　　　whoever the JU:DGES may
46.　　　be that's THEIR decision (1) we're we're only to REPresent
　　　　　those people *not*
47.　　　uh to say that they're guilty or not
　　　　　↑Although we may have it in mind
　　　　　((quickly, louder　　))
48.　　　although we know it ↑ you know that's not our (3)
　　　　　((quickly, louder))
49. Lyle: Are you allowed to just discharge anybody from
50.　　　the union?

In comparison to both the speakers who preceded her and her own subsequent statements, Georgia begins her turn quietly. She does, however, stress the terms "stewarts," "jump," "as well," and "union," all in reference to the union disciplining its own members. At line 60, Georgia uses "but" as an internal adversative (Halliday and Hasan, 1976: 235) to convey the message "as against what the current state of the communication process would lead us to expect, the fact of the matter is . . ." At this point she used tone 5 (rising–falling) over obligation (line 60) which conveys the message of certainty when speaking with respect to the union's obligation to represent its members. When Georgia counterchallenges Lyle in (lines 64–65), again following the use of "but," she concludes her utterance with tone 1, stressing her point by using marked drop in pitch and increased emphasis of the term "supervisors." Thus far in her turn, Georgia is using contrastive stress to underscore her point that union and management have the same problems and engage in the same practices and to argue against Lyle's one-sided approach. Georgia's subsequent backing off (lines 67–75) is signalled through her greater use of mitigation and accompanying rising intonation (tone 2) conveying tentativeness. Following "but" in (line 75), Georgia's new counterchallenge to Lyle is marked prosodically with greater variation in pitch, increased volume and stress. The text follows:

75. Georgia: on the circumstances but it's *not* so much that you feel the person is
ʊ
76.   ↑RIGHT but (1) you're like an at↑TORney you have to take
ʊ
on a ↑ CASE and
77.   they're en*tit*led to represen↑TAtion and uh we can't necessarily

Georgia uses tone 4 over the words "RIGHT" and "CASE" (line 76), a tone which is generally associated with tentativeness. In this instance, Georgia's intonation choice underscores her own and Sam's previous point, that the union is obligated to represent members without necessarily knowing of their guilt or innocence.

Overall, the interactional rhythm of this episode is uneven, with mixed tempos within speakers' turns, frozen and formal at turn junctures where the Chair generally selects speakers.

Turn structure.   Episode 1 is characterized by long chunks of uninterrupted, primarily non-narrative "position turns." Speakers' turns at talk are seen as representative of organizational positions in meeting talk with two or more official sides when issues concerning both sides are the topic at hand. In such a context, whole chunks of talk refer to earlier segments, and attention to overall emerging themes and structures across turns becomes more important than attention to immediate sequencing. For example, in responding to Lyle, Georgia makes reference to his challenges and assertions and organizes her turn according to statements that she had heard during his three-and-a-half-minute turn and Sam's one-minute statement. (Later in episode 2, in a segment not analyzed here, Hart [the city superintendent] follows a similar pattern, and organizes his turn to respond to issues that Lyle had raised six to seven minutes earlier.)

There are very few interruptions and overlaps in this talk. No interruptions occurred during a person's position turn. While the chair called on union members and management members between turns, during turns the interactants did not attempt to take the floor.

For the following discussion of the dispute between Lyle and Hart the reader should refer to the full text printed in appendix 4.

4.3 Episode 2: interpersonal conflict

Pronominalization. During his challenge to Hart (lines 189–208), Lyle makes reference to Hart using the second person singular "you" nine times. He uses "I" once in the context of reporting (line 205) and "we" once to refer to the people who work in the Water shop with him (line 205). "We" here refers to union and management members.

Hart used the first person singular "I" seven times during the same period. In his one brief turn, Sam uses "we" twice to refer to the people in the Water shop. During their exchanges, Lyle and Hart rarely refer to people ("someone else"; "garage boy") but rather to things like running boards, trucks, cars, and bells.

Modality. In episode 2, very little indeterminacy is expressed via modality. Hart and Lyle argue in polar terms: situations exist or they don't exist. When Sam intervenes in the dispute (line 208), modality once again comes into play as he says "if I may: correct/"

Strategy choice. Episode 2 immediately follows episode 1; there is no intervening talk. Hart is in a difficult position; he is as Ned says (line 98) "on the hot seat." Lyle's earlier comments were problematic for both the union and management. From Hart's point of view, the company must minimize offending the union in order to promote good work relations and insure maintenance of municipal services. From a superintendent's point of view, Lyle had overstepped the legitimate authority structure by taking so strongly an anti-union stance. That Hart considers Lyle to have done so is evident in Hart's later remarks to Lyle concerning the union's rights (lines 117–156), management irresponsibility (lines 172–188), and responsibility (line 6). (My field interviews both with Hart and Lyle and with others revealed that the two men had frequently disagreed over work-related issues and had quite different management philosophies.)

Hart takes a very long initial turn (lines 112–164) which, while sequentially a response to Ned's immediately preceding question, includes a number of other interactional moves as well. Much of his talk is devoted to support and indirect remedial work (Goffman, 1971) and to reminding his audiences of the importance of responsibility. In so doing, he is indirectly hinting to Lyle to make amends.[4] Lyle fails to comply, and continues his previous line of argument at which point Hart directly challenges him (line 184). A fully fledged dispute emerges as Lyle challenges Hart's factual claims. Both men challenge and counterchallenge via question–answer sequences until Sam chimes in with information supporting Hart's assertions (line 208).

205. Lyle: //tha that's what I'm sayin (1) you hea:rd in the meeting that
we didn't *have* any
206.   bells on em
207. Hart: No, I didn't hear tha:t (1) did not hear that (1)
((quickly   ))
208. Sam: We daw uh: if I may: correct that uh we have uh (1) four five
that doesn't have bells on . . . uh:://
((softer   ))

Upon hearing Sam's remarks, Hart returns to the theme of responsibility
(lines 210, 212) and concludes by setting a policy goal for the Waterworks
(line 213).

209. Lyle: // on the boom trucks you don't need one (my good-
((low   ))
ness you . . .) // (dump trucks)
(Group laughter.)
210. Hart: //well (1) MY ONLY *POINT* BE: IN (3) getting back (1)
((louder))   ((soft background chat-
to responsibility (2)
ter and laughter))
211.   *WE: KNOW: MANAGEMENT* knows that that is a *serious*
situation (1) and we have *KILLED* one
212.   person as a result of it (2) there's a *POLICY* that trucks are
supposed to have
213.   bells or at least those trucks that you feel (1) that its *necessary*
(1) some trucks

Prosody   Lyle begins his challenge (line 189) of Hart's facts with a
question delivered in a tempo quicker than that of episode 1, slightly
increased volume, emphasis, and in tone 1, a tone not usually associated
with questions but with statements. His next challenge (lines 191–192) is
also delivered in a similar tone, but most of his subsequent utterances end
with rising intonation (tone 2), signaling uncertainty. Hart delivers his
statements with little variation in pitch or volume. He uses stress to emphasize the fact currently being disputed. Hart follows up Lyle's initial question/
challenge (line 189), with a minimal agreement in tone 3 indicating that
Hart recognizes that while he did not *personally* see the item in question, he
believes his sources are valid. If Hart had disagreed with Lyle's challenge
(line 189), he would have countered the contrastive stress that Lyle had
used on the terms "you" and "see." The remainder of Hart's utterances end
in tone 1, conveying certainty. In contrast to the more frozen interactional
rhythm of episode 1, the interactional rhythm is smooth and even throughout the series of question–answer exchanges. Lyle's style is moderate in

comparison to his remarks to the union. There is no recurrent use of tone 4, signaling reservation. Lyle often uses a questioning intonation. Lyle's comments exhibit little prosodic intensity until Sam chimes in with some new information, which Lyle misinterprets, as he doesn't allow Sam to finish his sentence. Following the exposure of problems in his shop, Lyle's intensity again drops. Throughout this exchange, Hart displays very little prosodic intensity. It is only after Hart has won the dispute, that he displays his greater power by using an expletive and tapping on the table to underscore his emphatic proposal for changed organizational policy.

Turn structure. Once Hart's long initial turn has been completed and Lyle introduces the issue of drunkenness on the job, the conflict between Lyle and Hart is manifested in the form of increasingly brief, rapid and frequently latching turn sequences. No interruptions or overlaps occur until Lyle interrupts Sam when Sam self-selects. While the Chair had initially called on Hart to respond to the outcome of episode 1, during the conflict sequence analyzed here Lyle and Hart self-select. While I have not analyzed textual cohesion in this chapter, it is important to note that Lyle and Hart respond to each other with partial sentences and do sentence completions for each other. The ability to do so is based on shared organizational and interactional knowledge. The text below illustrates this point:

197. Hart: one I think it was the tan one (2)
        ((quickly   ))
198. Lyle: But that all the rest of em had it?
        ((quickly, condensed   ))
199. Hart: All the other *dump* trucks
200. Lyle: had bells
        ((lower))
201. Hart: That was what that's what I was told

4.4 Summary

Episodes 1 and 2 involve conflicts, but the way the disputes are argued varies considerably and systematically. Analysis of tone, grammar, and turn structure reveals that the first dispute centers on organizational points of view. In episode 1, there is less reciprocity with respect to modality, pronominalization, or speech strategy than between the interactants in episode 2; this difference reveals the greater power/status differentials which exist between the interactants in episode 1. Lack of reciprocity is correlated with asymmetrical power relations. Similarly, there is greater variation in amplification in the union/management dispute than in the manager's interpersonal conflict. Greater prosodic intensity occurred with organizational positional statements, indicating either positive or negative affect of the speaker toward the topic at hand or toward his/her listener(s). Episode 2 was less marked by intense linguistic realizations. Finally, interactants in episode 1 had to spell out their organization's position; the necessity to make issues explicit emerges in all conflict contexts but is more critical among those with greater social distance. If a speaker is confronted with the necessity of taking a stance and being cautious simultaneously, she/he can do so using various forms of implicature or by going off-record with respect to specific claims. The social distance between Lyle and the union representatives Sam and Georgia is recreated through lengthy "position turns," used to explain an organizational point of view. In contrast to the interactants of episode 1, Lyle and Hart share background organizational and personal experiences and this familiarity is expressed interactionally by brief, rapid, interrupted and latching turn structures, and less need to elaborate on their respective positions. They can take more for granted.

5. Conclusion

In this chapter I have examined how various configurations of interpersonal social structural relationships are linguistically realized in conflictual encounters. In episode 1, the power semantic prevailed and produced asymmetry across linguistic and prosodic channels; social distance was evident in tone and turn structure. Episode 2 was characterized by speech forms indicating greater reciprocity and less social distance between Lyle and Hart; the solidarity semantic was in operation. Still, several issues with respect to the effect that organizational contexts have on this particular talk remain unresolved.

First, my analysis has not specified the extent to which the ideology of QWL programs influences contemporary labor management discussions and this meeting's talk in particular. Future attention to the category of field would allow me to specify this process. Second, while my analysis suggests that labor and management discourse vary systematically in conflict situations, more research is needed to establish the extent to which different registers are employed by these groups. Third, gender, class, race, and individual stylistic differences interact with and in part constitute relations of power and solidarity. I have not specified the interplay of these factors in this chapter.[5] Finally, because I have utilized a synchronic framework, I have left implicit and unexamined the extent to which the history of labor/capital relations has left its traces on the discourse at hand.[6]

Appendix 1   Key to transcription conventions

(3.5) Time – denotes elapsed time, unfilled pause, (laughter) vocalizations.
/ = / Latching – two utterances joined with minimal terminal juncture between.
((Soft, trailing off)) Voice quality – descriptions appear beneath utterances.

// Indicates the point at which a current speaker's talk is interrupted by the talk of another. An overlapped utterance is followed by the talk which overlaps it.

[indicates simultaneous talk and is placed at the point of overlap.

:, :: Indicates prior syllable is prolonged.

MORals Capitalization marks emphatic stress, with increased volume.

why Italic type marks stress without increased volume,

ʊ Tone 4 falling rising.

ɔ Tone 5 rising falling.

? Tone 2 rising (question)

– Indicates a cut-off of a prior word or sound.

= Indicates that two utterances are joined with minimal terminal juncture between.

↑ Rise in pitch.

↓ Drop in pitch.

Adapted from transcript conventions developed by Gail Jefferson.

Appendix 2   Official minutes – August 23 meeting
September 1, 1978

Division of Water
Minutes of Quality of Working Life
Division Committee
August 23, 1978

The minutes of last meeting were accepted by consensus, but it was decided that future minutes need to be submitted only within a week or ten (10) days of each scheduled meeting. In this way any changes and additions for the next meeting can be enclosed with the minutes. N and Mr. M should be contacted relative to any requested changes or additions to be included for discussion at each meeting.

The meeting opened with a discussion to determine common goals and objectives of Union and Management.

An effort was made to define what was meant by "Peace and Harmony" with the conclusion being that it meant working in an atmosphere of respect and understanding attempting to identify and resolve common problems.

Before the discussion could continue L conditioned his active participation in the QWL program, upon resolving of question as to why the Union defended members, right or wrong. The issue was resolved with the understanding that the Union had a commitment towards its members not to necessarily judge but to take the position of any lawyer who feels all have the right to defense. This position on the part of the Union was concurred in both by management and the Union.

It was decided that specific incidents should be taken care of in the Working Level Committee and active participation is required of all people on the Divisional Committee and not conditioned on resolving specific incidents between Union and Management.

Goals decided upon were as follows

1.   Honest and open Communication flowing between Union and Management, Union and Union, Management and Management.

2. Identify common concerns.
3. Improved committment to Public Service.
4. Mutual respect of *responsibility* and *accountability* to job roles.

The goals as decided upon seemed to combine all of the previous ten (10) goals decided upon in the separate meetings of Union and Management.

The meeting was concluded with it being decided that at our next meeting, we would decide on the formation of the working-level committees. Will they be on site committees or committees formed along areas of responsibility? Are people to be selected, elected, or appointed? How do we maximize participation?

Answers to these questions should be thought out and ready for presentation at our next meeting which is to held September 13, 1978, at 9:30 a.m.

Respectively submitted,

Secretary
QWL Division Committee

Appendix 3
Transcript – Episode 1

00. Ned:	Well let's pick on management for a side (2) for a minute
0.	the ident the identify common concerns (4) L (3)?
1. Lyle:	N I'm uh (2) I'm still back to one thing 'hat
2.	you said last week that I've been trying to kick out and
3.	kick around my mind and find out what you meant by it↓uh::
	((low))
4.	you said that you had to wear two hats or two cloaks which
5.	ever colloquial you u:sed on that (1) that uh *what you say te ME::* (1) eh eh
6.	over a bottle of beer may be different than what you say
	ʊ
7.	in my↑OFFICE and↑I would like to know↑WHY (2) the union
8.	has (1) to have *two* you know it's it's either right or *it's* wrong (1)
	ʊ
9.	WHY do you have to: be on the side of WRONG (1) uh: if it's WRONG (1)
10.	WHY do you have↑WHY I th I the the reason I the reason I bring it
11.	up is because let me get back let me let me get this thing straightened out a little bit
12.	when I was a young man I belonged to a union (1) and I got
13.	thrown↑outa that union (1) uh the REASON I was thrown outa ((quickly))
14.	that union was was a *just*↑reason because I didn't agree with
15.	what they↑SAID (1) and I stood up and I told em I *don't* I *don't*
16.	BE↑LIEVE in what you're doing they wanted to strike
17.	for two cents (1) I DIDN'T wanna strike for two cents because I
	ʊ
18.	knew I'd loose a couple weeks work and at two cents an

19.	hour it takes a hell of a long time to make back your weekly
	((quickly, low
20.	wage (1) *anywhere they threw ME out* (1) now I have never HEA:RD
	)) ʊ ((condensed))
21.	of ANYONE in THIS union being thrown out for *ANYTHING*
	((·quickly))
22.	*drunk*edness (1) *fighting* (1)↑*ANYTHING* (1) eh it just seems that (1)
	((low))
	as
23.	you say you wear two cloaks (1) you run to the aid of the guy
	((quickly))
24.	who does the↓wrong, and I (1) and and I just don't think that's right
	((slowly, deliberately))
25.	uh and and I I for that reason I'm not gonna answer any of your
	questions until I get a
26.	REASONABLE ANSWER OUTA *THAT* because I don't I I think that
	((quickly))
	the meetings are
27.	we're having here are a WASTE of time (1) if we continue with
	((quickly))
28.	the fact that the union will stand up and say this man just
	((quickly)) ((quickly
29.	because he was drunk fallin down drunk couldn't get on the
30.	back ( ) hit the guy on the head with a that doesn't
	))
31.	mean he's *guilty* he's he's a WONDERFUL↑guy cause he's payin
	ʊ
32.	us ten bucks a month or whatever they pay (1) *THAT* I don't
	ʊ
33.	think is right I think there should be some change
34.	there to where the union will stand up and say hey
35.	you were *wrong*↓pal (1) and we're not gonna stand here and
36.	uh help you OUT and protect your JOB any longer (3)
37. Jack:	I think that's one of the goals of // number 7 here would be (2)
?:	// seven
38. Lyle:	Yeah but I wanna sp I wanna he asked me a question
39.	and I wanna I wanna an answer te that first (1)
40. Ned:	uh: S you started to answer that part of LAST time you wanna
	( )=
41. Sam:	=what about its a//
Ned:	//two hats
42. Sam:	The union is similar to the lawyer that goes and
43.	takes the case of a person, that uh in OUR MIND we are the way WE
	think we know that
44.	the person is guilty but that's not for us to decide that's
42.	for uh (2) whoever has (1) uh MADE the complaint and whoever the
	JU:DGES may
46.	be that's THEIR decision (1) we're we're only to REPresent those
	people *not*

47.	uh to say that they're guilty or not↑Although we may have it in
	mind ((quickly, louder
	))
48.	although we know it↑you know that's not our (3)
	((quickly, louder))
49. Lyle:	Are you allowed to just discharge anybody from
50.	the union?
51. Sam:	Are we allowed? through the executive board yes
	((louder))
52. Ned:	Georgia?
	((quietly))
53. Georgia:	Well (1) as far as: we always stand up and tell
	((quietly))
54.	em they're right *that*'s not necessarily true because management
	((quickly))
55.	doesn't necessarily know that union does chastise members (1)
56.	and *stew*arts *jump* on em too when they're chronic because they
57.	can also be a ha*bit*ual person who is a problem can be a
58.	problem for the union as *well* as for management because they
59.	create problems that other *union* members sometime will git on us
	ᴜ ᴖ
60.	about (1) but at the same time we have an obliGAtion to
	ᴜ
61.	represent that person as far as we↑can now if that person is
62.	totally uh guilty of something and if things are done right
63.	then they'll probably have to suffer uh their↑*consequences* (1)
64.	but as far as the UNION standing behind uh their *members*
65.	I don't feel that the union stand behind their members
	((quickly, voice constriction
	(intake of air)
66.	anymore than management uh stands behind their↓ *super*visors
	))
	because we have had
67.	uh some chronic supervisors and some chronic union members uh
	(1) down through the years and I think that in (1) of the record
	((quickly
68.	conversation with some management we have both recegnized this
	))
	but there's
69.	certain problems that you have to live with and sometime try te solve
	(1)
70.	you know *ONE* in my department//
Sam:	// uh huh
	been workin on for a long time but
71.	it's just one of those things that we have te to LIVE with and it's not
	that
72.	you think that person is *RIGHT* (1) and uh in fact sometimes you (1)
	kinda think

73.   that maybe somebody DOES need a little discipline maybe uh it will

74.   ↑happen (3) and sometimes it has been arranged (1) so it just
                    ((quietly)) ((quickly
          depends
           ))

75.   on the circumstances but it's *not* so much that you feel the person is
          ℧

76.   ↑RIGHT but (1) you're like an at↑TORney you have to take on a↑
          ℧
          CASE and

77.   they're en*tit*led to represen↑TAtion and uh we can't necessarily
          can't ↑ ( ) for them//

78. Sam: //uhm

79. Georgia: //can't ↑ *lie* for them//

80. Sam: //uhm

81. Vern: *I* have one less union member and I don't believe that he left by his
          ℧
          own wheel (will) (3)

82. Georgia: Yeah

83. ?:   Yeah

84. ?:   Yeah

85. Vern: I believe he left the *un*ion but on his own
          (mild group response)

86. Lyle: Well we got *two* you get rid of *one* and I'll I'll go along with ( )

87.   (group laughter)

88. Lyle: You know you know who they//

89. Sam: //I'll say like this

90. Lyle'   //are and you know I I you guys WORK with em

91. Sam: I'll say like this we () *we* represent em (1) it's left up to

92.   Mr. H, you uh Mr. R, Mr. M ( ) you're the judges (2) OK if you
                            ℧   ℧   ℧   ℧

93.   case is legitimate e enough er there's nothin we can do we have to
          ℧
          ac*cept* it

94.   (I can) like I sa:id uh we only there to *re*present↓em it's not that we
          think they're

95.   right or wro:n ya know (1) we can know that they're DEFINATELY
          wron but is

96.   nothin we can do about it's left up to *YOU* to make that uh ( )

97.   ( )

Appendix 4
Transcript–Episode 2

98. Ned: Let me (1) put Hart (1) on the hot seat here for a

99.   minute in the same way I'll forewarn you you know
                    ((quickly, lower

100.   you're gonna be hot taking the situation of the *MANAGER* (1)
          ))
101.   a *SUPERVISOR* (1) who does something that is WRONG (1)
102.   and charges or whatever are brought to YOU (4)
103.   would you in your position and d'you think in any
                              · ((quicker))
104.   *respon*sible (1) management position should that person
105.   should the supervisor be criticized (1) and publicly
106.   flogged for saying you know anything wrong or would that be a
                              ((softly))
107.   situation where you will say oh no that's something that
108.   I wanna handle in *my* office in *my* manner (2)
109.   wouldn't you (1) necessarily defend your supervisor
110.   basically publicly (1) taking whatever action you
          ((quickly   ))
111.   wanted to privately (1) depending on the situation ( )
                              ((low, quickly   ))
112. Hart: Yes that's very true (1) in many situations (2) uhm: (2)
          ((softly   ))
113.   I I *think* (1) the *thing* (1) that's bothering L (1) is you say wearing
          ((voice constriction))
          different
114.   *cloaks,* wearing different *hats* (1) OK (1) and I think that's just a
                              ((quickly
          reality
115.   of *life* that you *cannot* a*void* (1) *personally* (1) now your
                              ))
116.   your MORals your conVICtions your resPONsibility (1) all play a
117.   *part* in how you play those *roles* (4) I'm su:re (1) that you've
118.   probably experienced the situation (1) both of us have (1)
119.   even with regard to our own children (1) where we know DARN n
          good
120.   n well: that we have do:ne as teenagers let's say (2) things
121.   that we don't want them doing (1) and we're going to *TELL* them
122.   and di*RECT* them and in*STRUCT* them not to do those type of
123.   things (1) but you did em yourself (1) OK (1) you *LEARNT* from that
124.   experience (1) and it was as a re*SULT* of that learning you now:
125.   in ma*tur*ity you now have a different attitude towards (1)
126.   what you think is proper action for ↑ them (4) you: (1) are
          ((quickly   ))
          in a sense
          ((slower, deliberate))
127.   playing two different roles one is a teenager and one is
128.   a *parent* (3) responsi*bility* (1) plays a big part in it
129.   I think in other words as a manager or as a supervisor (2) S
          ((low, soft))((quickly))

130.   for example if you: (1) ask him to perform a certain ta:sk he *ha:s* a

                  ʊ

131.   responsibility to carry it ou:t (1) whether he agree:s necessarily with

132.   your decision or↑*not* (1) and I would say: (1) uh he would *do* that

         ʊ   ((faster   ))

        because of

                                ʊ

133.   responsi*bili*ty he'll carry that out in his RO:LE *A:S* a *FORE*man for the

        ((quickly   ))   ((slow, deliberate

134.   water shop so in a sense he's playin a role there (1) he may disagree:

        ))   ((quicker))   ((softer)

135.   but he carries it out because of responsibility I *don't* think you can

         ʊ   ʊ

136.   AVO:ID (3) ACTing in ROLES (1) now: (1) what YOU'RE concerned

        ((stretched))((slowly, deliberately))

        about is how: (1)

          ((slow, delib-

137.   sincere: and how HONEST somebody is going to be with you (3)

        erate))   ((slower, clearly enunciated   ))

138.   take the situation (1) where the union is representing someone (1)

        that you feel

139.   is not a ideal employee (1) that *opinion* (1) may *well* come from *many*

                                                        ((higher

140.   circumstances and instances (1) that don't relate to the *specific*

        pitch, voice constriction   ))   ((swallowed))

141.   circumstances being grieved (2) they: ↑ *I* feel uh: ha:ve the ↑ *right* to be

142.   represented (1) te develop facts (1) relative te that one ↑ circumstance

143.   you *CAN'T solve all your problems* at one time in *most* cases you have

144.   to do things a *step* at a time (1) and if you're having a uni*que* problem

                                  ((quickly))

145.   that comes to a head through a grievance or some other action (2)

146.   *I* think we have a responsibility to primarily to address

        ((quickly   ))

147.   that *one* action (1) the *OTHER* items (2) have *not* come to a head

        ((clearly enunciated))

           ʊ

        or↑*WE* have

148.   not initiated an appropriate action (1) uh: I I don't have any (1) real

                                         ((softer, voice

        problems

        constriction))

                                            ʊ

149.   with the union doing uh the BEST THEY↑CAN to represent that

                                 ((quickly))

        individual (1) uh: with

150.   regard to that spec-particular set of circumstances (1) I think that's a

151.   necessary part of gitting *facts* out on a table to aid us in making

152. a decision (1) now (2) there are times certainly when it seems to be
153. done with more vigor than we would hope to see it (1) there's times (1)
154. when (1) uh certainly you can resolve some of these items by setting down
155. and *talk*ing to the union rep and I I have done that and it and it is
      ((quickly   ))
156. *work*able uh:: but I *think* as I said when we when I recommended
      ((quickly))
157. that we use Ned in the r a as as a↑chairman for example (2) uh:: I think

                                                                    ᴜ
158. he can for inst- uh::at times play the devil's↑advocate (1) and I think
      ((voice constriction))
159. that's↑*nec*essary to our dis↑*cuss*ion particularly if the discussion
160. comes down to a lull where we're not↑gitting anywhere (1) I think it's
161. helpful to *have* that type of uh discussion going on te te to uh git
162. everybody's↑viewpoint out on the table now, I don't know whether
      ((low, quickly, soft   ))
163. that I *THINK* the main thing you're concerned about Lyle was
      ((swallowed))
164. whether people are being sincere and honest (1)
      ((getting lower, softer, trails off)
165. Lyle: Yes =
166. Hart: = We're *ALL* concerned about that (1)
167. Lyle: Yeah (1)
      ((low, choking, voice constriction))
      the thing the thing I would like to do is uh if: (2) we've had we've *had* cases
168. where a possibility of a man↑being killed uh: has loomed very (1)↑largely in the
      ((voice constriction)
169. division (1) because of a man on the job *drunk* (1) uh: running a piece
      ((voice constriction))   ((quickly
      of

                                                                    ᴜ
170. machinery and I↑just wanna just wanna make sure that the
            ))   ((accusatory tone   ))
      responsibility
                  ᴜ
171. of something like that eh goes to the right person or persons (1)
      ((accusatory tone   ))
172. Hart: I *could*n't agree mo:re (1) and I can also tell you of a situation (1)
      ((deliberate, soft))   ((like reading a report – monotone, low))
173. where we ALL KNOW I think (1) setting here that we HA:VE in fact
      ((clear))((slowly))((quickly   ))   ((slower))

            ʊ
killed a man (1)
174. Lyle: Ye[s
           ((low, soft))
175. Hart: on [the job (2) backed over the top of im (1) and I: can point out a
           ((soft, quickly)) ((quickly, low   ))
           situation where we had (1)
                  ((slowly))
176.   *trucks* that shoulda had bells on em that didn't have em and that's
           ((quickly   ))
           a↑*man*agement
177.   responsibility (2) uh: so↑you have both sides to that: (1)=
                       ((voice constriction))
178. Lyle: =at that time (1) [uh:
           ((low, quickly))
179. Hart: [story (2)
180. Lyle: bells were not (1) used =
           ((getting softer, slows down, trails off)
181. Hart: =I can even point out (1) I have seen (1) and I: have to share in part
           ((quickly   ))   ((slowly))
           of that
182.   responsibility since that time it's a*maz*ing the number of *back*ing
           ((quickly   ))
           accidents
183.   we've had *back*ing over tricycles in somebody's private yar:d these
                ((listing intonation, low   ))((lower
           types
184.   of things I↑don't see any action being taken by management (4)
           ))
185. Lyle: Really? (2)
           ((voice constriction, rising pitch))
186. Hart: We had a hearing the other day and I found out that there was a
           ((quickly   ))
           running
187.   board on a *truck* (1) that (1) was more of a problem than it should
                       ((voice constriction, clear
           have been and
           enunciation))
188.   it got attention (1) im↑*me*diately the following day
                    ((voice constriction, quickly))
189. Lyle: Well uh (1) you: you're not *you* didn't *see* the running board (down
           ((softer))   ((quickly, louder   ))
           there)
190. Hart: I understand that (1) (   )
           ((quickly, condensed))
191. Lyle: you got you gotta now just like the ba the cars that don't ha:ve *BELLS*
           ((quickly   ))
           on em (1)

192.   that you he:ard from someone else that↑no one of em that↑none of
              ((condensed)) ((rapid
              em had bells on em
                           ))
193. Hart: No: I didn't hear any such thing I heard it was one
              ((low, quickly, tense sounding
              truck (1) [(   )
                    ))
194. Lyle: [One truck does *not* have bells?
195. Hart: *One* truck (1) it *now* has it (2) I'm told
196. Lyle: *ONE* bell you you heard that that *one* truck did not have bells
              ((tense, aggravated tone))   ((voice constriction))
197. Hart: one I think it was the tan one (2)
                   ((quickly   ))
198. Lyle: But that all the rest of em had it?
              ((quickly, condensed   ))
199. Hart: All the other *dump* trucks
200. Lyle: had bells
              ((lower))
201. Hart: That was what that's what I was told
202. Lyle: Whos you told that by =
                        ((softer, lower))
203. Hart: = by your *garage* boy (1)
204. Sam: That's wrong (   ) //
              ((soft   ))
205. Lyle: //tha that's what I'm saying (1) you hea:rd in the meeting that we
                 ((quickly, voice constriction))
              didn't *have* any
206.   bells on em
207. Hart: No, I didn't hear tha:t (1) did not hear that (1)
                   ((quickly   ))
208. Sam: We daw uh: if I may: correct that uh we have uh (1)
              four five that doesn't have bells on. . .uh::://
              ((softer   ))
209. Lyle: //on the boom trucks you don't need one
              ((low   ))
              (my goodness you. . .)//
              [(dump trucks)
          [(Group laughter)
210. Hart: //well (1) [MY ONLY *POINT* BE:IN (3) getting back (1) to
              ((louder   ))   ((soft background chatter
              responsibility (2)
              and laughter))
211.   *WE: KNOW: MANAGEMENT knows* that that is a *serious* situation
              (1) and we have *KILLED* one
212.   person as a result of it (2) there's a *POLICY* that trucks are supposed to
              have

213. bells or at sleast those trucks that you feel (1) that its *necessary* (1) some trucks

                                             ʊ
214. don't have them as I understand it (2) to↑me that: is: *I* think   the
                     ((lower   .))   ((higher pitch)
      policy as far as I know
      ((quickly
215. is well established (3) a:nd there is an area where I feel both *YOU* and
))   ((slowly   ))   ((quickly   ))
      the↑*FOREMAN* of that
216. *CREW* (1) has a DAMN REAL reSPONsiBILity to see that that thing
                      ((tap on table accompanies each word))
      happen (2)↑but it goes on
                    ((high pitch, mocking,
217. nonchalantly unTIL somebody makes an issue of it (2)
      sarcastic tone)) ((slow)) ((quickly   ))
218. I've HIT on one thing that I is going to become a GOAL as far as I'm
                                                       ((soft, low))
219. concerned (1) and that is (1) to give more responsibility and as
      necessary the
220. au*thority* down to those (1) foreman 1's I *really feel* (1) that they are
                ((slow, low   ))
      not
      ((
221. *held* respo*ns*ible enough (1) for what they're assigned
      slow, deliberate   ))
      (someone in audience clears throat)
222. Allen: I think uh if I can interject
             ((quickly, with hesitation   ))

Notes

This paper was prepared for presentation at the Eleventh World Congress of the International Sociological Association, New Delhi, India, August 18–24, 1986.

1   Halliday's work is based on the analysis of British English. For a key intonation contour in my data, the falling–rising configuration (tone 4), Halliday (1985) and Labov and Fanshel (1977) provide parallel interpretations although Labov and Fanshel use American English data. It is difficult to say with certainty how British and American English correspond to each other with respect to tone as no systematic comparative studies exist on this subject.

2   I did not attend this meeting. I did, however, have audio records (recorded by the QWL observer), the observer's notes, and the "official" minutes. During the course of my research I visited Midwestern City and was able to interview the principals in the talk studied; I also talked with members of the QWL "team." I am grateful to all those involved for their cooperation and encouragement; they are not, of course, responsible for what I have done with the several records I have employed in my analyses.

3   Brown and Levinson (1978: 134–5) define negative politeness as "redressive action addressed to the addressee's negative face: his want to have his freedom of action unhindered. It performs the function of minimizing the particular imposition that the face threatening act unavoidably effects." Forms of "negative politeness" also serve a social distancing function.

4   For a detailed analysis of Hart's use of indirection see O'Donnell (1983), pp. 152–204.

5   For a discussion of the role of Black English Vernacular (BEV) in constructing relations of power and solidarity see O'Donnell (1983), pp. 97–122; p. 248.

6   An analysis of labor/capital relations and discourse across time would allow me to account for the extent to which contemporary industrial relations talk is a product of as well as a departure from that of earlier historical epochs.

11 The management of a co-operative self during argument: the role of opinions and stories

DEBORAH SCHIFFRIN

1. Co-operation and conflict

Everyday forms of talk are guided by norms of co-operation and competition. Even argument, a form of talk which might seem to be the paradigm example of conflict talk, can be a co-operative way of speaking as well as (or instead of) a competitive way of speaking. In this chapter, I describe how two speech activities – giving an **opinion** and telling a **story** – help individuals to co-operatively manage themselves during conflict talk. More specifically, I suggest that opinions and stories adjust the **participation framework** of talk, and that these adjustments allow individuals to negotiate two of the idealized standards (**truth** and **sincerity**) underlying argument.

I begin by clarifying what I mean by participation framework, and how truth and sincerity are relevant to argument. I then turn to my main discussion of opinions and stories. After highlighting those features of opinions and stories which make them useful in the management of conflict, I analyze each speech activity within an argument to suggest its role during conflict talk. The arguments on which I focus are about intermarriage, a topic of controversy in the lower-middle-class Jewish community in Philadelphia in which I did sociolinguistic fieldwork.[1]

1.1 Participation frameworks

A participation framework is comprised of a set of positions which individuals within perceptual range of an utterance may take in relation to what is said.[2] Although both producers and recipients of talk can occupy such positions, I will focus here mostly on the participation statuses occupied by those at the production end of talk: **animator, author, figure,** and **principal.** Although these positions can be filled by different people (Goffman, 1974, 1981b), I am interested here only in how a single individual can alternate among these positions during the course of his or her own talk.

An **animator** is that aspect of self involved in the actual physical production of talk: "the talking machine, a body engaged in acoustic activity ... an individual active in the role of utterance production" (Goffman, 1981c: 144). Self repairs, for example, show the individual as animator for they display him/her as monitoring and adjusting the production of sounds and their intended meanings. An **author** is that aspect of self responsible for the content of talk, "someone who has selected the sentiments that are being expressed" (Goffman, 1981c: 144). For example, when a speaker quotes his/her own prior words, he/she is at once the animator and the author of that quote; but when a speaker quotes another's prior words, he/she is assigning the authorial role to the original source of those words. A **figure** is that aspect of self displayed through talk; in a story for example, a speaker presents a particular image of him/herself through the construction and rendition of events in the story. A **principal** is "someone whose position is established by the words that are spoken, someone whose beliefs have been told, someone who is committed to what the words say" (Goffman, 1981c: 144). Our tacit understandings of talk include the assumptions that what is being said is the speaker's position, that the speaker is committed to his words, and that the speaker does believe in what is being said – such that evidence to the contrary is expected to be explicitly marked (e.g., by explicitly framing a statment as a joke). In short, the animator produces talk, the author creates talk, the figure is portrayed through talk, and the principal is responsible for talk.

Each position within a participation framework is associated with codified and normatively specified conduct (Goffman, 1981a: 3). In other words, we expect animators, figures, authors, and principals to conduct themselves in routine ways, and we can recognize these aspects of the self because of our normative expectations about the conduct appropriate for each position.

Norms of conduct, however, are not the only link between participation frameworks and social interaction. The related concepts of **footing** (Goffman, 1981c) and **frame** (Goffman, 1974) provide two additional links. Footing concerns "the alignments we take up to ourselves and the others present as expressed in the way we manage the production or reception of an utterance" (Goffman, 1981c: 128); frames are the organizational and interactional principles by which situations are defined and sustained as experiences (Goffman, 1974). Frames and footings are closely related, since one source of the definition of a situation (the frame) is the sort of alignments taken up by participation (the footing): we experience a situation as a "friendly chat" or a "hostile discussion", for example, because of the different stances which individual take with regard to one another and to what is being said. Similarly, changes in footings are related to shifts in frame: a change in participant alignment may motivate a change in the interactional definition of the situation as an experience, or *vice versa*. And, finally, footing and frames are related to participation frameworks, because alterations in such frameworks result from changes in our alignments and in our definitions of situations.

In sum, a participation framework is the set of positions which individuals take in relation to an utterance. Such a framework is related to participant footings and experiential frames.[3]

1.2 Truth and sincerity

Truth and sincerity have a role in argument which is similar to their more general role in co-operative conversation. The philosopher Grice (1975) has observed that individuals bring to conversation assumptions about each others' rationality and co-operative nature.[4] These assumptions are differentiated into four specific maxims which address the truth (maxim of quality), informativeness (maxim of quantity), relevance (maxim of relevance), and orderliness (maxim of manner) of all conversational contributions. Together the maxims form a "co-operative principle" which allows interactants to both convey and infer each others' intended communicative meanings – especially when such meanings go beyond the semantic content of what is actually said. A key part of Grice's theory is that individuals routinely violate the specific maxims. Despite such violations, however, individuals still assume each others' co-operative intent, and it is this assumption that leads them to search for some other understanding of what has been said. Because actual behavior is **expected** to differ from the guidelines of the specific maxims, then, the maxims are idealized norms whose routine violations are strategies which allow people to mean more than they say.

Grice's (1975) maxim of quality is the maxim most relevant for argument:

Try to make your contribution one that is true, specifically:
do not say what you believe to be false
do not say that for which you lack adequate evidence.

This maxim suggests that speakers assume each other not only to be presenting utterances in whose truth they believe, but utterances in whose truth they have reason to believe, i.e. utterances about which they are sincere. Because it is the truth of a proposition, and the sincerity of a speaker, which are adjusted by opinions and stories, it is the maxim of quality which is most relevant to my analysis.

2. Speech activities in argument

Let us turn now to opinions and stories. In section 2.1, I discuss how the general characteristics of opinions contribute to their function in argument, paying special attention to the way they adjust the participation framework of talk. An example of an opinion during an argument illustrates. Section 2.2 follows the same format for stories.

2.1 Opinions

Consider, first, that is is not always possible to find linguistic features which mark a declarative statement as the presentation of an opinion. The most straightforward linguistic cue is metalinguistic (e.g., prefacing a statement with *my opinion is*), or the use of verbs (e.g., *I think, it seems*) which show that the speaker cannot claim with absolute confidence the factuality of what is about to be said. Other opinions are marked internally by modals conveying degrees of likelihood that a particular situation holds, e.g., both *could* and *should* can mark opinions, since the former can convey the speaker's feeling of uncertainty and the latter the speaker's feeling of certainty. Except for the metalinguistic *my opinion is*, however, the linguistic devices just identified are not used solely in the statement of opinions. *I think*, for example, has not only the meaning suggested above, but also its more literal meaning as a verb of cognition; *should* can convey a meaning of obligation rather than certainty (compare *Customers should pay by cash* to *It should rain tomorrow – just look at that sky!*). In short, there is not always an absolute linguistic criterion by which to differentiate opinions from other statements.[5]

The lack of a linguistic definition for opinions means that we need to look elsewhere for a way to define this speech activity.[6] I will define an opinion as **an individual's internal, evaluative position about a circumstance.** There are three critical features in this definition. First, opinions are not available for observation. This means that "it is not clear what kind of substantiation would be sufficient to ground an opinion in an external reality" (Goffman, 1974: 503), i.e. opinions are not available for external verification. Second, opinions are individual, subjective positions rather than objective statements of fact.[7] Third, although opinions are internal cognitive states at one level of analysis, they are also representations of an *external* situation – the circumstances to which the opinion is addressed. This means that at one level of analysis, opinions depict an internal state, but, at another level of analysis, opinions also depict an external state.

These features suggest that, when presented in a conversation, opinions remain in the special informational preserve of the speaker which "can be as little established as disconfirmed" (Goffman, 1974: 503.) They also suggest that the very existence of an opinion implies general uncertainty over the circumstances addressed by the opinion. This explains, for example, why we are more likely to understand *That flower is pretty* as an opinion than *That flower is red*: the state of "beauty" has a lower degree of certainty – because it is less open to objective verification – than the state of "redness."[8]

Let us consider, now, how opinions adjust the participation framework of talk. Recall that when individuals make statements about an external world, they are usually seen as displaying a principal: "someone whose position is established by the words that are spoken, someone whose beliefs have been told, someone who is committed to what the words say" (Goffman, 1981c: 144). As I suggested above, there seems to exist a set of tacit understandings that what is being said is the speaker's position, and that the speaker is committed to his words, and **does** believe in what is being said. What opinions do is **modify that tacit understanding about speaker commitment to words.**

Suppose someone prefaces a statement by saying *my opinion is*, or ends a statement by saying *That's my opinion*. There are two ways of interpreting such brackets. First, they may be interpreted as **decreasing** the speaker's commitment to a statement, as if the speaker had said *That's my opinion; I don't know for sure*. Alternatively, they may be interpreted as **increasing** the speaker's commitment to a statement, as if the speaker had said *That's my opinion; I don't care what anybody else thinks*. These two interpretations are radically different subjective alignments toward what is being talked about: the former **mitigates** the speaker's commitment and the latter **intensifies** the speaker's commitment. But there is also an underlying similarity: changing one's commitment in either a mitigating or an intensifying direction is a modification of the speaker's display of a **principal** – of that aspect of self through which commitment is assumed to be expressed. Another way of saying this is that opinions propose a new subjective alignment to a proposition, and thus, a modification in footing.

The footing change displayed by an opinion involves not only the principal, but also that aspect of self referred to as the author, "someone who has selected the sentiments that are being expressed" (Goffman, 1981c: 144), i.e., someone who is responsible for the factual content of talk. So, when opinions mitigate a speaker's commitment to a position, it is the principal who displays the reduced commitment to the facts put forth by the author; similarly, when opinions intensify a speaker's commitment to a position, it is the principal who displays the extra commitment to the facts put forth by the author. In both cases, then, it is as if the principal is saying: "I am committed to the facts put forth by the author in a way which you would not otherwise expect."

It is because opinions shift a speaker's participation status that they can be used to negotiate truth and sincerity in argument. More specifically, opinions allow speakers to shield themselves from the truthfulness of the facts by focusing on their own stance toward what is being said. Another way of saying this is that opinions free the speaker (as author) from a claim to truth, by emphasizing the speaker's claim (as principal) to sincerity.

The argument in example 1 highlights some of these features of opinions (for transcription conventions, see appendix, p.257). Three people are involved in the argument. Henry and Zelda are a lower-middle-class, Jewish couple in their mid sixties; they have two sons (both married) and an unmarried teenage daughter. The third person is Irene – Henry and Zelda's neighbour, in her mid thirties, also lower-middle-class and Jewish; she has four children, ranging in age from five to sixteen.[9] Prior to example 1, Henry and Irene had been arguing about intermarriage between Jews and Gentiles. Henry does not approve of intermarriage and he has just told several stories about how he was able to influence his sons' choices of Jewish wives, and how his mother was able to prevent her son (Henry's older brother) from dating a Gentile woman many years ago. Irene had said earlier that although she doesn't like intermarriage, she is willing to accept it in her own family, not only because she thinks that religious differences are disappearing (see discussion of Irene's story in example 3), but because she feels unable to prevent her children from doing whatever they want. Example 1 begins as Henry emphasizes the importance of the role that parents can (and should) have in influencing their childrens' decisions. (*He* in (a–c) refers to Henry's older brother, who was the object of a story that Henry has just completed.)

Example 1

Henry: (a) But he– the fact is that he listens. T'my mother.
       (b) And, he did her wishes.
       (c) We respected our mother to the hilt.
             [   ]
Irene: (d) But that was *yea::rs* ago.
Henry: (e) But *why* shouldn't you respect your mother   today:?
                               [   ]
Zelda: (f)   Wait a– wait a minute.
       (g) That's *his* opinion!
                   [   ]
Henry: (h)   Why   should it be different?
                               [   ]
Irene: (i)   All right. Right.
       (j) That was *years* ago.
       (k) I don't feel that   the kids–   I don't think=
                                 [   ]
Henry: (l)   D'you agree with me?
Irene: (m) =the kids: today . . .
             [[   ]
Zelda: (n) Heh?
Henry: (o)   D'you agree with me?
Zelda: (p) No *I* don't agree with him.
       (q) He has his own beliefs.

The argument in (a) to (e) revolves specifically around Henry's claim that children should obey their parents. As I noted above, this claim is relevant to Henry's position against intermarriage – since it is his belief that Jewish childrens' obedience to their parents helps prevent them from intermarrying. As I also noted, Henry's claim (a-c) figures as the point of a story (not included in example 1) describing how his parents had prevented his older brother from dating a Gentile girl. Irene's challenge in (d) is that the circumstance Henry has described is no longer relevant.

Henry defends himself in (e) with a question: *But why shouldn't you respect your mother today:?*. His question has two effects. First, it shifts the direction of the argument from the outcome of respect (respect leads to obedience which leads to children not going against their parents' wishes, i.e., not marrying out of their religion) to the reasons for respect (he asks *why shouldn't*). Second, it shifts the burden of defence away from himself and onto Irene because the form and content of his question (a WH-question with a negative, and the model *should*) presupposes that Irene has said that children should not respect their mothers. However, this is not what Irene has said and it is not her challenge to Henry. If we look back at the placement of Irene's challenge, we see that it starts just as Henry begins to mention his family's respect for his mother ((c, d)). It seems unlikely, then, that Irene was challenging the importance of respect *per se*; rather, what she was challenging was Henry's prior point that children obey their parents (a, b). (This interpretation is also consistent with Irene's expressions of belief elsewhere in our conversations: she states that children are more independent than they used to be and less afraid of risk.) Since Irene has not challenged the importance of respect, Henry's question need not force her to defend the position that children should not respect their mothers. What we might expect, then, is for Irene to clarify her challenge, e.g.: *I didn't mean that they shouldn't respect their parents, I meant that they don't respect them anymore*, or *But can't children respect their parents without obeying them?*

However, what happens next in the argument is that Zelda overlaps Henry's question with *Wait a– wait a minute. That's his opinion!* (f-g). Thus, Zelda seeks to interrupt the argument in order to frame Henry's claim as an opinion. Henry continues to challenge Irene (in (h), *why should it be different?*), but note that Zelda's identification of Henry's position as an opinion has added a new proposition to which Irene can respond: not only can she respond to the content of Henry's position (that children should respect mothers), but she can respond to the definition of that position as opinion. This is precisely what Irene does in (i) and (j): her *All right. Right.* affirms the status of Henry's claim as opinion, and her *that was years ago* reissues her attack on the content of Henry's position. Thus, Irene does not grant Henry's position its substantive content, although she does grant the position its status as opinion.

As Irene begins to support her position in (k) – children today are different than they were when Henry was young – Henry turns his attention to Zelda to ask *d'you agree with me?* (l, o). Zelda responds that she does not agree and that *He has his own beliefs* (p, q). Thus, like Irene, Zelda has assigned to

Henry's position its status as opinion without agreeing with its substantive content.

In sum, both Zelda and Irene have allowed Henry his right to be committed as principal to an opinion. But since both have different substantive views of the circumstance to which the opinion is addressed, they are simultaneously denying his view as author to the content of that opinion. The effect is to emphasize Henry's claim to sincerity and to free Henry from his claim to truth. Thus, example 1 illustrates that identifying a statement as an opinion can change the course of an argument by adding a proposition ("what I say is an opinion") to prior substantive propositions ("this is what I say"). This makes it possible for individuals to both agree and disagree – to agree with the sincerity with which the principal is committed to a substantive proposition, but to disagree with the truth of that substantive proposition as put forth by the author.

These characteristics of opinions give them somewhat paradoxical roles in argument: they may either begin or end conflict talk. Because opinions free the speaker from a claim to truth (since they are unavailable for proof), another's right to doubt the validity of an opinion cannot be denied. This means that speakers often justify their opinions through evidence or reasoning even when those opinions have not been openly disputed. (We see an instance of this in example 3.) And, for the same reason, opinions will often provoke a disagreement.

Since opinions are the speaker's own informational preserve, however, the speaker's right to maintain an opinion cannot be denied by others. This means that individuals may respond to attacks on their opinions by admitting uncertainty over the facts, but stressing their right to present an opinion (*I may be wrong, but that's my opinion*). And although they may even recognize faults in their own reasoning, or concede to others the validity of a challenge, they may still keep their own opinions (*I can't help it, that's my opinion*). Similarly, individuals can defend themselves against another's challenge by redefining an assertion as an opinion, and by then defending their right to that opinion – simply because they can count on their opponent's willingness to grant them that right to an opinion. And as we saw in (1), opponents in an argument who support contradictory positions may actually defend each other's rights to different opinions, without forsaking all of their own positions, and therefore, without losing total ground in their dispute. All of these are ways that opinions can help terminate – rather than initiate – conflict talk.

In sum, opinions are unverifiable, internal, subjective depictions of an external world. Their presentation in talk displays a participation status in which a principal modifies the commitment of an author toward a proposition. This footing change creates a partial sacrifice of claims to truth for claims to sincerity: the facts presented by the author cannot remain undisputed, but the principal's stance toward that proposition cannot be disputed. It also gives opinions a paradoxical status in argument, such that they can either initiate or end an argument.

2.2 Stories

Since stories and opinions are very different speech activities, it is not surprising that their roles in argument differ. I will suggest that stories of personal experience create participation shifts in both speaker and hearer. The speaker is portrayed in a triple capacity as author, figure, and animator; the hearer is transformed into a specialized recipient role, that of an appreciative audience that can react to author, figure, and animator. Since several features of story telling underlie these shifts in participation framework, I describe these features before focusing more on the actual shifts.

First is selective interpretation: stories of personal experience recount events from an individual's life which have been selectively interpreted from the perspective of that individual. The most vivid illustration of this is stories which report personal confrontations (Johnstone, 1987; W. Labov, 1981): such stories allow an individual to justify the correctness of his or her prior actions to an audience who may not have been present during the actual confrontation – and thus is less able than the actual protagonist to challenge the narrator's rendition of "only one side of the story." Although confrontation stories are the most obvious example of selective interpretation, all stories do this to a certain degree – if only because external events are always interpreted from subjective standpoints formed on the basis of past individual experience.

A second factor leading to a shift in participation framework is a shift in deictic center – a shift from the time, place, and participant co-ordinates of the conversational (or storytelling) world to the co-ordinates of the story world. Such a shift may actually reflect the speaker's own reorientation: a friend with a three-year-old son, for example, was recently describing her pregnancy to me, and referred to her son as *it* – the same way in which she referred to him prior to his birth, and prior to her knowldege of his gender.

Many linguistic devices used in stories reflect (and create) this deictic shift. Even the temporal ordering found in most stories – the matching between the presentation of clauses and the inferred order of events (W. Labov, 1972a) – can be seen as a deictic shift which transforms past events into the storyteller's perspective, and allows the audience to see those events from that perspective. For example, narrators often report pre-existing states in introductory orientation clauses. However, when they are reporting states which existed, but about which they themselves did not know during the initial stages of their experience, they frequently delay mention of those states until the story has reached their own point of discovery. In other words, narrators may allow their initial point of discovery to be displayed in its original temporal sequence, thus moving their audience back to the initiation of their own involvement and carrying it along with their own viewpoint, perspective, and information state. It is in this sense that temporal ordering reflects a deictic shift which transforms the audience from a passive recipient of information to a vicarious participant in an experience.

The third way that stories adjust a participation framework is through evaluative devices. Such devices are phonological, grammatical, and textual modifications of the discourse norms which highlight parts of the experience from the narrator's perspective, and thus show the speaker taking a particular orientation toward what is being talked about (W. Labov, 1972a; Polanyi, 1979). For example, in Schiffrin (1981), I compared three stories with parallel plot structures and similar evaluations. Each story concerned the way in which a mother was able to solve her child's problem when more knowledgeable authorities had failed, and in each story the most highly evaluated section was the mother's discovery of the solution for her child's problem. I found a particular evaluative device – the historical present tense – used only when the speaker was justifying her **own** role as mother, not when she herself was the child reporting on her **mother's** role as mother. Thus, it was the speaker's orientation toward the problem situation which influenced her use of evaluation: when she was using the past to justify her **own** competence as mother (a competence, incidentally, which was frequently challenged by her neighbors), she highlighted that part of her past which best supported her position – her claim to being a good mother.

Finally, stories contextualize an event: they frame an event within a reported reality (the story world) which supplements the reality simultaneously being created through the conversation (the storytelling world). A brief example illustrates. Example 2 is a story in which Ira and Jan (a lower-middle-class, middle-aged, Jewish couple who live across the street from Henry, Zelda, and Irene) are jointly explaining their position against intermarriage between Jews and Gentiles to me. Immediately prior to example 2, Ira had mentioned that his son had *brought home a Puerto Rican girl*, and that the son *saw no difference*. Neither Ira nor Jan, however, believe that there is *no difference* between ethnic groups, and they develop and support this position later in our conversation. In example 2, they are contrasting their daughter Beth's experience dating a young man of a different religion with their son's experience with the Puerto Rican: because Beth's experience is more in line with their own view, their retelling of this experience can be used to contextualize their own position.[10]

Example 2

Ira: (a) Now my daughter went out with eh– she went out with a couple Gentile kids,
     (b) and she said that=
Jan: (c)   ⌊she wouldn't go out with them=

Ira: (d) ⌈=she wouldn't go out with them again.
Jan: (e) ⌊=again. ⌉   ⌈She ⌉ said they're too
          different.
Ira: (f) She said that uh . . . they're just eh–the–⌉
Jan: (g)   ⌊they're⌋ different.
Ira: (h) They're different.
Jan: (i) She says, "It's not what I'm used to.
Ira: (j) So em . . . s– ⌈he ⌉
Jan: (k)   ⌊One⌋was a . . . his father was a friend of my
          husband's.
     (l) And when I heard she was goin' out with him,
     (m) I said, "You're goin' out with a Gentile boy?"
     (n) She says, "Well Daddy knows his father."
     (o) I said, "*I* don't care."
     (p) So she introduced him,
     (q) and they went out,
     (r) and she came home early,
     (s) and I said, "Well, y'goin' out with him again?"
     (t) She says, "Nope."
     (u) I said, "Did he get fresh?"
     (v) She said, "No!"
     (w) She says, "But he's *diff*erent!"
     (x) She says, "I'm not *used* t'Gentile boys."
     (y) That⌈cured her!   ⌉
Ira: (z)   ⌊hhhhhhhhhhh⌋hhhhh
Jan: (aa) She'd never go out with one again.

Prior to Jan's story, both Jan and Ira report their daughter Beth as having stated that she would not go out with Gentiles again (Jan in (c) and Ira in (d)). Both also report Beth's statement of their very own position: Gentiles are *different* from Jews (Jan in (e) and (g), Ira in (h)). Jan also directly quotes Beth's reason for not wanting to date Gentiles again before she begins her story: *It's not what I'm used to* (i).

All three of these propositions are contextualized in Jan's story. In (t), Beth responds to Jan's question (*Well, y'goin' out with him again?* in (s)) with *Nope*. Then in (w), Beth gives her reason: *But he's different*. And finally, in (x), Beth embellishes her reason: *I'm not used t'Gentile boys.* Thus, Jan tells her story in a way which not only presents Beth's experience as a confirmation of her own view, but also allows Beth to actually present Jan's very own views – but in her own individual words. It is in these ways that Jan's story contextualizes her position about intermarriage.

Note, also, that Jan allows Beth to "see for herself" that Gentile boys are different (note that in (o), Jan reports herself as saying *I don't care*).[11] That Beth then came to the very same conclusion as Jan – without Jan having forced her into this conclusion – also strengthens Jan's own position. In other words, if Jan had forbidden Beth to go out on the date, Beth's conclusion would not have been nearly so convincing.

I have suggested that four factors – selective interpretation, deictic shifts, evaluation, and contextualization – all help transform the person who listens to a story into an audience that vicariously participates in the narrator's experience. It is this transformation which could lead a listener to be sympathetically aligned with whatever position a story is being told to support. In other words, the advantage created by stories is this: once a particular experience is seen from another's point of view, so, too, can the more general proposition which the particular experience is supporting be seen from that individual's point of view.

Because reports of vicarious experience (e.g., relaying the plot of a film or transmitting a news item) are similar in some ways to personal stories (Chafe, 1980), some of the same participation shifts occur in both types of stories. For example, an author (that part of the self whose sentiments are chosen for expression) is displayed through the selective interpretations and deictic shifts occurring in both personal and vicarious stories. This is because the selection and organization of events into a story is not an objective process; rather, it is strongly constrained by the sentiments which the speaker holds toward the experience. It does seem, however, that one's sentiments about an experience are less objective if the experience is one in which the individual has participated; thus, perhaps, an author is more visibly displayed in personal stories.

Personal stories also allow another dimension of the narrator's self to be displayed, simply because they display both the narrator's current competence as a story teller, and his or her prior competence in whatever role and status had been occupied in the prior experience. The simultaneous view of the narrator's competence in two domains means that the narrator is displayed in two capacities besides that of author. First, the narrator is seen in the story-telling world as an **animator**, as "the talking machine, a body engaged in acoustic activity . . . an individual active in the role of utterance production" (Goffman, 1981c: 144). Second, the narrator is seen in the story as a character in the story, as a **figure**, someone "who belongs to the world that is spoken about, not the world in which the speaking occurs" (Goffman, 1981c: 147).

To summarize, personal stories create the opportunity to present oneself in three capacities. First is animator – the producer of talk. Second is author: the author can interpret an experience, arrange evaluative devices, and create story events which contextualize a position in order to convey just those sentiments which highlight that version of the experience most in line with the position being argued for. Third is figure: the figure can act in the story world precisely as he or she might have wanted to act had there been the chance to do so. In short, the audience gains an idealized view of the experience (through the author), and an idealized view of the narrator (through the figure). And the narrator's hope is that these idealized views will lead the audience into acceptance of the position being argued for.

How, then, do stories allow a speaker to negotiate the truth and sincerity of an argument? Stories can be used to support a speaker's claim during argument because they lead the listener toward a sympathetic alignment with the position being argued. Another way of saying this is that stories create a testimony for the position – a testimony which invites the listener to join in an interactional allegiance and endorse the speaker's position. Thus, what a story can create is a *widened base of support* for the position. It is this widened base which frees the speaker as author from sole responsibility for the truth of the position, at the same time that it frees the speaker as principal from being alone in his/her commitment to, and sincerity in the belief of, the position. In other words, stories delegate much of the supportive work in an argument – including responsibility for truth and sincerity – to different parts of the self, and to the audience.

The argument in example 3 highlights some of these features of stories. Again, the speakers are Henry, Zelda, and Irene. Henry has just completed a fairly long monologue about anti-Semitism. (His belief that Gentiles are prejudiced against Jews is one reason why he does not favor intermarriage.) Irene, who had left Henry and Zelda's kitchen to return to her own house for a moment, has just re-entered.

Example 3

Irene: (a) Fill me in.
Debby: (b) We're talking about whether Jewish people should marry people who aren't Jewish.
Irene: (c) Oh *you:* want t'start a fight here. If you know me!
Zelda: (d) ⌊We know! Yeh! ⌋
Well see she's taping it.
(e) That's why I said . . .
Irene: (f) ⌊Uh: ⌋Well, let's put it this way.
(g) *I* feel that my children should marry within their religion.
(h) But if they choose . . . *not* to, it wouldn't be the worst thing in the world for me.
(i) So we had a long discussion, my neighbor's Italian.
(j) We had a long discussion a couple weeks ago,
(k) all the kids and I were sittin' . . . and *her*, we were sittin' on the patio.
(l) And when her daughter tried t'express herself that you're not marrying a religion, you're marrying a person.
(m) Anita's very strong on that.
(n) Yeh she says, "You are not mar–"

(o) Which is *true.*
(p) You're not marrying somebody's religion.
(q) And *I* feel, eventually, and it may not be in *my* day,
(r) maybe it'll be in my children's, *I* don't know, or *their* children's,
(s) that there will only be one religion in this world.
Henry: (t) No. Never be.
Irene: (u) Well I feel there will. Because–
Henry: (v)   ⌐Never.⌐ ⌐Do you know⌐ [continues]

As I noted in discussion of (1), Irene is less bothered by intermarriage than Henry. Their disagreement is common knowledge to Henry, Irene, and Zelda: note Irene's *Oh you: want t'start a fight here. If you know me! (c)* and Zelda's response *We know! (d).* Irene's story in (i) to (p) presents one reason why she is willing to accept (even though she doesn't desire) her children's intermarriage (g, h). Note that her story supports a reason for an opinion: she states in (g) and (h) what she "feels" about what her children "should" do, and how if they didn't, it wouldn't be the "worst thing" (an evaluative term) for her. The reason for this opinion is given at the end of the story: *You're not marrying somebody's religion* (p).

How does Irene use her personal story to support her opinion? First, Irene has her neighbor's child, Anita, state her very own view (1, n) as something in which she really believes (m). The reported speech (1, n) and the intensifier *very strong* (m) both contextualize and evaluate Anita's (and Irene's) belief.[12] Second, Irene embeds Anita's view within her own everyday experience: it occurs during *a long discussion* in which she herself took part (*we had a long discussion* (i, j), *all the kids and I . . . we* (k)). It is also important that this experience is reported as an ordinary part of Irene's life: *sittin' on the patio* (k) is a routine activity for summer evenings in Irene's neighborhood. This everyday nature of the experience heightens the story's sense of authenticity, that is, Irene did not have to force Anita to state her views, she just happened to do so in the course of an ordinary conversation. Third, Irene makes clear that Anita is not Jewish (*my neighbor's Italian* (i)). This is important to Irene and Henry's overall argument. Recall that Henry had just finished a long monologue in which he claimed that one reason he is against intermarriage is that Gentiles are anti-Semitic. (Although Irene was not present to hear Henry's monologue, she is familiar with his general position about anti-Semitism.) Anita's expression of indifference toward religion is thus one piece of evidence against Henry's belief in anti-Semitism. Fourth, Irene evaluates Anita's view as *true* (o) and then uses that evaluation as an introduction to her own view: *You're not marrying somebody's religion* (p). This view then becomes a pivot from which to state an even more extreme view about the eventual disappearence of all religious differences.

What is the role of Irene's story in her argument with Henry? Irene's story reports someone else's **endorsement** for why she believes that intermarriage *wouldn't be the worst thing in the world* (h). The reason is that *You're not marrying somebody's religion* (p)). The story thus widens the base of support for Irene's belief and frees her from sole responsibility for either its truth or her own sincerity in holding that belief. Its interactional effect is to invite Henry to join in an allegiance not only with Irene herself, but with another person (Anita) who shares Irene's belief.

Henry does not agree with Irene even after her story. But note that the story itself is somewhat immune to attack: Henry does not dispute Anita's reported statement that *you're not marrying a religion*. What he does challenge (in (t) with *No. Never be.*) is the more extreme view expressed by Irene **after** her story (*there will only be one religion in this world* (s)). Henry combines this challenge with his own views about anti-Semitism (conveyed in his monologue prior to Irene's story) to describe how assimilated Jews in pre-war Germany were taken to concentration camps, and thus to argue that even those Jews who had acted as if there were one religion were victims of anti-Semitism. Thus, Henry relates the story to his prior topic only by attacking the more extreme belief that the story has allowed Irene to state. But because the story itself is insulated from attack, Henry's challenge does not force Irene to totally retreat from her position; rather, she is allowed to maintain some of her prior ground in this argument.

Of course there are other roles played by stories during argument. In Schiffrin (1985), for example, I describe an argument between Henry and Irene in which Henry again leaves intact the details of Irene's story, but challenges the ability of the story to stand as an appropriate example for the general position being argued. And sometimes stories actually end a dispute: in an argument between Henry and Irene over the value of professional help for personal problems, two of Irene's stories about the help provided her son and niece by a school counselor prompt Henry to admit that *Well then they're good to have.* Thus, in contrast to opinions, which may either begin or end an argument, stories are likely to be used as efforts to end an argument.

In sum, stories are speech activities used during argument to strengthen speakers' claims. They have four characteristics – selective interpretation, deictic shifts, evaluation, and contextualization – which help transform the listener of a story into a vicarious participant in an experience, and which allow the narrator to present him/herself as animator, figure, and author. Because they create a widened base of support for the speaker's position, they free the author from sole responsibility for the truth of a position, and allow the principal to share responsibility for commitment to a position with the audience.

3. The management of co-operation during argument

We have seen that two speech activities – stating opinions and telling personal stories – can be used in argument to negotiate the truth of a position being argued and the sincerity of a speaker. These two activities work in different ways. Opinions sacrifice the absolute truth of a position for the sincerity of its speaker, and stories widen the speaker's claim to both the truth and sincerity of the position. Although these alterations give opinions and stories very different roles in argument, what makes them possible is the same for both speech activities: the speaker draws upon different relationships between the self and talk (different footings) to display multiple participation statuses which figure in the continual framing and reframing of talk.

The participation statuses that I have discussed allow the speaker to align him/herself with some of the idealized standards of cooperation which underlie talk. I stated above that Grice's maxim of quality ("do not say what you believe to be false, do not say that for which you lack adequate evidence") was the idealized standard of co-operation most relevant to argument. We have now seen how both opinions and stories address this maxim of quality: opinions separate the speaker's belief from the truth or falsity of what is said, stories create what the speaker believes to be adequate evidence. The dynamic nature of the alignments displayed by opinions and stories shows how truth and sincerity cannot be considered as taken-for-granted, static features of argument; rather, they are potentially emergent features of argument which are open to participant negotiation.

It is not only the local norms provided by speech activities such as opinions and stories which allow individuals to negotiate the truth and sincerity of their arguments. Other co-operative norms in argument are relatively global, i.e., they are sustained during the entire course of an argument. For example, arguments may have cultural meanings other than "conflict", and they may be interactionally motivated by ends other than the negotiation and resolution of disagreement. In Schiffrin (1984), I describe how Jewish Americans use argument as a means of sociability, that is, as a form of talk in which "the common search for the truth, the form of the argument, may occur; but it must not permit the seriousness of the momentary content to become its substance" (Simmel, 1961: 161). Sociable argument is thus a co-operative enactment of conflict which actually demonstrates the solidarity of a relationship – simply because it displays the ability of that relationship to tolerate features of talk typically associated with conflict, e.g. disagreement, challenge, interruption, insult (cf. Bateson, 1955; Kochman, 1983; W. Labov, 1972b).

Certainly there are other ways of speaking through which individuals manage the co-operative side of their selves during conflict talk. Perhaps the analysis of such forms of talk will not only help us appreciate the co-operative norms that exist during conflict talk, but help us learn how to build on those norms, so that we can direct people who disagree away from intensification of their conflict and toward resolution of their conflict.

Appendix   Key to transcription conventions

. Falling intonation followed by noticeable pause (as at end of declarative sentence)
? Rising intonation followed by noticeable pause (as at end of interrogative sentence)
, Continuing intonation: may be slight rise or fall in contour (less than "." or "?");
   may be followed by a pause (shorter than "." or "?")
! Animated tone
... Noticeable pause or break in rhythm without falling intonation (each half-second
   pause is marked as measured by stop watch)
– Self-interruption with glottal stop
: Lengthened syllable
italic type Emphatic stress
CAPS Very emphatic stress
When speech from A and B overlap, the starting point of the overlap is marked by a
lefthand bracket, and the ending point of the overlap is marked by a righthand
bracket.

A: Do you know what time the party's supposed to start?
B: ⌊Six o'clock.⌋

When lack of space prevents continuous speeh from A from being presented on a
single line of text, then " = " at end of A1 and " = " at beginning of A2 shows the
continuity.

A1:   Do you know what time the party's supposed to start? =
B: ⌊Six o'clock.⌋
A2:   = Because I have to work late tonight.

When speech from B follows from A without perceptible pause, then Z links the end of
A with the beginning of B.

A: Do you know the time? $_Z$
B: Six o'clock.

Notes

An earlier version of this chapter was presented at the American Anthropological
Association Meetings, December 1985, during a session organized by Gillian Sankoff
and Bambi Schieffelin on "Framing discourse: truth, lies, and deception."

1   Fieldwork was done as part of a project on linguistic change and variation
     (NSF Grant 75–00245). I thank William Labov, principal investigator, for
     generous access to this material.
2   This section compiles (and of course greatly reduces) ideas in Goffman
     (1974, 1981a, b, c).
3   Also crucial to the establishment, maintenance, and adjustment of partici-
     pation frameworks in social interaction are the verbal and nonverbal
     devices through which people indicate interpretive contexts for what they
     are saying. Gumperz (1982a: 131) calls these devices contextualization
     cues: "any feature of linguistic form that contributes to the signalling of
     contextual presuppositions" (see Goffman, 1981c: 126–127.) Equally
     important is the ability of the self (as either speaker or hearer) to adopt

multiple positions within a given encounter. Two points are important here. First, participation statuses could not exist if the self were not already socially constructed as a multi-faceted entity. That is, individuals do not have holistic, undifferentiated selves (although they may of course believe themselves to); rather they have sets of selves which are created and managed during the different interactions in which they are involved. The differentiation of speakers as animator, author, figure, and principal is possible, then, only because speakers are already divided selves. Second, participation statuses could not exist if social interaction did not provide structured opportunities for the emergence and management of selves. Such opportunities are closely linked to the organization of the conversations and encounters in which talk occurs, and to the organization of the gatherings and social establishments in which social occasions are housed.

4   I do not address here two isssues: the possible cultural relativity of the Gricean principles, the difference between assumed and negotiated cooperative rules. On the former, see Keenan, 1979; on the latter, see Schiffrin, 1987b.

5   Consider, also, that there is a partial functional overlap between opinions (at least when they mitigate speaker commitment, see discussion below) and hedges (as reflected in the use of certain expressions, e.g., *I think*, in both speech activities). And since statements of opinion are about disputable events, they also coincide with Labov and Fanshel's (1977) D-events.

6   Faced with the need to search further than language for the means by which to recognize particular speech activities, linguists often turn to the philosophically motivated body of work known as "speech act theory" (Austin, 1962, Bach and Harnish, 1982; Searle, 1969). A key insight of this work is that speech acts (such as promising, requesting, warning, and giving opinions) are constituted (i.e., created) because speaker and hearer share knowledge of the underlying conditions which allow a particular utterance to be used as an action. The utterance *Okay*, for example, can count as a "promise" as readily as the utterance *I promise* just so long as its speaker is understood to have intended through its utterance the acceptance of an obligation to perform a future action which will benefit the hearer. Atelsek (1981) analyzes opinions within such a framework.

7   A recent court decision ruling that a statement is an opinion if it "cannot objectively be proved or disproved" points out the importance of this second feature (*Washington Post* editorial, "Libel: facts and opinions," May 29, 1985.)

8   The general uncertainty presupposed by an opinion, however, can challenge those who believe in the verifiability of a particular circumstance. A dramatic illustration of this challenge is the movement in many conservative political circles against the educational approach known as secular humanism, an approach which emphasizes the relativity (at cultural, social, and personal levels) of many moral decisions: a parents' group in the small town of Plano in Texas forbade local teachers to request their students' opinions – simply because if students were found to actually have opinions, that implied the existence of uncertainty and relativism, that is, that there was no absolute truth (*New York Times*, May 17, 1981, p.1).

9   I describe these speakers (and others in the community) in Schiffrin 1984, 1987a.

10 This example is clearly not an argument in the sense of conflict talk, i.e. co-present interlocutors are not disagreeing with one another, and it is not intended as such. However, it is an argument in a rhetorical sense (Schiffrin, 1985): Jan and Ira are supporting their positions on a disputable issue (intermarriage) after having just reported the position (taken by their son) to which they are opposed. So even though Jan and Ira are not themselves in opposition, they are jointly oriented toward disputing the validity of an opposing position.

11 That Jan's *I don't care* is a statement that she – as opposed to her daughter Beth – does not care about Beth's date is signalled by the contrastive stress (indicated by italics) on *I*.

12 Direct quotes (as in examples 2 and 3) actually produce a more complex footing than I am here describing, since the animator of the quote is presenting another person as the author.

12 Silence as conflict management in fiction and drama: Pinter's *Betrayal* and a short story, "Great Wits"

DEBORAH TANNEN

A recent collection of papers (Tannen and Saville-Troike, 1985) presents a range of investigations of the meanings and functions of silence in cross-cultural perspective. A number of papers in that collection demonstrate that silence can be associated with conflict or negative emotion. My own chapter (Tannen, 1985) suggests that many of the components of a conversational style I characterize as "high involvement" can be understood as ways of avoiding silence in casual conversation, since silence, for these speakers, is seen as evidence of lack of rapport.[1] Scollon (1985) surveys a broad range of research by others as well as himself to indicate that silence is often regarded negatively, metaphorically seen as a mechanical breakdown of a machine that should hum steadily along.

Saunders (1985) investigates the role of "Silence and noise as emotion management styles" in an Italian village. He suggests that "exuberant noise and grim silence are in some respects functional equivalents" as they both "may be used in the management of strong but problematic emotions . . ." Saunders finds that "in the Italian case, the more serious the potential for conflict, the more likely it is that people will choose the silent mode" (p.165).

The main body of the present chapter shows how this perspective on silence provides the basis for understanding the use of silence – and minimal instances of silence, that is, pauses – in managing potential conflict in Harold Pinter's play, *Betrayal*. Analysis of the play supports Saunders' finding that silence and noisy speech can be functional equivalents. Whereas pauses written into the dialogue of *Betrayal* mark mounting conflict between characters, the playwright calls for silence at the points where potentially explosive information is confronted.

Following analysis of *Betrayal*, a somewhat briefer analysis is presented of silence as conflict management in another literary genre: a short story. In "Great Wits," by Alice Mattison, silence prevents conflict from erupting into damaging confrontation. When the young protagonist breaks the silence and openly expresses frustration with her parents, permanent damage results.

Before presentation of these analyses, a word is in order about the status of literary examples in the study of interaction.

1. The use of literary dialogue for analysis of interaction

Robin Lakoff (Lakoff and Tannen, 1984) suggests that literary dialogue – the dialogue in fiction and drama – constitutes a competence model for interaction. It is not equivalent to the dialogue spontaneously produced in interaction. Paradoxically, however, the dialogue in drama or fiction often strikes audiences as extremely realistic. For example, a reviewer (Kendrick, 1983) observes that in Judith Rossner's novel *August*, "The give-and-take of real conversation, its hesitations, repetitions, and Freudian slips – all are reproduced with exact fidelity." Yet a conversational analyst familiar with accurate transcriptions of conversations need only glance at the dialogue in that novel to see how different from real conversation it actually is, containing occasional rather than pervasive repetition, hesitations, slips, false starts, and so on. In contrast to the impression of realism made by the contrived dialogue of some fiction and drama, accurate transcripts of actual conversation often strike unaccustomed readers (as distinguished from professional conversational analysts) as repetitive, obscure, inarticulate, and generally unrealistic.

If audiences respond favorably to the contrived dialogue of literary productions, then such dialogue represents something that rings true to them. Lakoff suggests that, like the human ear and human memory, literary dialogue distills the wheat of conversation from the chaff of hesitations, fillers, hedges, and repetitions. In this spirit, the current chapter is offered as an analysis not of what actually occurs in human interaction – the relationship between the literary and the actual remains to be discovered and shown – but of a type of representation of human interaction that has at least symbolic significance for members of the culture that appreciate the artistic production.

2. Pauses and silences in the plays of Pinter

The plays of Harold Pinter make an art of silence as a way of masking (and, because the mask can be seen, revealing) strong unstated feelings. Whereas all plays make use of pauses and silences in their performance, Pinter's plays have pauses and silences printed in the dialogue.

Much has been written about pauses and silences in the works of Pinter. Donaldson (1985) has identified some key passages from commentaries as well as from remarks made by Pinter himself. I draw upon her excellent work in presenting two key accounts of pauses and silences in Pinter's plays. In examining Pinter's *Betrayal*, I found that the critics' accounts do not accurately describe the functions of pauses and silences. Rather, they describe conventional wisdom: how most people think silences and pauses are used in conversation.

Esslin (1970) suggests:

> When Pinter asks for a pause . . ., he indicates that intense thought processes are continuing, that unspoken tensions are mounting, whereas silences are notations for the end of a movement, the beginning of another, as between the movements of a symphony. (Esslin, 1970: 237–8, cited in Donaldson, 1985: 9)

Hollis (1970) makes a similar observation:

> There are many ways in which Pinter uses silences to articulate, but the first, and perhaps most common, is simply *the pause*. The pause occurs when the character has said what he has to say and is waiting for a response from the other side, or it occurs when he cannot find the words to say what he wants to say. . . . He is caught up short; he has reached the limits of language and now waits in silence for something to happen. . . . Although they may fill the air with words, *the silence of these characters is the result of their having nothing to say*. (Hollis, 1970: 14–15, emphasis his, cited in Donaldson, 1985: 9)

There is a satisfying scene in Woody Allen's film *Annie Hall* in which Allen, standing in line for a movie, overhears a man speaking authoritatively about the works of Marshal McLuhan. In the film, as rarely in life, Allen fishes the real McLuhan out from behind a billboard to pronounce the man's pronouncements nonsense. Without editorial comment, Donaldson manages a comparable feat, following these foolish accounts of Pinter's pauses and silences with a comment by Pinter himself, in response to a question by an interviewer who borrowed the interpretation of Esslin quoted above:

> Interviewer: You're very clear about the differences between a pause and a silence. The silence is the end of a movement?
>
> Pinter: Oh, no! These pauses and silences! I've been appalled. Occasionally when I've run into groups of actors, normally abroad, they say a silence is obviously longer than a pause. Right. O.K., so it is. They'll say, this is a pause, so we'll stop. And after the pause we'll start again. I'm sure this happens all over the place and thank goodness I don't know anything about it. From my point of view, these are not in any sense a formal kind of arrangement. The pause is a pause because of what has just happened in the minds and guts of the characters. They spring out of the text. They're not formal conveniences or stresses but part of the body of action. I'm simply suggesting that if they play it properly they will find that a pause – or whatever the hell it is – is inevitable. And a silence equally means that something has happened to create the impossibility of anyone speaking for a certain amount of time – until they recover from whatever happened before the silence. (Gussow, 1971: 132, cited in Donaldson, 1985: 9)

I was delighted to find this quote because it pulled Pinter out from behind a billboard to support what I had observed in his play: far from showing that the character is waiting, or has nothing to say, a pause shows that a character is reacting to what has been said, is feeling something. Put another way, rather than indicating that they can't find words to say what they want to say, pauses show that the characters do not want to say what they are thinking. In a sense, they show it by not saying anything else. And finally, far from representing the end of a movement, a silence represents climaxes of emotion in interaction, the point at which the most damaging information has just been introduced into the dialogue, directly or indirectly. In the context of potentially explosive conflict in *Betrayal*, pauses and silences prevent the conflict from exploding and destroying the possibility of continuing the relationship.

A final excerpt from Pinter himself draws a parallel similar to that of Saunders on the Italian cases: a functional equivalent of silence is a long outburst of words that stands out against the normally sparse turns at dialogue that make up the play:

> There are two silences. One when no word is spoken. The other when perhaps a torrent of language is being employed. This speech is speaking of a language locked beneath it. That is its continual reference. The speech we hear is an indication of that which we don't hear. It is a necessary avoidance, a violent, sly, anguished, or mocking smoke screen which keeps the other in its place. When true silence falls we are still left with echo but are nearer nakedness. One way of looking at speech is to say that it is a constant stream to cover nakedness. (Pinter, 1964: 579, cited in Donaldson, 1985: 8–9)

The following discussion demonstrates the use of pauses and silences (including wordy silences) in Pinter's *Betrayal*.

Betrayal

Betrayal is about a love triangle among Jerry, Emma, and Robert. The lovers are Jerry and Emma. Jerry, a literary agent, is the best friend and colleague of Emma's husband, Robert, a publisher. The most remarkable aspect of this play is that most of its action moves backward rather than forward in time, thus violating the conventions of dramatic art but paralleling the constraints of human memory. That is, the action depicted in the first scene of the play is chronologically the last: a meeting between Emma and Jerry two years after their love affair has ended. The last scene of the play depicts the earliest action: the beginning of their affair. Thus when the audience regards the moment at which the affair begins, they recognize it as such, seeing telescoped in this single and final cameo the subsequent affair and its complex consequences – just as one is able to look back, years later, on a first meeting from the perspective of later knowledge of the relationship that developed. This is in contrast to the limited knowledge that one has at the moment of a meeting, or on viewing a first meeting in a play which is presented chronologically. T.S. Eliot observed in his poem "Portrait of a Lady" that "our beginnings never know our ends." By putting the beginning of Emma's and Jerry's affair at the end of his play, Pinter allows us to see its beginnings while knowing its ends.

As its title suggests, this play portrays a series of painful betrayals: hidden, revealed, and uncertain. Jerry betrays his best friend Robert by seducing Robert's wife, Emma. Jerry also betrays his own wife, as Emma betrays her husband. But Emma and Robert also betray Jerry: neither one tells him when Robert learns of the affair. Rather, the affair continues, and Jerry continues to socialize and work with Robert, compounding and dramatizing his betrayal of Robert because he believes Robert doesn't know about it.

At the end of the action (but the beginning of the play), Emma reports to Jerry that Robert just told her he has been betraying her for years. Since this is not seen, however, one cannot know whether Robert has told her the truth or has simply given her misinformation to hurt her and/or to ensure her agreement to a divorce. A motivation for such deception is that Emma is now having an affair with a writer named Casey, and Robert knows about it.

All these betrayals and their revelations take place without the raising of voices, without verbal expressions of emotion. The most emotionally tense scenes are distinguished not by yelling or running about the stage but by understatement and indirectness – the acute tension created by continual insignificant chatter in the face of emotionally explosive information – and the increased use of pauses and silence.

Appendix 1 provides a brief synopsis of scenes to make discussion comprehensible and to serve as a reference. As this appendix shows, most of the dialogue in the play consists of two-party conversations among dyads: Jerry and Emma, Robert and Emma, or Robert and Jerry. Only twice do all three interact on stage at once: for most of scene 4 and very briefly in scene 9, the last.

Simply counting the occurrences of *Pause* and *Silence*, as printed in italics in the screenplay (Pinter 1978), provides a barometer of the tension in the various scenes (see appendix 2). The last four scenes, which present the earlier action, include no instances of *Silence* (in scenes 6, 7 and 9) or a single one (in scene 8). In these scenes, Robert and Emma begin their affair, and are enjoying the early heady romance of it. Scene 4 also contains no *Silence*. This is the scene in which Jerry pays a surprise visit to Robert and Emma, and the talk is social chatter. The largest number of *Silences* occur in scenes 3, and 5. Scene 3, with seven silences but only twelve pauses, is the one in which Jerry and Emma end their seven-year affair. Scene 5, with six silences and twenty-two pauses, is the dramatic as well as numerical center of the play: the scene in which Robert learns that Emma has been having an affair with his best friend Jerry. Although this discovery does not lead to the immediate break-up of their marriage, it is a point of potential break-up and the revelation of the most damaging and shocking betrayal. I am arguing that it is the silence itself that prevents this revelation from breaking up the marriage. Furthermore, it is Emma's and Robert's silence in not telling Jerry that Robert has learned about it that allows the affair to continue.

Let us now see how pauses and silences are used to manage (and reveal) conflict in *Betrayal*. First, I will consider the scenes which contain the greatest number of silences.

Scene 5 takes place in a hotel room in Venice, where Robert and Emma are on vacation. While in American Express the previous day, Robert was handed a letter addressed to Emma from Jerry. Robert has waited until this moment to tell her that he knows about the letter, which he left at American Express for her to retrieve. (Stage directions are rendered in italics, as in the script.)

Silence

ROBERT

By the way, I went into American Express yesterday.
She looks up.

EMMA

Oh?

Indirectness and understatement are the dialect of this world. Knowing that she received a letter from Jerry in care of American Express, Emma has reasons to suspect that her affair with Jerry may now be known. But her response is limited to a terse movement ("*She looks up*") and a minimal response ("Oh?").

Robert then tells Emma that the employee at American Express had handed her letter to him. He explains that he declined to take it, and asks Emma whether she got it. His first response to her affirmative answer is understated and indirect. But after a pause (during which his emotions must be churning), he launches into a long burst of speech about the character of Italians who would give a letter to someone other than the addressee:

ROBERT

Oh well, I'm glad you got it.
Pause
To be honest, I was amazed that they suggested I take it. It could never happen in England. But these Italians . . . so free and easy. I mean, just because my name is Downs and your name is Downs doesn't mean that we're the Mr and Mrs Downs that they, in their laughing Mediterranean way, assume we are. We could be, and in fact are vastly more likely to be, total strangers. So let's say I, whom they laughingly assume to be your husband, had taken the letter, having declared myself to be your husband but in truth being a total stranger, and opened it, and read it, out of nothing more than idle curiosity, and then thrown it in a canal, you

would never have received it and would have been deprived of your legal right to open your own mail, and all this because of Venetian je m'en foutisme. I've a good mind to write to the Doge of Venice about it.
Pause
That's what stopped me taking it, by the way, and bringing it to you, the thought that I could very easily be a total stranger.
Pause
What they of course did not know, and had no way of knowing, was that I am your husband.

As noted earlier, such a long turn by a single speaker is extremely marked in the play and occurs only at points of maximum distress. As Pinter was quoted to observe, it is a variant of silence: a torrent of words that are not addressing the true issue, but are dramatizing it nonetheless. The invective aimed at the Italian national character is carrying the emotional burden more properly aimed at Emma. But expression of rage at Emma might unleash a comparably emotional response from her, and the ensuing exchange of recriminations might pose a threat to the continuation of their relationship on any terms. The expression of rage at the Italian employee at American Express has no consequences.

The drama is heightened by the *Pauses* which punctuate Robert's diatribe. Then comes the confrontation:

Pause

EMMA
It was from Jerry.

ROBERT
Yes, I recognised the handwriting.
Pause
How is he?

EMMA
Okay.

ROBERT
Good. And Judith?

EMMA
Fine.
Pause

ROBERT
What about the kids?

EMMA
I don't think he mentioned them.

ROBERT
They're probably all right, then. If they were ill or something he'd have probably mentioned it.

Pause
Any other news?

EMMA

No.
Silence

ROBERT

Are you looking forward to Torcello?
Pause

Each time Emma could be expected to tell Robert what was in the letter –
or, more to the point, why she was receiving a letter from Jerry – there is a
Pause. The tension mounts as the audience anticipates a confrontation, and
builds further when no confrontation comes. The indirectness – that is, the
not talking about what is obviously on both their minds – contributes to the
tension. When all obvious diversions have been uttered (customary inquiries about the health of spouses and children – conventional chatter found
throughout the play), the *Pauses* become *Silence*.

Robert then changes the apparent topic of talk, but the real topic (or
subtext) is still the same, pursued indirectly through talk about Jerry. Once
more the crescendo of the tension comes when *Pause* becomes *Silence*:

ROBERT

Pause
He wasn't the best man at our wedding, was he?

EMMA

You know he was.

ROBERT

Ah yes. Well, that's probably when I introduced him to you.
Pause
Was there any message for me, in his letter?
Pause
I mean in the line of business, to do with the world of publishing. Has he
discovered any new and original talent? He's quite talented at uncovering
talent, old Jerry.

EMMA

No message.

ROBERT

No message. Not even his love?
Silence

EMMA

We're lovers.

Emma utters the most damaging revelation of the play after the preceding
silence makes clear that the information is there and can no longer be
avoided, covered up by displaced anger or irrelevant commonplaces.

Rather than explode, Robert responds, civilly, "Ah. Yes. I thought it might be something like that." The strength of his emotion comes out soon after, in silence and repetition. Emma asks when Robert first suspected, and he replies, when he saw the letter in American Express. Then:

EMMA

Ah.
Pause
I'm sorry.

ROBERT

Sorry?
Silence

In the movie version of *Betrayal*, the actor Ben Kingsley portrays the strength of Robert's emotions by the distraught expression on his face and a choking tone of repressed emotions on the point of explosion, in the way he utters the single word, "Sorry?" The implication is that the apology is shockingly inadequate, given the magnitude of the offense. The brink of emotional outburst here reached is maintained, but not crossed, by the maintenance of a state of not speaking: silence.

The effect of the pauses and silences on readers of the play depends on their imaginations. In performance, it is the job of the actors to portray strong emotions in their facial expressions and body movements, and in the quality of their voices when they utter their few words. Throughout, the pauses and silences work to cover up emotion – but also, paradoxically, to show that strong emotion is there to be covered up.

The other scene which is characterized by numerous *Silences* is scene 3, in which Emma and Jerry end their affair. They meet in the flat they had rented and furnished as a meeting place when their affair was in full swing. Acknowledging that they have not used the flat in months, they agree to give it up, thus officially ending their seven-year affair. The difficulty of such a separation is represented in the frequent silences which follow realizations that they had been very much in love but are no longer, that for years they met regularly to share love and will no more.

The scene opens, significantly, with a *Silence*. The next *Silence* occurs immediately following Emma's calling attention (indirectly) to the fact that the affair is over:

EMMA
We were going to get another electric fire.

JERRY
Yes, I never got that.

EMMA
Not much point in getting it if we're never here.

JERRY

We're here now.

EMMA

Not really.

Silence

The silence is not a transition, but an action: Jerry and Emma are experiencing the loss of their love, the realization that although they are meeting in their flat, they are not meeting as lovers. Although space does not permit the presentation of the remaining five instances of *Silence* in this scene, they all follow the same pattern.

Silence appears with just the same function the only time it is used in scene 1. In this scene, Jerry and Emma meet alone for the first time in two years, that is, the first time since the events depicted in scene 3, just discussed. (Recall, however, that this scene has not yet been seen by the audience.) They meet in a pub, and Emma tells Jerry that she and Robert were up all night talking, that Robert told her he had been unfaithful to her for years, and that they are getting a divorce. In answer to Jerry's question, she tells him that she told Robert about their affair.

In this scene, Jerry and Emma have a wistful attitude toward each other and their past affair. But this emotional distance is disrupted, at one moment, by a memory which recalls to both of them their former intimacy. It is a memory from the height of their happiness, before Robert learned of their affair, when all of them – including their spouses and children – seemed to be a harmonious unit. The memory is described in scene 6, when Jerry and Emma are happily together in their flat:

JERRY

Listen. Do you remember, when was it, a few years ago, we were all in your kitchen, must have been Christmas or something, do you remember, all the kids were running about and suddenly I picked Charlotte up and lifted her high up, high up, and then down and up. Do you remember how she laughed?

EMMA

Everyone laughed.

JERRY

She was so light. And there was your husband and my wife and all the kids, all standing and laughing in your kitchen. I can't get rid of it.

EMMA

It was your kitchen, actually.

He takes her hand. They stand. They go to bed and lie down.

Why shouldn't you throw her up?

She caresses him. They embrace.

Here, the memory of Jerry's and Emma's families blended together in a kitchen (whose kitchen is never known, contributing to the symbolic merging of their families) is integrated into their love for each other. His throwing her daughter up in the air seems to symbolize both the blending of their families and the easiness of their affair. When, in scene 1, after their affair has been over for two years, Jerry tells Emma that he saw her daughter Charlotte, now grown, he recalls the same event, and that recollection recalls their former intimacy and occasions a (painful) silence:

JERRY

Pause
Yes, everyone was there that day, standing around, your husband, my wife, all the kids, I remember.

EMMA

What day?

JERRY

When I threw her up. It was in your kitchen.

EMMA

It was in your kitchen.
Silence

JERRY

Darling.

EMMA

Don't say that.

Jerry's calling Emma "Darling" grows out of the memory of their intimacy, the recollection of which is represented by the silence.

The scene with the third largest number of *Silences* (three) is scene 2, in which Jerry learns that Robert has known for years about his affair with Emma. The number of silences indicates the significance of the emotional impact of Jerry's learning that he too was betrayed. Jerry thought he had carried on his affair with Emma in secret, whereas in fact Robert had learned about it four years earlier. In this sense, Jerry was betrayed by Robert and Emma. (This is dramatized in scene 4, in which Jerry pays them a surprise visit. Although everyone is labouring under heavy emotions, they all chatter sociably as if they were not. At the end of the scene, when Jerry leaves, Robert and Emma embrace, and he holds her as she weeps. Their shared knowledge is a bond from which Jerry is excluded by being kept in ignorance.)[2]

Scene 2 occurs because Jerry, believing that Emma has just told Robert about their seven-year affair, called Robert and asked him to come over. Whereas the silence in scene 3 represented Jerry's and Emma's realization of the loss of their love, the silences in scene 2 represent Jerry's realization that he has been a fool, as well as a cad: for four years, while he acted like Robert's friend, Robert knew that Jerry was having an affair with his wife. The first *Silence* marks his receipt of this information:

JERRY

And she told you . . . last night . . . about her and me. Did she not?

ROBERT

No, she didn't. She didn't tell me about you and her last night. She told me about you and her four years ago.

Pause.

So she didn't have to tell me again last night. Because I knew. And she knew I knew because she told me herself four years ago.

Silence

JERRY

What?

The shocking quality of this information is evidenced not by shouting or talking but by Jerry's silence.

There follows an ironic role reversal in which it is Jerry who is emotionally distraught, feeling betrayed, whereas Robert takes the role of comforter:

JERRY

She told you . . . when?

ROBERT

Well, I found out. That's what happened. I told her I'd found out and then she . . . confirmed . . . the facts.

JERRY

When?

ROBERT

Oh, a long time ago, Jerry.

Pause

JERRY

But we've seen each other . . . a great deal . . . over the last four years. We've had lunch.

ROBERT

Never played squash though.

JERRY

I was your best friend.

ROBERT

Well, yes, sure.

Jerry stares at him and then holds his head in his hands.

Oh, don't get upset. There's no point.

Silence

Again, silence occurs at the point when the most damaging and potentially conflict-inducing information has been confronted.

Scene 1, the reunion between Emma and Jerry in the pub, has only one *Silence*, as discussed above. However it has a very large number of pauses: thirty six. This is partly because it is the longest scene in the play: nineteen pages of script. (The others are between nine and thirteen, with the exception of the last, with only five pages.) Even allowing for its length, it has a great many *Pauses*, as Jerry and Emma remember but do not talk about their former intimacy – emotionally loaded enough for pauses, but not cataclysmic enough for silences.

The scene with the next largest number of pauses is scene 2, in which Robert and Jerry, for the first time, confront the fact of Jerry's betrayal of Robert. The next is scene 5, the Venice scene, in which Robert and Emma confront this betrayal. Thus the number of pauses per scene provides an indication of the level of potential conflict portrayed in each scene.

A final example from *Betrayal* shows the second kind of silence discussed by Pinter: the use of excess verbiage about something other than what is at issue. (The same device is used in Ingmar Bergman's screenplay for his film *Scenes From a Marriage*, as shown and discussed in Lakoff and Tannen, 1984.) In scene 7, Robert meets Jerry for lunch, following his return from Venice. This is an emotionally laden encounter for Robert, who has learned in Venice that Jerry is having an affair with Emma, but not for Jerry, who does not know this. The scene is marked by no silences and only four pauses. Instead, Robert's distress is shown in a wordy silence: an outburst not about Jerry's affair with Emma but about books and publishing. For Robert, this is all bound up with Emma and Jerry: while in Venice, Emma was reading a novel by an author named Spinks whom Jerry had discovered and Robert had declined to publish and who has since become a great success. After noting this (financial) failure of judgment, Robert says,

ROBERT

I'm a bad publisher because I hate books. Or to be more precise, prose. Or to be even more precise, modern prose, I mean modern novels, first novels and second novels, all that promise and sensibility it falls upon me to judge, to put the firm's money on, and then to push for the third novel, see it done, see the dust jacket done, see the dinner for the national literary editors done, see the signing in Hatchards done, see the lucky author cook himself to death, all in the name of literature. You know what you and Emma have in common? You love literature. I mean you love modern prose literature, I mean you love the new novel by the new Casey or Spinks. It gives you both a thrill.

JERRY

You must be pissed.

ROBERT

Really? You mean you don't think it gives Emma a thrill?

JERRY

How do I know? She's your wife.

Pause

Robert here comes face to face with Jerry's dissembling. What "you and Emma have in common," he now knows but does not say, is far more than a love of literature. Robert soon launches a second, though shorter, diatribe, against the waiter and the restaurant, as he chooses not to confront his friend directly with the knowledge he has gained. If Robert confronted Jerry with this knowledge, he could not continue to be friends with him, so the silence is a way to manage the conflict and preserve the friendship. As Pinter observed, wordless silences are nearer "nakedness" than wordy ones. I suggest that this explains why Robert employs only the wordy type of silence in this scene with Jerry. Whereas Jerry realizes something is wrong ("You must be pissed," i.e. drunk), Robert's diatribe succeeds in throwing up "a smoke screen" which camouflages "the language locked beneath it" – the truth about his reaction to Jerry's betrayal. The outburst can be dismissed by Jerry as attributable to a physical condition: inebriation.

3. The cultural component in conflict management style

Betrayal is staggering in its contrast to contemporary American plays in which characters express strong negative emotion loudly and explicitly. (Two of the most popular contemporary American playwrights who come to mind are David Mamet and Sam Shepard.) The papers collected in Tannen and Saville-Troike (1985) demonstrate that the meanings and functions of pausing and silence vary widely across cultures. It is probably not by chance that Pinter, whose play uses silence as a substitute for direct expression of negative emotion in a conflict situation, is British. The British novelist, John Fowles, frequently contrasts American and British characters by the verbosity of the former and the taciturnity of the latter. In the novel *Daniel Martin* (Fowles, 1977: 139), the narrator observes of the British upper middle class, "No other caste in the world . . . are so certain that public decency and good breeding is silence." That the use of silence to manage conflict is partly culturally conditioned is suggested by Pinter's observation, quoted at the outset, that when he finds actors mistaking pauses and silences for breaks in the action, it is "normally abroad."

Though the particular guise of silence as conflict management in Pinter may be culturally related, the use of silence to manage potentially conflict-inducing emotion is certainly not limited to British culture. An American short story published in *The New Yorker* makes similar assumptions about the potentially destructive effect of expressing negative emotions. Whereas silence prevailed in *Betrayal* until the end of the action (but the beginning of the play), "Great Wits" depicts a family drama in which silence gradually gives way to verbal expression of conflict which results in permanent hurt. Like Pinter, the author of this story highlights the role of silence by writing it into the dialogue.

4. Silence as conflict management in fiction

"Great Wits" is a short story by Alice Mattison (1986) about a recollected conflict between a college student living at home, named Anne, and her parents. The first part of the story recounts Anne's mounting conflict with her mother, confrontations with whom are deflected by the strategic use of silence. The story's climax occurs when silence breaks down: at a party in their home, Anne's frustration with her father leads her to lose her temper and argue with him, provoking him to retort angrily and in turn leading her to say something whose damaging effects remain forever, along with Anne's regret for having said it.

The first instance of silence in this story occurs when Anne meets her mother in a Manhattan art gallery, eager to show her her favorite paintings. They meet following the mother's appointment with an eye doctor. Anne begins by inquiring about her mother's visit to the doctor.

> "Does he think you need new glasses?'
>
> "Yes, but I'm not going to get them," her mother said. "I don't like getting used to new glasses. And they're expensive."
>
> "But if you need them?"
>
> "Oh, I probably can do without them. I'm getting along now, after all."
>
> Anne turned impatient. "Then why did you go to see him – if you weren't going to do what he said? What's the point?"
>
> Her mother was silent. It was not a good start.

Anne's mother is modeling the use of silence to defuse conflict. Soon Anne herself uses silence in this way, when her mother does not display the expected appreciation of the paintings Anne shows her, but rather talks about other things or makes only vague comments:

> Anne stopped in front of Vermeer's "Officer and Girl". . . . She waited for her mother to exclaim over the painting.
>
> "I've been thinking about Daddy's study," her mother said. "I don't see how we can have all those people in, if he won't clean it up."
>
> Anne persisted. She pointed out some of the details in the painting – the elegant design of the girl's sleeves, her happy eyes. It was her third-favorite painting in the collection, but she didn't feel able to say that.
>
> "It's very real," said her mother tentatively.
>
> . . .

They looked at several more paintings, but her mother didn't seem much interested, and finally Anne led her to a bench in the Garden Court, with its plants and skylight, and they sat down. "I'm tired," her mother said. Anne was silent. (p.35)

Anne's frustration mounts and the protective wall of silence begins to crumble when she "tried and failed not to answer":

Then her mother said, "How long do you think it will be before the drops wear off?"

"He put drops in your eyes?"

"Of course he did. How could he examine my eyes without putting drops in? My old ophthalmologist always put drops in."

"You mean you can't *see*?"

"Of course I can see," said her mother. "But things are blurry. I'd have told you, but I knew how much you wanted to show me the museum."

Anne tried and failed not to answer. "So if I took you dancing and you had a broken leg, I suppose you'd just dance?" she asked bitterly. "And if I cooked you a meal and you were throwing up –" She held back tears. "How old do you think I am? Three?"

In the next event in the story, the breaking of silence leads to confrontation. Anne's father has sent her to the New York Public Library to look up a fact for him. Anne had to request that the required book be brought from the stacks – a service to which college students, but not high-school students, were entitled. Angered by being asked to prove she was a college student, Anne refused to produce the I.D. she was carrying, arguing instead that she should not be singled out by being asked to produce it. She ended up shouting and then crying, making a scene in the library, but not getting the book.

This outburst, and its unproductive result, prefigures the story's denouement. At a long-awaited family party at their home, Anne joins a conversation in which her best friend Harriet is telling Anne's father about a teacher's reaction to something Harriet wrote. When her father offers an unlikely interpretation of why Harriet's written assignment sparked the teacher's response, Harriet responds, "Oh, no. I don't think so," and is "not much disturbed." But Anne is very much disturbed by what she perceives as her father's illogic:

But Anne, totally surprised, was almost incoherent. "How do you know what Harriet writes? How can you say such things?" she cried at her father. "And that's not what she means. You haven't even been listening. No wonder you think artists are crazy – you can't make any sense yourself."

Her father shouts in retort, accusing her: "You can't keep control of yourself – just like your mother."

The father goes on to refer to an earlier event: Her mother had bought a rose-colored dress to wear at the party, and had paid a seamstress to alter it, but decided not to wear it because her husband disapproved. The comparison with her mother further angers Anne, who protests in a way that insults her mother:

> "Just like your mother," her father said. "Always losing control of herself. She buys a dress in a ridiculous color, designed for someone trying to attract a man–"
>
> "I'm not the least bit like Mommy," Anne protested. "Just because you make some remark about her perfectly O.K. dress, she goes out among her guests in some dowdy old thing – I'd *never* do that. I'd never let you get to me like that." (p.42)

Anne did not really believe her mother looked dowdy; earlier that evening she had thought (to herself), "The brown dress, to tell the truth, was becoming to her" (p. 39). But the effect of the words spoken in anger was lasting, the fact that they were overheard giving them an undeserved air of truth: "In all the years since the party – almost fifteen years now – Anne's mother has never dropped the notion that she looked dowdy that night" (p. 42);[3] the memory remained, at the time of the story's narration, "still painful." Thus silence had been the cap on conflict. When it gave way to verbal expression, the conflict erupted with everlastingly destructive results.

5. Conclusion

The story "Great Wits" concerns family conflict of a less potentially cataclysmic nature than the adultery in Pinter's *Betrayal*. This may be seen to support Saunders' contention, based on his observation of Italian villagers, that the more potentially divisive the conflict, the more likely silence is to be used. In any case, the American short story supports the view of silence as conflict management found in the British play in that, in both works, disruption of relationships is avoided so long as silence rather than direct expression is the response to potential conflict. This may explain, as well, a scene that is portrayed in the movie version of *Betrayal*, but is not found in the printed screenplay – a scene which puzzled and disturbed me at first, since it seemed so out of keeping with the spirit of the rest of the play. The movie opens with a distant view (the camera's vantage point is outside the house, so the audience sees without hearing) of a party at Emma's and Robert's house. After the guests leave, Emma and Robert are shown to be having a violent argument, in which he strikes her. This violence contrasts sharply with the muted interchange in Venice when Robert discovered

Emma's affair with Jerry. Whereas the first revelation did not result in Robert and Emma separating, the violent argument does. The violence of this argument is out of keeping with the indirectness and suppressed emotion that characterizes the rest of the play, but it also provides an explanation, perhaps a motivation, for the break-up of the marriage which did not occur earlier, despite the betrayals that the play documents.

I do not wish to suggest that this pattern characterizes the function of pausing and silence in conflict management in all stories and plays, let alone in real interaction. I am suggesting only that this is the pattern found in these two literary representations of family conflict. The papers collected in Tannen and Saville-Troike (1985) make clear that conflict management is only one of many functions of silence, and there are certainly many means other than silence to manage conflict. The present analysis is proffered as an illustration of one means of managing conflict as found in two examples of literary discourse. The parallel of these findings with the conclusions of Saunders based on observation of real interaction suggests that literary dialogue can provide a useful symbolic representation of human communication.

Appendix 1. Sequence of scenes in *Betrayal*

Scene 1: 1977. Jerry and Emma meet in a pub. It is two years since their affair ended. Emma tells Jerry that she and her husband Robert are getting divorced, and that Robert has just told her that he has been betraying her for years and that she told him about her affair with Jerry.

Scene 2: 1977. Time follows scene 1. Robert visits Jerry at home in response to Jerry's phone call. He tells Jerry that he has known about Jerry's affair with Emma for four years.

Scene 3: 1975. Two years earlier. Emma and Jerry meet in their flat and agree to give it up (and end their seven-year affair).

Scene 4: 1974. One year earlier. Jerry pays a surprise visit to Robert and Emma at their home.

Scene 5: 1973. One year earlier. Venice. Robert and Emma are on vacation. Robert discovers that Emma is having an affair with Jerry.

Scene 6: 1973. Time follows scene 5. Emma returns from Venice, meets Jerry in their flat, but does not tell him that Robert has learned of their affair.

Scene 7: 1973. Time follows scene 6. Robert and Jerry meet in a restaurant for lunch.

Scene 8: 1971. Two years earlier. Emma and Jerry meet in their flat. They are in love.

Scene 9: 1968. Three years earlier. A party at Emma's and Robert's home. Jerry waylays Emma in her bedroom. He declares his love for her. Robert comes upon them but leaves shortly, suspecting nothing.

Appendix 2 Pauses and silences in *Betrayal*

	Pauses				Silences			
Scene	Robert	Emma	Jerry	TOTAL	Robert	Emma	Jerry	TOTAL
1								
(Pub)	—	13	23	36	—	1	0	1
2								
(Jerry's house)	20	—	8	28	3	—	0	3
3								
(Flat: break-up)	—	6	6	12	—	4	2	6
4								
(Robert and Emma's house)	2	1	3	6	0	0	0	0
5								
(Venice)	18	4	—	22	4	2	—	6
6								
(Flat: after Venice)	—	3	5	8	—	0	0	0
7								
(Restaurant)	2	—	2	4	0	—	0	0
8								
(Flat)	—	7	12	19	—	1	0	1
9								
(Robert and Emma's house: affair begins)	0	0	0	0	0	0	0	0

Notes

Three dots indicate ellipsis, except in excerpts from *Betrayal*, where they are reproduced as in the original.

1   My book on conversational style (Tannen, 1984) has been criticized by some for explaining away conflict as misunderstandings resulting from style differences. In this chapter, I confront the issue of conflict head on, suggesting that there are stylistic differences in ways of dealing with potential conflict. Silence and pausing are presented as one such stylistic means.

   This study is part of a larger, ongoing research project comparing conversational and literary discourse. Research on this project in general and on Pinter's play in particular were begun with the support of a Rockefeller Humanities Fellowship. I gratefully acknowledge this support. I would also like to thank Allen Grimshaw and Susan Kay Donaldson for helpful comments on earlier drafts.

2   Goffman (1974: 172) discusses the paradoxically layered nature of betrayal in a love triangle so directly as to sound like a template for Pinter's

play: "Over time, the errant spouse is likely to find reason to goad her husband with what she has done, or, perhaps more commonly, to confess in order to provide evidence that a sincere effort is now being made to give the marital relationship another chance. This betrayal of the betrayal is sometimes not betrayed, in which case it is the lover, not his loved one's spouse, who ends up in the dark, not knowing who knows what."

3   Elsewhere (Tannen, 1986) I discuss the .peculiar nature of overheard remarks, such that they seem to represent the real truth. Quite the contrary, their nature and impact are utterly distorted when they are perceived by a party and in a context other than the ones for which they were intended.

Acknowledgement

Excerpts from *Betrayal* © 1978 by H. Pinter Limited. Reprinted by permission of Grove Press, Inc. and Methuen, London.

The words "our beginnings never know our ends" are from "Portrait of a Lady" in *Collected Poems 1909–1962* by T. S. Eliot, copyright 1936 by Harcourt Brace Jovanovich, Inc.; copyright © 1963 by T. S. Eliot. Reprinted by permission of the publisher.

Excerpts from "Great wits" reprinted by permission of William Morrow and Company, Inc.

13 Research on conflict talk: antecedents, resources, findings, directions

ALLEN D. GRIMSHAW

1. Introduction

Corsaro and Rizzo, in their contribution to this collection, observe that early studies of the phenomenon generally focused on the form or structure of disputes to the exclusion of what they accomplished socially and that many of a second "wave" of studies attended to pragmatic considerations – but less to structure or devices employed. They also observe that many of both sorts of these early studies were of researcher-instigated disputes in dyads and that both of these latter features led to overestimation of the proportion of disputes which are in some way "resolved" (M.H. Goodwin [1982b] made a similar observation). They have also suggested that many early students of conflict talk were concerned about the disruptive consequences of such talk and thus tended to underestimate more positively valued outcomes such as the creation of social organization and the training of participants in valued social skills. Both of these last were long ago anticipated, of course, by Georg Simmel. The data, analytic concerns, conceptualization, modes of analysis, substantive findings, and theoretical conclusions of the research reported in the chapters above vary quite considerably from those of earlier studies; there are also important continuities.

With the exception of Tannen's piece (a study of a dramatic scripting in which there are usually only two parties talking at a time – or even on stage together) all of the studies above are based on sound or sound-image records of interactions involving multiple participants. With the exception of the studies by Schiffrin and Mehan, each of the corpuses investigated would have occurred without researcher intervention (in Mehan's case, the intervention was that of a documentary film-maker). While Corsaro and Rizzo looked at children in what might be called "classroom" settings and Vuchinich at the increasingly familiar venue of the family dinner table, other contributors have examined conflict talk in a range of settings (the street, meals at school, a mental hospital, courts, business meetings of a food

Co-op, the workplace, and living rooms) which have not been much attended in previous research.

While several of the studies reported in the pages above attend to such formal (in the conversational analytic sense of that term) features of the talk examined as sequencing (e.g., especially, the papers of Vuchinich, the Goodwins, and Philips), and all of them to sociolinguistic and linguistic devices such as "footing shifts" and grammatical and prosodic features, respectively, employed by participants in conflict talk, these studies differ from many earlier ones in at least four significant ways.

First, in contrast to past practices of conversation analysts, speech-act philosophers and many linguists, and in consonance with the practice of the *ethnography* of communication, each contributor has attempted to take the social (ethnographic–historical, situational [Halliday]) context of the talk studied into account and, where available, the context of text (Halliday) as well. Second, while not uninterested in the mechanisms (devices, forms, structures; see, especially, the Goodwins' chapter with its careful attention to sequencing) employed by social actors to accomplish their ends in talk, contributors to this volume are generally more interested in participants' interactional agendas and the outcomes of interaction than in full specification of the actual apparatus of talk employed. This leads to a focus on what I have called "disambiguation" (1987, 1988a) of participants' own interpretive and inferential practices and attribution, to participants, of goals (purposes, intentions). This last, i.e., attribution of purposiveness to participant behaviors, will be sharply criticized by those students of talk (e.g., conversation analysts) who argue that this implies the ability to "get into people's heads" and requires unwarranted inferences and claims. The researchers whose work is reported here do not contest the position that what is in people's heads is accessible neither to analysts nor to interlocutors (nor even, ultimately, fully accessible to those whose behavior is under investigation). I believe most of them will also argue, however, that the availability of ethnographic context *and* of an optimally complete behavior record permits analysts to make such inferences and attributions which are "for-most-practical-purposes" (paraphrasing Garfinkel) no less plausible than those of actual participants.[1] This claim is subject to qualification but the disambiguation process is that which we ourselves employ in interaction – where, it must be conceded, we sometimes err.

Third, it follows from the first two differences that the kinds of researches reported here can attend to participants' *hierarchies* of interactional agendas and to outcomes of extended interactional events rather than – or as well as – to the short-term goals, tactics chosen, and the *immediate* outcomes of fragments of behavior extracted from the ongoing "streams" of interaction in which they are embedded. I noted above Corsaro and Rizzo's observation that many previous studies of conflict talk have overestimated the proportion of disputes which are in some way "resolved." It is now a commonplace of interactional analysis (and that of conversational discourse) that different behaviors may be directed to same ends, that similar behaviors may be directed to different ends, that multiple means can be employed to individual ends, and single behaviors to multiple ends, and that behaviors may have multiple consequences – intended, unwanted, incidental, and so on. There are certainly disputes in which "winning" is the primary goal of the parties involved; even in litigation, however, personal vindication, or acknowledgement of one's competence, or vindictiveness – can compete with the desire for redress in intentional hierarchies. The reports above demonstrate that in many instances such superordinate ends (sometimes manifest, sometimes latent) as socialization, play, identity-marking, establishment and/or reaffirmation of social structure, claims of solidarity, and resolution of one's own ideological priorities may be more important than "winning."

Finally, and again implied by the differences already identified, the studies above focus with varying degrees of explicitness on *sociological* dimensions in and understanding of conflict talk. This does not mean that the non-sociologist contributors have abandoned the perspectives of their home disciplines or professions; it implies rather that they share the view that investigation of social processes and of the features of social structure that severally facilitate and constrain those processes should be a central concern for all the social sciences and humanities. In recent years students from across the range of disciplines studying discourse have increasingly come to agree on the central importance of what I have called, somewhat imperialistically, the "sociological variables" of relations of power, relations of affect, and of considerations of utility (stakes, goal salience and costs for participants, etc.), in determining interactional outcomes. The sociological variables, foregrounded with varying degrees of explicitness and identified in diverse manifestations, are incorporated into the analyses and interpretations of each of the studies reported above.[2]

As Whitehead (1925) told us long ago, taxonomic organization of phenomenal diversity is a necessary first step in research on a new (or newly defined) topic. Chomsky (1965) says much the same thing, in a different way, in his dictum that observational and descriptive adequacies are prerequisities for viable explanatory efforts. A considerable proportion of what we know about conflict talk can be summarized by identification of: (1) dichotomies and continua which differentiate instances of conflict talk in terms of, e.g., participants, manifest and latent ends, behaviors (including the particulars of talk), and outcomes – and the interaction of these several elements; and (2) the social, sociolinguistic, and linguistic resources available to conflict-talk participants in circumstances defined by varying combinations and interactions of the differentiating features or elements just listed. In the pages following I sketch such a summary – as will be seen, I will have more to say about the nature and course of conflict talk than about the resources available to participants.

2. What we have learned. 1: distinctive/distinguishing features

When ordinary "members" (as contrasted to analysts) talk about conflict in general and about specific disputes, they most often attend to substantive issues seen as "causes," to participants' motivations, to whether the dispute might have been avoided, to the course and character of the dispute(s) in question (including, in at least some instances, attention to specific devices [legal and other] employed by parties to the conflict), and to outcomes or resolutions. In this section I will discuss the goals or ends (Ends $_1$ in Hymes' [1974] sense) of, occurrence of, and participant orientations to, conflict talk. In the next section I review findings on the course (in terms of unfolding characteristics and of constraints on those characteristics), and the outcomes (Hymes' [1974] Ends$_2$) of conflict talk. In section 4 I will turn very briefly to available resources and devices employed in that talk and in section 5 to some implications of the work reported.

2.1 Ends$_1$ (goals, purposes)

Just as beauty is "in the eye of the beholder," so the critical dimensions of conflict talk are seen/heard differently from the perspectives of contenders, allies, disinterested audiences, and observers. Whatever one's "footing" or "participant status" (Goffman, 1981) with reference to a particular conflict event, however, it seems likely that at least three sets of elements will be taken into account in assessing and interpreting the ends of a dispute, namely: (1) content; (2) occurrence/visibility, focus and hierarchy; (3) participant orientation. Space constraints will permit me to do no more than to suggest some of the more obvious distinctions defining these sets of elements which are emerging from studies of conflict talk.

"Content": Although the substantive issues which may precipitate conflict talk or emerge in its course are infinite, they can be roughly sorted into four principal categories. There are, first, conflicts in which the matter at dispute is the central concern of participants – and where their goals are to "win." These disputes are, in turn, analytically separable into conflicts about: (1) things or "rights" (toys or territory, authority or precedence, respectively); (2) beliefs (ideologies, values, opinions); (3) factual claims (usually historical – when personal attributes becomes a focus another variety of conflict is occurring, i.e., that over identity claims); or (4) some combination of things, beliefs, claims, and so on. Table 13.1 provides a very rough gloss of some representative issues disputed in events reported in chapters above; I fully realize that the categories overlap and that some of the assignments may be problematic, the entries are intended to be illustrative and suggestive – not definitive.

Table 13.1 *Some representative conflict issues*

Focus	Things, rights	Beliefs	Facts
Author			
Corsaro and Rizzo	Toys, access	Existence of wolves	Who said what to whom
Eder	"Best friend" status	Rules for loyalty among friends	What was promised
Vuchinich	Garbage duties; truck-driving	Rules for spending money	Historical facts
Labov	Parking space[a]	Priority of co-op values or those of anti-racism	Theft[a]
O'Donnell	Control of workplace	Proper role of unions	What trucks have bells
Conley and O'Barr	Money; self-esteem	Priority of social or contractual obligations	What was promised
Mehan	Release from hospital	Rules for medical decisions	Patient's health status
Goodwin and Goodwin	Leadership, followership roles		
Philips	Pre-trial release	Rules for admissibility of evidence	
Schiffrin		Inter-ethnic contact appropriateness norms	
Tannen		Fidelity norms	

[a]Reported conflicts which did not occur in the data record studied.

A second variety of conflict talk revolves around claims about and negotiation of personal identities, i.e., about what kinds of persons participants and their interlocutors *are* and about what the nature of their social relations should be. Whatever the putative stakes in terms of the tripartite typology just suggested may be, it appears that *all* conflict talk involves *some* negotiation of identities and of the appropriate nature of interpersonal (i.e., structural, organizational) arrangements. This is evident even in those instances in which analysts do not explicitly address the matter; it it true both of the papers above and of others I have reviewed in writing this chapter. Labov remarks (personal communication) that ethnic slurs and other derogatory labeling, such as some of talk reported in the talk in the Co-op meetings she studied, can be deeply implicated in negotiation of identities.

While the third and fourth varieties of conflict talk are less frequent in their occurrence, they are critically important and perhaps less rare than may initially seem to be the case. One of these has socializing functions, three sub-varieties of which are touched upon in the reports above i.e.: (1) inculcation of skills in argument and in negotiation of identities (Corsaro and Rizzo, Eder, the Goodwins, Vuchinich); (2) instruction (implicit as well as explicit) about both the realities and different perceptions of social structure (the same four papers plus those of Mehan and of Labov and/or Conley and O'Barr); (3) instruction concerning normative proprieties of talk and of interaction (Corsaro and Rizzo, Vuchinich, Mehan, O'Donnell, and possibly Schiffrin). The other is the use of conflict talk in "play"; in the chapters above, this function is most evident in the *discussione* of Corsaro and Rizzo's Italian children and in some of the exchanges Schiffrin reports (see, more particularly, her 1984), it is discernible in some of Vuchinich's materials and may be latent in other conflict talk reported. Much of such play is directed to solidarity enhancement and the generation of preferred social relationships; some may be more serious than one or both parties may wish it to be – that some is "play" may not be evident to audiences or analysts. The fact remains that conflict talk approaches the status of a major "sport" in some circles.[3]

2.2 Occurrence/visibility, focus and hierarchy

Whether or not disputes occur, and the course of those that do, depends upon interaction of: (1) the stakes involved (content of ends), (2) the attributes and orientations of, and relations among, participants, and (3) initial and evolving contexts of situation. While the disputes analyzed in this volume *did* occur, they varied on some dimension of avoidability-inevitability. The *discussioni* of Corsaro and Rizzo's Italian children, the sometimes ambivalently playful contentions of Eder's adolescent girls, and the amiable arguments of Schiffrin's spouses and their friends were by no means inevitable – although they might be characterized as "waiting to happen" quite different foci might have emerged from the ongoing interaction. Contrastively, stakes such as continued incarceration in a hospital or not (Mehan), or the nature of a marital infidelity and a dissolving relationship (Tannen), or of union–management relations (O'Donnell), increase the probability that disputes will occur – just as does the presence of participants with personal attributes and orientations like those of Vladimir (Mehan) or Lyle (O'Donnell) or of different race or ethnicity (Labov). In some instances, of course, disputes may be avoided in spite of high immediate stakes because of superordinate ends – such as the maintenance of a social relationship which would be threatened by conflict (Simmel); in others with lower stakes someone "spoiling for a fight" may "pick" one. Whatever the "inevitability" of a dispute, moreover, situational constraints such as emergencies or the appearance of certain audiences may cause a dispute to be delayed – or even "tabled." Just as conflict may be delayed or tabled, moreover, and in spite of the fact that both (or all) parties may intend to avoid conflict (at least for the time being), some conflicts are genuinely spontaneous and incidental to the main focus of the ongoing – or "accidents" resulting from unintended insults (e.g., failures of interactional "engagement" [Goffman, 1967]) or other delicts.

While occurrence of any dispute minimally requires co-presence, the rigidity of "scheduling" is highly variable. Trials (Conley and O'Barr, Philips), meetings of medical review boards (Mehan), the Quality of Working Life meetings (O'Donnell), and Co-op meetings are scheduled in advance; family meals and childrens' after-school play are presumably more casually arranged. The *discussioni* among Corsaro and Rizzo's Italian children often erupted, predictably, during periods when children were "drawing" (see also Maynard 1985a, 1985b) – apparently facilitated by a conjunction of high interpersonal density and relaxation of adult supervision. Vuchinich's family dinners provide a regularly occurring setting in which complainants and offenders *and* powerful adult "judges" will be together; his findings appear to confirm the stereotype that Americans (at least) find the dinner table an optimal setting for disputes. Working spouses must be home before at least some of Schiffrin's "sociable" arguments can occur; they apparently occur with some regularity when the condition of co-presence is met. School lunches (Eder) and after-school play (Goodwin and Goodwin) also provide regular *opportunities* for disputes to occur. The "showdown" between Emma and Robert in the Pinter play (Tannen) may have been inevitable and increasingly so, but nothing that Pinter allows us to know would permit us to say why it occurred exactly when it did. Only in *reports* of conflicts with "outsiders" in Labov's material do we hear of totally "unscheduled" disputes – those reports occurred in the course of regularly scheduled Co-op meetings in which contending ideological principles occurred with high predictability. While there are studies of disputes which occur when the right combination of potential disputants and stakes co-occur (because of the very unpredictability of such conflicts, such stories have usually been based on reports of past conflict; see, illustratively, Bower, 1984; W. Labov, 1972b; Dittmar, Schlobinski, and Wachs 1988), the studies above show that the scheduling of the occurrence of conflict talk is far more regular – and predictable – than we may have thought.

Two final caveats. Consideration of the three elements identified at the beginning of this section may permit us to make asessments of the probability of conflict and attention to scheduling constraints may permit us to anticipate when it is most likely to occur. These facts notwithstanding, both participants in interaction and analysts of interaction must confront and deal with interpretive problems stemming from the inherent ambiguities of human behaviors, including talk. There is, first the danger of "discovering" conflict where it does not exist; W. Labov and Fanshel (1977) warn analysts about the "paradox of aggression" – the fact that close analysis of almost any talk appears to reveal an underlying entanglement of claims, counter-claims, challenges and counter-challenges; friends and cointeractants similarly warn us about the dangers of "paranoia." The complementary danger, more of a threat for conversational co-participants than for analysts, is that the ambiguities of talk may prevent them from realizing that conflict is present.[4] Conflict may be obscured by indirection or overt politeness or spurious playfulness or even by apparent solicitude. Goffman argued that extremely subtle "reframings" and "rekeyings" can massively change the interactional meaning of the ongoing (1974); our own everyday lives continuously validate his observation. Convincingly virulent staged disputes may end in laughter; "shared" laughter may be only manifestly so. Bailey (1983) has demonstrated how displays of "passion" are quite dispassionately employed to obtain instrumental ends. The continua of occurrence and non-occurrence and of overt and covert conflict interact complexly with others of foolhardiness and fear or altruism and greed.

2.3 *"Participant orientation"*

While the possible orientations of participants in conflict are empirically no less diverse than are the ends of disputatious talk, it is again possible to roughly categorize what might be called "sectors of orientation." Participants' orientations are even less accessible than is "content" to direct observation; and contenders, audiences and analysts may make different assessments of orientations – indeed, the nature of orientations may itself become a focus of conflict. This fact makes specification of the boundaries and internal organization of the sectors of orientation very difficult. I offer the following four "bundles" of relevant distinctions as an exploratory heuristic; other bundles could doubtless be useful.

Nature of involvement. A first bundle of such features and distinctions, that of perception of nature of involvement, is related to – but not exhausted by – the families of distinctions of "footing" and of "participant status" described by Goffman (1981). Participants in conflict talk may see themselves as speaking "for" themselves or for others (T. Labov, 1980, and this volume) and, if for others, variously as official or unofficial representatives, surrogates, or even as reluctant (but morally compelled) "public defenders." This last suggests a distinction between participant senses of participation as being voluntary or involuntary, i.e., that they are severally themselves initiators of a dispute (if only in the sense that something has been said which they "can't let go by"), or defendants, or "innocent victims." Non-contenders may also see themselves in a variety of roles. Judges may see themselves as disinterested rule-interpreters, parents as interested but impartial arbitrators, and friends as mediators; there are also, however, "trouble stirrer-uppers" (some of Corsaro and Rizzo's children or Eder's adolescents) and "advantage-takers" or "exploiters" (per Simmel's [1950, pp.154–162] notion of *tertius gaudens*).

Consideration of another distinction, i.e., Parsons' (1951) between self-orientation and collectivity-orientation, suggests an interesting paradox. Parsons asserted, quite logically, that all human behaviors are directed to maximization of own self-interests or those of the collectivity; he was not unaware that social actors may have stakes in defining the two sets of interests as isomorphic. There are surely instances in which both parties to a dispute recognize self-interests as central issues (though each may invoke maintenance of social norms as a goal); there are just as surely instances in which both parties claim collectivity-orientation as their central motivation (i.e., certain ideological arguments) even while possibly acknowledging an interest in "winning" an argument. But in a large number of instances each party will claim a collectivity-orientation while assigning a self-orientation to their opponent. The paradox is the breakdown of the principle of complementarity around which role theory is organized. While there are exceptions, as in the case of acceptance of the "troublemaker" label (I have a friend whose talk is sprinkled with the phrase, "Speaking as the Devil's advocate"), it is more generally the case that not only do conflict talk participants not accept the roles (and orientations) assigned to them by their opposite parties – they are likely to assign, and claim for themselves, roles the reverse of those claimed and assigned by opponents. Patients may argue with their doctors about diagnoses, they don't ordinarily argue with them about whether they *are* doctors or by what authority they make a diagnosis at all; disputants argue about who started an argument, about the authority with which each speaks, about their disinterestedness, etc.

Perception of stakes.   Participants may or may not recognize in their own involvement in disputation the sorts of ends listed above in the brief review of "content"; whether or not they recognize such variation in content in their own and in their fellow disputants' conflict moves, they are likely to have orientations toward outcomes whatever the content of the talk. Some disputes will be seen as more important (or salient) than others; some will be seen as "all or nothing" (zero sum) and some as subject to compromise (non-zero sum). Relatedly, and in part because one party's compromise "offer" may be seen by her/his opponent as no compromise at all, contending parties will see stakes as variously negotiable. Conley and O'Barr's and Philips' judges and other third parties may see compromises and non-zero sum outcomes as preferable to protracted and possibly costly extended disputes; contending parties, with differing views of salience and of the moral dimensions of points at issue, may differ in willingness to negotiate. These differences in willingness to negotiate constitute another dimension, i.e., that of "commitment" or "non-commitment" to an ongoing conflict.

Finally, related to participants' perceptions of their involvement as well as of the stakes involved and perhaps obscure to conflict participants, audiences and analysts alike, there is a sense in which the former are driven by perceptions of stakes as embodying, variously, principles, preferences, or some combination of the two. Equity in the abstract (i.e., for unknown others) is presumably at least primarily a matter of "principle." What movie to attend would seem to be a matter of preference – though it may be advantageous to attempt to find equity dimensions. "Rights" may involve considerations of both preference and principle; the latter considerations may be employed to minimize one's commitment to the former. Because we often do not know ourselves, a participant's priorities may be more evident to opponents and audiences than to themself. Because of the malleability of talk, participants may be able to leave opponents and witnesses (and especially analysts) uncertain about the priorities reflected by their behaviors. (It is this last, of course, which makes conversational analysts suspicious of attempts to assign "intent" to talk.)

There is no stable weighting of outcome priorities; they shift with maturation through the life course (adults who don't learn this are characterized as "childish" or "adolescent"), they shift through the course of disputes – as new information becomes available, as alliances shift, as ennui replaces passion, as "real" passion replaces the feigned (see, on this latter, Bailey, 1983). There are also instances, of course, in which individual (or organizational) priorities are both initially clear and robust over time. The patient whose case is being reviewed in the materials examined by Mehan consistently sees the stakes in this case as zero sum, non-negotiable, principled *and* preferential, highly salient and as his major focus of commitment. Although in practice a combination of principled and preferential goals is routinely given salience, however, Labov's Co-op members find themselves unable consistently to assign priority to one set of ideological principles over another set, i.e., they use commitment to the Co-op as a device which legitimates segregation-fostering actions while simultaneously deploring that segregation.

The materials examined by O'Donnell are particularly instructive. A reading of the lengthier corpus from which O'Donnell's illustrative texts are drawn reveals that *all* of the four categories of "content" identified just above are disputed by conflict-talk participants i.e., (1) authority (in the plant), values (about unions), and factual claims (which trucks had "back-up beepers"); (2) identity claims and the appropriate nature of social relationships; (3) socialization (of Lyle); and (4) play (or, at the least, displays intended to be seen as less than "fully serious"). The interaction by its very mode of inception is defined as oriented toward compromise and nonzero sum, "win-win" outcomes. While acting as official representatives of officially contending parties (union and management), most participants agree in defining two goals, i.e., "harmony" and "the protection of life" as goals of particularly great salience to which they are committed; their discussion displays mutual assessments of the two goals as combining both preferential and principled dimensions. Lyle, however, even in the face of this apparent consensus and without openly challenging it, assigns greater salience to and is personally more committed to what can be glossed as "anti-union" values and a goal of getting his fellow interactants to concede a basis for those values in past union behaviors. He adheres to his personal agenda and priorities in spite of their disruptiveness *and* an openly critical response from his fellow management representative. Lyle's behavior can be interpreted only through knowledge of the ethnographic–historical *and* textual contexts; that same behavior (and its antecedents) shows why there can be no stable weighting of outcome priorities.

Affectual/emotional orientation.   While contemporary students as diverse as Kemper (1978) and Hochschild (1983) have demonstrated the wide range of individual emotions (feelings, sentiments) which may be incorporated into affectual orientations, they do not seem to disagree with Freud and even earlier students in assessing such orientations (whether towards individuals or toward events) as being *generally* positive or negative (or indifferent). Once again, however, apparent simplicity dissolves under scrutiny. Aside from whatever ambivalences participants may bring with them into the interactional arena, economies of emotion are, as the three authors just mentioned have so nicely demonstrated with quite different data and starting from quite different analytic and theoretical perspectives, continuously being renegotiated. Relations of liking or disliking may long perdure; they remain vulnerable, however, sometimes to modest (or unintended) slights – or kindnesses – invisible to all but a recipient or a surprised but attentive third party.

Whatever the subtleties of initial participant orientations toward those with whom they engage in conflict talk and their sense of nature of the talk itself, and whatever the subtleties of shifts or orientations and of assessments of the ongoing talk in its course, participants are likely to have at all times some sense that interpersonal relations and the talk *itself* are hostile, friendly or neutral. Analytic assessment of these orientations and "sense" is a most uncertain enterprise, however, for at least three reasons. First, it cannot be assumed either that affect is symmetrical or that assessments of the nature of the ongoing are shared. Vladimir (the patient in Mehan's paper) appears to be angry and hostile toward the doctors on the review board and to consider the interaction as directed "against" him; the doctors would presumably deny any personal animus toward him and claim disinterestedness in the outcome of the hearing – or even hopes that Vladimir could be discharged (i.e., that they are friendly). Similar asymmetries characterize the apparent emotional orientations of the litigants in Conley and O'Barr's small-claims cases and of Lyle and his several opponents in O'Donnell's materials. All of us are familiar with instances in which insistence by one party in conflict talk in treating that talk as "play" (or at least as non-serious) elicits increasing outrage from the (self-seen) victim; such scenarios are most likely, of course, where there are also sharp differences in power and/or where stakes are seen very differently by contenders. In such instances the asymmetries in orientation or the different assessments of the nature of the talk may themselves become the focus of disputation.

Second, and generative of another sort of asymmetry, there are both individual and group differences about norms both of production and of interpretation (Hymes, 1974) of conflict orientations, perceptions, and behaviors. Kochman (1981, see also 1986) has nicely limned differences in black and white "styles" of conflict which can cause potentially critical misperceptions of anger, propensities for violence, and commitment.[5]

Finally, as noted above, whatever the initial emotional orientations of participants and whatever the initial definitions of the ongoing talk, the "framing" of conflict talk is no less vulnerable than that of other discourse to blatant or subtle, intended or unintended, abrupt or gradual, benign or malign, ambiguous or less so, "refabrication, rekeying, frame breaking, reframing," (Goffman, 1974).

An "instrumental-expressive" dimension. This dimension is closely related to but analytically quite distinct from that just discussed. In the years before air-conditioning I lived in an apartment which opened onto a shared courtyard. In the summer a young couple across the courtyard regularly had bitter arguments in which they reviewed, very loudly, each other's defects and those of their families. At some point, just as regularly, one or another neighbor would yell at them to "shut up" – or at least "close your windows." And, just as regularly again, both members of the couple would come to their open window(s) and respond to their neighbors' suggestions with both colorful characterizations of the latters' antecedents and attributes and scatological and sexual counter-suggestions. Unlike the amiable disputes of Schiffrin's couples those of the couple were truly rancorous and threatening. At the same time, however, they had some of the elements of *discussione* in that they were highly predictable in both course and content. The arguments were never so engrossing, moreover, that the principals could not stop long enough to castigate neighbors who asked them to make their battles less public. I do not have the impression that even the couple expected to "resolve" their problems through their pyrotechnics; middle-class white Americans refer to what they did as "blowing off steam." (Some families have code terms for such behaviors; family members and some friends said of an adult and putatively patriarchal adult male I once knew, "He's got the 'blood.'")

All of us learn, sometimes at quite considerable costs of embarrassment and sorrow, that appearances *can* deceive and that the presence or absence

Table 13.2 *The distributive interaction of instrumentality/expressiveness and manifest affect/emotion*

Conflict talk "purpose"	Instrumental	Expressive
Level of emotion displayed		
High overt affect	Possession contests (Corsaro/Rizzo)	*Discussione* (Corsaro/Rizzo)
	Family dinners (Vuchinich)	Family dinners (Vuchinich)
	Eighth graders (Eder)	Eighth graders (Eder)
	"Relational" litigants (O'Barr/Conley)	Lyle (O'Donnell)
	Vladimir (Mehan)	Members vs "outsiders" (Labov)
High (undisplayed) affect[a]	QWL meeting (O'Donnell)	Emma and Robert (Tannen)
Low affect[b]	Family dinners (Vuchinich)	"Sociables" (Schiffrin)
	"Contractual" litigants (O'Barr/Conley)	
	QWL meeting (O'Donnell)	
	Doctors (Mehan)	
	Attorneys (Philips)	
	Sling shotters (Goodwin/ Goodwin)	

[a]O'Donnell observes that while some of this affect can be discerned in the prosodic channel it was not "heard" by all participants; open emotional displays were presumably suppressed because of sharp discrepancies in power, etc. Tannen argues, of course, that silences and pauses actually display tension and high emotion.
[b]May or may not be "affectively-neutral" in Parsons' (1951) sense, i.e., emotions may be present but suppressed.

of emotions can be simulated. As Bailey (1983) has so nicely demonstrated, some of us learn to employ emotion "tactically"; all of us, again, are taught an "etiquette of simulation" which includes such rules as "sounding as if you mean it" when we express apologies or thanks, and other niceties of what Hymes (1974) labels "key." This knowledge and our further awareness of the subtleties of "impression management" (Goffman, 1959b) and "emotion management" (Hochschild, 1983), notwithstanding, fore-warned is not always forearmed, and the danger of misreading is always present. The situation is further complicated by the fact, often remarked above, that orientations and emotions can shift rapidly and simulated anger turn ugly. Still additional laminations are consequent from both idiosyncratic ("cool" versus "hot" anger) and cultural differences in emotional expression.

Fortunately for us as social actors (and as analysts) the world is not totally random. This is true for two reasons. First, the effects of the sociological variables are consistent and we are able to interpret "new" situations because they are much the same as "old" and more familiar ones. Second, while some people and some groups *do* behave quite differently from others, we learn, to the extent that we have repeated interaction with those people and/or these groups, to expect and appropriately anticipate and respond to, those differences. (Some of us don't learn, of course – and those with whom we interact may learn to anticipate behaviors constrained by our "unteachability.") Taken jointly, these two factors allow us to take the roles of others; more often than not most people are, most of the time, able to distinguish instrumental and expressive behaviors and real and simulated emotions.

Table 13.2 displays how an "outsider" who knows about the disputes described and analyzed in the chapters above only from reading about them might make surface assignments of the location of the disputes along the dimensions of instrumentality-expressiveness and manifest affect-emotion. My assignments may be wrong; I think I have probably used the same sorts of cues and indicators that all of us employ – as ordinary participants – in interpreting what cointeractants are "doing" in conflict talk. I find it doubtful that Lyle believed that he would change union practices by his attack; I strongly suspect that none of his cointeractants would disagree (indeed, O'Donnell [1983] provides ethnographic documentation for this view).

3. What have we learned. 2: the nature and course of conflict

Considerably more has been written about what happens in the actual course of conflict than about the topics sketched in the sections above (see, illustratively, Coleman, 1957; Gouldner, 1954 Hiller, 1928; Simmel, 1955 [1908]). It is neither necessary nor possible to review the rich literatures on conflict here; I will limit my discussion to brief commentary on three questions: (1) what is the nature of social relations/interaction in conflict and conflict talk? (2) How is conflict (talk) done and how does conflict change, developmentally, over its course? and (3) What cultural, ecological, ethological (bionomic), psychological, and sociological constraints condition conflict's (conflict talk's) nature and course?

3.1 Dimensions of variability in conflict behaviors

The nature of conflict behaviors is jointly determined by features discussed above (i.e., ends, particularities of occurrence and participant orientations) and the sociological and other constraints to be discussed below (pp. 297ff.); as will be seen, it is often difficult to clearly identify sources of behaviors. Many conflict dimensions are co-determining (or at least interactive); in the O'Barr and Conley study, for example, the behaviors of litigants tend to be either relational *and* diffuse *or* rule-oriented *and* specific. This complication notwithstanding, it is possible to suggest a heuristic distinction between features/dimensions of focus, form(at), and intensity-tone-direction.

Focus: Conflicts may focus on beliefs, objects (things), persons, groups, or institutions.[6] If any of the latter three is the focus, conflicts may be directed to behaviors or to attributes. The focus may be highly specific, it may be (or come to be) diffuse. The focus will not always be clear, both because we don't always know what is "bothering" us and because of uncertainties about optimal resolutions. These unclarities are often exacerbated by the ambiguities of discourse itself (Grimshaw, 1987) and, perhaps, by the presence of unconscious motivations. Because of the operation of the sociological variables the "official" or manifest focus of disputation may differ sharply from what is actually at issue; normative considerations may also cause conflict participants to obscure focus. These complexities notwithstanding, and admitting the possibility of strategic (or tactical) denials of actual focus, I think it likely that conflict participants and analysts will often agree on what conflicts are about. (How often is an empirical question; how validly may be partly a philosophic one.)

Form (at). In section 4 I identify a few of the numerous and diverse linguistic and other devices employed in conflict talk. It can be noted here that conflict talk, like all discourse, can be: (1) direct or indirect; (2) "cool" or "passionate"; (3) based on facts or opinions (though each may appear in the garb of the other); (4) procedurally formal or informal; (5) based on appeals to morality or to codified norms (including law) or both; (6) based on appeals to reason or threats of force, etc. As the researches reported above have demonstrated, these distinctions are continua; as the reports have also shown, location on one continuum is neither independent of nor determined by location on another. Finally, as the studies by O'Barr and Conley, O'Donnell and Mehan, show, the formats and styles of adversaries in conflict talk are not necessarily symmetrical; Mehan underlines, however, that Vladimir and the review board "reason" in the same way.

Intensity-tone-direction. The operation of the sociological variables of power, affect and utility and of those features of participant orientation which combine to produce "commitment" are particularly visible in their influence on this also more visible feature of conflict talk. Conflict talk can be seen, both by participants and by non-participants (including analysts) as being in some general sense more or less benign or malign. This sense is determined by two sets of related but analytically separable features, namely, is the talk friendly, neutral, or hostile and is it pleasant, neutral, or threatening. Shifts along these continua are sometimes signaled by shifts along another dimension, namely that of coolness-emotionality; these latter shifts are sometimes indicated/displayed by prosodic features (shifts in amplitude or tempo, "troubles" in talk [hesitations, recyclings, word searches, etc.]), increased kinesic activity, and the appearance of, e.g., "challenging" or "defending" postures (Scheflen, 1973), or (again sometimes) involuntary physiological behaviors such as tears, "blood rushes," trembling, or excessive perspiration. They are sometimes signaled more openly, of course, by the introduction of negative verbal characterizations of adversaries' behaviors, motives and/or persons. The modifier "sometimes" is necessary for at least two reasons. First, there are both individual and cultural differences in the *expression* of the same emotions, e.g., some persons may show anger by becoming more voluble and others by becoming taciturn. (Cultures vary additionally, of course, in what emotions are normatively appropriate in response to what situational stimuli.) Second, we must as always keep in mind Goffman's caveats about genuine as contrasted to spurious or managed emotional displays (see also, again, Bailey, 1983). (There is again a cultural dimension, Americans sufficiently alarmed by *discussione* among adult Italians to attempt intervention would find themselves minimally reacted to with puzzlement and perhaps with rebuff or something stronger.)

These important qualifications notwithstanding, familiars of participants in conflict talk and even "members" more generally are usually well attuned to shifts in the tone and intensity of disputatious discourse. Familiars may interpret shifts along one or another dimension as being more threatening than that along another; as has been noted, increasing anger can be variously signaled by politeness or its obverse – we are sensitive to the passing of combined thresholds of the several continua which warn us that "things have become 'ugly.'" It is at that juncture that witnessing strangers to disputes in public places become, variously, open or covert spectators, embarrassed "ignorers," panic-stricken or more casual escapees or, more rarely, reluctant or variably officious (and sometimes "official") intervenors. The options available to witnessing cointeractants, who sometimes are unable to withdraw, may be more limited, they may also be constrained by cultural, or group, norms. (In some instances, of course, conflict talk participants may themselves withdraw – as was the case with some of Eder's middle schoolers and of Vuchinich's dinner participants.)

So long as conflict talk is sustained (i.e., if participants do not withdraw) it does not seem to be the case that hostility ("ugliness") will increase without some concomitant increase in intensity. Friendly disputes can get quite "hot"; at least to some point they can apparently increase in intensity without the occurrence of hostility. Both the relationship betweeen increasing hostility and increasing intensity and the occurrence or not of "rekeying" (Goffman, 1974) of increasingly intense friendly arguments into less friendly ones are determined by participants' orientations, their interpersonal relations of power and of affect, and their stakes in the ongoing, and, of course, institutional and other (including normative) constraints of the situation/setting. Vladimir (Mehan) and Lyle (O'Donnell) and litigants Rawls and Webb (O'Barr and Conley) and even some of Vuchinich's diners perceived stakes as high and do not have appear to have had very positive affect for their adversaries (a short-term condition, hopefully, for Vuchinich's family members); it seems likely that in the absence of greater power of their opponents or of third parties both intensity and hostility might have escalated. Such an outcome seems less likely for Schiffrin's "sociables" or Philip's attorneys or Conley and O'Barr's other litigants.

3.2 The developmental course of conflict talk

First, and obviously, each of the features already discussed may change over the course of a dispute. Coleman (1957) noted of community controversies that they: (1) tend to *expand* in focus, moving from initial precipitating issues, sometimes to the point where the latter are submerged or forgotten; (2) tend to *change* in focus, moving from dispute over material interests or ideological positions to increasing personalization, with attribution of specific defects to opponents being replaced by globally negative characterizations of opponents (individuals or groups or categories, etc.); and (3) tend to *spread* along pre-existing boundaries of classes, categories, groups, institutions (i.e., churches, schools, businesses) and more informal (e.g. friendship) networks. Coleman and others (e.g. Lambert, 1951; Williams *et al.*, 1964) have further observed that both cross-cutting social and organizational memberships and idiosyncratic patterns of friendships and loyalties and interests may serve to constrain the spread of conflict, inhibit or facilitate expansion or change in focus, and so on. Other constraints may be introduced by custom or by law, and by such mundane considerations as available resources of energy, wealth, or time. Similar dynamics and similar constraints seem to be present in conflicts as different in scale as those between spouses and those between nation states and, presumably, in the conflict talk displayed in each.[7] In the paragraphs following I will comment briefly on the dynamics of and constraints on the conflict talk described in some of the studies reported above.

The developmental course; some variable dimensions. On reflection, the conflict talk reported above is generally fairly mild, relatively low in intensity (or at least in overt displays of intensity), and generally not highly personalized. Even though there are instances in the disputes above where participants become sufficiently distressed to withdraw from interaction in "huffs" (W. Labov and Fanshel, 1977), none of the disputes starts from some simple "opposition move" (Vuchinich) and escalates into a full-blown "knock down drag 'em out fight" in which adversaries are characterized as globally bad and initial issues submerged or forgotten. This does not mean that there are not changes in intensity or expansion and change in focus, and/or spread of disputes to involve additional participants. There are apparently increases in intensity of involvement for at least some participants (but not necessarily all) in all of the kinds of disputes studied except for those examined by Goodwin and Goodwin, Philips, and Schiffrin; these increases are not symmetrical. New issues are raised over the course of several of the dinner arguments, in the interactions of the middle-school girls, by the unsuccessful litigants in the small claims court cases, and by the sling shotters as they prepare for battle. Allies volunteer or are recruited in most of the cases involving children, in Labov's Co-op discussions, by Philips' attorneys, and even in Schiffrin's sociable arguments; they are sought unsuccessfully by some of the children, by Lyle, and by both Rawls and Webb in the small-claims court.

Some of the disputes studied, however, seem as much or more characterized by oscillation between features as by linear shift toward different features. Thus, while some conflicts continued until resolved or otherwise "finished," other conflict talk was discontinuous (Emma and Robert [Tannen], QWL meeting [O'Donnell] or even episodic [the Goodwins' sling shotters].) (Retrospectively it can be seen that while Emma and Robert's dispute was discontinuous it moved inexorably to plateaus of greater intensity – however civil the actual talk itself may have been.) Thus, too, some participants and some talk moved from lesser to greater directness and back again – and with variable degrees of subtlety; Emma and Robert, and perhaps Lyle, are again exemplaries. Some arguments are characterized by the recycling of charges, claims, and putative evidence, others by the insertion of new "information." There may also be oscillation as well as linear shift in the extent to which charges, claims, and putative evidence are seen by adversaries (and audiences and/or analysts) as "on" or "off" topic. Assessments of topicality vary; Philips' attorneys and judges would probably agree that their arguments stayed on topic – Conley and O'Barr's "relational" litigants would have argued that they stayed on topic but their "rule-oriented" partners in the litigation – and the judges – apparently disagreed. Conflict talk differs, ultimately, in the extent to which it is in some sense well designed, or not, to move toward outcomes based on the talk itself as contrasted to outcomes based on features of the situation extrinsic to the discourse. I turn now to brief discussion of some of those features.

The developmental course; some constraints.   Some disputes are highly predictable in occurrence and course; some expected disputes never "break," or are delayed or tabled, minor spats swell into titanic struggles, major confrontations "fizzle out," apparent victors withdraw, intense disputes suddenly terminate without apparent reason. The reasons for these several different developmental courses and outcomes are not always recoverable from analysis of texts of discourse; they must be discovered instead in the presence and operation of cultural, social, and ecological constraints. These constraints are sometimes complementary and overlapping, sometimes contradictory, and variously salient in specific instances of conflict potential; conflict talk cannot be explained without taking them into account.

Cultural constraints.   Norms about when disputes are appropriate (or mandatory) and about how conflict talk should be conducted vary across cultures; each culture has both general and specific norms about disputes and the talk (and other behaviors) which may appropriately be employed in "doing disputes" – each culture also has additional rules about exceptions (Edgerton, 1985). No culture is monolithic, Kochman (1981) has shown the differences, within American society, of black and white "conflict styles," the Goodwins (1987) have documented differences in male and female "styles" and syntax in intragender disputes, and Tannen (1984, 1986) has elaborately shown how ethnicity, region, class, gender, and age in conversational styles can generate communicative non-success and set the stage for conflict. Such sub-cultural variations notwithstanding, American society has both positive and negative general norms about when conflict should or should not take place, e.g., "protect the weak" or "some principles are worth dying for" and "pick on those your own size" or "forgive the deranged or bereaved or obsessed, etc. (for 'they know not what they do')" and "defer to the dying," respectively. Responses to Vladimir and Lyle were presumably tempered because they were members of "forgivable" categories, i.e., the deranged and the obsessed, respectively. Emma and Robert, contrastively, presumably avoided more rancorous expression in their conflict because of Anglo-American class norms proscribing "unseemly incivility."

One set of more specific Anglo-American norms indexes class-specific constraints regarding a public–private dimension and other features of what Hymes (1974) calls "scene" or "setting." Most Anglo-Americans would consider it inappropriate to argue openly during a church service, because of the sacred nature of the event, out of consideration for others in attendance, and because of the difficulties in keeping such a dispute private. A smaller but still very large number of potential disputants would avoid *public* dispute visible/audible to "non-ratified overhearers" (Goffman, 1981) again out of consideration for the latter and again because of proscriptions concerning "washing dirty linen in public." The visible-audible modifier is important, some people feel it appropriate to engage in conflict talk in such public places as restaurants – if voices are "kept down" and the uninvolved spared vicarious participation. There are some persons, of course, for whom the public–private distinction seems to carry little weight, and whose disputes become public spectacles wherever delicts occur or opposition moves are made – thereby generating variously amusement, disdain, embarrassment, or even fear, amongst overhearers. The woman who was reported to have shouted "racist" in the Co-op (Labov) seems to have generated all these responses except amusement – amusement mixed with other emotions was often the response to the boisterous neighbors mentioned earlier.[8] Some people appear to find no place off-limits for conflict talk other than those, like courtrooms, libraries, and hospitals, where institutional sanctions (including forcible removal) can be invoked.

There are, of course, *ceteris paribus* conditions on these (and other) cultural norms; real or perceived stakes may be too high to permit conflict avoidance and some individuals may be either temporarily or perennially unconstrained by the normative considerations which inhibit their fellows. The warrantable exceptions are the cultural "exceptions" investigated by Edgerton (1985); some violations by individuals may fall within the purview of students of psychopathology.

Sociological constraints. Cultural norms may prevent some overt conflict and delay the occurrence of some conflict talk; the principal constraints on the occurrence or non-occurrence of conflict talk and of its course when it occurs, appear to be the operation of the sociological variables of relations of power and of affect and of considerations of utility. Union participants in the QWL talk may have tempered their dispute with Lyle because of his well-known and bitter anti-unionism; he was, in the last analysis, also a "boss." Corsaro and Rizzo's children disputed with one another; they did not undertake to substantially challenge teachers or others with authority. Parents remained the ultimate authorities in Vuchinich's family disputes and their children did not ordinarily "take them on." Lyle listened to *his* boss. The greater the discrepancies in power, the lower the likelihood that those of lesser power will challenge the more powerful and engage them in dispute. The greater the discrepancies in power, the greater the likelihood that if such challenges and engagement do occur they will be indirect, of lower intensity, and overtly neutral. The greater the discrepancies in power of a third party, the greater the likelihood that disputants will cease or modulate disputes at that third party's instance.

The operation of power is not unconstrained, of course. If the stakes are seen as sufficiently critical, subordinates may challenge superiors with much greater power; it has been reported that senior military officers were prepared at the height of Watergate to disobey orders from Nixon to initiate nuclear strikes (Wieseltier, 1986). More mundanely, Vladimir *did* challenge the medical review board; children sometimes *do* challenge parents or teachers. A perhaps more frequent response to major discrepancies in power is revision of tactics either through, e.g., substitution of "sniping" for "direct assault" or, more drastically, substitution of altogether different non-conflictual goal-oriented behaviors such as, for example, deceit, flattery, persuasion, or perhaps importuning.[9]

When relations of power and perceptions of utility are minimally influenced by considerations of affect, their interaction is relatively straightforward and their mutual effects, to some extent at least, calculable. The introduction of considerations of affect can immensely complicate whether or not conflict will occur and, if it does, its nature, course, and outcome. It is not surprising that the likelihood and course of conflict will be different when potential adversaries like or do not like one another – and that varying intensities of positive or negative affect have easily discernible effects. Complication results from the analytically discomforting fact that *positive and negative affect may have superficially similar effects on conflict and its course in conflict talk.* Anything like a full treatment of this apparent anomaly is beyond the scope of my discussion here; I can do no more than suggest some directions in which such a discussion would have to go.

A first paradox is that, independently of considerations of relations of power (but not necessarily of those of utility), high degrees of either positive or negative affect may increase *or* decrease the likelihood of dispute and, if it occurs, the further likelihood that it will be acrimonious. Simmel long ago observed that the absence of visible conflict did not necessarily mean that apparent harmony was real; he argued that interactants motivated to maintain a relationship and concerned that it was not a strong one would avoid conflict – while individuals confident about a relationship would more comfortably engage one another in dispute. Simmel's observation was an astute one, and many of us know people who love one another but who nonetheless engage in frequent and often acrimonious dispute. (The situation is complicated at one level, of course, by the fact that people who do not appear to love one another but stay together because of other [perhaps pathological or other dependencies] reasons, may also fight regularly and bitterly.) There are other instances, however, in which parties who ordinarily do not engage in conflict do – and precisely because they share high positive affect. Such disputes occur when a goal valued more highly than harmony comes to be at issue; that goal is frequently the well-being of one or another party, i.e., when a loved one embarks on what is seen as a self-destructive course, etc. (The analog to willingness to challenge a president when he embarks on a course seen as contrary to national interests will be evident.) Argument will be avoided, however, if by some calculation its occurrence, whatever its likely resolution, is seen as likely to be more hurtful than helpful. Life is complex.

Similar complexities occur at the other end of the positive-negative affect continuum. Some people dislike one another so intensely, or are at such ideological odds, or both, that their very co-presence is seen as a "guarantee" that rancorous dispute will occur; some Co-op members (Labov) apparently, and very reluctantly, came to conclude that this characterized their relations with some black neighbors of the Co-op. Others who dislike one another with equal intensity, however, may simply avoid interaction even when copresent and, if unable to avoid interaction and even confrontation, conduct their disputation circumspectly and even politely. These latter types may simply not want to interact with their "enemies," they may not be willing to manage the discomfort produced by conflict involvement, they may be unwilling to distress innocent bystanders. And, even in those instances where someone hates another so much that they "don't even want to fight with them", there may be some stakes of such a nature that that reluctance may be overcome. The re-introduction of the power dimension can make matters even murkier.

The world is not random and the effects of the sociological variables are, I believe, specifiable. At this juncture my belief is a matter of faith. Further studies of conflict talk of other varieties will be needed to validate my faith.

"Ecological" constraints. I use the term ecological as an imprecise gloss for those "opportunity constraints" on conflict talk which, while they may be socially defined, are in some sense "natural" and out of participants' control. Three such constraints, i.e., noise, comfort, and disaster are "natural" in the sense that they may be fully beyond participant control. If disputants cannot hear one another, whether because of machine noise, the roar of a waterfall or the din of gunfire, or because of the talk of others, they cannot argue – though they may well display rage kinesically or posturally, etc. Stakes must be high indeed for disputants to argue, unprotected from the elements, in bitter cold or pouring rain.[10] Disasters or emergencies, large (flood, fire, explosion), medium (coronaries, power failures, "no-show" wedding caterers), and small (burning main courses, spilled wine, running out of ice) may cause conflict talk to be terminated, tabled or truncated. Just as "accidents" may shape the course of conflict, they may also determine its occurrence or non-occurrence. Who knows what delicts may have gone unobserved in the last minutes of the *Titanic*, or what opposition moves ignored? There are also, of course, disputes which result from the unsought discovery of the disputable, as in the case of Watergate and Iranian arms sales profits going to the "contras."

Constraints introduced by the inexorability of the passage of time and by the presence of audiences of certain characteristics can be very strong; they are not totally beyond control of disputants. Temporal constraints are variously absolute, schedule-generated and allocative-competitive. There are only so many hours in a day or a week or a lifetime; while feuds may cross generations individuals can participate only just so long. Aside from the (analytically trivial) limiting case, however, cultural and sociological constraints can override temporal considerations. Stakes must be very high before a disputant will knowingly miss an airplane flight; flights *are* missed. Stakes need not be as high for some conflicts to spill over the boundaries of such scheduled activities as meals, or work, or classes; those boundaries often causes disputes to be postponed, tabled, or truncated, or, at the least, shifted to new venues. Conflict participants often exploit both scheduled and non-routine temporal constraints to end a current round of conflict talk; such exploitation is often marked by such expressions as "I have to go to school (work, another class, home, catch my plane, etc.) now", or "We'll talk about this next time (after work, tonight, tomorrow, when your father comes home, etc.)." While even the most heated disputes can sometimes be stopped by such moves, however, there are also such counters as, "You can catch a later plane", or "Not until we get this settled." Time can be simultaneously a topical focus, a constraint and a resource in conflict talk; its centrality in that talk mirrors its importance in our society.[11]

Some of us have internalized a norm that arguments should be private; we may be disinclined to argue in front of powerful others for more instrumental reasons (these cultural and sociological constraints may operate to dampen conflict among teachers in the presence of students and of the latter in the presence of the former, respectively). The audience constraints become more ecological, however, when *unanticipated* audiences of unwanted characteristics appear in what had been thought to be "safe" settings for conflict. In such instances, conflict talk will again often be postponed, tabled, truncated, terminated, moved, or modulated. In some cases, however, even the appearance of early guests will not stop a flourishing family fight.

Conflict talk outcomes

Our contemporary preoccupation with conflict outcomes is not a new one; Shakespeare has Lear talk of conversation concerning "who wins, who loses; who's in, who out", and Marlowe remarks our wish "that one would win, the other lose." Americans may have a particular penchant for definitive outcomes, sports contests are carried into overtimes and extra innings and we are certainly among the world's most litigious people. While we do not appear to agree fully with Herrick that, "Its the end that crowns us, not the fight" (if such were the case we would read about sports events after they are over and watch only the ends of films), we tend to see the world as one of "winners" and "losers." There are exceptions, of course; some of us at least find a fascination in the protracted mutual destructiveness of George and Martha in Albee's (1962) play, *Who's Afraid of Virginnia Woolf?* and of those we see as like them in our own lives. While we acknowledge that there are non-zero sum conflicts and that there can be "winner–winner" and "loser–loser" outcomes, however, we generally focus on outcomes which are both definitive and asymmetrical.

I was struck, in my reading of the analyses reported above, by the relative infrequency in these materials of the zero-sum resolution; I have been driven to re-examine my assumptions about the world in which I live. I say relative infrequency in the absence of any statistical benchmarks, we have no studies of random samples of conflict talk. It might be argued that we should discount the quantitative evidence of a high proportion of unresolved conflict events reported by Vuchinich and by Corsaro and Rizzo on the grounds that the disputes they studied weren't very "important." Such an argument is fragile, in part because we have no metric for assessing the importance of those disputes to those engaged in them, but more critically because definitive outcomes of "defeat" or "victory" occur rarely even in disputes of putatively greater moment. Some of Vuchinich's dinner participants, Corsaro and Rizzo's pre-schoolers, Goodwins' sling shotters and Eder's middle-school girls may have experienced temporary elation from victory or pangs of defeat; it is hard to believe that these individual outcomes much affected their lives (there are, of course, possibilities of cumulative corrosive effects). While Emma and Robert may have experienced distress over the gradual deterioration of their marriage it is hard to say that one or the other of them "won" a dispute. While Lyle may have experienced disgruntlement over his failure to get his opponents to admit his righteousnes or to agree with his characterization of unions, he certainly did not leave the QWL meeting feeling he had been bested in an argument. Only in the cases of Rawls and Hogan (Conley and O'Barr) and Vladimir can it be said both that disputants "lost" in conflict-talk exchanges and that their losses may have had immediate and obvious impact on the quality of their lives and – perhaps – more perduring effects on their self-concepts and esteem. In the case of the small-claims court "losers," moreover, O'Barr notes (personal communication) that there may be, even in losing, a sense of having confronted and exposed their adversaries and of having had their "day in court."

Several defining dimensions of conflict-talk outcomes are implicit in the two paragraphs with which I have begun this discussion. First, there can be different resolutions (including non-resolution) of the *explicit* focus of a dispute – adversaries may or may not gain possession of a disputed object, or may or may not concede the correctness of a fact or opinion. Second, there can be different effects on particpants themselves; self-esteem and the esteem of others may rise or fall. Third, whatever the outcome, it can be judged as more or less important – by participants, audiences, those who may come to learn about it, analysts. Fourth, the implications of outcomes may be immediately visible, they may be deferred, or they may never become fully visible to affected or interested parties – the same implications may be transitory or more perduring both for disputants and for the social structures in which they live their lives. Fifth, as the Goodwins observe in their paper, it can be the case that because of redefinitions of conflict in its course, the conflict which is ultimately resolved is not the conflict in which participants initially engaged. For this reason, and because of the variable nature and quality of conflictual interaction, disputes may have quite unanticipated subsidiary outcomes. These secondary outcomes may again

be more or less important and more or less lasting.
I can do no more than sketch some highlights of these distinctions.

Resolution of manifest or "official" issues.   Disputants can win, lose, or
draw in their own views, those of their opponents, and those of observers.
These several outcomes can be officially or unofficially ratified, consensual,
secret, implicit, and themselves subject to later dispute. Defeat may be
openly acknowledged with varying degrees of reluctance, signaled by withdrawal or tears or rage (and, possibly, physical assault) or even laughter,
imposed by third parties, "reportable" (W. Labov, 1968) or not. In some
instances the conclusion of a dispute will be marked verbally (i.e., a simple
"Okay," or "Allright, we'll do it your way," or "Take it if it's so important to
you"), sometimes a settlement will be put in writing (i.e., in the cases above,
legal judgments in the small claims cases or review board minutes in the
Titticut case), sometimes conflict-talk participants simply go on about their
business with their worlds somewhat differently arranged in terms of power,
affect, etc – this latter was the outcome in most of the cases above. In still
other instances, a temporary or final close of conflict talk may be marked by
withdrawal of one or both parties; some tablings or postponements will be
verbally marked ("We'll talk about this again tomorrow"); others cannot be
distinguished from terminations and will be seen to be tablings and
postponements only when a dispute is renewed. Sometimes disputants
maintain co-presence but simply stop conflict talk, perhaps with a topic shift,
perhaps trailing off with a "Well, . . ." In some such instances disputes may
trickle off because both or all participants have become bored with a dispute
increasingly perceived as "not worth fighting about," and termination may
indicate nothing more than ennui. In others, however, cessation may be
only temporary, and one or another party may recycle the matter at issue at
some later juncture in the ongoing talk – perhaps as new arguments come to
mind, perhaps because of "pent-up" frustrations, perhaps because a matter
of higher priority has been resolved, perhaps because an inhibiting audience
has left the scene. The cessation may in actuality be only apparent, moreover, since underlying contests can be continued in new topical guises. This
is particularly so to the degree that what are actually being contested are
often less the "official" foci of disputes (possession of things or historical
"facts") than locations in interpersonal hierarchies. I will turn to this matter
momentarily.

Some cautious generalizations can be essayed on the basis of this brief
discussion. First, there *are* "winners" and "losers" in conflict talk but
"winning" can be ambiguous and "victories" can be Pyrrhic, partial,
inconsequential, temporary, or false. Second, superficial appearances are
often misleading; this is true both in the sense that hidden agendas may be
more important to participants than "official" ones (see, again, below) and
in that conflicts that appear to be "over" may not be at all. Consider, for

example, the case of the Co-op members who ousted the black women but felt that they then had to repair their reputations as conscientious liberals by claiming that they had made efforts to increase black participation. These ambiguities, and others (see my 1987), put both disputants and analysts at risk.

"Secondary" outcomes. I use the quotes because "unofficial" outcomes of conflict talk, while they are often less visible to both participants and analysts, are also often more important over the long run that are "official" ones.[12] Collins (1981) has provided us with an extremely suggestive way of looking at secondary outcomes of conflict talk with his notion of "interaction ritual chains." He argues that social organization is continuously generated and re-generated by individuals' participation in endless streams of encounters in which they interact with others who, as they do, bring (1) conversational or cultural and (2) emotional resources to these encounters. Through the course of the interaction each participant's resources are enhanced or diminished as interactants, constrained by one anothers' resources and goals and by what Collins calls the "irreducible macrofactors" of time and space, seek to optimize their resources. Successful participants in talk, including conflict talk, leave encounters with both enhanced communicative competence and enhanced confidence. Even "losers" may learn new skills and, in some circumstances, such as doing better than they had expected even while losing, increased confidence. Both losers and winners can be disappointed with outcomes. The principal point is that we never leave *any* interactive encounter unchanged.[13] (It is harder to sustain this argument in the case of individuals with less than full social and communicative competence. Even Vladimir, however, may have been more paranoid after than before.)

Children and adolescents (Corsaro and Rizzo, Eder, Goodwin and Goodwin, and Vuchinich) learn models and tactics of conflict talk which they will employ throughout their adult lives; they also come to view themselves as more or less competent (and/or lucky) and to enter new encounters with greater or lesser confidence. (Michael, the sling shotter who negotiated and achieved dominance in the childrens' interaction studied by the Goodwins, has also been the most successful as an adult.) As readers, we have a sense that Rawls and Hogan will expect the world to treat them ill – and that it will do just that. Lyle's prospects for advancement are not good. Just as we make such assessments in reading these cases and in all the instances we witness in the course of our own lives, moreover, so too do participants in conflict talk make them about their cointeractants – and themselves. Assessments may sometimes err and both the gain and the loss of confidence may be hidden; I suspect that we are accurate more often than not; I am confident that the process is much as Collins has described it. There is work to be done.

Social *relationships* as well as individual resources are changed, of course.

Disputes can "clear the air" – solidarity (certainly respect and possibly even affection) may be a by-product of a "good fight."

4. Resources and devices

I have not left myself much room to talk about these matters; much of what could be said has been anticipated in the discussion above. Most important from the perspective of this book, of course, are the resources which collectively constitute *communicative competence*, i.e., (1) the knowledge of (a) language and how to use it *and* (2) knowledge of social and sociolinguistic "appropriateness constraints" on that use. Depending upon how broadly one defines communication (or language), similar knowledge of and ability to employ prosodic variation (in such features as amplitude, intonation, stress, rhythm, and tempo), kinesic behaviors (e.g. body movements and posture, facial expression, gaze, gesture, etc.) and proxemics (interpersonal spacing), are also a part of communicative competence; many if not most linguists would include prosodic features as a part of syntax, many sociolinguists attend regularly to kinesic and proxemic features of interaction. The taking into account of these last sets of features in the analysis of conflict talk is made more complicated by the fact that while most members of a speech community share understandings about how to *interpret* variations, individuals differ in the extent to which they can consciously *manipulate* their production of "key" (Hymes, 1974), "keying" or "framing" of the ongoing interaction (Goffman, 1974), and "tactically" employ "passion" (Bailey, 1983). This last suggests another "resource" or "competence," i.e., emotion (Kemper, 1978).

Additional complexities are encountered as the notions of "resources" and "competence" are further extended to incorporate power and *claims* of power (or displays of putative power) in interaction generally, and specifically in conflict talk. Some power is associated with location in the social structure and a consequent ability to enforce the bearers' wishes; this is the power of teachers (Corsaro and Rizzo), parents (Vuchinich), managers (O'Donnell), judges (Conley and O'Barr, Philips). In court cases power may be associated with both a litigant's social position and her attendant speech styles – whether "powerful-powerless" (O'Barr, 1982) or "relational" (Conley and O'Barr, in this volume). Power among putative equals results, in contrast, from differences in competences, whether those latter be physical (some of Corsaro and Rizzo's children) or communicative (most of the other cases). In American society, at least, greater communicative competence is often expected to be associated with greater structural power; military personnel learn to employ a "voice of command" and professionals "registers." Power can be claimed by symbolic displays of dress or demeanor and by talking like the more powerful – both sorts of claims can of course be challenged – dominance claims are often successful.

If power is recognized as multi-dimensional, it can be seen that all conflict resolved by victory or defeat (however defined) is so resolved because the "winning" party possesses great *usable* power on some dimension. Physical struggles are not always won by the physically strongest contestant – Davids can cut Goliaths "down to size" and individuals skilled in the "martial arts" can best much stronger opponents who do not have those skills. Similarly, sheer intellectual wherewithal may not be sufficient to prevail in contests where conflict partners have access to unshared knowledge – and disputants willing to employ emotional "blackmail" may succeed in conflicts with smarter, more knowledgeable and more principled opponents. It may be that "rule-oriented" litigants are ordinarily more successful than "relational" ones (O'Barr and Conley) and witnesses who use "powerful" as contrasted to "powerless" language more credible (O'Barr, 1982), but some users of less effective registers or styles of talk may be successful because of putatively extraneous considerations of sympathy or even because of physical attractiveness. Finally, and non-trivially, disputants "weaker" along any of a number of power dimensions may prevail simply because they care more about some outcome – whether through ideological commitment, personal self-interest or sheer stubbornness; the black man and woman who confronted the Co-op members did not prevail – but they persisted in the face of being both outnumbered and legally culpable.

These several qualifications (and others could be adduced) notwithstanding, power, *including linguistic and sociolinguistic competences* (and such less obvious language-related attributes as voice quality), of some sort will be the currency in conflict talk. Power can be invoked directly in "positional" self-attributions (Bernstein, 1971), e.g., "Because I'm your mother", or "*I'm* the teacher and *I'm* going to talk" (said during a floor contest in a graduate seminar), or in the claims of superiority made by children ("I'm smarter, stronger, older, etc."). It can be alluded to less directly by invocation of unshared knowledge or by claims of institutional authority displayed in pronominal use, as when a "we" claims a group membership from which an opponent is excluded (Labov, 1980 and this volume; Grimshaw, 1989). It can be asserted prosodically in assumption of rights to interrupt, or by increasing or decreasing amplitude, or by silence. Each of these and other power-claims will be variously credible and variously subject to counter-claim and challenge. Susan Ervin-Tripp somewhere reports an exchange in which a child retorts, "You can't call me 'honey,' you're not the mother" when given a command by an only slightly older child in play; conflict talk is replete with analogous ripostes. Such challenges invoke a power greater than that of individuals, i.e., sociological/sociolinguistic norms of appropriateness – and appeals to equity, precedent, solidarity and *noblesse oblige* can sometimes balance discrepancies in individual power. In fact, it can even be the case that in disputes in which weak parties argue before a stronger arbiter arguments can be effectively made of greater *weakness*.

5. Some implications.

All of the contributors to this volume find talk intrinsically interesting; all are committed to adequate observation and description of ongoing conversational discourse/interaction. While each may focus on different things that "get accomplished" in the talk they study, i.e., socialization for adult life or affect management or dispute resolution itself, and while each may focus on different sets of resources and different devices employed in "accomplishment" of these varying ends, I think that all are interested in *how things get done in/with talk*. As a sociologist, I am interested in the phenomenon of social conflict as a process. As an individual I am interested in the mitigation of species-threatening conflict. While these last two interests may not be explicit in the studies above, I believe that they may also be shared.

My reading of the contributions to this volume and my attempt to sort out some of the conclusions of my collaborators have led me to reach some conclusions of my own about promising directions for further research on conflict and its special manifestation and display in conflict talk. First, I believe that the studies above collectively provide a convincing demonstration of the value of naturally occurring conversation (and probably of any discourse, written or spoken) as a situs for research on sociological issues. Conversely, it seems to me that the introduction of sociological notions in discourse analysis facilitates the adequate description and interpretation of what goes on in talk, i.e., contributes to what W. Labov and Fanshel (1977) refer to as "comprehensive discourse analysis." Second, while I am not sure that all of my associates in this project will agree and am sure that some readers definitely will not, I am persuaded that the "sociological variables" of relations of power and of affect and consideration of utility will turn out to be centrally important in any set of conceptual notions employed in discourse analysis. Conversely here, it seems likely to me that many questions about the operations of these variables will be richly illuminated by further studies of talk. Third, I am more convinced than ever that, however elegant more formal linguistic and/or sociological-interactional (i.e., conversation analytic) analyses of talk may be, we will not be able to address the important questions of *language in use* until we fully take into account, as scholar-researchers as different as Corsaro and Halliday have enjoined us to, the details of ethnographic–historical (situational) and textual contexts. This implies "going beyond the text"; in contrast to our conversation analytic colleagues I do not believe it means "going beyond the data."

Fourth, and critically, richly instructive as I believe the studies reported above to be, I strongly believe that they and the other suggestive studies of "conflict talk" now available share, along with most sociologically informed analyses of discourse, a significant – but remediable – shortcoming. This shortcoming is, broadly stated, that discourse analytic studies (including those of conflict talk) are neither theoretically cumulative nor empirically methodologically systematic; the two dimensions are of course interdependent. They are not theoretically cumulative because they share neither a set of common questions, nor of conceptualizations of the phenomena of interest, nor even of determining variables. They are not empirically methodologically systematic because the several studies neither control for any of the elements identified in the pages above, e.g., ends, content, participant characteristics, outcomes, etc., nor systematically vary those elements. In most instances, students of conflict talk (and of conversational discourse more generally) have investigated one or a very few instances of some variety of event which is simultaneously intrinsically interesting and accessible to study; the extended corpuses of, e.g., childrens' and adolescents' talk, or family dinners, or Co-op meetings, or attorney–judge court-room negotiations, with multiple instances of a phenomenon of interest are still exceptional (there are others). While Corsaro and Rizzo look at differences between Italian and American pre-schoolers, however, most of the studies reported here and elsewhere look for commonalities in the talk studied rather than for possibly systematic differences. When differences are found and reported, moreover, they tend to be described – but without any attempt to interpret/"explain" them in terms of any systematic linguistic, sociolinguistic, or sociological theory.[14]

There is no shortage of theories or proto-theories which purport to explain all or part of what goes on in conflict talk; some of these conceptual apparatuses focus more on talk (as socially constrained or determined), others have focused more on social behavior abstracted from the talk which is its principal medium. Among the former one might look at: (1) so-called "critical" analyses of text, including Marxist variants, in the work of scholars as different as Althusser, Barthes, Derrida, Foucault, Habermas, or Marcuse; (2) phenomenology as represented by, e.g., Husserl, Schutz, Wittgenstein, and some of the ethnomethodologists (i.e., Garfinkel); (3) some of the more exotic (i.e., Harré, Totman, and some of the semioticians [e.g., Eco]), and of more "traditional" (e.g., Pike) "global" conceptual frames. Among the latter, one could look at theorists: (1) who have focused on the micro-macro intersection such as Bernstein, Cicourel, Collins, and Giddens;[15] (2) traditional students of conflict like Pareto, Simmel, and Weber; (3) "exchange" and related theorists from Heider to Blau, Homans, and Kemper. There are many others who might be included; I have not listed some of those students of language in use in social contexts whose theoretical formulations have been most useful to me in my own work. That there are theoretical formulations available is unarguable.

5.1 Some directions

At this juncture, however, I believe more modest steps towards theory-building and (perhaps) testing are in order. First, and quite possibly only as an interim move, I would suggest that students of conflict talk adopt the "sociological variables" of relations of power and of affect and considerations of utility as an organizing theoretical frame for their studies. There are very substantial problems of conceptualization and of measurement to which only partial answers are currently available (see, however, my 1980); power, affect, and utility have been explicitly employed with great profit both in studies of language in use and in construction of sociological theories of social conflict. While not always foregrounded, I believe they are at least implicitly invoked in each of the studies above. In conjunction with Collins' (1981) "irreducible macrofactors" of time, space, and numbers, I believe they can serve as an organizing frame for adequate observation and description of the discourse of social conflict; I further believe that examination of their systematic interaction can be a first step towards explanatory adequacy.[16]

Second, while "casual talk" about conflict processes in discourse (written as well as spoken) is possible through attention to the sociological variables and macrofactors in any study of conflict texts, any comprehensive, coherent, and valid sociological theory of conflict talk must attend to the requirement of observational adequacy far more systematically than has heretofore been the case. However important the disputes reported above and throughout the literatures may have seemed to be to participants during their ongoing course, all of them have tended to cluster toward the lower end of variable dimensions of power discrepancies, social distance between principals, real and perduring (as contrasted to perceived and transitory) significance of stakes, numbers involved, size of arenas of involvement, and temperal extension. Vladimir at his review hearing possibly excepted (and in the case of a reported dispute, the black man parked illegally outside the Coop), it does not appear to be the case that participants in the disputes discussed in the pages above felt themselves to be faced by implacable enemies intent on doing them serious injury. (Some caution may be required in making this claim with regard to, e.g., Rawls and Webb or some family dinner participants, *at least in the short term.*) Until we study the discourse of disputes of conflict partners of great power (of whatever sort) and hostility contending for genuinely important stakes we cannot know whether there are, for example, "threshholds" of resources, or of emotion, or of goal salience, etc., beyond which the interaction of the sociological variables and the nature of the elements identified in this chapter *qualitatively change.* We need studies of more intense "fights" in contexts of low values on the macrofactors. More importantly, we need studies of the conflict discourse which occurs when truly powerful contenders struggle over goals to which they are deeply committed, i.e., of such events as the "Cuban missile crisis" or arms negotiations or wrangles over Beirut, the Suez Canal, hostages, "lines of death," etc. Data records of such events are hard to come by; we must strive to find best approximations.[17]

In a situation in which we are unable to obtain access to data with high values on certain variables, we cannot generate a comprehensive theory of conflict discourse. Even within such a situation of constraint, however, it should be possible to so systematize our understanding of the kinds of disputes to which we do have access that when the data we need become available we will be able to determine whether conflict processes are or are not qualitatively changed in those more "major" conflicts. There are, it seems to me, two directions which might be pursued in research on conflict talk which will contribute to a more coherent if not a fully comprehensive (because not based on the full range of cases) theory of disputations discourse. (What follows draws on a somewhat fuller discussion in my 1988a, chapter 12.)

First, while the analysis of conflict talk is a sufficiently "new" arena of focused research (focused in the sense that researchers feel that they are working on a common topic and share interests) that any careful study is likely to produce new understandings of the phenomenon, my view is that we know enough about what we are studying to select data-collection sites or already available data records so as to optimize presumed-to-be *theoretically relevant* variation (or not) of the sociological variables, Collins' macrofactors, and other selected features (i.e., those identified in the discussion above or, e.g., "institutionalization" [see my 1988a, chapter 12]) of disputes to be studied. Such a program would hardly be novel, it is what social psychologists do all the time – though I am not proposing that we should intervene to "experimentally" change weights on the variables under study. Such purposive sampling of the conflict talk to be investigated would permit us to, for example, determine whether certain linguistic devices, or registers of talk, or "keys" (in Hymes' [1974] sense), or kinesic or proxemic behaviors, etc., etc., are employed only by disputants of very high or very low *relative* power, or with certain affectual relationships. Once identified, the presence or absence of the same devices and ways of talk, etc., could then be employed as *indicators* of relations of power or of affect. The findings of such more "focused" studies could then be tested cross-culturally to begin to determine whether there are "universals" of conflict talk; Corsaro and Rizzo's comparative study of American and Italian pre-schoolers suggests that some but not all features of children's disputes are common to at least those two speech-communities. Levine's (1985) discussion of ambiguity in discourse suggests that we will discover that feature of talk to be quite differently employed in different speech communities.

Second, while comprehensive theories of conflict discourse and/or of conflict as a social process cannot be essayed until we have access to the full range of the discourse of interest, we can begin to assemble a variety of *propositional statements* ("rules"? "hypotheses"?) summarizing and organizing what we are learning from our studies of data records to which we can gain access.[18] For my current exploratory and programmatic purposes it is possible to identify four varieties of such "rules" or "propositions", namely:

(1) discourse/(interactional) rules; (2) sequencing rules; (3) propositions regarding the interaction of the sociological variables with conflict talk elements; and (4) propositions about the process of social conflict. I can say no more than a few words about each.

Discourse/(conversational, interactional) rules. Labov and Fanshel's (1977) discourse rules take an "if...then" propositional form; they are of two principal types:

> 13.1 *Rule of overdue obligations.* If A asserts that B has not performed obligations in role R, then A is heard as challenging B's competence in R. (96)
>
> 13.2 *Rule for challenging propositions.* If A asserts a proposition that is supported by A's status, and B questions the proposition, than B is heard as challenging the competence of A in that status. (97)

Such rules all have in common that the subject identifies a discourse behavior by a speaker, A, and that the predicate usually identifies an interactional move; they differ in that the interactional move is variously attributed to speaker A or an initial hearer (subsequently) speaker, B. Labov and Fanshel identify more interactional moves than rules of discourse and some of the latter (i.e., those on narrative) do little interactional work; readers are nonetheless left with the impression that interactional moves are closely related to and perhaps constrained by the discourse rules – this is certainly the case for "major" moves like assert, challenge, deny and retreat – all of which are major currencies in conflict talk.

Many of the disputes above include instances of assignment of blame or responsibility (on this matter see also Fillmore's [1971] classic, "Verbs of judging"), a discourse rule for this behavior might look like the following:

> 13.3 *Rule for assigning blame (responsibility).* If A asserts that B should and could have performed a behavior X_1, but wilfully did not, or that B should and could have avoided performing a behavior X_2, but nonetheless willfully performed it, then A is heard as blaming B for the non-occurrence or occurrence of X_1 or X_2 respectively.

Similar rules could be written for, *inter alia*, absolving (or justifying), associating with (or dissociating from), insulting, and so on. The study of data records of purposively selected conflict-talk events will permit the writing of additional rules of this sort; as rules accumulate, similarities (and differences) will become evident and the task of identifying more general, subsuming, rules can be initiated.

Readers familiar with Sacks' (e.g., 1972a) hearers' and viewers' "maxims" will note the kinship of the latter to interactional rules; I cannot pursue that similarity here.

Sequencing rules. Conversation analysts (CA) have made three kinds of contributions to our understanding of what goes on in talk, each of which has directly or indirectly informed some of the analyses above – or could have. First, and most generally, CA have demonstrated the elegantly structured nature of talk through formal analyses of the orderliness of turn-taking, of question-answer sequences, etc. (see, representatively, Sacks, Schegloff, and Jefferson, 1974). Second, CA have shown the delicacy with which variations from fundamental ABABAB, etc., sequences are managed, i.e., how participants in talk place appreciations, corrections, disagreements, interruptions, etc. Third, CA have given us a rich conceptual apparatus for discussion of what goes on in talk, i.e., labeling such different phenomena as adjacency pairs and recyclings and "troubles in talk" and, more specifically, self- and other-corrections, pre-invitations or pre-disagreements, displays of understanding, etc. These orderlinesses and elements are sometimes combined into rules such as the following on turn-allocation:

> 13.4 For any turn, at the initial transition-relevance place of an initial turn-constructional unit: (a) If the turn-so-far is so constructed as to involve the use of a 'current speaker selects next' technique, then the party so selected has the right and is obliged to take next turn to speak; no others have such rights or obligations, and transfer occurs at that place. (Sacks, Schegloff, and Jefferson, 1974, p.704)

Other rules, which may constrain the operation of prior rules, are also specified. The CA argue that such rules can be simultaneously "context-free" and "capable of extraordinary context-sensitivity" (this apparent conundrum is explained in, Sacks, Schegloff, and Jefferson, 1974, pp.699 ff.); because of their principle that the organization and nature of talk is best studied by focus only on the text itself and not on social context(s), the CA generally invoke those contexts only when their more formal corpus-based analyses are questioned.[19] They do not appear to be interested, for example, in how sharp discrepancies in power – or high salience of stakes (in a dispute) – might lead to regularized (i.e., rule-governed) "violations" of turn-allocations rules (see again Edgerton (1985). Note also Sacks *et al* [1974] citation of Albert [1964] in their note 6).

Among the preceding chapters, those of Vuchinich and of the Goodwins are probably both most informed by and most congenial with the perspective of CA; neither offers formal rules for the sequential behaviors they identify. They do, however, integrate context-specific features of participants, settings, ends, etc., into their analyses. Here again, the study of data records of purposively selected conflict-talk events will permit the writing of such contextually specific rules; once again also, as rules accumulate similarities (and differences) will become evident and the task of identifying more general, subsuming, rules can be initiated.

The sociological variables and conflict talk. I have used the term *instrumentalities* as a gloss for the behaviors which participants in talk employ to get their conversational partners to do what they otherwise might not – or not do what they otherwise might; while not isomorphic to the behaviors of interest, certain speech-acts verbs, e.g. order, or persuade, or browbeat, etc., can serve as useful reminders of the sorts of behaviors used to such ends.[20] Examination of the interaction of the three sociological variables and several *instrumentalities* in a naturally occurring instance of verbal interaction and several hypothetical cases allowed me to specify several observations (postulates?), namely:

13.5   Efforts to manipulate are most likely when *result* has high *valence* for both *source* and *goal* and where *cost* will be low for both.

13.6   Mutual positive affect precludes use of some *instrumentalities*.

13.7   Mutual negative affect devalues some *instrumentalities*.

13.8   Subordinate or equal hierarchical position of *source* makes some *instrumentalities* unavailable.

13.9   *Ceteris paribus*, result determines whether an effort will be made.

13.10 Hierarchy constrains the range of *instrumentalities* available.

13.11 Within that range, interaction of affect and perceived cost to *goal* constrain specific selection.

13.5 to 13.11, stated in sometimes quite similar ways, have been validated by investigators using data of quite different sorts (see references in work cited in note 20.) They can also be seen, I believe, to have constrained the nature of conflict talk (i.e. registers, prosodic features, "key," kinesic and proxemic accompaniments, etc.) reported above. The observations (principles, postulates?) permit the logical deduction of considerably more refined and testable propositions concerning specific *instrumentalities* and social relationships (and by extension, modes, direction, intensity, etc. of conflict talk), e.g.

13.12 *Source* will not attempt to *cajole goal* (or need to) if *source* has power to obtain *result* through *order and* is willing to risk generation of negative affect (in self, in *goal*, in self-*goal* relations, or possibly in other interactants or bystanders).

While formulation of a set of observations/postulates on conflict talk analogous to those on *instrumentalities* just listed would require more careful study of the data and much more space than I have available, it is possible to suggest what some such propositions might look like. Consider the following:

13.13 Probability of an initial opposition move varies directly with potential initiator's perceived stake in a possible outcome and with initiator's power relative to a potential opponent.

13.14 The "taking up" of an oppositional move (i.e. occurrence of conflict talk) varies directly with an offended party's perceived stake in a possible outcome and with the party's power relative to the offending party.

13.15 Mutual positive affect is inversely related to probability of occurence of "self-oriented" conflict talk and directly related to that of "collectively- or other-oriented" (see Parsons, 1951) dispute.

13.16 *Ceteris paribus*, selection of more "confrontational" modes of conflict talk (e.g. threats or insults and increased amplitude or physiological rage displays or threatening kinesic postures or gestures) is directly related to increasing relative power.

13.17 Within the range of conflict-talk modes available because of power considerations, specific selection is constrained by the interaction of relations of affect, perceived stakes, likely third-party (audience) reactions, etc.

Such (and further) specification of observations from studies like those above and from other studies of social conflict allows formulation of testable propositions like the following:

13.18 A will not attempt to avoid a dispute (or need to) if A has the power to overcome B *and* is willing to risk generation of negative affect (in self, in B, in self–B relations, or possibly in other interactants or bystanders).

The study of data records of purposively selected conflict talk events will permit the specification of additional testable propositions of this sort; as such propositions accumulate and are tested similarities (and differences) will become evident and the task of identifying more general, subsuming, principles can be initiated.

5.2 Propositions about social conflict processes

Formulation of descriptive postulates and/or of testable propositions about the sources, nature and course, and outcomes of social-conflict processes is an enterprise which has attracted the efforts of students of society from at least the time that written records have been available.[21] I believe that attention to this literature, and particularly its specification of concepts and statements of propositional relations, could greatly strengthen the discourse analytic study of conflict talk. I have room here only for one illustration of a useful conceptual distinction and one of a proposition; I think they should demonstrate my point.

Intensity, hostility, violence. In my discussion earlier (pp. 294ff.) of "intensity, tone and direction" as dimensions of variability in conflict talk I asserted that within certain (unspecified) limits intensity and hostility can vary independently. If one defines violence as injury inflicted on individuals or property (and not, e.g., to egos), then there is none in any of the events analyzed in the chapters above. Violence does occur, however, in interpersonal disputes as well as those of groups and larger social entities (classes, ethnic groups, nations); a comprehensive theory of conflict talk should allow for its occurrence. Dahrendorf (1959: 211) observes that some students of social conflict have used intensity and violence as synonyms; he argues that they may vary independently and are "distinct aspects of any conflict situation."[22]

Dahrendorf defines intensity as referring to "the energy expenditure and degree of involvement of conflicting parties" (p.211) and to violence of conflict as relating "rather to its manifestations than to its causes . . . a matter of the weapons that are chosen by conflict groups to express their hostilities" (p.212). With regard to *class* conflict Dahrendorf argues (pp.213 ff.) that intensity is critically affected by: (1) the organizational complexity of a society and the extent to which boundaries of organizations are superimposed; (2) the structure of authority and of opportunity structures; (3) possibilities for mobility – and the occurrence of violence primarily by regulatory structures including both "values" and enforcement institutions. He further argues that intensity of class conflict *decreases* to the extent that: (1) classes are organized; (2) superimposition of class interests in different sectors is lower (e.g. that landlords are not members of one religious and/or ethnic group and tenants of another); and (3) that disputes in one arena (e.g. politics or labor relations or religion) are not easily translatable into those in another. Violence also co-varies with the extent of class organization and *decreases* to the extent that conflict is effectively regulated. The implications of Dahrendorf's discussion for conflict talk at all levels of Collins' macrofactors and for varying values of the sociological variables are obvious; the interaction of intensity, hostility, and violence in conflict talk has not been remarked, let alone investigated. The study of data records of purposively selected conflict-talk events which are likely to manifest variation in these three features will permit the identification and specification of variable rules central in importance to understanding of both the discourse of interest and of social conflict more generally.

External threat and internal cohesion.   Simmel (1955 [1908]) is usually credited with having first enunciated, for modern sociology, both the role of social conflict in the formation of social groups and its function in increasing internal cohesion when groups already extant are confronted with external threat. (He also observed, it should be noted, that conflict necessarily establishes relationships between adversaries and that these relationships may result in, at the least, conflict regulation and, in some cases, new positive relationships. I will not be able to elaborate on these possibilities here; readers will see such effects in some of the disputes analyzed above.) Contemporary students (especially Coser 1956) have argued the necessity of refining and qualifying Simmel's formulations, most particularly with regard to intensity and violence of conflict with "outsiders" required before effects on internal cohesion are discernible. It is highly likely, in my opinion, that analytical attention to the internal–external dimension across the full range of conflict-talk events which can be specified by the sociological variables and the macrofactors will permit further refinement and qualification of theories of both social conflict and socially constrained discourse production. I will not be able to rigorously demonstrate the kinds of interactions that I suspect obtain; I will suggest some kinds of things that might usefully be looked at.

While there are occasional references to environing social worlds (i.e., that of the "neighborhood" by Co-op members or that of social relations with Gentiles by Schiffrin's "sociables"), and while some of the events (i.e. the trials in O'Barr and Conley and the arguments about evidence in Philips) are explicitly about events which have occurred or will occur elsewhere), the disputes described in the analyses reported above appear at first glance to be largely self-contained. This fact notwithstanding it seems to me that attention to an internal–external dimension would make some of the data more easily interpretable. Indeed, it sometimes seems that conflict participants expend considerable efforts in attempting to redefine interpersonal disputes as conflicts in which they and some potential ally (possibly including a current adversary) should be joined against "outsiders." Such attempts are essayed, with varying degrees of "baldness" (Brown and Levinson, 1978) and of success and through use of variety of devices, by some of Corsaro and Rizzo's pre-schoolers (i.e., Enzo and Dante in their example 16), Eder's adolescent girls, Vuchinich's family diners, Goodwin and Goodwins' sling shotters, Lyle in his attempt to generate a management-versus-union axis (O'Donnell), and Labov's Co-op members. Devices employed include, non-exhaustively, invocation of shared memberships, pronominal usages (see Grimshaw, 1989) and attribution to an intendedly to-be-excluded other of negative characterizations of the potential fellow "in-group" member. It may also happen, of course, that a potential fellow will himself offer alliance when threat is seen to a weaker member of some already established collectivity, as when an older brother protects a younger one on grounds that sanctions can only be administered within a family – or students voluntarily put aside differences in the face of perceived violations of work norms by teachers (or, possibly, "rate-busting" peers).

Some possible instances of this principle are considerably more problematic. I have found myself perplexed as to why Emma and Robert kept their "secret" of Robert's discovery of Emma's affair with Jerry from the latter even while the affair continued (Pinter in Tannen) – and have concluded that some obscure dimension of the internal–external distinction is probably involved. (Tannen's own interpretation is that "telling" would have ended the affair because Jerry [the third party] would not have continued betraying his friend had he thought the latter had known. She attributes to Goffman the observation that the shared secret was a – perhaps fragile – basis of solidarity for the couple. The conflicts of loyalties which result in feelings of guilt when someone having an affair shares intimacy with a spouse are often a theme in fiction.) Other complexities result from the fact that conflict talk may be tabled, or continued but muted in the presence of audiences – but that in such instances it cannot be claimed either that internal cohesion has necessarily been enhanced or that all such audiences are necessarily defined as "external" and "threatening"; to note just one such complication, estranged spouses may conceal that estrangement from parents, particularly if the parents are perceived as being pleased with the relationship and even more particularly if the parents are "declining." Things get even more complicated when co-interactants (whether individuals or collectivities) jointly threatened by other parties are unable to ally because of mutual hostility (i.e., they would rather "hang separately" than "hang together").

How can all of this be codified into propositions (postulates? hypotheses?) which can direct us to appropriate sites for research? While it will not be possible either to formulate testable hypotheses or to rigorously specify postulates until an appropriate sample of conflict-talk events has been identified, collected, and analyzed, it is possible, on the basis of propositions in the social-conflict literature and what we already know about the discourse of disputes, to essay some preliminary propositions regarding what I will call "external threat claims." Consider, for example, the following:

13.19   *Ceteris paribus*, the lower the relative power of a dispute participant, the greater the likelihood that he/she will invoke claims of co-membership with copresent potential allies in some in-group faced by external "threat." *However*

13.19a dispute participants or audience members who are potential dispute participants who have greater relative power *may* invoke external threat claims when they feel that their own prerogatives (i.e. to administer sanctions) are being violated;

13.20   *ceteris paribus*, the more easily identifiable and the more credible an "external threat," the greater the likelihood that it will be invoked by conflict-talk participants *and* the greater the likelihood of successfully recruiting allies from among (also "threatened") co-participants or audience members;

13.21   *ceteris paribus*, the likelihood of invocation of external threat claims is directly related to the degree of positiveness in relations between invoker and potential ally; *However*

13.21a there is a to-be-specified threshold of external threat beyond which potential allies with whom invoker shares negative relationships are increasingly likely to be addressed with "in-group versus external threat claims"; *and*

13.21b potential allies to whom an invoker might address an external threat claim and with whom invoked shares positive relations, but who are seen as vulnerable to injury through participation in conflict talk, may be shielded from external threat claims;

13.22   the likelihood of invocation of external threat claims increases directly with perceived importance of stakes (utility); *however*

13.22a the presence of audiences perceived as likely to interpret the invocation of external threat claims as a manifestation of low relative power may dampen this effect.

All of these propositions (hypotheses, postulates) are imprecise – under some conditions some are probably false. We know, for example, that politicans of very considerable power quite regularly employ external threat claims (e.g. "Godless communism," "imperialist capitalist aggressors") without erosion of that power; this would seem to directly contradict 13.19 as it is now formulated. We know, also, that there is some interaction effect of source credibility, intrinsic credibility, audience size and characteristics, perceived danger(s) and attenuation (Goffman, 1971).

These and other qualifications notwithstanding, we also know that external-threat claims are invoked, that their use is constrained by the sociological variables and the macrofactors and that they therefore are differently likely to occur in different varieties of conflict-talk events, that they are variously expressed and variously successful when invoked, and so on. Their occurrence or non-occurrence clearly reflects the social organizational features of conflict-talk events. Sensitivity to those social organizational features should direct us to examination of disputes where they are likely to be found; explication of what is done in using them in discourse should help us to further refine our understanding of the same social organizational features and of social-conflict processes. The study of data records of purposively selected conflict-talk events will permit the writing of both new discourse rules and more clearly specified propositions on social conflict; as these rules and propositions accumulate similarities (and differences) will become evident and the task of identifying more general, subsuming, rules can be initiated.

6. Summary

The studies of conflict-talk events reported above and in a growing literature demonstrate that the behaviors of interest are simultaneously immensely complicated and a rich potential source for new understandings both of discourse itself and of social conflict. This is true even though records of some critically important conflict-talk events have not thus far been available for study. Following a long-established precedent I have argued that a first step in defining the study of disputes as an arena of professional (and socially relevant) research is identification of the features which identify and define conflict talk and determine its course and outcome. I have attempted to essay beginnings towards this step through the taxonomic exercise reported in sections 2 and 3 above. I have suggested that a next step is the preliminary identification and specification of regularities, rules, postulates, propositions, hypotheses, and so on, both on the discourse of disputes and on the sociological principles which constrain and guide that discourse. I have attempted to suggest what such rules, of several sorts, may ultimately look like.

There are, it seems to me, several directions of further work implied by discussion in this chapter. First, I think it should now be possible to *select* sites for the study of conflict-talk events which will allow us to specify, correct, and complete the proto-taxonomy of conflict talk suggested above *and* to similarly specify and perhaps test propositions of the several sorts proposed. Second, such more focused investigation should also allow us to discover how the propositions of the several sorts can be integrated – both with one another and with the larger enterprises of discourse analysis and of the construction of a viable and comprehensive sociological theory of social conflict processes. Third, and hopefully not as unattainable a prospect as it has sometimes seemed, I think we should bend every effort to obtain access to data records of the *full range* of conflict-talk events – both in order to complete our theories of discourse and of social conflict and because understanding of what goes on in the discourse of international disputes may be critical to our very survival.

Notes

Each of the colleagues who has contributed a study to this volume has read one or more drafts of this chapter; Corsaro, the Goodwins, Labov, and Mehan have provided me with extensive commentary and careful corrections. As I will note at various places below, there are several matters on which there is fairly strong residual disagreement; I have resisted the temptation to use our discussions and correspondence as data for another study. I am deeply grateful to my colleagues, both for their papers and for their support and co-operation (including provision of sometimes-ignored counsel) through the course of a protracted project.

1   The Goodwins remark (personal communication): "The issue of the importance of getting the participants' perspective has a long history in anthropology (going back at least as far as Malinowski). Moreover, it is deeply intertwined with the phonetic–phonemic distinction in linguistics, and the generalization of that distinction to social phenomena in general by Pike. Of crucial importance to Pike's reformulation is his framing of this issue in terms of functional elements of the system being studied (see C. Goodwin, 1984). Such a perspective does seem to deal with purposiveness without claiming that one has to get inside people's heads in order to do this. Moreover, the notion of getting the participants' perspective has long been a key focus of research in conversation analysis (see, e.g., Schegloff and Sacks 1973)." I do not dispute their point; I do not find it incompatible with my characterization.

2   Several of my colleagues don't like my notion of "sociological variables." My fellow sociologists Corsaro and Mehan are critical of an unwarranted "positivism"; the Goodwins are concerned that their work may be misrepresented and comment (personal communication): "We have long tried to focus on attributes of participants, social context, etc., that emerge within the data itself, and are attended to by participants as relevant to the organization of the activities they are engaged in. We do not start from a perspective that assumes a priori the overriding importance of particular sociological variables. Moreover, in the present chapter we argue that some of these variables (for example, hierarchy) are phenomena that should be analyzed within the detailed organization of the events that

make them visible and shape them. We don't start by assuming the importance of hierarchy, but rather show how it emerges from the details of the talk." I probably use the term "variable" more loosely than do my colleagues, I have in mind something more on the order of an orienting heuristic than a quantifiable, unidimensional "variable" such as age, income or education. This acknowledgment made, however, I must further confess my belief that measurement of these variables, *as they influence what goes on in talk*, is an appropriate long-range aspiration.

I hope, on the other hand, that I have not led other readers to worry that I am advocating that students of language in use should organize their research around "looking for" the sociological variables. As the Goodwins themselves report, the importance of hierarchy "emerges from the details of the talk." I mean to say no more than that most investigators find this to be the case.

3   Labov (personal communication) observes that the notion of "'play' seems to concern that most basic of all matters: when is talk to be taken literally, seriously" and remarks that the issue can be both more of a puzzle and of greater consequentiality in conflict talk. She continues by remarking that the consideration here may be of how well people learn to make appropriate distinctions as part of their communicative competence "that needs to be learned (and learned for each sort of social group in which people participate) and also be put into practice during each instance of (conflict) talk."

4   The question of whether conflict requires the awareness and participation of both (or all) parties or whether it is present when one party "attacks" an unknowing object is an ancient one. I will not address it here.

5   The Goodwins comment that fewer differences have been documented between the conflict talk of black and white children and adolescents than Kochman has reported for adults. More explicit comparative work, both across ethnic categories and within such categories by age, is clearly needed.

6   There are quite different dimensions of focus which must be neglected because of space considerations. Focus may be, for example, context-dependent (i.e. related to some immediate event) or context-independent (i.e., related to some extra-situational general principle).

7   The question of whether conflict processes are the same at the interpersonal, intergroup, international and interbloc (e.g.) levels has long intrigued students of the phenomenon. No one has as yet found any way to definitively demonstrate that they are – or that quantitive differences ultimately change the quality of these processes. This is not, fortunately, an appropriate place to address this issue.

8   Tannen (personal communication) reminds me of the 1977 Mel Brooks movie, *High Anxiety*, in which a couple fools customs officials by "making a scene," apparently squabbling so loudly that embarrassed officials rush them through to get rid of them.

9   I have examined some of these other "INSTRUMENTALITIES" and the constraints of the sociological variables on their employ elsewhere. See, e.g., 1980d, 1981a or 1988a, chapters 4 through 7.

10   Marvin Bressler reported some years ago that demonstrations against the first black residents in Levittown (Pennsylvania) occurred only on those days on which whites could walk to the site from their cars, and in comfort.

11   While temporal considerations have some importance in each of the disputes reported above, they are not central. A dispute about past gender discrimination in the degree-granting department which was embedded within a dissertation defense and which deeply engaged its principals was, contrastively, terminated without resolution so that the defense could be "wound up." Fairly detailed description of the dispute and some sociological implications drawn from its study can be found in Grimshaw, 1982a and b and 1988a, and Grimshaw *et al.* 1989a (the latter volume includes several studies of the segment of the defense which included the dispute, done by investigators from different disciplines and theoretical and analytic perspectives).

12   Often, not always. The outcomes of international negotiations and of major litigation and of disputes between the legislative and executive branches of governments have implications which far transcend the power strivings of individuals. There has been little research on such disputes. Even when world peace, for example, is at stake, moreover, individual participants will be involved in maximizing their personal identities.

13   Collins (personal communication) comments that he would try to analyze these changes by carefully distinguishing between "cultural capital" (CC) and "emotional energy" (EE). CC, he suggests, increases whenever new information or symbols, or modes of discourse, etc., are introduced. He continues: "insofar as conflict occurs more in culturally heterogeneous encounters than in homogeneous ones, I would predict participants are *especially* likely to increase their CC in conflictual conversation (provided the encounters aren't cut short by the conflict). On the other hand, EE may be lowered or in some way blocked by losing a dispute, or especially by stalemates." There is considerable exploratory work to be done here; he notes that he is engaged in work with Kemper in which they are trying to decompose emotional "processes." He notes that anger, an emotion often associated with conflict talk, is "especially complicated."

14   There are exceptions. M.H. Goodwin (1980a, 1980b) and the Goodwins together (1987) have attempted to demonstrate that gender differences in arguing are related to larger patterns of social organization such as hierarchical (male) vs egalitarian (female) groups.

15   Bernstein and Cicourel are, of course, very deeply interested and involved in research on talk; both Collins and Giddens accord talk central places in their theoretical formulations.

16   While my use of the notion of levels of observational, descriptive, and explanatory adequacy borrows from Chomsky (1965), it varies in several particulars. See my 1974.

17   Practitioners of negotiation have been extremely reluctant to record sensitive negotiations and, when they do record them, to release them to analysts for study. There seem to be five principal reasons for their nearly consensual reluctance, i.e.: (1) a "no benefits" argument; (2) a concern about "endangerment of trust"; (3) a belief that data collection and the

prospect of analysis would cause participants to hyper-monitor, thus preventing accomplishment of the goals for which negotiation is undertaken; (4) fear of litigation and judicial re-interpretation if a record is available; and (5) fear of "leaks." The last concern is probably the most important – I have the sense that negotiators are sometimes more concerned that their constituencies might learn what they are doing than that their adversaries would "hold them to the record." The overall posture seems to be, "It wouldn't do any good – and besides, it's dangerous." I am trying to sort out this problem with a view to offering a persuasive case for collection of data records of negotiations and analysis of such records.

18   Many students of human behavior (including discourse) argue that the notion of "rule" is not properly applicable to what they study.

19   Mehan comments (personal communication) regarding this characterization of CA: "They do not eschew context: instead, they take an agnostic view toward issues of identity, context, institutional setting and the like. Their rule of work is to start with formal matters and go to such features if and only if it is relevant for the analysis, where relevance is identified in terms made clear by the participants. They are clearly interested in using features of the background, but are starting with the systematic stuff of conversation, and seeing how hard they can push that before needing to 'go to the context.'"

Mehan agrees that the CA strategy has been productive for telling us about formal features of conversation *and* that it is weaker in addressing sociological questions. He notes that this last feature does not bother CA, who are not particularly interested in sociological questions as those questions have been *traditionally defined* (Sacks asserted that the questions he was addressing were at the very heart of sociology). I guess I am more immediately interested in some of the "old" questions.

20   See my 1980b and 1981b (reprinted as chapters 10 and 12 in 1981a) and 1988a, chapters 4–7. I have looted a number of literatures (particularly that of speech-act theory) in constructing my exploratory heuristic; I can neither review those literatures nor a number of critical qualifications in this place.

21   As might be anticipated, those of my colleagues who are uncomfortable with my use of the "variable" notion are also suspicious of my reference here to "postulates." The formulation of "propositions" does not appear to generate the same discomfort.

There are probably hundreds of propositional statements about social conflict; they vary very considerably in scope, specificity, elegance and rigor of formulation and are drawn from both contemporary and historical case studies, experiments, and statistical analyses and are informed by perspectives from all the social and clinical sciences as well as the humanities. R.M. Williams (1947) and Mack and Snyder (1957) contain extensive inventories. Contemporary formulations continue to be very heavily influenced by the work of earlier students, particularly, e.g., Marx, Pareto, Simmel and Weber. While discourse-analytic studies of conflict talk have generally focused on interpersonal and intergroup disputes with low values on Collins' (1981) macrofactors and outcomes which affect the lives of only a limited number of participants and in bounded ways, many students of conflict processes have been and are investigating conflicts at the other end of the scale, i.e. international disputes up to and including war (including potential nuclear war).

22 Dahrendorf has written a dense and lengthy monograph on class conflict; his treatment of the intensity-violence distinctions runs to many pages and can be neither properly explicated nor fully articulated with interests here in the short space available. Interested readers should examine the original.

References

Abel, Richard L. 1973. "A comparative theory of dispute institutions in society." *Law and Society Review*, 8: 217–347.

Abrahams, Roger D. 1970. In *Deep down in the jungle: negro narrative folklore from the streets of Philadelphia*, Chicago: Aldine.

Adger, Carolyn Temple. 1984. "Communicative competence in the culturally diverse classroom: negotiating norms for linguistic interaction." Unpublished Ph.D. dissertation, Linguistics. Georgetown University.

Albee, Edward. 1962. *Who's afraid of Virginia Woolf?* New York: Atheneum.

Albert, Ethel. 1964. "Rhetoric, logic and poetics in Burundi: cultural patterning of speech behavior." Pp. 35–54 in J. Gumperz and D. Hymes (eds.), *The ethnography of communication*. Washington, DC: American Anthropological Association. (*American Anthropologist*, 66, 6, Part 2).

Atelsek, J. 1981. "An anatomy of opinions." *Language in Society*, 10: 217–225.

Atkinson, J. Maxwell and Paul Drew. 1979. *Order in court: the organisation of verbal interaction in judicial settings*. Atlantic Highlands: Humanities Press.

Austin, John. 1962. *How to do things with words*. London: Oxford University Press, and Cambridge, MA: Harvard University Press.

Aüwarter, Manfred. 1986. "Development of communicative skills: the construction of fictional reality in children's play." Pp. 205–230 in J. Cook-Gumperz, W. Corsaro, and J. Streeck (eds.), *Children's worlds and children's language*. Berlin: Mouton.

Ayoub, Millicent and Stephen Barnett. 1961. "Ritualized verbal insult in white high school culture." *Journal of American Folklore*, 78: 337–344.

Bach, K. and R. Harnish. 1982. *Linguistic communication and speech acts*. Cambridge, MA: MIT Press.

Bailey, Frederick G. 1983. *The tactical uses of passion: an essay on power, reason, and reality*. Ithaca: Cornell University Press.

Barry, William A. 1970. "Marriage research and conflict: an integrative review." *Psychological Bulletin*, 73: 41–54.

Basso, Keith H. 1970. "To give up on words: silence in Western Apache culture." *Southwestern Journal of Anthropology*, 26: 213–230.

Bateson, Gregory. 1955. *A theory of play and fantasy*. American Psychological Association Psychiatric Research Reports, II. Reprinted as pp. 177–193 of

Steps to an ecology of mind. New York: Chandler, 1972.

1963. "A note on the double bind." *Family Processes,* 2: 154–161.

Becker, Howard. 1963. *Outsiders.* New York: The Free Press.

Bennett, W. Lance, and Martha S. Feldman. 1981. *Reconstructing reality in the courtroom: justice and judgement in American culture.* New Brunswick, NJ: Rutgers University Press.

Berger, Peter. 1968. *The sacred canopy.* Garden City, NY: Doubleday.

Berger, Peter and Hans Kellner. 1975. "Marriage and the social construction of reality." *Journal of Marriage and The Family,* 35: 24–32.

Berland, Joseph C. 1982. *No five fingers are alike: cultural amplifiers in social context.* Cambridge, MA: Harvard University Press.

Bernstein, Basil. 1971. *Class, codes and control 1: theoretical studies toward a sociology of language.* London: Routledge & Kegan Paul.

Boggs, Stephen T. 1978. "The development of verbal disputing in part-Hawaiian children." *Language in Society,* 7: 325–344.

Bower, Anne R. 1984. "The construction of stance in conflict narratives." Unpublished Ph.D. dissertation, University of Pennsylvania.

Brenneis, Donald. 1988. "Language and disputing." *Annual Review of Anthropology,* 17: 221–237.

Brenneis, Donald and Laura Lein. 1977. "'You fruithead': a sociolinguistic approach to children's dispute settlement." Pp. 49–65 in S. Ervin–Tripp and C. Mitchell-Kernan (eds.), *Child discourse.* New York: Academic Press.

Brown, Penelope and Stephen Levinson. 1978. "Universals in language usage: politeness phenomena." Pp. 56–289, 295–310 in E.N. Goody (ed.), *Questions and politeness: strategies in social interaction.* Cambridge: Cambridge University Press.

Brown, Roger and A. Gilman. 1972 [1960]. "The pronouns of power and solidarity." Pp. 252–282 in P. Giglioli (ed.), *Language and social context.* Harmondsworth, England: Penguin Books.

Burton, Deidre. 1980. *Dialogue and discourse: a sociolinguistic approach to modern drama dialogue and naturally occurring conversation.* London: Routledge & Kegan Paul.

Button, Graham and Neil Casey. 1984. "Generating topic: the use of topic initial elicitors." Pp. 167–190 in J. Maxwell Atkinson and John Heritage (eds.), *Structures of social action.* Cambridge: Cambridge University Press.

Carlton, Eric. 1984. "Ideologies as belief systems." *The International Journal of Sociology and Social Policy,* 4, 2: 17–29.

Chafe, Wallace L. 1972. "Discourse structure and human knowledge." Pp. 41–69 in R.O. Freedle and J.B. Carroll (eds.), *Language comprehension and the acquistion of knowledge.* Washington: Winston.

1980. "The deployment of consciousness in the production of a narrative." Pp. 9–50 in W. Chafe (ed.), *The pear stories: cognitive, cultural, and linguistic aspects of narrative production.* Norwood, NJ: Ablex Publishing Company.

Chase, Ivan D. 1980. "Social process and hierarchy formation in small groups: a comparative perspective." *American Sociological Review,* 45: 905–924.

Chick, John K. 1985. "The interactional accomplishment of discrimination in South Africa." *Language in Society,* 14: 399–426.

Chomsky, Noam. 1965. *Aspects of the theory of syntax.* Cambridge, MA: MIT Press.

Cicourel, Aaron V. 1973. *Cognitive sociology: language and meaning in social interaction*. New York: The Free Press.

Clark, Herbert H. and Thomas B. Carlson. 1982. "Speech acts and hearers' beliefs." Pp. 1–36 in Neil V. Smith (ed.), *Mutual Knowledge*. New York: Academic Press.

Cole, Michael, *et al*. 1971. *The cultural context of learning and thinking*. New York: Basic Books.

Coleman, James S. 1957. *Community conflict*. Glencoe: The Free Press.

Collins, Randall. 1975. *Conflict sociology*. New York: Academic Press.

1981. "On the microfoundations of macrosociology." *American Journal of Sociology*, 86, 5: 984–1014.

Conein, Bernard. Unpublished. "Peuple et pouvoir politique: la position du porte-parole pendant la revolution francaise (juillet-septembre, 1972)."

Conley, John M. and Mark B. Childress. 1985. *Index to a research collection of tapes and transcripts from a North Carolina small claims court*. Report distributed by National Institute for Dispute Resolution, Washington, DC.

Conley, John M., William M. O'Barr, and E. Allen Lind. 1979. "The power of language: presentational style in the courtroom." *Duke Law Journal*, 78, 6: 1375–1399.

Corsaro, William A. 1979. "'We're friends, right?': children's use of access rituals in a nursery school." *Language in Society*, 8: 315–336.

1981a. "Friendship in the nursery school: social organization in a peer environment." Pp. 207–241 in S. Asher and J. Gottman (eds.), *The development of children's friendships*. New York: Cambridge University Press.

1981b. "Entering the child's world: research strategies for field entry and data collection in a preschool setting." Pp. 117–146 in J. Green and C. Wallat (eds.), *Ethnography and language in educational settings*. Norwood, NJ: Ablex Publishing Company.

1982. "Something old and something new: the importance of prior ethnography in the collection and analysis of audiovisual data." *Sociological Methods and Research*, 11: 145–166.

1985. *Friendship and peer culture in the early years*. Norwood, NJ: Ablex Publishing Company.

1986. "Routines in peer culture." Pp. 231–252 in J. Cook-Gumperz, W. Corsaro and J. Streeck (eds.), *Children's worlds and children's language* Berlin: Mouton.

1988. "Routines in the peer culture of American and Italian nursery school children." *Sociology of Education*, 61: 1–14.

Corsaro, William A., and Thomas Rizzo. 1988. "*Discussione* and friendship: production and reproduction within the peer culture of Italian nursery school children." *American Sociological Review*, 53: 879–894.

1990. This volume. "Disputes and conflict resolution among nursery school children in the U.S. and Italy." In A. Grimshaw (ed.), *Conflict talk*. Cambridge: Cambridge University Press.

Coser, Lewis A. 1956. *The functions of social conflict*. Glencoe: The Free Press.

Coulter, Jeff. 1979. *Social construction of mind: studies in ethnomethodology and linguistic philosophy*. London: Macmillan.

Dahrendorf, Ralf. 1959. *Class and class conflict in industrial society*. Stanford: Stanford University Press.

Danet, Brenda, K. Hoffmann, N. Kermish, J. Rafn, and D. Stayman. 1980. "An ethnography of questioning." Pp. 222–234 in R. Shuy and A. Shnukal (eds.), *Language use and the uses of language*. Papers from the Fifth Annual Colloquium on New Ways of Analyzing Variation in English. Washington, DC: Georgetown University Press.

Dittmar, Norbert, Peter Schlobinski, and Inge Wachs. 1988. "Berlin style and register." Pp. 44–113 in Dittmar, Schlobinski and Wachs (eds.), *The sociolinguistics of urban vernaculars: case studies and their evaluation*. Berlin: de Gruyter.

Donaldson, Margaret. 1978. *Children's minds*. New York: W.W. Norton and Company.

Donaldson, Susan Kay. 1985. "The pause that threatens: a comparison of pause length and response to pause in a natural conversation and in Harold Pinter's *The Homecoming*." Paper presented at the Linguistic Society of America Linguistic Institute Summer Meeting, Washington, DC.

Dore, John and Ray P. McDermott. 1982. "Linguistic indeterminacy and social context in utterance interpretation." *Language*, 58: 374–398.

Douvan, Elizabeth, and Joseph Adelson. 1966. *The adolescent experience*. New York: Wiley.

Duranti, Alessandro. 1986. "Language in context and language as context: the Samoan respect vocabulary." Paper presented at the invited session on "Rethinking context" at the 1986 Annual Meeting of the American Anthropological Association.

1988. "Ethnography of speaking: toward a linguistics of the praxis." Pp. 210–228 in T. Newmeyer (ed.), *Linguistics: the Cambridge Survey, vol. IV, Language: the socio-cultural context*. Cambridge: Cambridge University Press.

Eder, Donna. 1985. "The cycle of popularity: interpersonal relations among female adolescents." *Sociology of Education*, 58: 154–165.

Eder, Donna and Maureen T. Hallinan. 1978. "Sex differences in children's friendships." *American Sociological Review*, 43: 237–250.

Eder, Donna and Stephanie Sanford. 1988. "The development and maintenance of interactional norms among early adolescents." Pp. 283–300 in P. Adler and P. Adler (eds.), *Sociological studies of child development*. Greenwich, CT: JAI Press.

Edgerton, Robert B. 1985. *Rules, exceptions, and social order*. Berkeley: University of California Press.

Edwards, Lyford. 1927. *The natural history of revolution*. Chicago: University of Chicago Press.

Eisenberg, Ann R. and Catherine Garvey. 1981. "Children's use of verbal strategies in resolving conflicts." *Discourse Processes*, 4: 149–170.

Elstein, Arthur S., Lee S. Shulman, and Sarah V. Sprafka. 1978. *Medical problem solving*. Cambridge, MA: Harvard University Press.

Erickson, Frederick. 1975. "Gatekeeping and the melting pot: interaction in counseling encounters." *Harvard Educational Review*, 45: 44–70.

1979. "Talking down: some cultural sources of miscommunication in interracial interviews." Pp. 99–126 in A. Wolfgang (ed.), *Nonverbal communication*. New York: Academic Press.

Erickson, Frederick and Jeffrey J. Shultz. 1982. *The counselor as gatekeeper: social interaction in interviews*. New York: Academic Press.

Ervin-Tripp, Susan and Claudia Mitchell-Kernan (eds.). 1977. *Child discourse*. New York: Academic Press.

Esslin, Martin. 1970. *The peopled wound: the work of Harold Pinter*. Garden City, NY: Doubleday.

Evans-Pritchard, E.E. 1937. *Witchcraft, oracles and magic among the Azande*. Oxford: Clarendon Press.

Feshbach, Norman and Gittelle Sones. 1971. "Sex differences in adolescent reactions toward newcomers." *Developmental Psychology*, 4: 381–386.

Festinger, Leon, Henry Riecken, and Stanley Schachter. 1956. *When prophecy fails*. New York: Harper and Row.

Fillmore, Charles J. 1971. "Verbs of judging: an exercise in semantic description." Pp. 273–289 in C.J. Fillmore and D.T. Langendoen (eds.), *Studies in linguistic semantics*. New York: Holt, Rinehart and Winston.

Fisher, Roger and William Ury. 1981. *Getting to yes: negotiating agreement without giving in*. Boston: Houghton Mifflin.

Fisher, Susan and Alexandra Todd (eds.). 1983. *The social organization of doctor–patient communication*. Washington, DC: Center for Applied Linguistics. Distributed by Ablex Publishing Corporation, Norwood, NJ.

Folb, Edith. 1980. *Runnin' down some lines: the language and culture of black teenageers*. Cambridge: Harvard University Press.

Fontenrose, Joseph E. 1978. *The Delphic Oracle*. Berkeley: The University of California Press.

Fowler, Roger, Bob Hodge, Gunther Kress, and Tony Trew. 1979. *Language and control*. London: Routledge & Kegan Paul.

Fowles, John. 1977. *Daniel Martin*. New York: Signet.

Frankel, Richard. 1983. "The laying on of hands: aspects of the organization of gaze, touch, and talk in a medical encounter." Pp. 19–54 in S. Fisher and A. Todd (eds.), *The social organization of doctor–patient communication*. Washington, DC: Center for Applied Linguistics. Distributed by Ablex Publishing Corporation, Norwood, NJ.

Frazer, James G. 1890. *The Golden Bough: a study in magic and religion*. London: Macmillan.

Garfinkel, Harold. 1967. *Studies in ethnomethodology*. Englewood Cliffs, NJ: Prentice-Hall.

Garfinkel, Harold and Harvey Sacks. 1970. "On formal structures of practical actions." Pp. 337–366 in J.D. McKinney and E.A. Tiryakian (eds.), *Theoretical sociology*. New York: Appleton-Century-Crofts.

Garvey, Catherine. 1984. *Children's talk*. Cambridge, MA: Harvard University Press.

Gasking, D. 1955. "Mathematics: another world." In A. Flew (ed.), *Logic and language*. Garden City, NY: Anchor Books.

Gelman, Rochel. 1978. "Cognitive development." *Annual Review of Psychology*, 29: 297–332.

Genishi, Celia and Marianna di Paolo. 1982. "Learning through argument in a preschool." Pp. 49–68 in L.C. Wilkinson (ed.), *Communicating in the classroom*. New York: Academic Press.

Giles, Howard and Mary Anne Fitzpatrick. 1984. "Personal, group and couple identities: toward a relational context for the study of language attitudes and linguistic forms." Pp. 253–277 in D. Schiffrin (ed.), *Georgetown University Round Table on Languages and Linguistics*. Washington, DC: Georgetown University Press.

Gilligan, Carol. 1982. *In a different voice: psychological theory and women's development*. Cambridge, MA: Harvard University Press.

Ginsberg, Herbert P. (ed.). 1983. *The development of mathematical thinking*. New York: Academic Press.

Gluckman, Max. 1955. *The judicial process among the Barotse*. Manchester: Manchester University Press.

Goffman, Erving. 1959a. "The moral career of the mental patient." *Psychiatry*, 22: 123–142.

1959b. *The presentation of self in everyday life*. Garden City, NY: Doubleday and Company.

1967. *Interaction ritual: essays in face to face behavior*. Garden City, NY: Doubleday and Company.

1971. *Relations in public*. New York: Harper and Row.

1974. *Frame analysis*. New York: Harper and Row.

1976. "Replies and responses." *Language in Society*, 5: 257–313.

1981a. *Forms of talk*. Philadelphia: University of Pennsylvania Press.

1981b. Introduction (pp. 1–4) to *Forms of talk*. Philadelphia: University of Pennsylvania Press.

1981c. "Radio talk." Pp. 197–330 in *Forms of talk*. Philadelphia: University of Pennsylvania Press.

1981d. "Footing." Pp. 124–159 in *Forms of talk*. Philadelphia: University of Pennsylvania Press.

Goodenough, Ward H. 1965. "Rethinking 'status' and 'role': toward a general model of the cultural organization of social relationships." Pp. 1–24 in M. Banton (ed.), *The relevance of models for social anthropology*. London: Tavistock.

1981. *Culture, language and society*. Menlo Park, CA: The Benjamin/Cummings Publishing Company.

Goodman, Nelson. 1978. *Ways of worldmaking*. Indianapolis, IN: Hackett Publishing Company.

Goodwin, Charles. 1979. "The interactive construction of a sentence in natural conversation." Pp. 97–121 in G. Psathas (ed.), *Everyday language: studies in ethnomethodology*. New York: Irvington Publishers.

1981. *Conversational organization: interaction between speakers and hearers*. New York: Academic Press.

1984. "Notes on story structure and the organization of participation." Pp. 225–246 in J.M. Atkinson and J. Heritage (eds.), *Structures of social action*. Cambridge: Cambridge University Press.

1987. "Forgetfulness as an interactive resource." *Social Psychology Quarterly*, 50, 2: 115–130.

Goodwin, Charles and Marjorie Harness Goodwin. 1984. "Audience as process." Paper presented at the 1984 Annual Meeting of the American Anthropological Association.

Goodwin, Marjorie Harness. 1978. "Conversational practices in a peer group of urban black children." Unpublished Ph.D. dissertation, Department of Anthropology, University of Pennsylvania.

1980a. "He-said-she said: formal cultural procedures for the construction of a gossip dispute activity." *American Ethnologist,* 7: 674–695.

1980b. "Directive/response speech sequences in girls' and boys' task activities." Pp. 157–173 in S. McConnell-Ginet, R. Borker, and N. Furman (eds.), *Women and language in literature and society.* New York: Praeger.

1982a. "Byplay: diversions on talk." Presented at the Tenth World Congress of the International Sociological Association, Mexico City, August.

1982b. "Processes of dispute management among urban black children." *American Ethnologist,* 9: 76–96.

1982c. "'Instigating': storytelling as a social process." *American Ethnologist,* 9: 799–819.

1983. "Aggravated correction and disagreement in children's conversations." *Journal of Pragmatics,* 7: 657–677.

1985. "The serious side of jump rope: conversational practices and social organization in the frame of play." *Journal of American Folklore,* 98: 315–330.

1988. "Cooperation and competition across girls' play activities." Pp. 55–94 in S. Fisher and A. Todd (eds.), *Gender and discourse: the power of talk.* Norwood, NJ: Ablex Publishing Company.

Forthcoming. *Language as social process: conversational practices in urban black children.* Bloomington: Indiana University Press.

Goodwin, Marjorie Harness and Charles Goodwin. 1987. "Children's arguing." Pp. 200–248 in S.U. Philips, S. Steele, and C. Tanz (eds.), *Language, gender and sex in comparative perspective.* Cambridge: Cambridge University Press.

Goody, Jack. 1977. *The domestication of the savage mind.* Cambridge: Cambridge University Press.

Gould, Stephen J. 1981. *The mismeasure of man.* New York: W.W. Norton.

Gouldner, Alvin. 1954. *Wildcat strike.* Yellow Springs, OH: Antioch Press.

Gramsci, Antonio. 1971. *Prison notebooks.* New York: International Publishers.

Greenwood, Davydd J. 1984. *The taming of evolution.* Ithaca: Cornell University Press.

Grice, H. Paul. 1975. "Logic and conversation." Pp. 41–58 in P. Cole and J. Morgan (eds.), *Syntax and semantics, Volume 3, Speech acts.* New York: Academic Press.

Grimshaw, Allen D. 1974. "Sociolinguistics." Pp. 49–92 in Ithiel de Sola Pool, W. Schramm, F.W. Frey, N. Maccoby, and E.B. Parker (eds.), *Handbook of communication,* Chicago: Rand-McNally.

1980a. "Sociolinguistics at the Council, 1963–1979: past and prologue." *Items,* 34: 12–18.

1980b. "Social interactional and sociolinguistic rules." *Social Forces,* 58: 789–810.

1980c. "Mishearing, misunderstandings and other nonsuccesses in talk: a plea for redress of speaker-oriented bias." *Sociological Inquiry,* 40 (3–4): 31–74.

1980d. "Selection and labeling of instrumentalities of verbal manipulation." *Discourse Processes,* 3(3): 203–29.

1981a. *Language as social resource.* Stanford: Stanford University Press.

1981b. "Talk and social control." Pp. 200–232 in M. Rosenberg and R.H. Turner (eds.), *Social psychology: sociological perspectives.* New York: Basic Books.

1982a. "Comprehensive discourse analysis: an instance of professional peer interaction." *Language in Society,* 11: 15–47.

1982b. "A cross-status dispute in ongoing talk: conflicting views of history." *Text,*

2, 4: 323–358.

1987. "Disambiguating discourse: members' skill and analysts' problem." *Social Psychology Quarterly*, 50, 2: 186–204.

1988a. *Collegial discourse: professional conversation among peers*. Norwood, NJ: Ablex Publishing Company.

1988b. "Secret openness: the need for electronically-recorded data on international negotiation – and resistance to research access." Paper presented to Research Council of the International Sociological Association, Ljubljana, September.

1989 "Referential ambiguity in pronominal inclusion: social and linguistic boundary marking." In A.D. Grimshaw *et al. What's going on here? Complementary studies of professional talk*. Norwood, NJ: Ablex Publishing Company.

Grimshaw, Allen D., P.J. Burke, A.V. Cicourel, J. Cook-Cumperz, S. Feld, C.J. Fillmore, J. Gumperz, R. Hasan, M.A.K. Halliday, D. Jenness, and L. Wong Fillmore. 1989. *What's going on here? Complementary studies of professional talk*. Norwood: Ablex Publishing Company.

Grimshaw, Allen D., Steven Feld, and David Jenness. 1989. "The Multiple Analysis Project: background, history, problems, data." In A.D. Grimshaw *et al., What's going on here? Complementary studies of professional talk*. Norwood: Ablex Publishing Company.

Gumperz, John J. 1977. "Sociocultural knowledge in conversational inference." Pp. 191–211 in M. Saville-Troike (ed.), *Linguistics and anthropology*, 28th Annual Round Table Monograph Series on Language and Linguistics. Washington, DC: Georgetown University Press.

1982a. *Discourse strategies*. Cambridge: Cambridge University Press.

1982b (ed.). *Language and social identity*. Cambridge: Cambridge University Press.

Gurwitsch, Aron. 1962. *Studies in phenomenology and psychology*. Evanston: Northwestern University Press.

Gussow, Mel. 1971. "A conversation [pause] with Harold Pinter." *New York Times Magazine*, December 5, 1971: 42–43, 126–136.

Halliday, Michael A.K. 1961. "Categories of the theory of grammar." *Word*, 17, 3: 241–292.

1973. *Explorations in the functions of language*. London: Edward Arnold, Ltd.

1978. *Language as social semiotic – the interpretation of language and meaning*. London: Edward Arnold, Ltd.

1985. *A short introduction to functional grammar*. London: Edward Arnold, Ltd.

Halliday, Michael A.K. and Ruqaiya Hasan. 1976. *Cohesion in English*. Bath, England: Longman Group, Ltd.

Halliday, Michael A.K., Angus McIntosh, and Peter Strevens. 1964. *The linguistic sciences and language teaching*. London: Longman, (Bloomington: Indiana University Press. 1966.)

Hallpike, Christopher R. 1979. *The foundations of primitive thought*. New York: Oxford University Press.

Haviland, John B. 1986a. "'Sure, sure': evidence and affect." Unpublished manuscript.

1986b. "'Con buenos chiles': talk, targets and teasing in Zinacantan." *Text*, 6, 3: 249–282. (Special issue on the audience, edited by A. Duranti and D.

Brenneis.)
1987. "How to talk: some Tzotzil ways: or, ritual speech with ritual." Paper presented at the University of Texas at Austin Conference on "Discourse in sociocultural context," April 9–11, 1987.
Headley, Bernard D. 1986. "Ideological constructions of race and the 'Atlanta tragedy'." *Contemporary Crises*, 10, 2: 181–200.
Heath, Christian. 1984. "Talk and recipiency: sequential organization in speech and body movement." Pp. 247–265 in J.M. Atkinson and J. Heritage (eds.), *Structures of social action*. Cambridge: Cambridge University Press.
  1986. *Body movement and speech in medical interaction*. Cambridge: Cambridge University Press.
Heath, Shirley Brice. 1983a. *Ways with words*. Cambridge: Cambridge University Press.
  1983b. "Processes of dispute management among urban black children." In *Ways with words: language, life and work in communities and classrooms*. Cambridge: Cambridge University Press.
Henry, Jules. 1965. *Pathways to madness*. New York: Random House.
Heritage, John. 1984. *Garfinkel and ethnomethodology*. Cambridge: Polity Press.
Heritage, John and J. Maxwell Atkinson. 1984. Introduction. Pp. 1–16 in J.M. Atkinson and J. Heritage (eds.), *Structures of social action*. Cambridge: Cambridge University Press.
Hiller, Edward T. 1928. *The strike*. Chicago: University of Chicago Press.
Hochschild, Arlie R. 1979. "Emotion work, feeling rules and social structure." *American Journal of Sociology*, 85: 551–575.
  1983. *The managed heart: commercialization of human feeling*. Berkeley: University of California Press.
Hollis, James R. 1970. *Harold Pinter: the poetics of silence*. Carbondale: Southern Illinois University.
Holmes, Dick. 1984. "Explicit-implicit address." *Journal of Pragmatics*, 8: 311–320.
Homans, George C. 1950. *The human group*. New York: Harcourt, Brace and World.
Horton, Robin. 1967. "African traditional thought and Western science." *Africa*, 37: 50–71; 155–187.
Hutchins, Edwin. 1980. *Culture and inference: a Trobriand case study*. Cambridge, MA: Harvard University Press.
Hymes, Dell. 1964. "Introduction: toward ethnographies of communication." Pp. 1–34 in J.J. Gumperz and D. Hymes (eds.), *The ethnography of communication*. Washington DC: American Anthropological Association. (*American Anthropologist*, 66,6, Part 2.)
  1974. *Foundations in sociolinguistics*. Philadelphia: University of Pennsylvania Press.
Jefferson, Gail. 1972. "Side sequences." Pp. 294–338 in D. Sudnow (ed.), *Studies in social interaction*. New York: Free Press.
  1984. "On stepwise transition from talk about a trouble to inappropriately next-positioned matters." Pp. 192–222 in J.M. Atkinson and J. Heritage (eds.), *Structures of social action*. Cambridge: Cambridge University Press.
Johnstone, B. 1987. "'He says . . . so I said:' Verb tense alternation and narrative depictions of authority in American English." Pp. 33–52 in N. Dittmar (ed.), *Variation and discourse*. Special volume of *Linguistics*, 25, 1.

Jules-Rosette, Bennetta. 1976. "The conversion experience." *Journal of Religion in Africa*, 7: 132–164.

Katriel, Tamar. 1985. "*Brogez*: ritual and strategy in Israeli children's conflicts." *Language in Society*, 14, 4: 467–490.

Kaufmann, John H. 1967. "Social relations of adult males in a free ranging band of rhesus monkeys." Pp. 73–98 in S.A. Altmann (ed.), *Social communication among primates*. Chicago: University of Chicago Press.

Keenan, E. 1979. "Universality of conversational postulates." *Language in society*, 5: 67–80.

Keenan, Elinor Ochs and Bambi B. Schieffelin. 1983. "Topic as a discourse notion: a study of topic in the conversations of children and adults." Pp. 66–113 in E. Ochs and B.B. Schieffelin (eds.), *Acquiring conversational competence*. Boston: Routledge & Kegan Paul.

Kemper, Theodore D. 1978. *A social interactional theory of emotions*. New York: Wiley-Interscience.

Kendrick, Walter. 1983. "The analyst and her analysand." Review of *August* by Judith Rossner. *The New York Times Book Review*, July 24, 1983: 1, 19.

Kitsuse, John. 1963. "Societal reaction to deviant behavior." In H.S. Becker (ed.), *The other side: perspective on deviance*. New York: Free Press.

Kitsuse, John and Aaron V. Cicourel. 1963. *Educational decision making*. Indianapolis: Bobbs-Merrill.

Kluegel, James R. and Eliot R. Smith. 1982. "Whites' beliefs about blacks' opportunity." *American Sociological Review*, 47: 518–32.

Kochman, Thomas. 1981. *Black and white styles in conflict*. Chicago: University of Chicago Press.

1983. "The boundary between play and nonplay in black verbal dueling." *Language in Society*, 12: 329–337.

1986. "Strategic ambiguity in black speech genres: cross-cultural interference in participant-observation research." *Text*, 6, 2: 153–170.

Kuhn, Thomas S. 1962. *The structure of scientific revolutions*. Chicago: University of Chicago Press.

Labov, Teresa. 1980. "The communication of morality: cooperation and commitment in a food cooperative." Unpublished Ph.D. dissertation, Columbia University, Department of Sociology.

Labov, William. 1968. *A proposed program for research and training in the study of language in its social and cultural settings*. Columbia University. Mimeo.

1972a. *Sociolinguistic patterns*. Philadelphia: University of Pennsylvania Press.

1972b. *Language in the inner city: studies in the Black English Vernacular*. Philadelphia: University of Philadelphia Press.

1972c. "The transformation of experience in narrative syntax." Pp. 354–396 in *Language in the inner city*. Philadelphia: University of Pennsylvania Press.

1972d. "Rules for ritual insults." Pp. 297–305 in *Language in the inner city*. Philadelphia: University of Pennsylvania Press.

1981. "Speech actions and reactions in personal narrative." Pp. 219-247 in D. Tannen (ed.), *Analyzing discourse: Text and talk*. Georgetown University Round Table 1981. Washington DC: Georgetown University Press.

Labov, William and David Fanshel. 1977. *Therapeutic discourse: psychotherapy as conversation*. New York: Academic Press.

Laing, Ronald D. 1967. *The politics of experience*. New York: Pantheon.

Lakoff, Robin T. 1975. *Language and woman's place*. New York: Harper and Row.

Lakoff, Robin T. and Deborah Tannen. 1984. "Conversational stategy and metastrategy in a pragmatic theory: the example of *Scenes from a marriage*." *Semiotica*, 49, 3/4: 323–346.

Lambert, Richard D. 1951. "Hindu-Muslim riots." Unpublished Ph.D. dissertation, University of Pennsylvania.

Lave, J. 1983. "Arithmetic practice and cognitive theory: ethnographic inquiry." Unpublished manuscript. School of Social Sciences, University of California, Irvine.

Lein, Laura and Donald Brenneis. 1978. "Children's disputes in three speech communities." *Language in Society*, 7: 299–323.

Lever, Janet. 1976. "Sex differences in the games children play." *Social Problems*, 23: 478–487.

Levine, Donald N. 1985. *The flight from ambguity: essays in social and cultural theory*. Chicago: University of Chicago Press.

Levinson, Stephen C. 1983. *Pragmatics*. Cambridge: Cambridge University Press.

Li, Charles (ed.). 1976. *Subject and topic*. New York: Academic Press.

Lind, E. Allan, John Thibaut, and Laurens Walker. 1973. "Discovery and presentation of evidence in adversary and nonadversary proceedings." *Michigan Law Review*, 71: 1129–1144.

Lofland, John. 1977. *Doomsday cult*. New York: Irvington Publishers.

Luria, Alexander R. 1976. *Cognitive development*. Cambridge, MA: Harvard University Press.

Lyons, John. 1972. "Human language." Pp. 49–85 in R.A. Hinde (ed.), *Non-verbal communication*. Cambridge: Cambridge University Press.

Maccoby, Michael and Nancy Modiano. 1966. "On culture and equivalence." Pp. 257–269 in J.S. Bruner, Rose R. Olver, Patricia M. Greenfield, and Joan R. Hornsby, Helen J. Kenney, M. Maccoby, Nancy Modiano, F.A. Mosher, D.R. Olson, Mary C. Potter, L.C. Reich, Anne McKinnon Sonstroem, *Studies in cognitive growth*. New York: Wiley.

Mack, Raymond W. and Richard C. Snyder. 1957. "The analysis of social conflict – toward an overview and synthesis." *Journal of Conflict Resolution*, 1, 2: 212–248.

Maroules, Nicholas. 1985. "The social organization of sentencing." Unpublished doctoral dissertation, University of California, San Diego.

Martin, J.R. 1984. "Grammaticalizing ecology: the politics of baby seals and kangaroos." Department of Linguistics, Sydney, Australia. Unpublished manuscript.

Mattison, Alice. 1986. "Great wits." *The New Yorker*, May 19, 1986: 34–42. Reprinted in *Great Wits*, by Alice Mattison. New York: William Morrow, 1988.

Maynard, Douglas W. 1984a. *Inside plea bargaining: the language of negotiation*. New York: Plenum.

1984b. "The structure of discourse in misdemeanor plea bargaining." *Law and Society Review*, 18: 75–104.

1985a. "How children start arguments." *Language in Society*, 14: 1–29.

1985b. "On the functions of social conflict among children." *American Sociological*

Review, 50: 207–223.

1986. "Offering and soliciting collaboration in multi-party disputes among children (and other humans)." *Human Studies*, 9: 261–285.

Maynard, Douglas W. and Don H. Zimmerman. 1984. "Topical talk, ritual and the social organization of relationships." *Social Psychology Quarterly*, 47, 4: 301–316.

Mehan, Hugh. 1983a. "Le constructivism social en psychologie et sociologie." *Sociologie et Societies* XIV, (2): 77–96.

1983b. "The role of language and the language of role in practical decision making." *Language in Society*, 12: 1–39.

Mehan, Hugh and Houston Wood. 1975. *The reality of ethnomethodology*. New York: Wiley-Interscience.

Merton, Robert K. 1966. "Dilemmas in voluntary associations." *The American Journal of Nursing*, 66: 1055–1061.

1972. "Insiders and outsiders: a chapter in the sociology of knowledge." *American Journal of Sociology*, 78: 9–47.

Mishler, Elliot G. 1985. *The discourse of medicine: dialectics of medical interviews*. Norwood, NJ: Ablex Publishing Company.

Mitchell-Kernan, Claudia. 1973. "Signifying." Pp. 310–328 in A. Dundes (ed.), *Mother wit from the laughing barrel*. Englewood Cliffs, NJ: Prentice-Hall.

Mitchell-Kernan, Claudia and Keith T. Kernan. 1975. "Children's insults: America and Samoa." Pp. 307–315 in M. Sanches and B.G. Blount (eds)., *Sociocultural dimensions of language use*. New York: Academic.

1977. "Pragmatics of directive choice among children." Pp. 189–208 in S. Ervin-Tripp and C. Mitchell-Kernan (eds.), *Child discourse*. New York: Academic Press.

Molotch, Harvey and Deidre Boden. 1985. "Talking social structure: discourse, dominance and the Watergate Hearings." *American Sociological Review*, 50: 273–288.

Myrdal, Gunnar. 1944. *The American Dilemma*. New York: Harper and Row.

Nader, Laura. 1969. "Styles of court procedures: to make the balance." Pp. 69–91 in L. Nader (ed.), *Law in culture and society*. Chicago: Aldine.

1984. "A user theory of law." *Southwestern Law Journal*, 38: 951–963.

Nader, Laura and Harry Todd, Jr. 1978. "Introduction." *The disputing process: law in ten societies*. New York: Columbia University Press.

O'Barr, William M. 1982. *Linguistic evidence*. New York: Academic Press.

O'Barr, William M. and Bowman K. Atkins. 1980. "'Women's language' or 'powerless language'?" Pp. 93–110 in S. McConnell-Ginet, R. Borker, and N. Furman (eds.), *Women and language in literature and society*. New York: Praeger.

O'Barr, William M. and John M. Conley. 1985. "Litigant satisfaction versus legal adequacy in small claims court narratives." *Law and Society Review*, 19: 661–701.

O'Donnell, Katherine. 1983. "Labor problematics: a sociolinguistic analysis of industrial conflict." Unpublished Ph.D. dissertation, Indiana University, Department of Sociology.

Parsons, Talcott. 1951. *The social system*. Glencoe: The Free Press.

Piaget, Jean. 1948. *The moral judgement of the child*. Glencoe: The Free Press.

Pinter, Harold. 1964. "Writing for the theatre." Pp. 574–580 in Henry Popkin (ed.), *The new British drama*. New York: Grove Press.

1978. *Betrayal*. New York: Grove Press.

Polanyi, L. 1979. "So what's the point?" *Semiotica*, 25: 207–241.

Pollner, Melvin. 1975. "'The very coinage of your brain': the anatomy of reality disjunctures." *Philosophy of Social Science*, 5: 411–430.

Pollner, Melvin and Lynn McDonald-Wikler. 1985. "The social construction of unreality." *Family Process*, 24: 241–254.

Pomerantz, Anita. 1978. "Compliment responses: notes on the co-operation of multiple constraints." Pp. 79–112 in J. Schenkein (ed.), *Studies in the organization of conversational interaction*. New York: Academic Press.

Qualitity of Working Life (QWL). 1977. *Agreement Handbook: A memorandum of mutual trust*. Pamphlet.

Rapoport, Anatol. 1960. *Fights, games and debates*. Ann Arbor: University of Michigan Press.

Rizzo, Thomas. 1988. *Friendship development among children in school*. Norwood, NJ: Ablex Publishing Company.

Rosenhan, D.L. 1973. "On being sane in insane places." *Science*, 179: 250–258.

Rothschild-Witt, Joyce. 1979. "The collectivist organization." *American Sociological Review*, 44: 509–28.

Ryno, Ronald J. 1985. "The pragmatics of religious belief: an ethnography of the Cursillo community in Palma Mallorca." Unpublished doctoral dissertation, University of California, San Diego.

Sacks, Harvey. 1963. "Sociological description." *Berkeley Journal of Sociology*, 8: 1–16.

1970. Unpublished class lectures.

1972a. "On the analyzability of stories by children." Pp. 325–345 in J.J. Gumperz and D. Hymes (eds.), *The ethnography of communication*. New York: Holt, Rinehart and Winston.

1972b. Unpublished class lectures.

Sacks, Harvey, Emanuel A. Schegloff, and Gail Jefferson. 1974. "A simplest systematics for the organization of turn-taking in conversation." *Language*, 50: 696–735.

Saunders, George. 1985. "Silence and noise as emotion management styles: an Italian case." Pp. 165–183 in D. Tannen and M. Saville-Troike (eds.), *Perspectives on silence*. Norwood, NJ: Ablex.

Savasta, M.L., and Brian Sutton-Smith. 1979. "Sex differences in play and power." Pp. 143–150 in B. Sutton-Smith (ed.), *Die Dialektik des Spiels*. Schorndoff: Holtman.

Savin-Williams, Richard. 1980. "Social interactions of adolescent females in natural groups." Pp. 320–343 in H.C. Foot, A.J. Chapman, and J.R. Smith (eds.), *Friendship and social relations in children*. New York: John Wiley and Sons Ltd.

Scheff, Thomas J. 1966. *Being mentally ill: a sociological theory*. Chicago: Aldine Publishing Company.

1968. "Negotiating reality: notes on power in the assessment of responsibility." *Social Problems*, 16: 3–17.

Scheflen, Albert E. 1973. *Communicational structure: analysis of a psychotherapy transaction*. Bloomington: Indiana University Press.

Schegloff, Emanuel A. 1968. "Sequencing in conversational openings." *American Anthropologist*, 70: 1075–1095.

1972. "Notes on a conversational practice: formulating place." Pp. 75–119 in D. Sudnow (ed.), *Studies in social interaction*. New York: Free Press.

Schegloff, Emanuel A., Gail Jefferson, and Harvey Sacks. 1977. "The preference for self-correction in the organization of repair in conversation." *Language*, 53: 361–382.

Schegloff, Emanuel A. and Harvey Sacks. 1973. "Opening up closings." *Semiotica*, 8: 289–327.

Schelling, Thomas B. 1963. *The strategy of conflict*. New York: Oxford University Press.

Schiffrin, Deborah. 1981. "Tense variation in narrative." *Language*, 57: 45–62.

1984. "Jewish argument as sociability." *Language in Society*, 13: 311–335.

1985. "Everyday argument: the organization of diversity in talk." Pp. 35–46 in T. van Dijk (ed.), *Handbook of discourse analysis. Volume 3: Discourse and dialogue*. London: Academic Press.

1987a. *Discourse markers*. Cambridge: Cambridge University Press

1987b. "Toward an empirical base in pragmatics." Review article of B. Levinson *Pragmatics*. In *Language in society*, 16: 381–395.

Schofield, Janet W. 1982. *Black and white in school: trust, tension, or tolerance?* New York: Praeger Publishers.

Schutz, Alfred. 1962. *Collected papers: the problem of social reality*. Vol. 1. The Hague: Martinus Nijhoff.

Scollon, Ron. 1985. "The machine stops: silence in the metaphor of malfunction." Pp. 21–30 in D. Tannen and M. Saville-Troike (eds.), *Perspectives on silence*. Norwood, NJ: Ablex Publishing Company.

Scott, Marvin B. and Stanford M. Lyman. 1968. "Accounts: inquiries in the social construction of reality." *American Sociological Review*, 33: 46–62.

Scribner, Sylvia S. and Michael Cole. 1974. *Culture and thought*. New York: Wiley-Interscience.

Searle, John. 1969. *Speech Acts*. Cambridge: Cambridge University Press.

See, Katherine O'Sullivan. 1966. "Ideology and racial stratification: a theoretical juxtaposition." *The International Journal of Sociology and Social Policy*, 6, 1: 75–89.

Serpell, Robert. 1976. *Culture's influence on behavior*. London: Methuen Ltd.

Shultz, Jeffrey J., Susan Florio, and Frederick Erickson. 1983. "Where's the floor? Aspects of the cultural organization of social relationships in communication at home and in school." Pp 88–123 in P. Gilmore and A. Glatthorn (eds.), *Ethnography and education: children in and out of school*. Washington: Center for Applied Linguistics. Distributed by Ablex Publishing Corporation, Norwood, NJ.

Shweder, Richard A. 1977. "Likeness and likelihood in everyday thought: magical thinking in judgments about personality." *Current Anthropology*, 18: 637–658.

1984. "Anthropology's romantic rebellion against the enlightment, as there's more to thinking than reasoning and evidence." Pp. 27–66 in R.A. Shweder and R.A. LeVine (eds.), *Cultural theory: essays on mind, self and emotion*. Cambridge: Cambridge University Press.

Silverman, David, and Brian Torode. 1980. *The material word: some theories of language and its limits.* London: Routledge & Kegan Paul.

Simmel, Georg. 1950 (1908). *The sociology of Georg Simmel.* Trans. and with an introduction by K.H. Wolff. Glencoe: The Free Press.

1955 (1908). "Conflict." Pp. 11–123 in Kurt Wolff (ed. and trans.), *Conflict and the Web of Group Affiliation.* New York: Free Press.

1961. "The sociology of sociability." *American Journal of Sociology,* 55, 3 (1949). Reprinted as pp. 157–163 of T. Parsons *et al.* (eds.), *Theories of society.* New York: Free Press.

Sloss, Leon and M. Scott Davids (eds.), 1986. *A game for high stakes: lessons learned in negotiating with the Soviet Union.* Cambridge: Ballinger.

Smith, A. Wade. 1981. "Racial tolerance as a function of group position." *American Sociological Review,* 46: 558–573.

Spiegelberg, Herbert. 1973. "On the right to say 'we': a linguistic and phenomenological analysis." Pp. 129–56 in G. Psathas (ed.), *A phenomenological sociology.* New York: John Wiley.

Szasz, T. and M.H. Hollender. 1956. "A contribution to the philosophy of medicine: the basic models of doctor-patient relationship." *AMA Archives of Internal Medicine,* 97: 585–592.

Tajfel, Henri. 1978. "Social categorization, social identity and social comparison." Pp. 61–76 in Henri Tajfel (ed.), *Differentiation between social groups.* London: Academic Press.

Tajfel, Henri and John Turner. 1979. "An integrative theory of intergroup conflict." Pp. 33–53 in W.G. Austin and S. Worchel (eds.), *The social psychology of intergroup relations.* Monterey, CA: Brooks/Cole Publishing Company.

Tannen, Deborah. 1984. *Conversational style: analyzing talk among friends.* Norwood, NJ: Ablex Publishing Company.

1985. "Silence: anything but." Pp. 93–111 in D. Tannen and M. Saville-Troike (eds.), *Perspectives on silence.* Norwood, NJ: Ablex Publishing Company.

1986. *That's not what I meant! How conversational style makes or breaks your relations with others.* New York: William Morrow; London: J. M. Dent.

Tannen, Deborah and Muriel Saville-Troike (eds.) 1985. *Perspectives on silence.* Norwood, NJ: Ablex Publishing Company.

Thibaut, John and Laurens Walker. 1975. *Procedural justice.* Hillsdale, NJ: Lawrence Erlbaum Associates.

Thorne, Barrie, Cheris Kramarae, and Nancy Henley (eds.). 1983. *Language, gender and society.* Rowley, MA: Newbury House Publishers.

Tuch, Steven A. 1981. "Analyzing recent trends in prejudice toward blacks: insights from latent class models." *American Journal of Sociology,* 87: 130–42.

Turner, Ralph. 1970. *Family interaction.* New York: Wiley and Sons.

US Bureau of the Census. 1970. Population, Table P-1. Washington, DC: US Government Printing Office.

1980. Population Data; Planning Board; Philadelphia, PA.

Vološinov, Valentin Nikolaevic. 1973. *Marxism and the philosophy of language.* Translated by Ladislav Matejka and I.R. Titunik. New York: Seminar Press. (First published 1929 and 1930.)

Vuchinich, Samuel. 1984. "Sequencing and social structure in family conflict." *Social Psychology Quarterly,* 47: 217–234.

1988. This volume. "The sequential organization of closing in verbal family conflict." In A.D. Grimshaw (ed.), *Conflict talk*. Cambridge: Cambridge University Press.

Wacker, Fred. 1981. "Culture, prejudice and an American dilemma." *Phylon*, 42: 255–61.

Waitzkin, Howard. 1983. *The second sickness: contradictions of capitalist health care*. New York: The Free Press.

Wason, Peter C. 1977. "The theory of formal operations: a critique." Pp. 119–135 in B.A. Gerber (ed.), *Piaget and knowing*. London: Routledge & Kegan Paul.

Wason, Peter C. and Philip N. Johnson-Laird. 1972. *The psychology of reasoning*. Cambridge, MA: Harvard University Press.

Watzlawick, Paul, Janet H. Beavin, and Don D. Jackson. 1967. *Pragmatics of human communication: a study of interactional patterns, pathologies, and paradoxes*. New York: W.W. Norton.

West, Candace. 1985. *Routine complications: troubles in talk between doctors and patients*. Bloomington, IN: Indiana University Press.

West, Candace and Don H. Zimmerman. 1985. "Gender, language and discourse." Pp. 103–124 in T.A. van Dijk (ed.), *Handbook of discourse analysis*. London: Academic Press.

Whitehead, Alfred N. 1925. *Science and the modern world*. London: Macmillan.

Wieseltier, Leon. 1986. "What went wrong? An appraisal of Reagan's foreign policy." *The New York Times Magazine*, December 7.

Williams, Robin. 1977. *Marxism and literature*. London: Oxford University Press.

Williams, Robin M., Jr. 1947. *The reduction of intergroup tensions*. New York: Social Science Research Council.

Williams, Robin M., Jr, John P. Dean, and Edward A. Suchman. 1964. *Strangers next door: ethnic relations in American communities*. Englewood Cliffs, NJ: Prentice-Hall.

Wolf, Kurt (ed.). 1950. *The Sociology of Georg Simmel*. New York: Free Press.

Woodbury, Hanni. 1984. "The strategic use of questions in court." *Semiotica*, 48: 197–228.

Yngvesson, B. and L. Mather. 1983. "Courts, moots, and the disputing process." Pp. 51–83 in K. Boyum and L. Mather (eds.), *Empirical theories about courts*, New York: Longman.

Youniss, James and Jacqueline Smoller. 1985, *Adolescent relations with mothers, fathers, and friends*. Chicago: University of Chicago Press.

Zabor, Margaret R. 1978. "Essaying metacommunication: a survey and contextualization of communication research." Unpublished Ph.D. dissertation, Indiana University.

Name index

The indexes have been prepared by Mrs. Mary Neumann.

Subject index

acceptance of concession offering, 122
access (to play): disputes over among children, 27, 33–36, 39, 46–51
accounts: as social proposals, 94–95, 96–97
accusations, 70–73, 79–81, 123; use in children's disputes, 22, 33; use in ritual insulting, 74–77
acting for, *see* representative role
activity structure, 86; of black urban youths' play, 89–95, 99–100, 108, 110–112
address: explicit/implicit, 93–94, 109–110, 113; official, 117n.21
adequacy: observational, descriptive, and explanatory, 310, 322n.16
adjacency pairs, 103–104, 105, 113, 116n.16
adjudicator, third party as, 208
adolescents (teenagers), 5, 14, 67–83, 305; involved in interracial conflict, 142–143
adversarial system, Anglo-American system of law as, 199
adversary, trial-court judge as, 198
advocate, trial-court judge as, 198
affect, 86, 118, 290–293; negative, *see* negative affect/emotion; positive, 300–301, 314–315; *see also* emotion
affect, relations of, 3, 9–10, 12, 18, 19, 282; changes in, 304; as constraint on development of conflict talk, 299, 300–301; effect on form of conflict, 210–211, 228; interaction with conflict talk, 310, 311; interaction with instrumentalities, 314–315; in organizational role relationships, 212
affiliation, 102–103, 105–106, 210
age, 51, 159n.5
aggravated disagreement, 51; *see also discussione*

aggravation, 67, 210
aggression, paradox of, 287
agreement, 103, 112, 121
alignment, 101, 116–117n.19; among urban black youth, 102–103, 108, 110, 112
alliances, formation of, 317–318
all or nothing, *see* zero sum decisions/ resolutions
alternative institution, food co-op as, 139, 158n.2
alternative solutions, 67
ambiguity, 149, 287
American Federation of State, County and Municipal Employees Union (AFSCME), 213
amplification, 218
amusement: as response to public disputes, 299
anger, 4, 290–291, 292–293, 295, 322n.13; simulated, 292
Annie Hall (film), 262
anthropology, 7–8, 320n.1; legal, 198–199, 208
animator: as aspect of self, 241–242, 249, 252, 257–258n.3
arbitrator, third party as, 208
argument, 85–115, 241, 249, 285; judge's role in, 198, 201; management of co-operative self during, 241, 243–256; as means of sociability, 256; in rhetorical sense, 259n.10; *see also* conflict talk
argumentation style, 33; *see also discussione*
assent: role in terminal exchanges, 121, 123–124, 127–130
assertiveness of black playsongs and cheers, 68–69
attack/submit patterns, 121
attorneys, *see* lawyers
audience, 15, 68; role in story telling, 252, 253, 255

345

management in, 260, 273–276
field: as situational determinant, 212, 218
figure: as aspect of self, 241–242, 249,
   252–253, 257–258n.3
focus, 283, 285–287, 294, 303; changes
   in, 296, 297
food co-operative, 158n.1, 159n.4;
   interracial conflict at, 15–16,
   139–158
footing, 10, 242–243, 256, 283, 287;
   modifications in, 18, 245, 248
form(at), 294; in the cantilena, 61;
   emphasis on, 22-23, 24; format tying,
   54, 55, 60
formulation, 137n.1, 145–146, 148–149
frame, 242–243, 247, 256, 291
friendliness, 290, 295–296
friendship, 46–47, 51–52, 71–73, 84n.2
functional grammar: and theory of register,
   210, 211–212, 218
functionalism, 6–8, 18

gaining the floor: in children's claim
   dispute, 51, 54
games: resolution of conflict during, 70
game theory, 120, 130, 136–137; *see also*
   zero-sum decisions/resolutions
gatekeeping encounter: psychiatric exam as
   example of, 165, 166
gender: as feature, 159n.5
gender differences, 3, 93; in accounts of
   task activities, 94–95; in resolution of
   conflicts, 70
goals (ends; intentions; purposes): of
   conflict talk, 15, 281–282, 283–285;
   in major conflicts, 310–311; in QWL
   program, 214, 216–217; valued more
   highly than harmony, 300
gossip, 68
government: outcomes of legislative- and
   executive-branch disputes, 322n.12
grammar, 210, 227, 250; and theory of
   register, 210, 211–212, 218
"Great Wits" (Mattison): silence as conflict
   management in, 18–19, 260,
   273–276

hair-combing: significance to adolescent
   girls, 70–71, 84n.2
harmony: and absence of conflict, 300; in
   ideology of food co-op, 140, 148, 150,
   154
hedges, 18, 220, 258n.5
hegemony and discourse analysis, 211
"he-said-she-said confrontation," 54
hesitation, 211, 223
hierarchy, 4, 86, 283, 285–287; as
   constraint on instrumentalities
   available, 314; as emerging from talk,

320–321n.2; as interactive activity,
   112–113, 281–282; maintenance
   through conflict talk, 67, 75, 82;
   among urban black youth, 14, 90,
   93–95, 108, 112–113
High Anxiety (film), 321n.8
hostility, 221, 310–311, 315–316; in
   inter-
personal relations, 215, 290;
   perceived in conflict talk, 295–296; as
   termination of verbal conflict, 118
humour: settlement of disputes through,
   36, 37–38; *see also* joking; laughter

iatrogenic theory of mental illness, 172
ideational function of language, 212
identity, 18, 289; personal, 284–285, 322
   n.12; social, *see* social identities
ideology: conflict over, 139–158, 286,
   148–155, 159n.4; presenting in talk,
   143–152
ignoring, 67
illocutionary structures: for accomplishing
   oppositional turns, 123; *see also*
   accusations; challenges; denial;
   disagreement; insult exchanges;
   threats
impersonal expressions: use by Italian
   children, 41
implicature, 8, 222
impression management, 292
inappropriate behavior or attitude,
   accusations about, 70–73
incorrigibility of propositions: maintained
   in oracular reasoning, 168
indirect speech, 294; use by nursery-school
   children, 35–36; use by Pinter, 264,
   265, 267, 277
indirect submission, 124
individuals, speaking as,143,145–146, 148
inevitability–avoidability of conflict,
   285–287
informativeness: as maxim of quantity, 243
inquisitorial system, continental European
   system of law as, 199
insertion sequences, 104, 114
insistence, 31–32, 67
institutional authority, 160, 173, 307
instrumentalities, 291–293, 313–315
insult exchanges (ritual insulting), 14,
   67–69, 73–83; among adolescent
   girls, 74–81; as oppositional turn,
   120, 123, 129; use of adjacency pairs,
   116n.16
intensity, 245, 315–316; as dimension of
   variability, 294–296, 297
intentions, *see* goals
interaction (social interaction), 2, 4–5, 7,
   8, 281–282; avoidance of as